VANESSA BELL

VANESSA BELL

The Life and Art
of a Bloomsbury Radical

WENDY HITCHMOUGH

YALE UNIVERSITY PRESS

New Haven and London

For my sister, Sally

For information about this and other Yale University Press publications, please contact:
U.S. Office: sales.press@yale.edu yalebooks.com
Europe Office: sales@yaleup.co.uk yalebooks.co.uk

Set in Linotype Sabon by Tetragon, London
Printed in China

Library of Congress Control Number: 2024940086

ISBN 978-0-300-26921-5

A catalogue record for this book is available from the British Library.

10 9 8 7 6 5 4 3 2 1

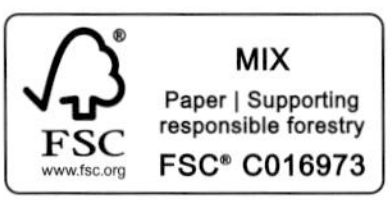

CONTENTS

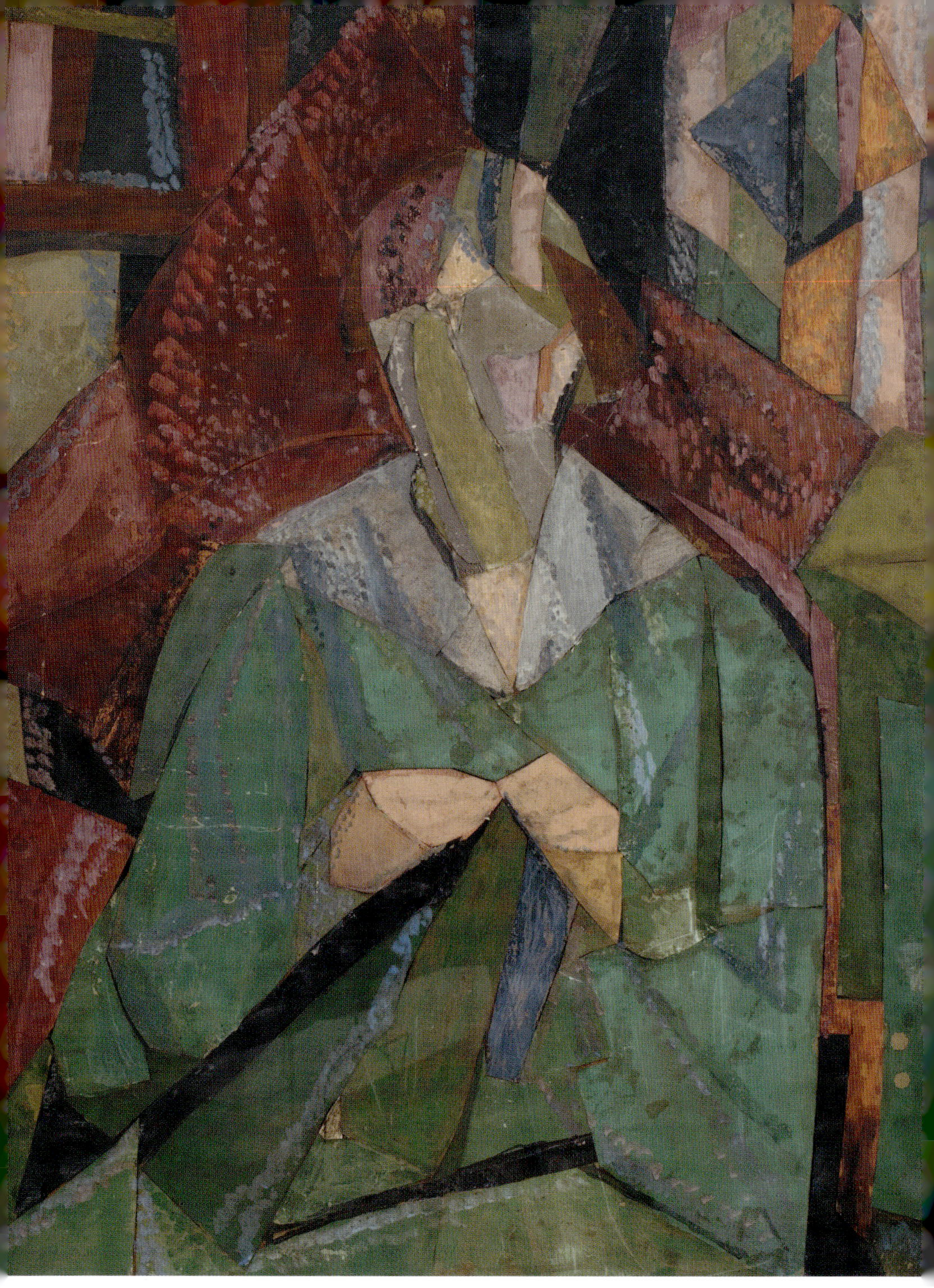

o.1. Vanessa Bell, *Portrait of Molly MacCarthy*
1914, gouache, oil and collage on board, 920 × 750 mm, Piano Nobile, London

INTRODUCTION

anessa Bell travelled to Paris in March 1914 with one of her husband's three current lovers, Molly MacCarthy (fig. 0.1).[1] There they would meet her husband, the art critic Clive Bell, and her lover and business partner, the artist and critic Roger Fry. The risk of scandal was deemed too great for Clive and Molly to be seen taking the train and ferry from London to Paris alone together.[2] All four belonged to the Bloomsbury Group, and although Vanessa was forging new pathways to sexual freedoms and equality she needed to tread a fine line between respectable appearances and the alternative values that Bloomsbury upheld. Vanessa's reputation as an artist has been overshadowed by a fascination with Bloomsbury sex lives. Her trail-blazing approach to art as well as life and her crucial role in shaping modernism have also been obscured by her own ability to cover her tracks. She cast an inscrutable veil over outrageously transgressive behaviour. Her rejection of conventions was integral to her work and to her life as a modernist but it was also potentially ruinous professionally and for her family. Vanessa grew up in a Victorian society that ostracised women who deviated from its standards.

Molly and Vanessa went shopping in Paris department stores, determined 'to revolutionize' their dress, but the main purpose of the trip was professional.[3] Vanessa was already familiar with the art dealers of London and Paris. Three years earlier the Bells had acquired a Picasso still life, the first to enter a British private collection, and on this trip they purchased a still life by Juan Gris and a landscape by Maurice de Vlaminck. They saw Michael and Sarah Stein's collection of Fauve paintings and Gertrude Stein took them to meet Picasso and Matisse in their Paris studios. Vanessa described Picasso's 'wonderful

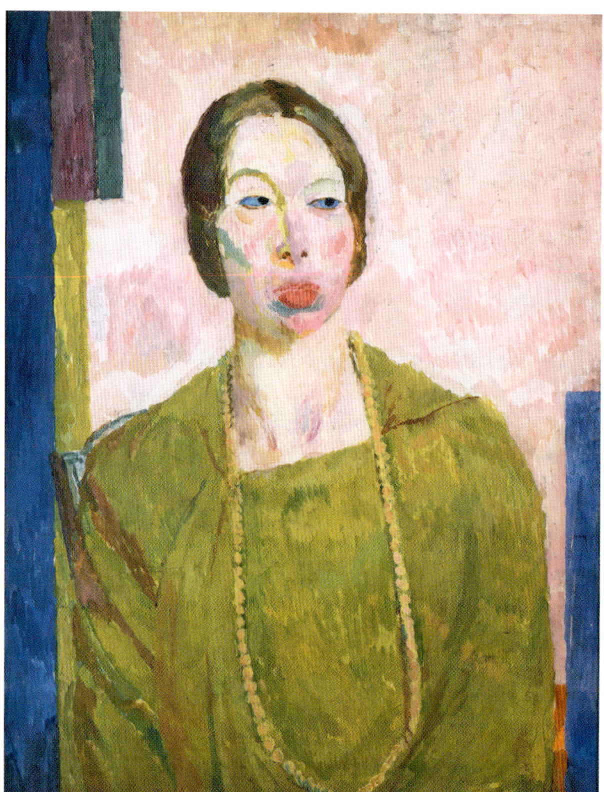

portraits of the blue period' in a letter to her fellow artist Duncan Grant, and the exhilaration of visiting his studio where boundaries between art and environment disintegrated: 'All the bits of wood and frames had become like his pictures.' The most recent ones, she wrote, 'are amazing arrangements of coloured papers and bits of wood . . . he is probably one of the greatest geniuses that has ever lived'.[4]

Vanessa was one of the most radical and influential artists working in Britain in the early twentieth century. She opened up professional opportunities for women, including her sister, Virginia Woolf. She was one of the first artists in Britain to produce fully resolved abstract paintings and collages. She exhibited in London and Paris alongside Wyndham Lewis, David Bomberg, Thérèse Lessore, Paul Nash, Edward Wadsworth and artists more closely associated with the Bloomsbury Group in the years immediately preceding the outbreak of the First World War. Nevertheless, her career was hampered by prejudice. Duncan was invited to show his abstract paintings with the Vorticists in 1915 but Vanessa was excluded from the show.[5]

'Let's not have any of these damned women', the artist Christopher Nevinson is reputed to have declared at the opening of their Rebel Art Centre.[6] She included her abstract paintings in the backgrounds to a self-portrait and a painting of Clive's lover, Mary Hutchinson, wryly reflecting her own relegated status within the bombastic, male-dominated field of British modernism (fig. 0.2). Her abstracts were ambitious and deliberate contributions to an international visual dialogue about the future of painting.

Vanessa's fortitude and her determination as a pioneer were rooted in a succession of tragedies early in her life. As a young woman she learned to model the Victorian values instilled in her by her family. She was born in 1879. Her father, Sir Leslie Stephen, was an eminent and well-connected figure in literary circles. He was a writer and the first editor of the *Dictionary of National Biography*. Her mother, Julia Stephen, had been the favourite model and niece of the photographer Julia Margaret Cameron, writing the entry on her for the *Dictionary of National Biography*. She published a short guide to nursing, *Notes for a Sick Room*, and Virginia described her charitable work 'visiting the slums'.[7] Both parents had children from previous marriages and were initially attracted to one another by their shared experiences of intense mourning following the deaths of their former partners. Vanessa's character would be profoundly influenced by the prospect of death and its aftermath. She grew up in the large London house where she and her three younger siblings, Thoby, Virginia and Adrian, were born. 22 Hyde Park Gate in South Kensington was also home to her two older half-brothers and her half-sister from her mother's first marriage, George, Gerald and Stella Duckworth. For the first seven years of her life her father's first child, her half-sister Laura, also lived with them. Laura was nine when Vanessa was born. Now understood to have been autistic with a co-morbid psychotic condition possibly induced by childhood sexual abuse, she was criticised by Leslie for her 'perversity' and 'backward' behaviour.[8] Laura was dispatched to a governess in Devon when she was 16, 'put away' in an asylum seven years later, and almost never referred to again.

Recalling her childhood, Vanessa wrote: 'I cannot remember a time when Virginia did not mean to be a writer and I a painter. It was a lucky arrangement for it meant that we went our own ways and one source of jealousy at any rate was absent.'[9] Their youthful ambitions were supported but they were expected to take their places in society primarily as wives and mothers. Weeks before Vanessa's sixteenth birthday, however, their mother died, and two years later Stella also died after a short illness. She had 'come to the rescue', Vanessa wrote, 'looked after us younger ones, and sacrificed herself as far as she could to my father'.[10] The trauma of these two deaths robbed Vanessa and Virginia of the maternal guidance that would have directed them towards conventional marriages and family lives. Virginia later acknowledged that there would have been no Jewish husband, no books or publishing house for her had their parents survived.[11] Equally, for Vanessa, there would have been no Post-Impressionist outrages on Victorian sensibilities, no Omega Workshops or alternative households with homosexual lovers and an illegitimate child. Initially, however, their resistance to family pressures was passive.

'Like all Victorian young ladies', Vanessa wrote, 'I had come out at the age of eighteen . . . but of course had gone in again when we were plunged into mourning.' She was made responsible for managing her father's complex household and for coping with his severe depressions and 'violent rages', described by Virginia as a 'temper that he could not control'.[12] At the same time she pursued her ambition to be a painter, enjoying the anonymity of 'the grubby, shabby, dirty world of art students at South Kensington' where she studied at a small art school. It was 'separate entirely', she wrote, and 'a great relief' from her life at Hyde Park Gate.[13] This ability to lead a double life was formative. It was complicated by George Duckworth, who, she later wryly observed, realised that she was unlikely to meet a 'rich old Etonian husband' at art school and insistently groomed and chaper-oned her, accepting unwelcome invitations to dinners and parties on her behalf.[14] Vanessa's childhood and family background are described in Chapter 1. They are vividly evoked in Virginia's autobiographical works, including two ruthless accounts read aloud to Bloomsbury's Memoir Club and a longer, autobiographical *Sketch of the Past*.[15] She described their 'close conspiracy' during the seven 'unhappy years' between Stella's death and that of their father when she and Vanessa were 'fully exposed without protection' to his emotional brutality.[16] The sisters may also have been exposed to sexual abuse. Virginia's memoir '22 Hyde Park Gate' includes a chilling description of George creeping into her bedroom after a long evening together. He had taken her to a dinner, followed by the theatre and then a party at the home of the elderly artist William Holman Hunt. She describes the 'confused whirlpool' of impressions as she undressed and began to fall asleep and then the door to her bedroom 'creaking stealthily' as George entered, 'flung himself on my bed, and took me in his arms'. Vanessa was almost certainly present when the memoir was read aloud and is clearly identified as a fellow victim. It concludes with the extraordinarily brave revelation: 'George Duckworth was not only father and mother, brother and sister to those poor Stephen girls; he was their lover also.'[17]

Vanessa's adult relationships with men were conditioned by an acceptance of selfish, unregulated behaviour and an absence of boundaries. She was a survivor of these experiences. Her life and work resonate today because she challenged the ways in which women engaged with the patriarchal structures of the early twentieth century. She pioneered new directions for powerful, independent women. She is the subject of a fascinating and substantial biography.[18] Here, however, the focus is on her art. Snapshots of her life offer new insights into the logistics and emotional labour of her work towards equality as a professional woman. Her defiance and resolve underpinned the inclusion of women within the Bloomsbury Group on an equal footing with men. Following her marriage to Clive, Vanessa's insistence upon absolute candour within the Group demolished society's expectations of chaste wives, passively accommodating the sexual initiatives and indiscretions of men. Her letters reveal open-mindedness and a profoundly experimental attitude to same-sex and heterosexual relationships that was central to Bloomsbury's evolution as a group. Her insistence that women's sexual freedoms should equal those of men and that Clive's relentless extramarital affairs should not be made more demeaning to her through dishonesty were consistent with Bloomsbury's commitment to the concepts of truth and reason. She was open with Clive about her affair with Roger. She rationalised with him and confronted his jealousy, urging Roger to be patient: 'he does know that we must both be free to have what friendships we like, & he will in time live up to his principles.'[19] She was inscrutable, however, with Clive's wealthy and conservative family, humouring their assumptions about her married life. While Clive's indiscretions were not so unusual, the Bells could have disinherited Clive if they had known about Vanessa's relationships. She delighted in gossip and in open discussions about the sex lives of her own family and friends, reporting after Christmas in 1917, for example, that Clive kept the company entertained with 'a lecture on fucking which lasted about 48 hours . . . & then we had a tree for the children'.[20]

Biographers of Vanessa and Virginia have explored their centrality to the Bloomsbury Group. This influential circle of friends transformed twentieth-century economics, literature, politics and the visual arts in Britain and took its name from the area of London where Vanessa established her family after the death of their father in 1904. The four Stephen siblings were all members of the Group and Vanessa's role as a matriarch within Bloomsbury was pivotal. It expanded her identity as the older sister and substitute mother to Thoby, Virginia and Adrian. She co-hosted Bloomsbury's initial meetings at 46 Gordon Square from 1905. Characteristically in her memoir, 'Notes on Bloomsbury', she credits Thoby with founding the Group:

> Thoby, not long down from Cambridge and now reading for the Bar, began to gather round him such of his Cambridge friends as were also starting life in London. It seemed to him a good plan to be at home one evening a week and though I do not think it had at first occurred to him to include his sisters in the arrangement, still there they were.[21]

Archival evidence documents that it was 'Miss Vanessa Stephen, and Mr J.T. Stephen, At Home' on Thursday evenings from 10 pm.[22] The gatherings were surely her initiative as the older sister, a riff on the respectable and conventional 'At Homes' over which she and Virginia had been obliged to preside in their father's household. The subterfuge gained access for these two young women to the intellectual freedoms and ambitions that their brother and his friends had enjoyed as undergraduates. Polite conversation and the tea table were abandoned in favour of whisky or unceremonious offerings of 'cocoa and biscuits'.[23] Even this risked compromising their reputations. Vanessa recalled the disapproval with which she was questioned 'at an ordinary conventional party as to whether we really sat up talking to young men till all hours of the night? – What did we talk about? – Who were these young men?'[24]

Vanessa subverted the gendered conventions of the Edwardian drawing room, the country house weekend and the 'club culture' of London's artists' groups to create alternative networks. The sleight of hand with which she operated would shape Bloomsbury's elusive identity as a group. She combined her social networking skills with professional acumen to establish environments that were stimulating, supportive and progressive, making spaces in which her own work and that of others could be shared. Following on from 'Thursday evenings' her invention of the Friday Club has to be pieced together as a consequence of her own obfuscations (as well as the prejudices that continue to obscure the mechanics of her leadership) to establish a fuller understanding of her importance as a modernist. She started the Club's weekly meetings in her own home in 1905 but soon needed to hire rooms, she wrote, 'to eradicate politeness'.[25] Through the Friday Club's annual exhibitions she established a degree of equality between the men and women artists with whom she chose to associate, drawing in artists such as Christopher Nevinson, Paul Nash, Henry Lamb and Mark Gertler as well as former art school colleagues Sylvia Milman, Sylvia Packard and Essil Elmslie. Non-exhibiting members included her friends Marjorie Strachey and Ka Cox, both graduates of Newnham College, Cambridge actively involved with women's suffrage, bringing together radicals from different disciplines.

Vanessa challenged Britain's xenophobia in the first decades of the twentieth century. She was central to modernist networks connecting British and European artistic practice. The Friday Club was started 'in a vain hope of creating something of the same kind of atmosphere in London' as the artists' studios and cafes that she frequented in Paris.[26] The birth of her second child, Quentin, and his illness prevented her from joining Roger and Clive there to select work for the ground-breaking exhibition *Manet and the Post-Impressionists* in 1910. But she exhibited in Paris in 1912 and 1920 and she took a studio there for a month in 1922. It concluded a three-month stay in the South of France to complete a body of work for her first major solo exhibition. She assimilated European as well as British influences and maintained an open engagement with the culture and personalities of the European avant-garde. When Picasso and Derain were in London in 1919, working with Diaghilev and the Ballets Russes, Vanessa was instrumental in arranging a celebrated dinner for them at 46 Gordon Square hosted by Clive. 'They want some of the beau monde & some artists if possible . . . I count absolutely on you, Roger, Duncan, and [Edward] Wolfe as a sort of committee – to organize and decorate', Clive wrote to her. 'It must be a great success in the half bohemian, half mondain style'.[27]

The arrangements for Picasso and Derain's visit illuminate Vanessa's centrality to the Bloomsbury artists' relationships with one another and with her husband, each promoting the others' interests. She created spaces for modernist interactions, and her influence as a 'place maker' is analysed in Chapter 4. This was no less profound for being, quite literally, self-effacing. The visit highlights Vanessa's frustrations and her balancing act as a mother of young children, struggling to maintain her family home at Charleston in East Sussex and to reassert her professional identity in London and Paris after the First World War. It was impossible in May 1919 for her to leave her five-month-old daughter Angelica and her two sons Julian and Quentin, aged 11 and 8, for more than 'nightmare dashes to London' lasting a day or two.[28] Vanessa had forfeited her home at 46 Gordon Square in 1916 when she moved to Charleston with Duncan, his boyfriend David Garnett and her two sons, so that the two men could work on a nearby farm as conscientious objectors. The economist John Maynard Keynes, a close friend and fellow member of Bloomsbury, had taken over the lease and made it his wartime base, sharing the house with Clive and his other Cambridge friends, the mathematician H.T.J. Norton and the classicist J.T. Sheppard. Vanessa now needed to ask Clive's permission to stay there.[29] She had just begun to paint again and, anxious to regain a London presence and protect her relationship with Duncan, the father of her new baby, she rented a flat in Regent Square that he could also use when he was in town. On Roger's suggestion she sublet this apartment to Derain while he was in London designing for the ballet. Roger took her to meet him there and to install new curtains that she had hurried to complete. She described the visit to Duncan: 'I saw your paintings there & thought them all lovely. Also the vases which are a priceless gift for which I'm very grateful. The mantel piece looked wonderful. In fact the flat altogether looked very nice.'[30] Evidently the interiors had been curated in her absence by Roger and Duncan for Derain's benefit.[31] Roger took her to the Ballets Russes and they went behind the scenes to see Derain and Picasso. It's likely that Vanessa also fine-tuned the arrangements at Gordon Square on this visit because a few days after her return to Charleston Clive hosted the first of at least three lunch parties there for Picasso and Derain. 'They came', Duncan wrote to her, 'to see Clive's pictures & you had a superb triumph. The picture they liked best in the house (they were unenthusiastic about the Cézanne and the Ingres) was your tray picture . . . Isn't it splendid?'[32] Vanessa was an absent presence, too, at a supper party, hosted by Clive and Maynard for Picasso and Derain. She withdrew at the last minute, unable to leave Charleston where Quentin had chickenpox. She wrote to Duncan, 'I like being here with the children better really than being in London but . . . I'd give anything to have no responsibilities for a short time'.[33]

Vanessa embodied conventional ideals of women as mothers, wives, sisters and models and she subverted and exploited them for her own professional purposes. She co-founded an influential design studio, the Omega Workshops, with Roger and Duncan in 1913. When Roger was away in France she took full responsibility for the Omega, comparing its management with her skills as a housekeeper. She wrote to him that the business of running the Workshops, 'all of which I despatch with great ability', was 'rather like ordering dinner I find'.[34] She developed two key strategies to elude the prejudices of hostile critics and to erode the gender inequalities of the London art world. The first of these, practised from childhood, was collaboration, and the second was anonymity. As a consequence, her agency has been underestimated. Her formative influence on the culture and design aesthetic of the Omega Workshops is inadequately understood because many of her ideas were channelled through her fellow directors, Roger and Duncan. The Omega principle that its designers should remain anonymous to clients and critics is likely to have been promoted if not initiated by Vanessa. It was crucial to the reception of her own work and that of her female colleagues but it robbed her of the credit for many of her most striking and influential designs. She worked so closely with Duncan to originate an Omega style that her extraordinary designs are almost indistinguishable from his. When her design for one of the painted panels that hung outside the Omega,

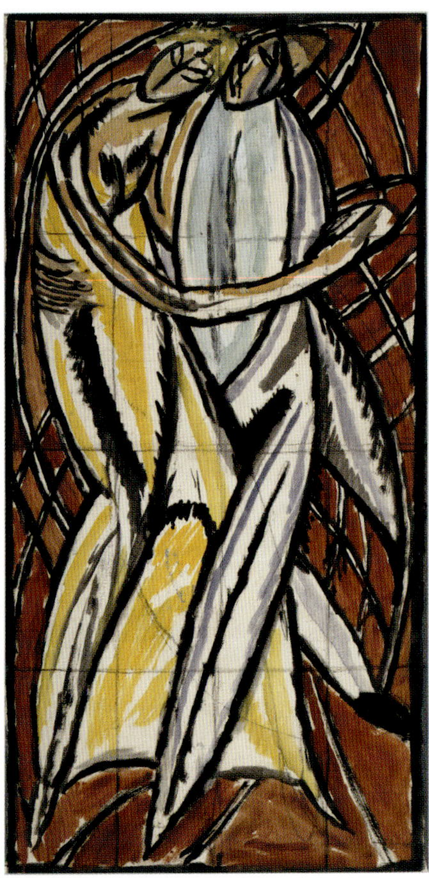

Dancing Couple, was acquired by the Victoria and Albert Museum in 1955 she did not challenge its attribution to Duncan, who couldn't recall whether he had painted it or whether Wyndham Lewis had done so.[35] It wasn't until 1999 that the art historian Richard Shone found incontrovertible evidence – a detailed description and a sketch for it, in one of her letters to Roger – and the design was credited to her (fig. 0.3).[36]

Vanessa became part of the arts establishment during the 1920s and 1930s, dividing her time between studios in London, Sussex and the South of France. She developed an interior design business with Duncan after the closure of the Omega Workshops, discussed in Chapter 12, and their work was popularised and promoted in *Vogue*. She was a founder member of the Society of Mural Painters in 1939, attracting commissions for the ocean liner RMS Queen Mary and the church of Saint Michael and All Angels at Berwick in Sussex. She was still representing her generation of painters and designers in *Britain Can Make It* in 1946 and the Festival of Britain in 1951.[37]

She deflected critical recognition during her lifetime, consistently championing Duncan's work. This may have been fundamental to the nature of their relationship. Together with the slippage between respectable appearances and the sexual freedoms that were essential to her early creative collaborations, it exacerbated her ambiguous status as an artist within the narratives that her family constructed around her. Discretion may have prompted Virginia to erase her sister from a spirited account of the Omega Workshops in her biography of Roger in 1940, knowing that the two artists were engaged in a passionate affair when Omega was conceived. Quentin, initially writing in Duncan's lifetime, reiterated gender stereotypes, positioning his mother as a secondary presence in his influential publications on Bloomsbury. 'Vanessa could offer Duncan an almost maternal devotion and at the same time accept him as a master', he wrote. 'It was her natural disposition to adore, to give, to submit, and in Duncan she found a man whom she felt to be worthy of her devotion; always she insisted upon his superiority'.[38]

Angelica observed that 'Bloomsbury was in the doldrums' at the time of Vanessa's death in 1961 and that both her parents were then underrated as painters.[39] Vanessa's work was problematic for historians because it was often unsigned and almost indistinguishable from that of Duncan. The concept that a work is by 'Vanessa Bell/ Duncan Grant' remains untenable. When the art dealer Anthony d'Offay began to shape and revive the two artists' reputations in the early 1970s and took many of their works from Charleston into his London store for safekeeping, the work of attributing paintings and designs to Vanessa or to Duncan began. It was conducted by a small team, including Anthony, Angelica and the Tate curator Richard Morphet, and it often depended entirely upon visual analysis.[40] It was fallible. Duncan outlived Vanessa by 17 years and remained at Charleston until 1978. There he entertained dealers, collectors and art historians, enjoying a revival of interest in Bloomsbury in the later 1960s and 1970s and assuming, perhaps, a disproportionate pre-eminence.

Seeing Vanessa through the eyes of her family is both revealing and problematic. As early as 1910 she complained that 'Virginia since early youth has made it her business to create a character for me according to her own wishes & has now . . . succeeded in imposing it upon the world'.[41] Twenty years later Virginia was still defining her sister in an unsolicited foreword to her 1930 exhibition: 'That a woman should hold a show of pictures in Bond Street', she began, and proceeded to validate Vanessa's reputation, to describe the inherent beauty, the emotional appeal of her paintings and their absence of narrative content. She was insistent on their inviolable reticence: 'Mrs Bell says nothing. Mrs Bell is as silent as the grave', she had 'no truck with words.'[42]

Vanessa's extensive and substantially unpublished correspondence belies such assertions. Her letters document her agency as an ambitious and autonomous artist, negotiating the terrain mapped out for her by her father, her elder half-brothers, her husband, her sister and the artists with whom she collaborated. They evidence the quiet strength and determination, described by Clive as 'a will of iron', with which she faced down the prejudices and stereotypes, even of her own family and friends.[43] Roger wrote to her that she had 'done such an extraordinarily difficult thing without any fuss: cut thro' all the conventions . . . got all the things you need for your own development and yet managed to be a splendid mother'.[44] In this book, her unpublished letters are quoted extensively so that her voice may be heard. Articulate and ironic, they reveal an incisive critical eye, observing and analysing her contemporaries and their work. She wrote openly about depression and mental health at a time when these subjects were stigmatised. References to menstruation, miscarriage and abortion in her letters to men as well as women challenged taboos surrounding women's bodies.

Much of Vanessa's most important work as a modernist – hosting, inventing, managing and supporting the creative contexts necessary for her own artistic practice – was invisible labour. Her emerging identity as a woman artist, threading her way through the training and travel opportunities of Edwardian society and positioning herself within the patriarchal cultures of the Paris and London art worlds, is explored in Chapter 2. Her choice of subjects and her dissolution of boundaries between art and life are discussed in subsequent chapters. As a Post-Impressionist, Vanessa experimented with technique and composition to explore modern subjects. Taking women and children as her theme, she responded to the nudes and pastoral scenes of Cézanne, Gauguin, Picasso and Matisse (discussed in Chapter 5) as well as Byzantine and Renaissance images of iconic women, to ground her own engagement with these subjects in her personal experience of motherhood and miscarriage. She demolished the traditional power dynamics of portraiture in her paintings of friends and family, sharing models with Roger and Duncan. Her career path and Duncan's coincided. Chapter 9 is dedicated to their portraits of one another and their exhibitions to highlight the gender disparities that shaped their careers. It details the societal expectations, the institutional support and the practicalities that underpinned their very different pathways to success.

Vanessa exploited her partnerships with Clive, Roger and Duncan to circumvent the prejudices that undermined professional women. Inevitably, working within a culture that withheld recognition, 'if one was that terrible low creature, a female painter', her letters are self-deprecating.[45] In private, however, the artists closest to her were unequivocal in their estimations of her work. Roger wrote to her: 'You have genius in your life as well as your art and both are rare things'. Duncan wrote: 'You do not know how important you are to the world besides individuals.'[46] Vanessa was central to the evolution of twentieth-century visual culture. Her life and work, as an entity, illuminate the role of women in the shaping of modernism.

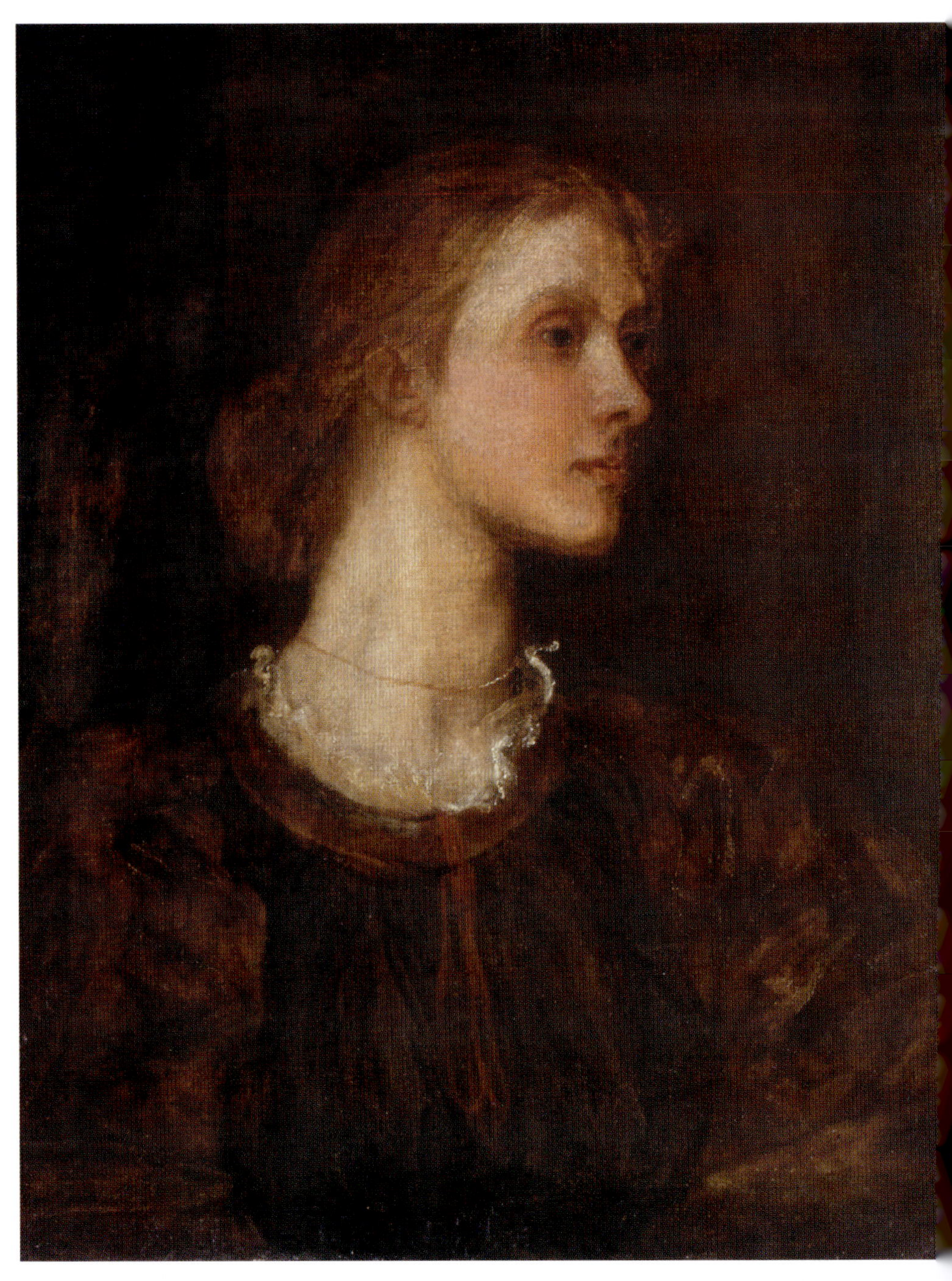

1.1. George Frederic Watts, *Julia Duckworth*
c.1870, oil on canvas, 710 × 595 mm, The Charleston Trust

1

FAMILY AND SOCIAL IDENTITY

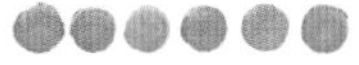

When she was 15 Vanessa, already determined to become an artist, would have visited the exhibition *Fair Women* at the Grafton Galleries. It included a portrait of her mother, Julia Stephen, by G.F. Watts.[1] Visiting galleries with her sisters and family friends was one of the ways in which she defined her independence as a modern young woman. Her family home at 22 Hyde Park Gate was a 15-minute walk from the museums on Exhibition Road and Virginia's diaries are peppered with references to their expeditions together: 'In the afternoon Nessa and I went to the South Kensington Museum [now the Victoria and Albert Museum], and went over for the 20th time the picture gallery'.[2] They travelled 'on the top of a bus to Trafalgar Square' to see paintings by Watts at the National Portrait Gallery.[3] *Fair Women* would resonate with Vanessa's subsequent work as the curator of pioneering exhibitions. She would exhibit at the Grafton Galleries and named the Grafton Group, one of the first artist collectives that she co-founded, after them.

Fair Women was organised by a network of formidable and predominantly aristocratic women who had access to private collections. The names of its all-female committee and their determination to show women 'possibly more celebrated for their historical interest, their influence, or their wit than for their beauty' were boldly published at the front of the catalogue. This innovative and immensely popular 'blockbuster' projected an alternative vision of powerful women exerting their agency as artists, collectors, rulers and prominent figures in the public domain. Portraits ranged from Hans Holbein's *Margaret Tudor, Queen of Scotland* and Joshua Reynolds's *Mrs Siddons as the Tragic Muse* to more contemporary paintings such as *Ellen Terry as Lady Macbeth*.[4] Although the majority of the artists were men, the show included portraits by Angelica Kauffmann, Elisabeth Vigée Le Brun and one of the organising committee, the Marchioness of Granby, Violet Manners.

Vanessa would have felt at home within the art world reflected in *Fair Women*. Watts was a family friend and one of the artists she had been raised to admire. 'W for Watts a painter is he' she wrote in the family newspaper that she produced with Virginia, promoting him to 'A great painter' in the next issue.[5] Julia disliked his portrait of her so much that Sir Leslie Stephen refused to go to the exhibition, but it was one of several Watts portraits at 22 Hyde Park Gate. Virginia recalled one of Sir Leslie in the drawing room, facing the door: 'a flattered, an idealized picture, up to which father would lead admiring ladies; and pause and contemplate it, with some complacency'.[6] Watts made portraits of Vanessa's grandmother, Maria Jackson, and her great-aunts as well as her mother, and for Vanessa these signified a matriarchal heritage that was empowering. She chose a Watts portrait of Julia as a determined young woman with a strong jawline and a resolute expression (fig. 1.1) for the drawing room at 46 Gordon Square, the home she set up with her siblings after Sir Leslie's death.[7] It hung above her bed at Charleston in the last years of her life and a Watts pencil portrait of Maria hung outside her bedroom door.

The family resemblance between Maria, Julia, Stella, Vanessa and Virginia was remarkable and would have been central to Vanessa's sense of identity when she was growing up (fig. 1.2).[8] Both Maria and Julia were renowned beauties and Vanessa knew her grandmother well. She often stayed at Hyde Park Gate. Vanessa and Virginia were ambivalent, however, about their own beauty: 'beauty is important', Woolf wrote of one of her characters in *Jacob's Room*: 'it is an inheritance; one cannot ignore it. But it is a barrier; it is in fact rather a bore.'[9] Vanessa's portraits consciously rejected 'prettiness', a disparaging term in her vocabulary. Nevertheless, beauty was a passport to influential and artistic circles in Victorian society for her mother and grandmother. Maria was one of seven 'Pattle sisters', all famous in Anglo-Indian society for their influence and, with the exception of

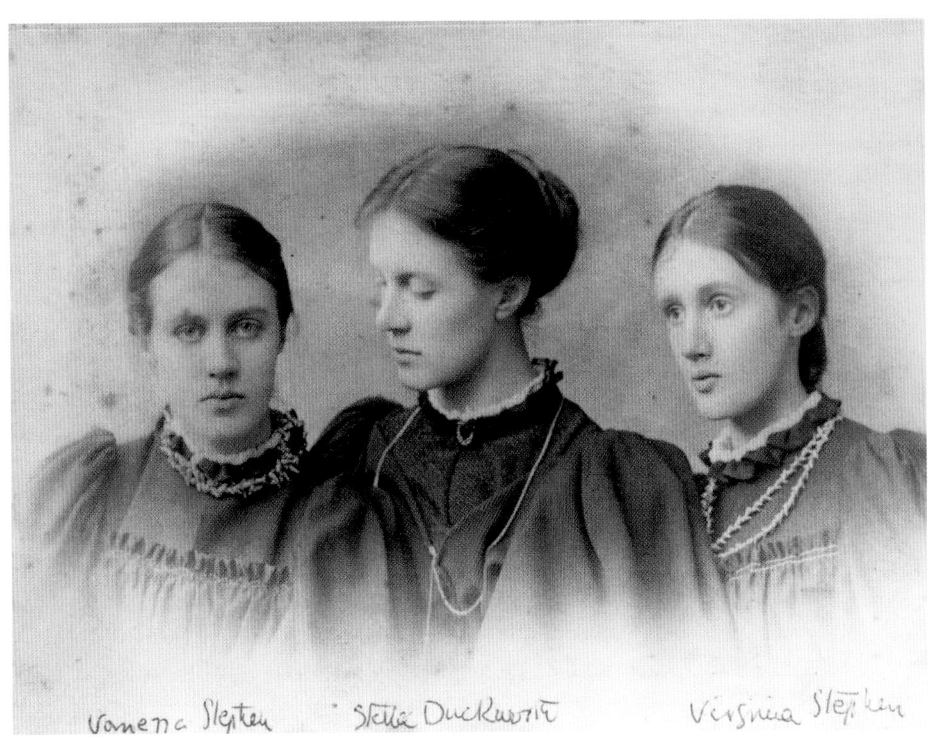

1.2. Photographer unknown, Vanessa, Stella and Virginia Stephen
The Charleston Trust

Julia Margaret Cameron (née Pattle), their beauty. Their grandfather, Antoine de l'Etang, had been exiled to India from the court of Louis XVI. He had served as a page to Marie Antoinette and subsequently as an officer in the royal Garde du Corps. His daughter and grand-daughters grew up in Calcutta and in Versailles, where his widow returned after his death. Virginia perpetuated the family story that de l'Etang was banished because he was Marie Antoinette's lover and both sisters romanticised their maternal heritage and mocked its pretentions.[10]

Women and children in Anglo-Indian families were often sent 'home' for their health and education, living apart from their husbands and fathers for many years at a time. Maria was educated in Paris with her older sisters, Julia Margaret and Sara. She married an eminent physician, John Jackson, and joined Sara and her husband, Thoby Prinsep, in London, leaving her husband to his work in Calcutta when Julia was two. Julia did not see her father again until he retired to England seven years later.

The Pattle sisters, and Vanessa's great-aunt Sara in particular, coordinated a community of Anglo-Indian families who socialised together, intermarried and promoted one another's interests in India, London and Paris. They were outsiders, to some extent, everywhere they lived. Vanessa belonged, whenever it suited her, to this powerful, intergenerational colonial network of Anglo-Indians. She inherited their sense of entitlement and their social acumen. She also inherited the ruthless determination and resilience that enabled her grandmother and great-aunts to move continents and establish alternative households with or without their husbands. Two of her great-aunts married into the aristocracy, Julia Margaret defied professional and technical challenges to forge a reputation as a formidable photographer, and Sara created an important cosmopolitan salon at her Kensington home, Little Holland House, which was frequented by all her glamorous sisters. They accentuated their otherness by rejecting Victorian corsets and crinolines in favour of long, flowing robes and cashmere shawls.[11] Vanessa's grandmother had a house in Hampstead but much of her time was spent at Little Holland House and Julia grew up there. She was closer to her uncle Thoby than to her own father.

The idea of this bohemian female stronghold where Maria made a life apart from her husband had a profound effect on Vanessa. When she was 50, a year older than her mother at the time of her death, she made a portrait based on one of Julia Margaret's photographs of Julia. *The Red Dress* was a direct response to Virginia's monograph on their great-aunt, *Victorian Photographs of Famous Men & Fair Women by Julia Margaret Cameron* (which referenced, in its title, the blockbuster exhibition), and her evocation of their parents in *To The Lighthouse* (fig. 1.3).[12] The woman's identity in *The Red Dress* is ambiguous. Her idealised features articulate the family likeness between Maria, Julia, Stella, Vanessa and Virginia but the red dress and blue cloak emblematise the Pattle sisterhood, a mantle subsequently adopted by Julia for the Watts portrait of her in Vanessa's collection. The painting and its title are an assertion of Vanessa's own claim to her maternal heritage.

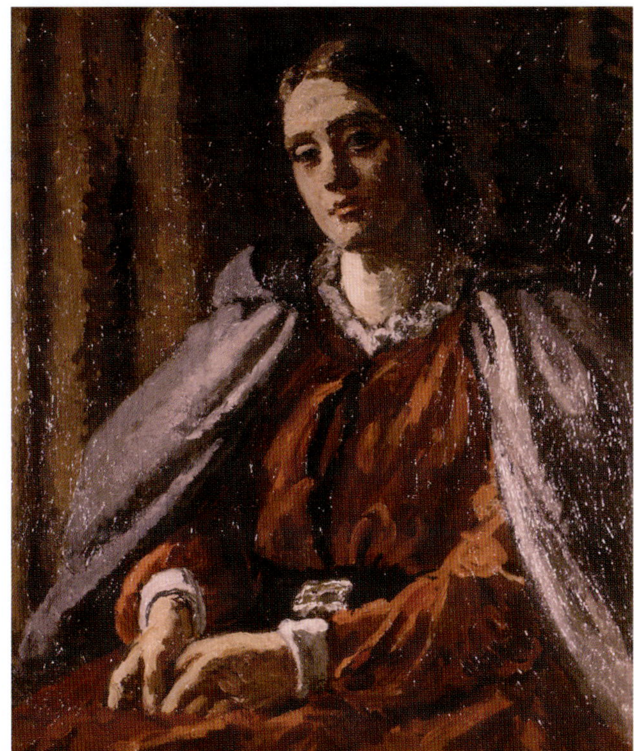

Virginia created word pictures of Julia's early life at Little Holland House and the eccentric, artistic community that Julia Margaret assembled at Freshwater on the Isle of Wight. Watts made Little Holland House his home and Virginia imagined his teenage bride, 'Ellen Terry dressed as a boy', there, and the 'eminent men . . . rulers of India, statesmen, poets, painters' who visited on Sunday afternoons.[13] They included Gladstone, Disraeli, Browning, Thackeray and Ruskin as well as many of the Victorian artists whose work was exhibited in *Fair Women* such as Rossetti, Leighton and Millais. Tennyson (whose poem 'A Dream of Fair Women' was playfully referenced in the exhibition title) was a close family friend. Julia modelled from childhood for Watts and in her late teens and twenties she became her aunt's favourite photographic subject. Two founding members of the Pre-Raphaelite Brotherhood, William Holman Hunt and Thomas Woolner, proposed marriage to her, and Edward Burne-Jones, who described Sara Prinsep as 'the nearest thing to a mother that I ever knew', immortalised Julia's languid beauty as the Virgin in his *Annunciation*.[14]

As an art student, intent on proclaiming her own creative identity, Vanessa would denounce the work of Watts and Burne-Jones. Her changing attitude is significant because it exemplified a rejection of Victorian culture and her emerging identity as a radical. Soon after they moved to Gordon Square, Vanessa and Virginia visited Watts's retrospective exhibition: 'Nessa and I walked through the rooms almost in tears,' Virginia wrote, describing the show as 'atrocious: my last illusion is gone'.[15] As children, however, they took their Pre-Raphaelite connections for granted. They were entertained at the imposing studio house Philip Webb designed for Val Prinsep in Holland Park. Val was their mother's cousin. Vanessa described a birthday party there for his son who was named, like her brother, after Thoby Prinsep, with tea 'elegantly served' in the studio.[16] As modernist women both Vanessa and Virginia referred back to their maternal heritage repeatedly, reordering it, simultaneously celebrating and critiquing it. In her autobiographical memoir Virginia recalled that they were always taken to Little Holland House on Sundays and that 'the honour and the privilege' of their association with its illustrious figures (she listed Watts and Burne Jones but not Cameron) were impressed upon them. She defined the concept of 'greatness' there as masculine and remote: 'something to which I am led up dutifully by my parents'.[17] In her only play, *Freshwater*, drafted in 1923 and performed for friends in Vanessa's London studio in 1935, she parodied the artistic community at Little Holland House and Freshwater. Vanessa took the character of her great-aunt Julia Margaret in the play. Ellen Terry (played by her daughter Angelica) abandoned her role posing as Modesty for her aged husband Watts (played by Duncan Grant) and exchanged her veils for trousers to run away with a sailor to a life of freedom at Gordon Square.

Humour and irony were coping mechanisms that Vanessa developed with her younger siblings from an early age and they would be central to Bloomsbury's self-fashioning as a group. This is evident in *Hyde Park Gate News*, the weekly paper that she and Virginia produced as children with occasional contributions from Thoby. Virginia's posthumous reputation, overshadowing that of her older sister, has resulted in mistaken assumptions that she was substantially responsible for the *News*. Vanessa retained two volumes of the paper in her archive at Charleston.[18] The cover of the first is stamped with her initials, 'VS', beneath the title, 'Hyde Park Gate News'. The second volume, bound to match, bears both sisters' initials, 'VS' and 'AVS' for Adeline Virginia Stephen. Vanessa was nearly 12 when the venture was launched and Virginia was 9. Although in her memoir 'Notes on Virginia's Childhood' she recalled with typical modesty that 'Virginia wrote most of it', Vanessa was unlikely to have simply copied out her younger sister's drafts.[19] The contents were devised collaboratively. The paper is wittily laid out in columns to replicate a newspaper and most of the issues are in Vanessa's neat, rounded handwriting. The first 'Cristmas Number' includes her illustrations, including 'a picture of the celebrated author Mr Leslie Stephen'.[20]

Hyde Park Gate News offers a vivid insight into Vanessa's interests as a young adolescent. Unlike Vanessa and Virginia's memoirs, for which it provided a source, it pre-dates the deaths of Julia and Stella and is unfiltered by memory. The *News* is parodic in tone, interspersing fictional letters and diary columns with items of family news. Even as a child Vanessa was acutely aware of the contractual nature of marriage for women and its consequences for their social and financial status. One fictional letter 'from Lucy's Mama to Lucy' advises her to 'put forth all your powers of snobsnubbing' to rebuff a suitor as 'your position in life does not permit you to marry a school-master with so small a salary'.[21] When Stella visited Bayreuth with George in 1892 'The Principal object', the *News* reported, was 'to hear a certain German opera', but Gerald 'has made prophesies as to which German baron is going to be Miss Duckworth's future one'.[22] Thoby's returns from boarding school were eagerly anticipated and a few days before Vanessa's thirteenth birthday, 'Miss Virginia and Miss Vanessa Stephen went to tea with their intimate friends the Misses Milman'.[23] Sylvia Milman would go to art school with Vanessa and lived nearby.[24] They played croquet before 'sitting at the table and discoursing upon various subjects'. According to the *News*, 'Miss Vanessa's mother gave her a handsome bag' for her birthday, and 'Miss Duckworth gave her some painting materials'.[25]

The paper was written in a small sitting room 'handed over' to Vanessa and Virginia at Hyde Park Gate, and at Talland House in St Ives where the family spent their summers. Vanessa's acutely visual understanding of light and interiors informs her account of the process: 'It was a cheerful little room, almost entirely made of glass – with a skylight, windows all along one side, looking on to the back garden . . . In this room we used to sit, I painting, and she reading aloud.' They spied on their parents through 'another window cut in the wall between the little room and the drawing room . . . I remember putting the paper on the table by my mother's sofa while they were at dinner and then creeping quietly into the little room to look through the window and hear the criticisms.' She recalled Virginia's excitement when their mother, 'quietly sitting near the fire, my father on the other side with his lamp, both reading', noticed the *Hyde Park Gate News* and picked it up. '"Rather clever, I think," said my mother, putting the paper down without apparent excitement. But it was enough to thrill her daughter'.[26]

Vanessa remembered most of the interiors at Hyde Park Gate as 'pitch-dark. Virginia creeper hung down in a thick curtain over the back drawing-room window, the kitchen and other basement rooms could only be seen by candle or lamp light and most of the paint was black.'[27] In a lecture given at her sons' school she later exemplified her sense of isolation as an artist in a literary household by describing an occasion when, 'fired . . . one day with a desire to reform', she cleared away a number of 'hideous' family photographs in plush frames 'in the darkest corner of a dark room'. She was immediately condemned as 'a heartless desecrator of the most sacred sentiments of family'.[28] But on another occasion when she removed a blackened chandelier with Thoby's help – 'you see I was already a revolutionary' – the change went unnoticed:

> Light flooded the room and we felt horribly exposed in our guilt. But . . . the chandelier had only been a mass of colour and reflected lights and semi-transparencies – it had no particular human associations – and so, although everything else in the room now stood revealed as colour and form where before all had been veiled in shade, for the writers there was no difference.[29]

Vanessa spent her early childhood in two rooms on the third floor at Hyde Park Gate, the 'day' and 'night' nurseries, with Thoby, Virginia and Adrian:

we four children and a nurse slept and had our baths and did
all else in what I think must by modern standards have been a
very unhealthy atmosphere. Was the window ever open at night?
I doubt it. There was a lovely bright fire to go to bed by: coal,
food, hot water and babies being carried up many times a day;
we were very snug.

She was educated at home, initially with Thoby, who was less than
16 months her junior, and then with Virginia. Thoby was sent to
preparatory school at the age of 10. She became responsible for supporting his education after their mother's death when he was 14 and
they remained close. Adrian, too, was sent to school while Vanessa
and Virginia studied French, history and Latin with their mother
and maths with their father. Sir Leslie believed that women should
be as well educated as men, writing to Julia, 'I hate to see so many
women's lives wasted simply because they have not been trained well
enough,' but he deferred to his wife's determination that her daughters should be committed to the service of others and ultimately this
served his own purposes because Vanessa became committed to caring
for him.[30] In 'Notes on Virginia's Childhood' Vanessa reiterated her
sister's complaint:

> She always said that she had no education and I am inclined to
> agree with her, if by education is meant learning things out of
> books. If she had none however, I had less, for she did at least
> teach herself or get herself taught Greek and was given books
> to read by my father.[31]

One of Vanessa's earliest memories of Virginia was her critical
appraisal of their parents when they were still young enough to be
'jumping about naked' in the bathroom. 'She suddenly asked me
which I liked best, my father or mother. Such a question seemed to
me rather terrible – surely one ought not to ask it. I felt certain Thoby
would have snubbed the questioner'. The conversation, in which
she instinctively replied that she preferred their mother and Virginia
proceeded to analyse her own feelings for both parents before opting
for their father, marked a turning point in their relationship. 'If one
could criticise one's parents, what or whom could one not criticise?

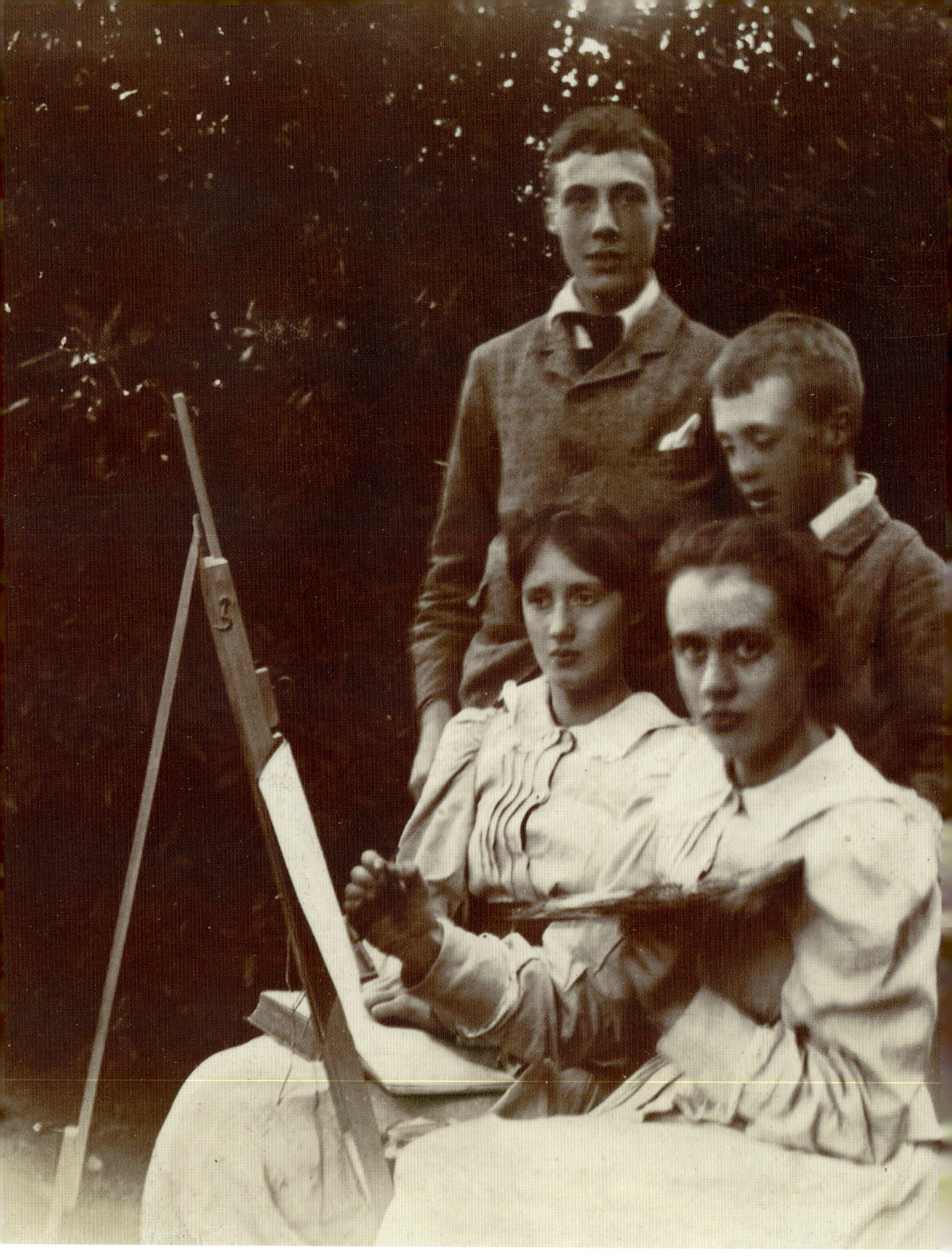

1.4. Unknown photographer, 'Vanessa, Thoby, Virginia and Adrian Stephen'

*c.*1893–5, Henry W. and Albert A. Berg Collection of English
and American Literature, New York Public Library

Dimly some freedom of thought and speech seemed born'.[32] Later, she rationalised her preference for Julia. Sir Leslie, she wrote, never entered an art gallery or ventured down from the Alps into Italy's museums and churches, while 'life apart from human beings was almost completely visual for me'.[33]

Stella supported Vanessa's interest in the arts and although she was a dutiful daughter Stella was a 'New Woman'. She encouraged Vanessa and Virginia to pursue progressive hobbies such as cycling and photography. Her photographs, as well as those of Vanessa and Virginia, complement the *Hyde Park Gate News* in documenting Vanessa's privileged and relatively liberal family life. Stella was given 'a photographing machine' in 1892 as the craze for amateur photography among young women gathered momentum.[34] She learned to develop and tone her own photographs, initiating a new family passion that would compete with cricket for their attention on holidays. That summer at Talland House the *News* reported that Gerald had 'taken to photography like his sister and declared his intention of photographing Sophia the cook'.[35] The siblings wrote that 'Miss Stella Duckworth and Mr Gerald Duckworth . . . keep a visitor's list by photographing everyone who comes to the palatial residence' and the following year Stella noted in her diary that she mounted photographs in an album before packing up ready to return to London.[36] Her photographs invariably show Vanessa and Virginia in identical dresses, despite the three-year difference in their ages, undermining their separate identities. Vanessa learned her skills as a young photographer from Stella. An early photograph shows her seated at an easel with her Stephen siblings behind her (fig. 1.4).[37] She holds a palette in her left hand and stares intently at the camera, as if in the act of portraying the photographer. Her raised right hand holds a small object rather than a brush or pencil and this may have been a remote shutter release, making her both the subject and creator of the image.

Painting and photographing were profoundly associated with the long summers that Vanessa spent in Cornwall. Every year for three or four months, like many Victorian families in their circle, the Stephens relocated their entire household of servants, pets, clothing, equipment and visitors to the seaside. Sir Leslie found Talland House on a walking holiday when Vanessa was two. After Julia's death he 'instantly decided that he wished never to see St Ives again'.[38] The lease was sold and childhood summers in St Ives came to an end. For Vanessa and Virginia, therefore, Cornwall and the photographs that Stella and Sir Leslie pasted into albums of their family at Talland House were mnemonic triggers. St Ives in the 1880s was becoming fashionable among artists such as Whistler and his assistant Walter Sickert, who would later tell Vanessa that he remembered seeing Julia and Sir Leslie there.[39] In her diary Stella describes painting in the rose garden with Vanessa and their mother, while their father took a boat out, and Virginia would create the character of Lily Briscoe, a serious young artist, painting on the lawn in full view of the house in her evocation of their childhood, *To the Lighthouse*. As a young mother, Vanessa replicated the practice of spending summers by the sea, organising advance parties of servants and trunks of luggage to travel by train to lodgings in Studland Bay in Dorset between 1909 and 1911. She invited friends and family to join her there, making them the subjects of photographs and of paintings that were deeply rooted in memory.

Vanessa's life as the eldest of the four Stephen siblings as well as her prospects for becoming a professional artist shifted irrevocably in 1895. A few weeks before her sixteenth birthday her mother died of rheumatic fever following a brief illness. She was 49. The family was plunged into mourning. Sir Leslie was agnostic, encouraging his children to be pragmatic in their approach to death. He channelled his grief into a text written 'to you personally, my beloved children . . . simply to talk to you about your mother'.[40] Dubbed the Mausoleum Book, it summarised Julia's biography and his own before describing their life together. His initial intention was to create a fair copy 'bound in a volume with some photographs'.[41] In the event a separate photograph album was compiled, possibly with the help of Stella or Vanessa, and bound to match that of the text in green Moroccan leather. It provided a model for Vanessa's own albums in which photographs were grouped together to suggest visual narratives.[42] The first 15 pages of the album were dedicated to Julia Margaret Cameron's photographs of Julia as a celebrated beauty, but subsequent pages were titled 'Julia with the 4 younger children' and 'At St Ives'. They show Vanessa in her mother's arms as a baby and as a small child. The album immortalised their holidays at Talland House, showing

Vanessa with her younger siblings taking lessons with their mother, and in larger family groups. Her close relationship with Thoby is evident in these snapshots. When Vanessa became the keeper of her family's archive she kept the Mausoleum Book at Gordon Square and then at Charleston. Evidently it assuaged her sense of loss and it may have been a source of pride in her mother's beauty and family connections. When spending Christmas away from Clive and their children in 1912 she wrote to him that Duncan had called round to Gordon Square on Boxing Day 'and lay on the floor and talked in a desultory but cheering way of the Mausoleum Book'.[43]

Vanessa's earliest surviving album, made in 1896 after the watershed of her mother's death, is meticulously produced with snapshots carefully aligned, cut into the cream paper of the album pages and captioned. It begins with a visual record of a family visit to Haslemere in Surrey in September 1896, followed by her first trip to France that November with Virginia and George, who paid for the trip. 'We took lots of photographs, but we haven't had time to develop any yet,' she wrote to Thoby on their return. A snapshot that Virginia must have taken of Vanessa and George wrapped in a blanket together on the crossing home is characteristic of photographs of him with his half-sisters. His presence seems invasive and uncomfortable. He is always standing or sitting too close.[44] Cameras and photographs were passed between the siblings to some extent, but Vanessa and Virginia owned their own camera by February 1897, when the subsequent album pages record a holiday to Bognor in which they chaperoned Stella and her fiancé Jack Hills.[45]

George assumed a quasi-parental responsibility for Vanessa after their mother's death and he was anxious to secure her position in society. She was introduced into Victorian society, briefly, following her eighteenth birthday and with Stella's marriage impending she was taught to manage her father's household:

> On me, naturally, fell the housekeeping and though this meant
> very little in some ways, for Sophy allowed me hardly any choice
> in the question of food, all had to be what it had always been
> during her fifteen or twenty years of service, still it did mean that
> I had to face the recurring horror of 'weekly books'.[46]

As a consequence of this early responsibility Vanessa was interested in her servants throughout her life, often sketching or painting them. Having managed a complex Victorian household, she was confident in her understanding of their respective roles. Even in the last years of her life at Charleston she maintained a formal relationship with her housekeeper, Grace Higgens. Every morning she would go into the kitchen where there was only one chair so that 'Mrs Bell' could be seated while 'Grace' stood to take her instructions for the day. She took responsibility for the smooth running of her own homes and for Clive's various residences. She arranged for rooms to be cleaned and decorated, for houses and apartments to be leased and sublet in London, Sussex and the South of France. Her practical engagement with the details of property management would underpin her creative work as an interior designer. This invisible and time-consuming labour became central to her identity and authority within the Bloomsbury Group as well as her practice as an artist.

The process of compiling the 'weekly books' of housekeeping costs and presenting them to her father in the seven years between Stella's death and that of Sir Leslie is given a disproportionate emphasis in a memoir Vanessa wrote, 'Life at Hyde Park Gate after 1897', because it was an abusive ritual. 'These almost always led to groans, sighs and then explosions of rage,' to which she responded by waiting in silence, 'acutely unhappy and rather terrified', for her father to sign the necessary cheque.[47] She avoided confrontation throughout her life and tolerated even outrageously unreasonable behaviour in men. She suffered, too, from a complicit acceptance of sexual abuse within her family and a determination to conceal it. Virginia's biographers have analysed the evidence for George and Gerald's abuse of both sisters but there is a telling absence of documents.[48] In his memoir of Vanessa, Quentin wrote a lengthy denial of what he described as 'wild speculation' about George, who, he argued, 'was certainly guilty of stupid and inconsiderate behaviour . . . but wasn't it possible that George himself was unaware of the seriousness of what he was doing?' He cites a letter from Vanessa to her cousin Fredegond Shove which, he wrote, 'discussed the business; clearly it had all been very horrible', but because there was no explicit account of abuse he concluded that 'George did not actually rape his sisters'.[49] Vanessa's correspondence was censored during her lifetime and subsequently.

As early as 1904, when both sisters were reading their parents' letters and Virginia was writing about their father for Frederic Maitland's biography of him, Vanessa wrote to her, 'I would rather that no one, not even Fred, should see the more intimate bits. I should like them burnt.'[50] Her own letters containing sensitive or confidential material are often headed in capitals 'BURN THIS' and evidently some were deliberately destroyed. The relevant letters to Fredegond Shove are missing, but in December 1918, when Vanessa was in the last weeks of her pregnancy with Angelica, Fredegond wrote to her:

> your letter was such a very interesting one . . . We never knew that you were going through such living nightmares. I can dimly see how horrible it must all have been and I would so like to know all the truth about that George affair . . . Some day will you tell me all about it.[51]

Fredegond subsequently repeated 'an amazing description of Virginia and Vanessa when they were young' to Dora Carrington. She was full of 'whimsical bawdy and scandal', Carrington wrote to Lytton Strachey.[52] Vanessa and Virginia's shared history of abuse was intrinsic to their relationship, and as the elder sister, Vanessa would have felt responsible for protecting Virginia. She made a lifelong commitment to caring for her mental health.

Vanessa's memoir about her childhood home begins with Stella's death in July 1897, which she described as a catastrophe: 'the second and more appalling of the two tragedies which had wrecked our normally cheerful family life.'[53] She and Virginia had followed Stella's courtship with Jack Hills closely. Stella was already ill when they returned from their honeymoon in Florence. Vanessa described the next three months as 'a time of horrible suspense, muddle, mismanagement, hopeless fighting against the stupidity of those in power'.[54] The family doctor, who would continue to treat Vanessa and Virginia, diagnosed peritonitis and operated too late but there were also rumours that Stella's acutely painful condition was a consequence of sexual intercourse or of pregnancy.[55] After her death Vanessa's relationship with Jack transitioned from one of consoling sister-in-law to a romantic attachment, reinforcing the concept that the Stephen sisters were interchangeable. A law that criminalised marriage between a man and his late wife's sister made their relationship a potential source of scandal. George was violently opposed to the match and rallied the family in opposition to it. Although Sir Leslie was relatively benign on the subject, giving Vanessa the option to marry abroad, she was trapped and alienated by an outdated family law.

Vanessa's Victorian upbringing taught her to internalise trauma and despair, to shoulder responsibility and to compartmentalise. Her days were divided, after Stella's death, between training to be an artist, discussed in the next chapter, and meeting her family's expectations. After a suitable period she was 'taken by George, one was always taken by him' to a dressmaker and bought a gown that would qualify as mourning: 'exquisitely pretty, transparent black over transparent white and all sewn with tiny silver sequins . . . I came to dread the sight of it', she wrote, because she wore it to the innumerable society parties, dinners, dances and weekends that she was coerced into attending with George.[56] Duckworth family money as well as age and gender gave George and Gerald a financial advantage over their Stephen siblings. 'George's generosity knew no bounds', Vanessa wrote sardonically, as the gift of a 'lovely grey Arab mare' obliged her to begin her 'social day' with him every morning at eight o'clock, 'trotting solemnly up and down the Ladies Mile' in Kensington Gardens.[57] After breakfast he would go to his work at the Treasury as Austen Chamberlain's private secretary while Gerald worked at the publishing house he established in 1898.[58] Vanessa would give her instructions for the day 'below stairs' before cycling or taking the bus to art school. 'From ten to one Victorian society did not exert any special pressure upon us,' Virginia later wrote. 'For three hours we lived in the world which we still inhabit.' However, from 4.30 p.m. she and Vanessa set aside their writing and painting and adopted the mannerisms of Victorian young ladies. 'In the first place, we must be in . . . And we must be tidied and in our places, she at the tea table, I on the sofa . . . for father could not give himself his tea in the society of those days.' As soon as the doorbell rang, Virginia recalled, 'instantaneously we became young ladies possessed of a certain manner. We learnt it partly from remembering mother's manner; Stella's manner, and it was partly imposed upon us by the visitor who came in.'[59] Although Sir Leslie was only 62 when Julia died and he continued his work as a writer and biographer to the end of his life, he indulged in the dependencies of a much older man. 'My father could only be spoken to through a tube', Vanessa wrote, 'and it was shy work doing this in front of the family, it was worse with strangers there'. He sighed and groaned in company, which, she wrote 'did not lead to cheerfulness'.[60] When Lytton Strachey, one of Thoby's Cambridge friends, first encountered Vanessa and her family on holiday in 1901 he described the oddness of 'Leslie with his ear-trumpet and tam-o'-shanter. What is rather strange is the old man – older than he really is – among so young a family.'[61] He was 'well kept in check by them', Strachey wrote, and this role of managing his eccentricities and pandering to his needs primarily fell to Vanessa.

She processed her emotional involvement with people, to an extent, through portraiture. Vanessa painted her father in his tam-o'-shanter, perhaps in response to a request from Thoby for an image of him when Sir Leslie was awarded an honorary doctorate from Oxford in November 1901 (fig. 1.5). Her portrait is an accomplished early work, echoing the restrained palette and composition of the much earlier Watts. It assimilates John Singer Sargent's teaching at the Royal Academy Schools and the work of Charles Wellington Furse, a family friend. The loose brushwork, dashing in highlights across the forehead and around the bridge and tip of the nose, emulates Furse's technique, although Vanessa later claimed to have found him 'formidable and crushing'.[62] Sir Leslie's piercing blue eyes are painted with deliberation and the handling of the moustache and beard, rapidly sketched in, suggests that the portrait was painted from life. The expression is pensive but the work reveals Vanessa's affection for her father.

In the last two years of Sir Leslie's life, Vanessa's role as a carer intensified. She was 22, still living at home with Virginia and their half-brothers and studying at the Royal Academy Schools, when her father became ill with abdominal cancer in April 1902. Thoby and Adrian were at Trinity College, Cambridge. Vanessa organised the medical care and budgeted for the considerable cost of daily doctors' visits and a succession of live-in nurses. Cancer wasn't openly discussed in Edwardian England, even with the patient. She maintained a semblance of normality, telling nobody outside the family until the following April, when she confided in her lifelong friend and fellow student, Margery Snowdon:

the only thing to do is to go on with all one's ordinary things &
be as cheerful as possible to him so that he may suspect nothing.
I mean to work at the figure at the R.A. 3 days a week & to
hire models & draw from the figure at home the other 3 days.[63]

She shielded Thoby and Virginia from the onerous psychological
weight of her responsibilities until this time when, she wrote, 'I settled that I ought to tell them all I know'.[64] Adrian was not told that
his father was dying until he came home for Christmas: 'poor little
boy', Virginia wrote, 'he had guessed nothing'.[65]

The first 24 years of Vanessa's life, before her father died at
home at Hyde Park Gate in February 1904, equipped her to manage
socially and psychologically complex situations. She developed an
astute understanding of patriarchal systems and double standards
that were beyond her control. She learned to present an appearance
of conformity to Victorian conventions that she would subsequently
undermine. She developed strategies of passive resistance to achieve
her own ends without confrontation. While she assumed the authority of a dutiful Victorian, managing her father's household and his
care, taking her place in the affluent and influential society that her
half-brothers insisted upon, Vanessa remained unmarried. She performed her domestic responsibilities whilst sustaining a detached
and unwavering ambition to be an artist. 'Nessa preaches that our
destinies lie in ourselves', Virginia wrote in her diary on New Year's
Day in 1898.[66] Virginia described her sister's 'exalted' position at 22
Hyde Park Gate, 'full of power and responsibility'.[67] By the time she
cleared the family home and left South Kensington for Bloomsbury,
Vanessa's identity as the influential and capable matriarch that the
Bloomsbury Group would revolve around was set.

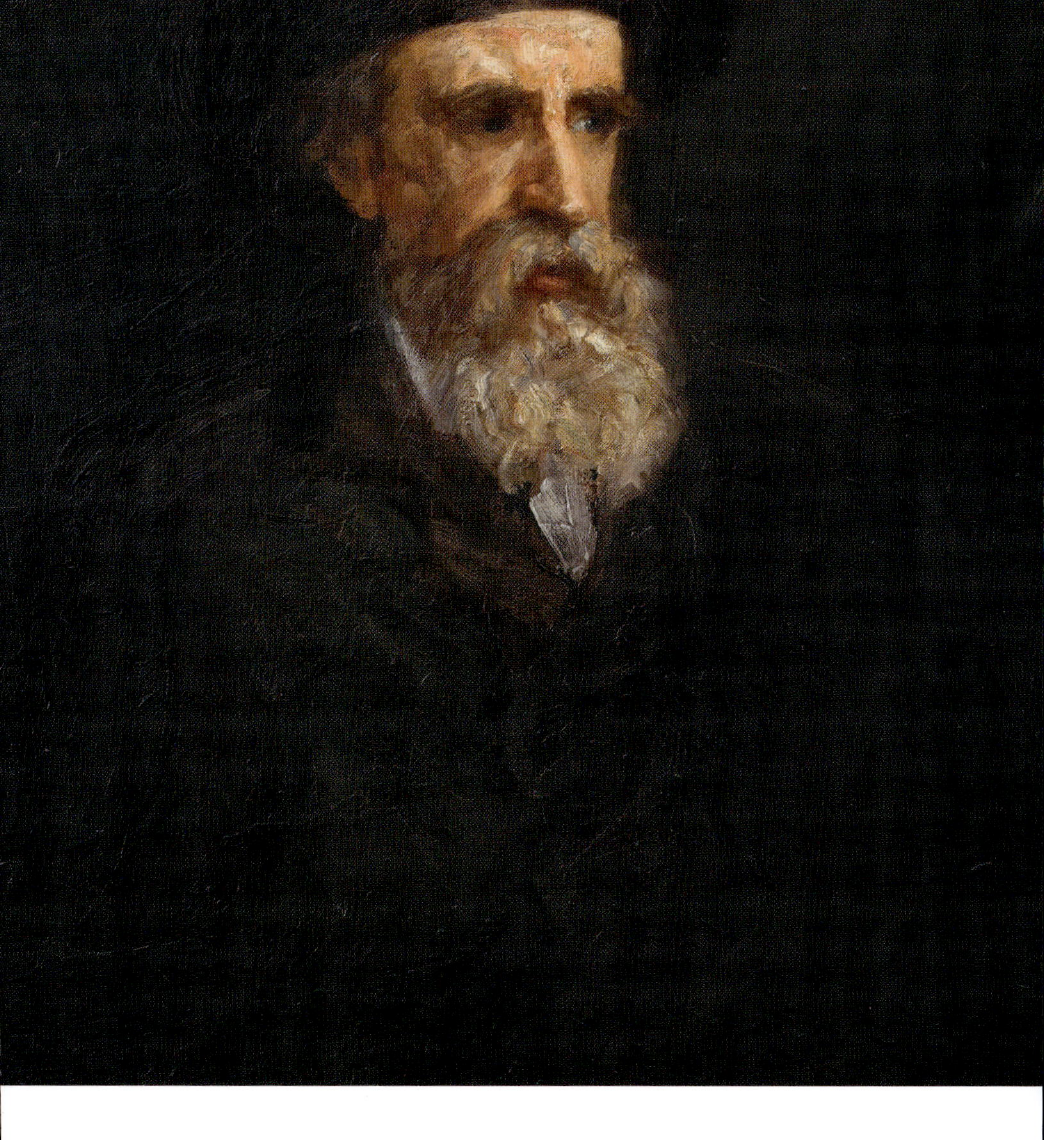

1.5. Vanessa Bell, *Leslie Stephen*

c.1901, oil on canvas, 670 × 600 mm, Piano Nobile, London

2

TRAINING AND TRAVEL

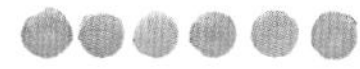

When Vanessa was pregnant with her first child, Virginia began a narrative for the unborn baby. 'Reminiscences' is an experimental biography, reasserting her close relationship with Vanessa and their shared experiences as sisters. Neither of them had established reputations when the manuscript was completed in 1908 but it describes the ambition that made Vanessa exceptional: 'Once I saw her scrawl on a black door a great maze of lines, with white chalk. "When I am a famous painter—" she began, and then turned shy and rubbed it out in her capable way.'[1] Vanessa and Virginia belonged to a generation of women who had to strive, even to imagine equality. There were no famous women painters to serve as professional role models.

Vanessa's formal training began in 1896, the year following her mother's death, when she studied drawing with Ebenezer Cooke and then enrolled in the Cope and Nicol School of Painting. Cooke was a reforming figure in art education. He had studied under John Ruskin at the Working Men's College in 1855 and succeeded him as the drawing master there. Soon after the Working Women's College was founded nine years later Cooke became responsible for its Ruskin Drawing Class.[2] By 1885 he was teaching drawing and botany in Belgravia at 'Grosvenor Select Classes for Ladies' as part of a wider programme to prepare students for London University and for Newnham and Girton colleges at Cambridge.[3] Vanessa is likely to have studied with him at this or a comparable institution where he taught one drawing class a week. She was already familiar with

Ruskin's work, including *The Elements of Drawing*, a cornerstone of Cooke's teaching.[4] Virginia described her at St Ives 'painting in water-colours, and scratching a number of black little squares, after Ruskin's prescription'.[5] His first exercise in *Elements* directed his reader to draw a series of squares and fill them 'with crossed lines'. The art of shading would be accomplished when each box was filled 'so completely and evenly that it should look like a square patch of grey silk or cloth'.[6]

Like Ruskin, Cooke was reverent in his approach to nature and he promoted a connection between drawing and learning. He was involved with the emerging Arts and Crafts movement and may have instilled an interest in design and the decorative arts in Vanessa. He taught 'men and boys engaged in the building, furnishing and kindred trades' at the Whitechapel Craft School in London's East End.[7] Women were excluded until 1898 when a Housekeeping School for girls was opened. Cooke developed the theories of the educational reformers Johann Heinrich Pestalozzi and Friedrich Froebel. His observations about the innate creativity of children would have a lasting impact on Vanessa. She encouraged Roger's exhibition of children's art at the Omega Workshops in 1917 and, as an established artist lecturing at her sons' school, she described very young children as 'dangerously like artists' because they 'saw the world as colour'.[8]

She soon progressed to a private art school for male and female students, recently established by Arthur Stockdale Cope. Three days a week, having dispatched her domestic duties, 'the day began', she recalled, 'by bicycling down Queen's Gate to Mr Cope's School of Art, in a long skirt and a large floppy hat which was apt to fly off near the draughty cross-roads at South Kensington Station'.[9] Cope and his fellow principal, John Watson Nicol, were successful Academicians. Both men had trained at the Royal Academy Schools, Cope also taught there and their school was designed to prepare students for the Academy. Each year Nicol formally recommended students for admission to the Painting School at the Royal Academy, ensuring a steady stream of graduates from his own establishment. Vanessa's lifelong friend Margery Snowdon was one of these, accepted into the Academy Schools on Nicol's recommendation in 1900. She was a friendly ally when Vanessa and Sylvia Milman arrived in a cohort of eight students recommended by Nicol the following year.[10]

Vanessa was diligent, intent upon passing the entrance exam to the Royal Academy Schools. There was a strong work ethic at 22 Hyde Park Gate and Stella was still presiding over the household when she enrolled. Stella had taken Vanessa to look at the school, writing in her diary on 1 April: 'to Cope & Nicols' studio. Nessa liked the looks of it. She begins on the 27th'.[11] 'Nessa went to her drawing' on Mondays, Wednesdays and Fridays, Virginia recorded in her diaries, sometimes returning home for lunch with Sylvia: 'Nessa and Sylvia came. Luncheon passed very peaceably and the art students departed soon after it.'[12] If she was obliged to miss classes, she made the time up: 'I am going to the Studio every day next week so as to make up for our week at Bognor', she wrote to Thoby in 1897.[13] Her time at the school was compromised by the emotional impact of Stella's sudden death. Virginia's mental health was already fragile and she became increasingly dependent upon Vanessa during Stella's illness, writing in her diary, 'I slept with Nessa, as I was unhappy'.[14] Vanessa later described her own acute depression at Cope's: 'I felt so utterly mean and despicable. I looked around the room and thought that any one of the people working there must despise me.'[15]

The teaching was conventional, with an emphasis on drawing from antique casts and from models. 'Line! Line!' Cope would shout at his students.[16] Although Vanessa was a prize-winning student, the pressure became intense as the Academy entrance deadline approached: 'I don't quite know what to do about the Trinity ball', she wrote to Thoby at Cambridge, 'we shall . . . be having a model for the drawing of a head & arm for the R.A. & if I miss him I shan't get the drawing done in time. . . . I must do this horrible Academy thing properly'.[17] She was more assured of her progress in a subsequent letter, explaining that she could miss a half day's class: 'We are now all trembling in the midst of doing our head & arm for the Academy & the model for it unluckily sits on Saturday . . . However such is my cleverness that I am further on than any one else'.[18] Evidently she was confident of her success because she wrote again the following month: 'On Tuesday I shall know my fate . . . I shall soon be wildly excited.'[19]

Many of Vanessa's fellow students were young women whose families, like her own, regarded art school as a pleasant diversion from their main purpose of finding husbands. Vanessa and Virginia were escorted by George on their visits to Cambridge, including to the Trinity College ball. 'Do you want us to be <u>very</u> smart?' Vanessa wrote to Thoby. 'Georgie has bought us a good many fineries from Paris which we shall put on for your benefit.'[20] Several of the women with whom she studied would go on to have moderately successful careers, but the Academy's patriarchal infrastructure did little to encourage their expectations.[21] All of their tutors were men. Vanessa's family connections reinforced this limiting prospect. Her great-aunt Julia Margaret Cameron and the Victorian artist Marie Spartali Stillman had moved in the same Pre-Raphaelite circles and Marie's stepdaughter, Lisa, was a friend of Stella's.[22] She stayed at Talland House, making portraits of Julia and Stella.[23] She and her sister, the sculptor Effie Stillman, shared a studio at the top of a house opposite the family home in Kensington, and Vanessa visited her with Stella and modelled for her.[24] She remained in contact with 'Old Lisa' although she described her in 1918 as 'a depressing figure. She says since her nervous breakdown 8 years ago she hasn't been able to see to draw'.[25]

Gendered approaches to art education were reiterated for Vanessa on Tuesdays when another family connection, Elizabeth Weston Flower, guided her 'and a party of other girls' through the National Gallery collections.[26] Vanessa regarded the National Gallery as an essential study resource, writing to Thoby around 1897, 'Tomorrow I'm going to begin going to the National Gallery with Mrs Flower again.'[27] She studied and copied from Old Masters throughout her life but she used professional photographs and prints to do so. The Gallery's 'Student Days' – when current students could set up their easels an hour before the general public were admitted and learn from the collection by making 'oil-colour copies' – were on Thursdays and Fridays. Vanessa saw Mrs Flower on Tuesday afternoons.[28] Young women performed their identities as artists for one another and for the public on these student days, but Vanessa does not appear to have been among them.

Mrs Flower was a flower painter and a friend of Whistler's. She and her husband owned several of his paintings, including *Nocturne in Blue and Silver*, and Vanessa would have seen their collection at the extraordinary house that Richard Norman Shaw designed for them in Chelsea, Swan House.[29] Whistler would influence Vanessa's early work. She analysed his method of building up layers of thin paint: 'he didn't put the right colour on at once. It was probably almost a monochrome to start with and I suppose he only got the right colour in the end.' Although she didn't emulate his style – 'I can't paint thinly enough' –, she understood and admired his technique: 'I expect that the most beautiful surface is got his way'.[30] His *Arrangement in Grey and Black, No. 2: Portrait of Thomas Carlyle* made an enduring impression and she kept a print of it in her collection.[31] Mrs Flower took Vanessa to exhibitions as well as the national collections and again these reinforced her family's Pre-Raphaelite heritage. Visiting a Ford Madox Brown exhibition at the Grafton Galleries they were delighted to meet Holman Hunt, who showed them round.[32]

The Stephen family supported Vanessa's ambition by cultivating the artists in their circle who might help her. She was a bridesmaid when Charles Furse married the daughter of a family friend.[33] Stella took her to Adrian Stokes's studio.[34] G.F. Watts and his wife Mary were entertained to lunch and they in turn invited Vanessa to see his London studio and then to stay with them at their home and studio in Surrey.[35] For Vanessa, this was a mixed blessing. Her professional insights were a social accomplishment which she was obliged to share with her family's South Kensington circle: 'Yesterday morning I went to the Watts exhibition for the third time with Lisa Hoby, which was rather beastly,' she wrote to Thoby.[36] She resented 'having to go to the first Impressionist paintings I ever saw in company with Alice Pollock and being aware that she enjoyed the paintings no more than I did her company'.[37] George accompanied her to stay with Watts in Surrey in 1901 and again two years later, by which time Vanessa was a student at the Royal Academy Schools. She was charged by Margery Snowdon to 'put down most of the great man's remarks', and although she regarded Watts as 'a very kind old gentleman' she was already ambivalent about his work and the 'long lecture upon Art' that he gave her.[38]

The deadpan tone of Vanessa's letters, simply recording 'scraps of what he said', reflects the power dynamics of the visit. When Watts asked, 'Now what do you mean by style?' she 'gibbered feebly', she wrote, 'about its being one's individual expression. "No. Now I will tell you what it is,"' the master replied.[39] He criticised the work of Sargent, who Vanessa admired: 'The whole idea of modern portrait painting is wrong. They try to make their sitters stand out from the frame & every picture should really seem to be some way inside & away from it', he explained to her. There is little evidence in Vanessa's account that her own opinions were encouraged, and statements that she and Margery would have challenged are recorded without comment: 'When I paint a picture I want to give a message,' Watts told her, and 'no art can be great unless it's beautiful'. He 'never did anything from a model', criticised modern French pictures as indecent and thought it wrong 'to paint the nude simply for its own sake'. George embarrassed Vanessa with his remarks '(you can imagine it) that he had been ashamed to look at the drawings at the RA prize giving & had felt in want of a fan all the time'.[40] After dinner she and George entertained the company in traditional Victorian style: 'we played their Pianola.'[41]

Vanessa's influence as a critic, shaping and informing the opinions of more outspoken men in her circle, is seldom recognised because she reserved her opinions for private conversations and letters to family and friends. They are reflected in Virginia's writing and in Thoby's letters to his friend from Cambridge, Clive Bell. Although Virginia and Stella regularly accompanied Vanessa to galleries, Thoby and Adrian had never visited the National Gallery when Vanessa began her training as an artist.[42] She and Thoby visited the Louvre together in 1900 when George took them to Paris during the *Exposition Universelle*. Thoby learned more about painting through discussions with Vanessa in the museums and churches they visited together with Virginia and Adrian in Italy after their father's death in 1904. He immediately engaged in a bombastic correspondence with Clive in which his opinions echo those of his more knowledgeable elder sister. Describing Venice to Margery Snowdon, Vanessa wrote: 'We spend our mornings seeing pictures, and the afternoons churches.'[43] She listed the artists whose work she had admired – Bellini, Titian and Carpaccio – but concluded emphatically:

> Tintoretto is simply splendid & finer than anyone else . . . One knows pretty well what Titian & Veronese & the others will be like from pictures in London & at other places, but Tintoret [sic] one gets no idea of anywhere but at Venice, & there one suddenly sees all his finest things. It was an absolute revelation to me.[44]

While she was writing to Margery, Thoby was lampooning Clive, who had recently moved to Paris and was spending his days at the Louvre:

When I wrote to you from Venice I was under the erroneous impression that you had been there . . . had you visited the Scuola San Rocco and the Academia [sic] you could not have uttered those blashphemies [sic] against Tintoret with which your letter is defiled. Until a man has been there he has no more right to speak of painting than a man who has read neither Sophocles nor Shakespeare to criticize literature. For Tintoret is the Shakespeare . . . of painting.[45]

The differences between Thoby's sparring correspondence with Clive and Vanessa's letters to Margery are informative because they exemplify the gender disparities that restrained her. As a Cambridge graduate embarking on a career in law, Thoby assumed a command of cultural history, grandly contextualising the paintings he had seen that week within a European canon of art and literature. He dismissed Clive's admiration for Velázquez over Tintoretto: 'even the limited knowledge of painting attainable in the Louvre would have enabled you to distinguish between diabolical dexterity and the grand style of the master – between Pope and Milton'. He was combative, using his knowledge to undermine: 'About Bellini . . . you misplace him – and I suspect are confusing him with his brother Gentile or his father Jacopo.'[46] Vanessa's letters discuss the same artists and paintings but they are very different in tone. Both siblings evidently had a copy of Ruskin's *The Stones of Venice* to hand but by this time Vanessa had formed her own opinions: 'There are beauties by Bellini and Carpaccio. Ruskin raves about them, but I don't think he's any good at all as a critic, though he's generally amusing.' She objected to his insistence that art could be symbolic or have 'several deep meanings, which doesn't seem to me to be what one wants'.[47] She and Thoby were agreed that Tintoretto's portraits were dull: 'he doesn't seem to have taken any interest in them', Vanessa wrote, and they both drew comparisons between *The Origin of the Milky Way* in London (his *Titus Andronicus* and *Troilus and Cressida* according to Thoby) and the larger paintings that they had seen together in Venice ('his *Lears* his *Othellos*').[48] Vanessa described these as 'splendid in colour and composition, and there's a tremendous sort of force about them'.[49] She wanted to share her experience with Margery, promising to show her photographs of Tintoretto's paintings in the Scuola Grande di San

Rocco: 'There's a huge crucifixion which takes up the whole of one wall and is quite splendid . . . I shall bring back some photographs to show you as its useless to try to describe them.'[50] A faded print of the *Crucifixion* is one of many such photographs in her collection at Charleston.[51]

> When I come back we will go to the National Gallery together, where one can really get a very good idea of all the different schools & painters. I feel now as if I should be able to understand them better . . . We will really go & see them properly & I will tell you what I have seen here.[52]

As an Edwardian traveller, negotiating the elaborate conventions that constrained women of her class, Vanessa was initially dependent upon her brothers as chaperones. Her first trip abroad, to Boulogne with George and Virginia after the death of their mother, was characterised by stereotypical prejudices: 'we went to a very improper French play,' she wrote to Thoby. 'The French are most disgusting people I think. They never seem to wash and they spit everywhere'.[53] Her letters to Margery eight years later reveal a transformation in her confidence and curiosity as a traveller. She wrote from Florence decrying the Grand Hotel, 'an enormous place full of English & Americans which was rather tiresome . . . I believe one ought to go to a small quiet place & stay there some time so as to do things in a leisurely way instead of rather rushing about as we did.'[54] This would remain her philosophy. Her travels were allowed to evolve. She wrote that they would remain in Florence for another fortnight before travelling to Sienna and Genoa '& then we might possibly go to Paris for a week or two'.[55] Violet Dickinson had recently joined them: 'a good person to have as she . . . has a friend here who writes about painters, & is going to go round with us & show us things'.[56] The friend was Vernon Lee. Vanessa's particular interest in portraiture is evident in her admiration for one of Titian's paintings but she was also excited by a portrait of Lee by Sargent: 'it was interesting to see her beside it, as I hardly know any of the people he has painted.'[57]

Luggage was the enemy of spontaneity for women travellers. Edwardians did not travel light and on her first visits abroad with George, Vanessa packed an extensive wardrobe including her evening dress (fig. 2.1). 'It's such a mercy not to be staying with people as I did last time', she wrote to Margery in 1904; 'one needn't think about dress, so you have heard nothing this time of my clothes'.[58] Nevertheless she was hampered by 'a good deal of small baggage which makes travelling difficult'.[59] Her travelling clothes, even as a relatively seasoned traveller setting out for Greece two years later, are indicative of the formality and decorum required of Edwardian women: 'You can imagine me in a grey felt hat, blue spectacles, white linen jacket & skirt, white boots (made for male use! None to be had for females) carrying a green lined white umbrella – not a beautiful but a most business like apparition.'[60] Invariably, as the only artist in her party, she was too self-conscious to paint. She took her paints and pinafore with her to Venice and Florence but wrote to Margery, 'I have done nothing . . . it's quite impossible to settle down to work & I can only hope that seeing pictures is educational.'[61] Undeterred, she described her painting kit for Greece two years later: 'I am reducing sketching necessities to their lowest limit now, & shall carry everything, except my palette which will be strapped outside, in a small leather case'. Her easel, she wrote, could

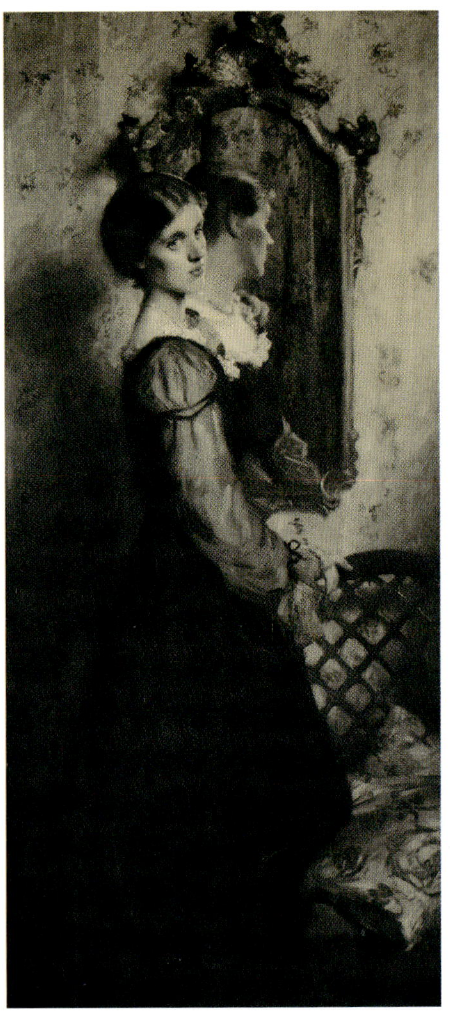

2.1. Vanessa in her evening dress in Rome
1902, The Charleston Trust

be packed with the umbrellas.[62] Her letters describe the planning and organisation as well as the intrepid determination that travel required.

Clive introduced Vanessa to contemporary artists and cafe society in Paris in May 1904. Adrian had already returned home from Italy and Thoby had left her to travel independently with Virginia and Violet ('our lady courier') while he walked in the Apennines.[63] He joined them in Paris, lodging with Clive while his sisters stayed at the Hôtel du Quai d'Orsay. By this time Virginia's mental health was approaching a complete breakdown: 'Oh Lord, how cross I have been, how dull, how tempersome,' she wrote from Paris.[64] She would make a suicide attempt later that summer while staying with Violet in Welwyn. Vanessa was also preoccupied with the sale of 22 Hyde Park Gate, again foregrounding her family responsibilities and obliging her to cut short her time in Paris. Clive's biographer has outlined his ignorance of the Paris avant-garde.[65] He was unaware that Picasso had returned to Paris in April 1904. He didn't visit Gertrude and Michael Stein's salon or Matisse's first solo exhibition at the Ambroise Vollard gallery that June. Vanessa already knew him as one of Thoby's Cambridge friends and was seemingly unimpressed. 'Your little friend Bell is here,' she wrote to Margery, who encircled the 'Your' and annotated it with an exclamation mark and a note, 'pure hypocrisy'.[66] Clive was ostensibly in Paris for research purposes. By chance, a letter of introduction had taken him to 'a warren of studios, just off the Boulevard Montparnesse [sic]' a few weeks earlier to meet a fellow Englishman, the artist Gerald Kelly, and he was soon intoxicated by the cafe society to which Gerald introduced him: 'That first evening turned my head.'[67] He was almost incapable of communicating in French and later recognised that the British and American artists who frequented an upstairs room at the Chat Blanc with their friends and models were 'anything but young lions: they were of the tame kind who worshipped Whistler and Velasquez, Rodin and Veronese, who went to the Louvre and paid their rent'.[68] Nevertheless this bohemian community gave Vanessa an insight into an alternative culture in which women artists were free to live and work independently. Her contemporary Eileen Gray had moved to Paris with fellow Slade students Kathleen Bruce and Jessie Gavin in 1902. They were among the artists she would have met or heard about at the Chat Blanc. The Irish painter Roderic

O'Conor was there and confessed that Virginia 'put the fear of God into me'.[69] One of their friends, Beatrice Thynne, invented theories about Wagner in the heat of the moment and when Kelly 'actually shook his fist at her across the table' Virginia had to hold her down.[70] Vanessa and Virginia revelled in their own outrageousness, smoking cigarettes and talking about art until nearly midnight at a 'common café'. 'We have been horrifying George with accounts of our doings at cafés & elsewhere,' Vanessa wrote to Clive on her return.[71] And to Margery she wrote: 'One thing I see you and I must do some day. We must come and work here.'[72]

She was interested in the painters Clive introduced her to: 'he knows a lot of the young artists and tells us of all the latest geniuses. I went today to see one of them called Kelly. He is only 24 and has 5 pictures in the Salon'.[73] Gerald Kelly was almost the same age as Vanessa. He was a close friend of Eileen Gray's and had been living in Paris since 1901. He spoke French fluently and had sought out Degas, Cézanne and Monet, whose work Vanessa knew principally through 'Mauclair's tiny book about the Impressionists' which her brother Gerald had published the previous year: 'How one pored over those absurd little reproductions'.[74] Together with Clive he took the Stephen sisters to Rodin's studio. Vanessa judged Kelly's paintings to be better than her own but she wrote to Margery: 'I think I am beginning to know what I want to do, and as it's not the same quite as what I think I can see that these other people are trying to do, I don't mind how well they succeed!'[75] She was curious to see a Paris studio when she was invited to 'watch him paint' and also planned to visit the Académie Julian, where Eileen Gray studied. The Salon, she observed, was 'much the same as the R.A.' and the paintings she admired there were by familiar artists: Whistler, Furse and Sargent, whose work she discussed in detail with Margery.

Sargent was one of the visiting tutors at the Royal Academy Schools where Vanessa had registered in October 1901. She was one of 20 students admitted to the Painting School that year. Margery was already a close friend and students from different year groups were taught together so they attended the same classes. Vanessa had passed the entrance examination with her full-scale drawing from life of a head and arm and three other formal drawings. To ensure that students had the requisite drawing skills and a thorough understanding of human anatomy these included two studies from antique casts, one anatomised to show muscles and tendons and the other to show the skeleton, all correctly labelled. The final drawing was a nude, again from an antique cast rather than a model. She would have adapted easily to the teaching at the Academy. It had barely changed in over a century and employed the same methods as at Cope's. Almost nothing of Vanessa's early work and juvenilia survives, with the exception of her portrait of her father (see fig. 1.5). As she was the keeper of her family archive this may signify a lack of sentimentality or professional embarrassment on her own part. However, student pieces and important early paintings may have formed part of the body of work that was destroyed by fire during the Second World War when her London studio was bombed.

The Royal Academy Schools had been a location for feminist provocations, closely associated with women's suffrage, since the mid-nineteenth century.[76] A concerted campaign and an element of deception saw the first woman admitted in 1860 and from 1893 women were included in life drawing classes. These were still segregated in Vanessa's time: 'if women painters were elected as associates of the R.A. they could superintend that class, and one more barrier would be removed from the feminine path to knowledge and distinction', one painter wrote as late as 1908.[77] Women were not elected to the Academy until 1922 and Laura Knight was the first full Academician to be elected in 1936. Vanessa benefited, throughout her career, from the political activism of her feminist predecessors and contemporaries. She was astute in recognising discrimination and side-stepping it where possible but she was careful not to be pigeonholed as 'a woman artist'. The majority of her fellow students were women, and many of them went on to exhibit in the Royal Academy's Summer Exhibitions, but the teaching represented and perpetuated a patriarchal hierarchy. Tutors included Val Prinsep and Sir Lawrence Alma-Tadema, men of her parents' generation and aesthetic circle. Vanessa was taught composition, perspective and portraiture in addition to drawing from life and the antique. A typical day there, she wrote soon after she started, began by: 'getting to the R.A. at 9.30 & staying till 1.15. You would come back & have a late lunch which you wouldn't eat much of, because you would think "In 2 hours I shall have tea".'[78] She would preside over the tea table at Hyde Park Gate before rushing back to the RA for an evening drawing class at 6 p.m. Then home in time to dress for dinner.

Sargent's painting and instruction as a visiting tutor influenced her most profoundly: 'Sargent is teaching most astonishingly well,' she wrote to Margery. 'He gives lessons . . . that would apply to any painting. They're chiefly about tone. He insists upon thick paint and makes one try to get the right tone at once.' This was in contrast to Whistler's technique. He taught her to strive for truth: 'The one thing he is down upon is when he thinks any one is trying for an effect regardless of truth.' He criticised her palette: 'He generally tells me that my things are too grey' and although he was relentlessly negative – 'I don't think anyone has had any praise' – she learned from his critiques of her fellow students' work as well as her own.[79]

Vanessa's training at the Royal Academy Schools equipped her with the confidence as well as the technical and critical skills to operate professionally. Her letters from Italy and Paris describe an open engagement with the canon, a determination to locate her studies and her own work within a broader context, and the independence to reject the aesthetics of the Salon and the Academy. The Schools were also small enough to provide her with an enduring professional network. She was one of 139 students in the schools of painting, sculpture and architecture in 1904 (fig. 2.2). Several of her closest colleagues, including Sylvia Milman, joined her Friday Club and fellow students also gave her access to a broader network of artists and designers. Many of them belonged to families of artists who would attend prize-giving evenings and other events. The designer Ada Louise Powell and Thérèse Lessore, for example, whom Vanessa would encounter at the Slade and later at the London Group, were Frederick Lessore's sisters. He studied sculpture at the Schools from 1903. They contributed to a loosely woven web of connections that supported Vanessa's career.

Soon after she returned from Paris, Vanessa left the Royal Academy for the Slade School of Fine Art, extending her network further. Several of her colleagues, including Margery and Sylvia, enrolled for a two-year 'Second Term of Studentship' at the Academy after their initial three years but Vanessa, having missed most of that year's teaching due to her father's illness and her subsequent travels, took matters into her own hands. She returned for the last month of term before

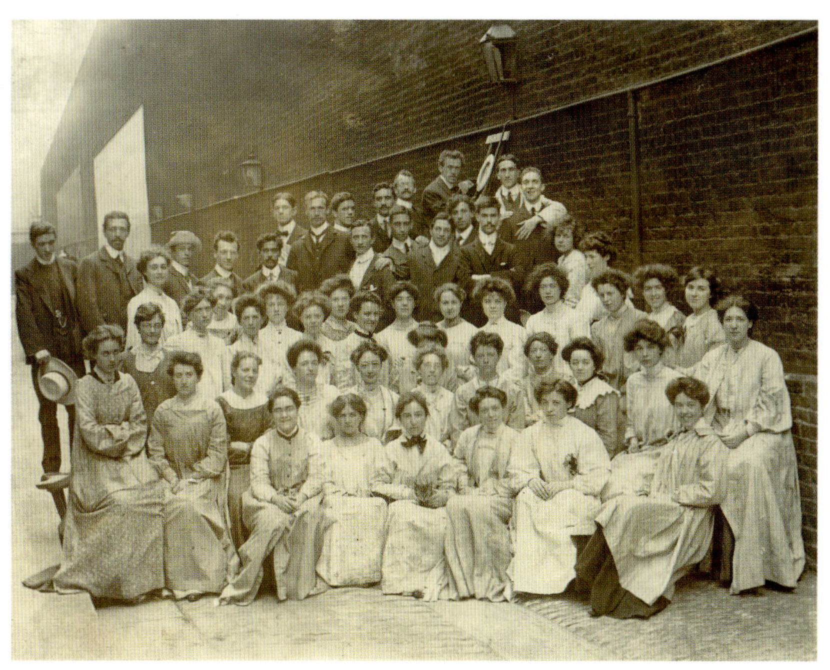

2.2. Royal Academy Group photograph
The Charleston Trust

enrolling briefly at the Slade. Her decision coincided with a radical shift in living arrangements. She 'wound up Hyde Park Gate' when she returned from Paris and established a new home for herself and her three younger siblings in Bloomsbury at 46 Gordon Square. Virginia's mental health was still a cause for concern and she was recuperating at Violet's home. She later described the decisiveness with which Vanessa dismantled the past: 'She had sold; she had burnt; she had torn up.'[80]

The Slade was only a few minutes' walk from Gordon Square and although Vanessa was disappointed by her experience there it gave her common ground with slightly younger painters including Duncan Grant, Paul Nash, Henry Lamb, Mark Gertler and Dora Carrington, who trained there after her and with whom she would work and exhibit. Virginia created a Slade student and model, Fanny Elmer, as one of the characters in *Jacob's Room*. In the novel, she took Jacob to a Slade fancy dress ball. It was the most progressive art school in

London at the time and although Vanessa stayed only a term, recalling that 'I made no friends there and soon left', her enrolment denotes a new direction, away from the Academy.[81] She was in awe of the Slade's leading professor, Henry Tonks, who was a member of the New English Art Club, 'which then seemed the most go-ahead group in modern art', she later recalled. All its members 'seemed somehow to have the secret of the art universe within their grasp', a secret that, as a woman, 'one was not worthy to learn'.[82] 'I haven't dared show my works to Tonks yet,' she wrote to Virginia in December 1904, and when she did so she recalled being 'squashed' rather than 'taught' by him.[83] A few weeks later she wrote to Margery that the Slade's prescriptive regime of drawing and painting had nothing new to teach her: 'I have decided not to go back to the Slade at all because I think I should waste my time there'. Working independently in her new studio at 46 Gordon Square, she determined to follow Tonks's advice and to write to him at the end of the spring term, 'I mean if I am bold enough . . . and [to] ask him to look at my things'.[84] The decision marked a significant shift in power dynamics. In March 1905, having 'cast off the Slade', Vanessa invited Tonks to visit her as an independent artist in her own home. Virginia waited with her in the studio to help steady her nerves. She noted Tonks's 'look of mingled severity & boredom' and his social awkwardness. On this occasion when he 'reviewed the pictures' there was a good deal of criticism 'but also some praise'.[85] Vanessa's initiative, exploiting her domestic power base for professional purposes, would become a strategy.

3

EARLY WORK, ART CLUBS AND EXHIBITIONS

'Of course the business of arranging furniture in new, clean, empty rooms is delightful to me,' Vanessa wrote to Virginia.[1] Her move to 46 Gordon Square with her three younger siblings, away from family and friends in South Kensington, distinguished her from Margery, Sylvia and her other student friends. While Margery had a room in a hostel for women students and Sylvia was still living in her family home, Vanessa was the head of her own household by the age of 25.[2] She had endured the deaths of both her parents and Stella. She had managed the care of her dying father and taken responsibility for Virginia's uncertain recovery. The process of arranging and decorating the rooms at Gordon Square materialised her work as a carer and homemaker as well as her originality as an artist. In her first six years in the house her beloved brother Thoby would die there; she would marry his close friend Clive and give birth at home to their two sons. The interiors at 46 Gordon Square were curated. They were repeatedly redecorated and rearranged as settings for the artistic and social experiments that she staged there. Even after Vanessa relinquished the house as her own home, it continued to resonate with her identity as a matriarch and creative force.

'We knew no one living in Bloomsbury then and that I think was one of its attractions,' she later recalled. 'It seemed as if in every way we were making a new beginning in the tall, clean, rather frigid rooms, heated only by coal fires in the old-fashioned open fireplaces.'[3] She had chosen a district that was already associated with feminists and free-thinking radicals. Bloomsbury was home to

University College London, of which the Slade was a part, and the British Museum Reading Room. Artists and intellectuals, including educated single women, were also attracted by its boarding houses, run by resident landladies, where they could rent affordable rooms. Between the wars, many of Bloomsbury's large houses were divided into flats, enabling Vanessa and her friends to further disrupt the conventions of the nuclear family and coexist in alternative configurations. Cheap rents made the district a centre for progressive charities and small businesses. Virginia helped with a mailing for the People's Suffrage League in 1910. It operated cheek by jowl in Reform House in Mecklenburgh Square with organisations such as the National Federation of Women Workers, the Working Women's Legal Advice Bureau and the Women's Trade Union League.[4] Bloomsbury, then, provided a fertile environment in which to establish an alternative creative and intellectual household.

Vanessa shared her vision for 46 Gordon Square with Virginia. In October and November 1904, while the house was taking shape, she insisted that Virginia remain in the country against her wishes and follow doctor's orders to rest: 'I am quite sure London would do you harm now . . . Any amount of boredom & tiresomeness is worth going through if it will prevent another breakdown – & I do think you were near one here'.[5] Virginia described Gordon Square as 'a dream of loveliness' when she was briefly allowed to stay there and complained that Vanessa had 'a genius for stating unpleasant truths in her matter of fact voice'.[6] Vanessa wrote to her daily and visited her, involving her in the arrangements for their new home as an inducement to recovery. She broke with convention by recognising her own need and that of her sister for separate living and working spaces, anticipating Woolf's polemic, *A Room of One's Own*. It was rare as a young woman, she later recalled, 'to have one's own rooms, be master of one's own time'.[7] 'At Hyde Park Gate', Virginia wrote, 'one had only a bedroom in which to read or see one's friends. Here Vanessa and I each had a sitting room'.[8] There was also a more public drawing room on the first floor. Virginia described 'the extraordinary increase in space' as exhilarating. Ruthlessly, Vanessa disposed of much of the family furniture, selling the better pieces to Harrods and replacing them according to her own taste. 'Your sofa has come', she wrote to Virginia; 'I think it ought to be comfortable'.[9] Spaces in Victorian houses were gendered. Sitting rooms were regarded as 'feminine' and as well as tripling their number at 46 Gordon Square Vanessa appropriated the 'masculine' dining room on the ground floor. She bought a plain red carpet and a dining room table: 'it's coming on approval so you can see if you like it', she wrote to Virginia.[10] Adrian was at Cambridge and Thoby, she wrote, was out every night: 'It will be very nice when you & I have luncheons & dinners alone in our little white dining room.'[11]

The distempered white walls and brightly coloured textiles that Vanessa introduced were strikingly modern after William Morris wallpapers and the 'gloom and depression' of Hyde Park Gate.[12] Virginia described the interiors as their 'Sargent-Furse era . . . We were full of experiments and reforms.'[13] When George, who had recently married and established his own household, invited himself to tea before sofas and chairs had their new covers Vanessa 'routed out some Indian shawls of brilliant colours & put them on some things. They look rather fine & barbaric against our white walls,' she wrote.[14] The permanent arrangement was more conventional. She chose white and green chintzes for the furniture and curtains, again involving Virginia by sending her a sample: 'They have all the old patterns & very good colours,' she wrote.[15]

The effect on visitors to the house was calculated. Passage through a conventional Victorian townhouse was choreographed to filter guests by gender, status and intimacy. The front door was opened by one of the servants from the basement and guests were obliged to remain in the entrance hall until their hosts were ready to receive them. Thoby and Adrian's friends could be entertained in the 'masculine' spaces on the ground floor, the study at the front of the house and the dining room at the back for those invited 'to luncheon' or 'to dine' (as Clive was often invited by Thoby). 'Callers' for either sister would be taken upstairs to the first-floor drawing room. Although Vanessa did use the drawing room as a studio on occasion this space, inseparable in the Victorian consciousness from the delicacy of the tea table and polite gatherings around the piano after dinner, had always to be tidy and prepared for unexpected guests.

Pictures were hung strategically. 'I have been hanging pictures in the hall – I hope you'll approve,' Vanessa wrote to Virginia. 'On the right hand side as you come in I have put a row of celebrities . . .

Then on the opposite side I have put 5 of the best Aunt Julia photographs of Mother.'[16] These striking, large-format photographs would have been unexpected in a hallway and Vanessa and Virginia could determine how long their visitors were kept waiting there. The repetition of Julia's image reflected the matriarchy at Gordon Square. A central portrait of their father on the opposite wall, flanked by Julia Margaret Cameron's portraits of Darwin, Lowell and Herschel on one side and Tennyson, Browning and a portrait of Meredith by Watts on the other, displayed their family's literary and intellectual connections. Visitors such as Tonks would have been left in no doubt as to Vanessa's cultural standing.

Vanessa turned society's expectations of her as a hostess to her own advantage on 'Thursday evenings' soon after Virginia was 'discharged cured' and the four siblings were settled together in Gordon Square.[17] She created a bohemian intellectual salon with Thoby at the unconventional hour of 10 p.m. Initially she had cards printed – 'Miss Vanessa Stephen and Mr J. T. Stephen, At Home. 10 P.M.' – and addressed them by hand to his friends.[18] Invitations to 'dine with us on Thursday next at 8 o'clock' secured the key participants for an evening and others would arrive casually after they had dined elsewhere.[19] The facility with which Vanessa operated as a hostess, drawing people into the Group and effecting introductions, is substantially unrecognised because, as a woman, she exercised her agency below the radar. In her memoir, 'Notes on Bloomsbury', she was characteristically self-effacing about the origins of the Group. 'So it happened that one or two of these friends began to drift in on Thursday evenings after dinner.'[20] There was whisky, she recalled, and 'cocoa and biscuits' were offered at around midnight, releasing Vanessa and Virginia from the conventions of serving their guests. She listed 'the young men from Cambridge' and described their liberation from polite conversation. They were 'full of the "meaning of good"', she wrote.

> I had never read their prophet G.E. Moore, nor I think had Virginia, but that didn't prevent one from trying to find out what one thought about good or anything else. The young men were perhaps not clear enough in their own heads to mind trying to get clearer by discussion with young women who might possibly

see things from a different angle. At any rate talk we all did, it's true, till all hours of the night.[21]

Encouraged by the success of Thursday evenings, Vanessa launched the Friday Club later in 1905 to focus on the visual arts, but she was developing a very different network at the beginning of the year. Violet Dickinson had introduced her and Virginia to Lady Robert Cecil, daughter of the second earl of Durham, and to Lady Beatrice Thynne, daughter of the fourth marquess of Bath. Lady Robert supported Vanessa's determination to forge a career as a portrait painter: 'I want to start on you and on Lady Robert as soon as possible', she wrote to Margery in January 1905.[22] Known as Nelly, Lady Robert had married Lord Robert Cecil in 1889 and became an influential supporter of women's suffrage. She chaired the Marylebone and Paddington branch of the Conservative and Unionist Women's Franchise Association (CUWFA) and overcame her profound deafness to appear on suffrage platforms, chair meetings and write for the monthly *CUWFA Review*.[23] An extraordinary photograph of Vanessa apparently poised in the act of painting her documents a deliberate campaign to launch her career as an artist (fig. 3.1). She stands at her easel, glancing demurely over her shoulder at the camera. Dressed in her painting smock, with a palette confidently held in the crook of her arm, she gives the impression – reinforced by the chintz-covered armchair in the foreground – that she

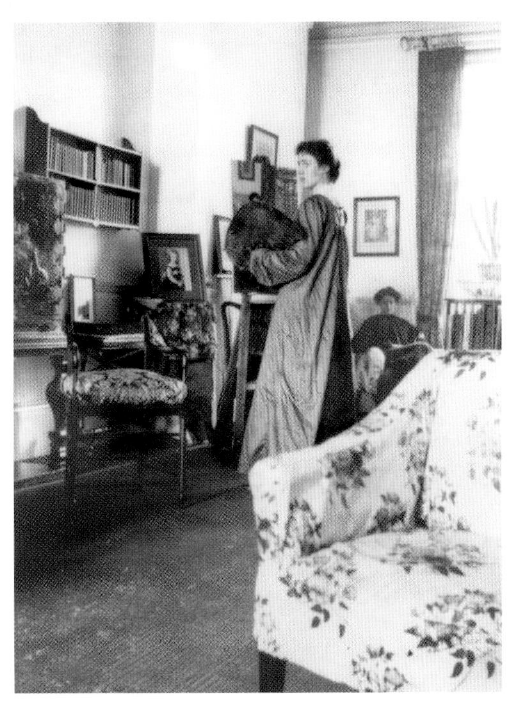

3.1. Anon., Photograph of Vanessa Stephen painting *Portrait of Lady Robert Cecil* from life

1905, The Charleston Trust

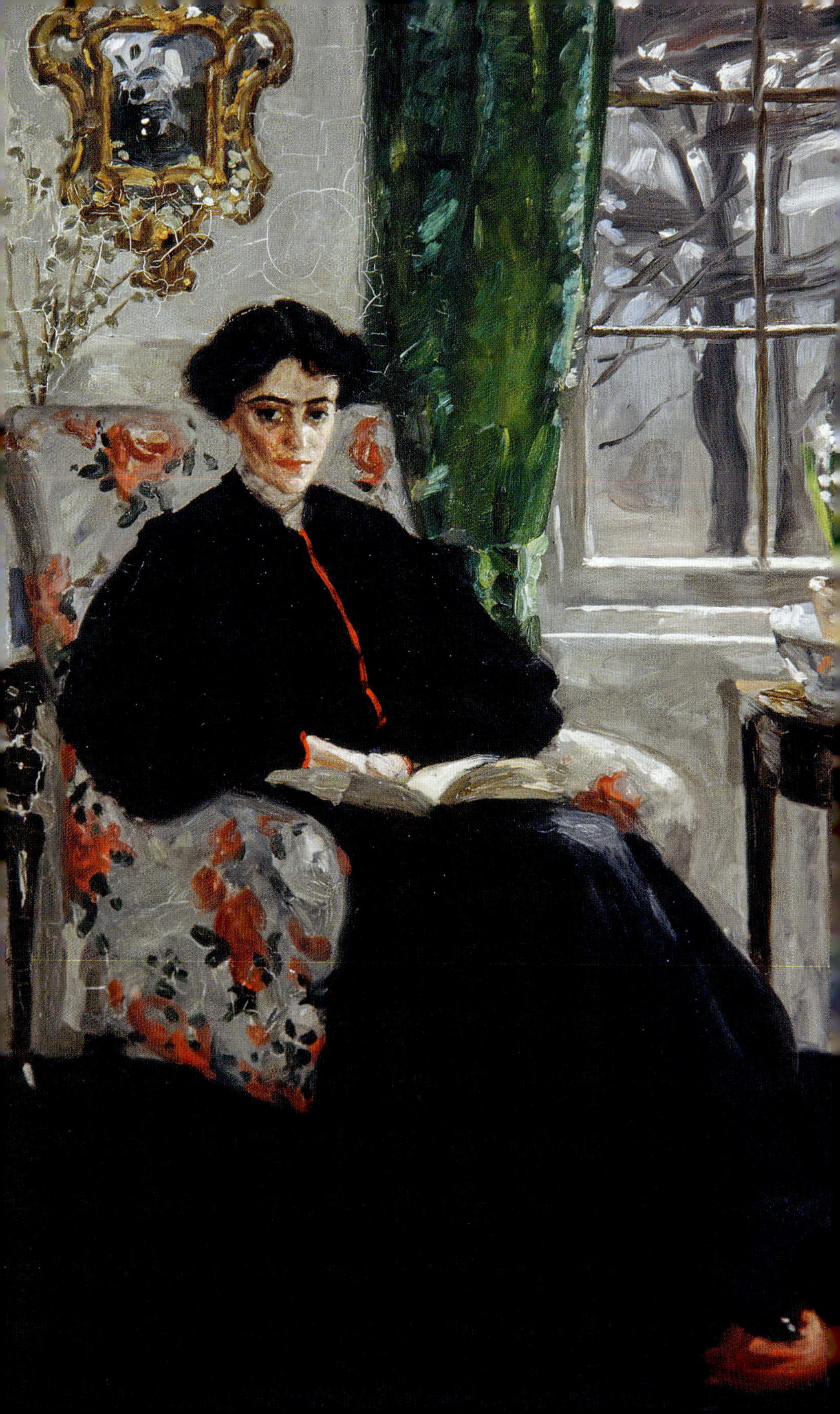

could be trusted to paint in her subject's comfortable drawing room, posing no danger to the upholstery. Nelly, barely inconvenienced by the process of modelling, sits reading by the window. The photograph offers an alternative to more conventional promotional images of male artists, immaculately dressed in suits within the grandeur of their own studios where subjects would be positioned on a model's throne. Here the setting was domestic, the sitter's own home, and the power balance between the two women, artist and sitter, was redefined as a consequence. *Portrait of Lady Robert Cecil* was the first painting that Vanessa exhibited (fig. 3.2).

A comparison between the photograph and the finished version of *Portrait of Lady Robert Cecil* shows the editorial process through which Vanessa arrived at her composition. The photograph was probably taken in the first-floor drawing room of Nelly's London home where Vanessa had initially been invited 'to tea'.[24] Balcony balustrades are visible through the full-height window next to which she sits and the unfinished portrait on Vanessa's easel shows the splayed upper branches of a tree outside. Vanessa was subsequently invited to stay with the Cecils at their Sussex home in Chelwood Gate to paint Sir Robert.[25] The portrait of Nelly may have been reworked there because she sits by a sash window in the finished portrait and the winter landscape outside indicates a ground-floor sitting room. A side table bears a hyacinth within a porcelain bowl, Vanessa substituted a mirror for the picture on the wall behind Nelly and a single spray of honesty completes the effect of aesthetic refinement. 'Nelly is really artistic and has very good taste,' Vanessa wrote to Virginia.[26] She had visited Sargent in his studio at the beginning of April 1905, where she admired his society portraits. Her painting of Nelly is modest in scale and ambition by comparison but her fascination with colour and light demonstrates the influence of Sargent's teaching. Unlike the Sargent portraits with their generic backgrounds, Nelly's interior is handled with the same care as her face and figure. The vibrant emerald green of her curtain and the rose-patterned chintz of her chair serve as foils to the stylish simplicity of her black dress with its crimson lines articulating a front opening and cuff. The warm light from the window contrasts with the wintry scene outside and Vanessa traces its fall across the sill, the curtain and the arms of the chair as well as its radiant effect on her subject's face.

3.2. Vanessa Bell, *Portrait of Lady Robert Cecil*
1905, oil on canvas, 765 × 510 mm, photo © Sotheby's 2024

Nelly continued her support for Vanessa and Virginia on her return from an extensive world tour with Violet. She read Virginia's manuscripts and commissioned Vanessa to paint her husband after he was elected as a Conservative MP. Only an outline for the portrait is known to have survived in Vanessa's correspondence but the process of painting it is recorded. 'This morning I just started the portrait', she wrote to Virginia on Good Friday from Chelwood Gate, where she stayed with the Cecils for a week. She liked Lord Robert but complained that he 'sat only for a very short time . . . he doesn't sit at all even when he is sitting if you understand. But it oughtn't to be difficult to do a characteristic sketch which I suppose is all Nelly wants'.[27] The following day the portrait was progressing slowly and by Tuesday it was nearly finished: 'I should stay on another day, for it seems a pity not to do it properly', she wrote to Virginia. 'I'm afraid it isn't at all a work of genius for I have done very little work . . . & then Lord R. never sits.' She wrote that it was 'atrociously painted . . . not very original' and a poor likeness: 'However I hope to get it like tomorrow . . . I would give a good deal to do him well'.[28] On Wednesday morning the painting was completed: 'I don't know what it's like – sometimes I shiver at the sight & sometimes I think it's d—d good! . . . Nelly says she likes it, but then she would in any case.'[29] A few months later she commiserated with Margery about the difficulties of getting a portrait 'all done in one visit, never having seen the person before. It takes so long to see what one wants to do.' She wrote that she couldn't 'bring it off successfully all at one go . . . with Lord Robert'. The solution, she wrote, was 'always to go back & work at a thing later'.[30] She used the Friday Club to exhibit the commission.

An important aspect of Vanessa's work as a modernist woman was the making of collaborative, creative environments where she could establish a reputation on her own terms and position herself as a professional. She invented the Friday Club as a forum for thinking and talking about art and as an exhibition society. It enabled her to attract the artists she admired and show alongside them. She took Margery to Paris in April 1905, subsidising her friend's expenses with a cheque from Virginia.[31] On their return she established 'the great club'.[32] 'Do you remember', she wrote to Margery from Paris many years later, 'how I started the Friday Club in a vain hope of creating something of the same kind of atmosphere here in London! Here the whole thing is alive & encouraging'.[33] She began by creating a committee, drawing her various networks together and hosting the first meetings at Gordon Square. Clive was 'dragged' into the enterprise as a friend who understood the Paris culture she hoped to emulate: 'You can still refuse to be on the committee if you like', she wrote to him. 'If not we will elect Adrian instead, so don't feel that you have to. I think that after the first meeting the rest of the business can be left to 2 or 3 members'.[34] Clive's involvement in founding the Club has been overestimated. When he suggested that it might restrict itself to meeting in private houses Vanessa explained her determination to be 'more ambitious'. 'We can get to the point of calling each other prigs and adulators quite happily when the company is small and select,' she wrote, 'but it's rather a question whether we could do it with a larger number of people who might not feel that they were on neutral ground.' She resolved 'to stick to the plan of having an occasional exhibition and for that we should have to hire a room'.[35] She was also planning to hire a studio for the Club.[36]

The Friday Club has been neglected in the historiography of modernism, not least because Vanessa denied its significance when she was approached by historians. 'I don't want to be brutal', she wrote to Leonard in 1950, 'but I simply cannot go on telling people about such things. They always and inevitably get it hopelessly wrong.' She told a historian that the Friday Club was small, short-lived and 'quite unimportant'.[37] She knew the reverse to be true. The Club's evolution, as a consequence, must be pieced together from fragments of evidence. Vanessa was already actively engaged in setting it up when she enlisted Clive's support in July 1905. 'I am trying to get everyone to come here on Monday at 3 – a horrible hour but I don't think the Academy people will be able to manage any other,' she wrote to him, planning to do 'room hunting' the following month.[38] Clive described the 'platitudinous gibberings of opaque inanity' at a committee meeting in a letter to Lytton. He endured it solely for the pleasure of a 'charming and continuous view of Vanessa's superb profile'.[39] She rejected a marriage proposal from him in August and took a holiday in Cornwall, revisiting Talland House with her siblings. 'Nessa produces 2 canvases a day; and is mad with the difficulties of the sea,' Virginia wrote.[40] She described Vanessa's painting in tandem with her own writing about Cornwall: 'All this morning I have tried to spin out words about it', she wrote to Violet. The paintings were 'far and away' Vanessa's best work: 'I want her to hire a room and have a small show this winter. Her Club flourishes, and will begin immediately'.[41] They were back in Gordon Square a few days later on 5 October. Virginia wrote to Violet again the following month: 'Nessa has fairly got her Club started; and they are to have an Exhibition at once'.[42] She described a meeting in November to Nelly: 'Tonight we all go off with Beatrice Thynne to Nessa's Young Artists Club. They are very catholic in their tastes and call Thoby an artist because he doesn't paint . . . and me one because? perhaps because I write reviews.'[43]

In her second novel, *Night and Day*, Virginia contrasted the polite formalities of afternoon tea at Katharine Hilbery's family home with the 'fortnightly meeting of a society for the free discussion of everything' held at 9 p.m. in the rooms of Mary Datchet.[44] Katharine was one of Virginia's many fictional portraits of Vanessa.[45] The gathering, in which a paper was read and discussed by the assembled company, evokes the Friday Club. 'The room very soon contained between twenty and thirty people, who found seats for the most part upon the floor', Virginia wrote.

> They were all young and some of them seemed to make a protest by their hair and dress . . . Katharine Hilbery came in rather late, and took up a position on the floor, with her back against the wall . . . Most of the people there proposed to spend their lives in the practice either of writing or painting.

The paper and its subsequent discussion stimulated conversations and broke down barriers.

> One person after another rose, and, as with an ill-balanced axe, attempted to hew out his conception of art a little more clearly . . . As they sat down they turned almost invariably to the person sitting next them and rectified and continued what they had just said in public. Before long, therefore, the groups on the mattresses and the groups on the chairs were all in communication with each other.[46]

Virginia described her sister's 'genius' for organising exhibitions: 'Old Nessa goes ahead, and slashes about her, and manages the business, and rejects all her friends pictures, and don't mind a bit.' The Friday Club's first show was 'Nessa's exhibition' and she wrote to Violet that it was a success, 'except that the room was small and dingy and dark, and we had to carry round lamps when the light gave out. But I think people were interested in the pictures, and there were no very bad ones. Nessa's showed up well.'[47] *Cornish Cottage* may have been shown at this first exhibition (fig. 3.3).[48] Painted on board, it is small in scale and the bold handling of paint suggests that it was painted in situ. The palette is restrained and the browns and greys of thatched roofs, hedges and lane are rapidly sketched in. Vanessa reduces the white walls, windows and doors of the cottage to an abstract pattern. The diagonal line of the lane draws the viewer into the composition and she contrasts its tilting plane and disappearance down the steep hill with the emphatic verticals that define the building. She balances the stark vertical accent of white wall against blue sea with a softer horizontal above. Both sky and sea are toned with grey around the line of the horizon so that it recedes within the picture plane. 'I believe that my kind of painting must be done more or less directly,' she wrote to Margery from Cornwall:

> partly because of its being thick, but also because (this is the important point) it seems to me almost impossible to get good colour by putting one layer of grey over another layer of grey. But you can get good colour by putting one layer of grey over another of red or brown.[49]

Cornish Cottage is a sophisticated study in colour and composition for all its apparent simplicity.

Accounts of the Friday Club's meeting in early December by Vanessa and Lytton, as well as Virginia, describe it in very different terms. For Lytton, who attended with his sister Pippa 'as guests of the Stephen family', the evening's 'air of third-rate incompetence blindly aiming at it knew not what' was a depressing spectacle in which 'the Gothic family seemed strangely out of place. Poor people! They so hate propriety that they're driven out into this wretched sort of groove.' Thoby was known as 'the Goth'. The evening was held,

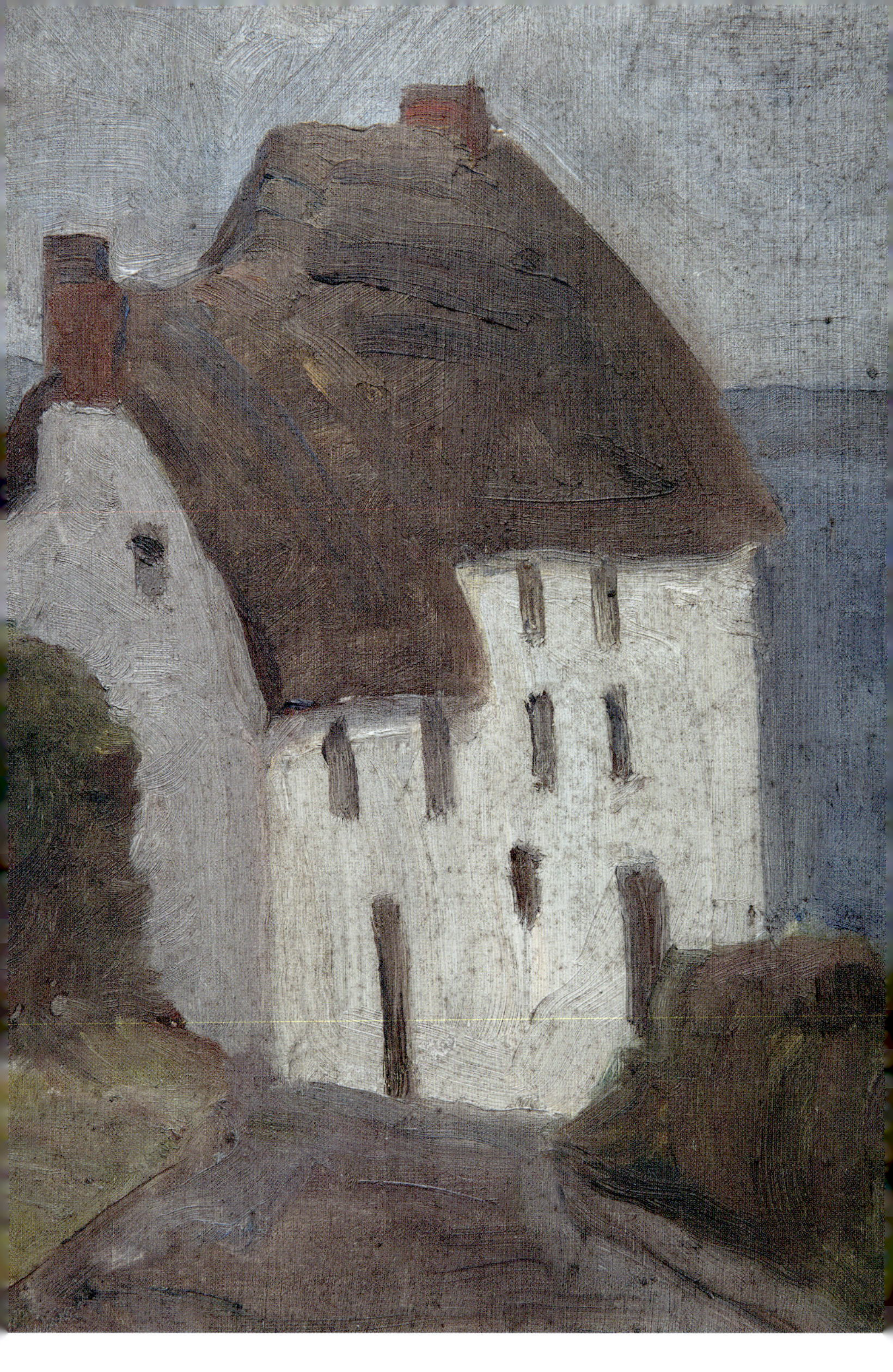

3.3. Vanessa Bell, *Cornish Cottage*
c.1905, oil on board, 225 × 175 mm, The Charleston Trust

Lytton wrote, 'in a flat belonging to Walter Creighton'. Walter's sister Mary studied with Vanessa at the Slade and exhibited with the Friday Club so it is more likely that she was hosting. 'The proceedings were curious and unpleasant. Nearly everyone – male and female – sat on the floor back to back, while Walter Creighton sang Brahms or posed with a cigarette'. Lytton noted Henry Lamb's presence, 'rather stupid and very slimy . . . and his quasi-mistress, a very young female dressed in the regulation harlot clothes'.[50] Vanessa was fascinated by Henry's companion, Nina Forrest, and by their situation: 'That Friday evening . . . was chiefly spent in a long conversation with Miss Forrest', she wrote to Margery. Nina told her a fantastic version of 'her most extraordinary past existence' and how Henry, a medical student in Manchester, had rescued her from an engagement to a Russian count that her family had enforced. They had run away together to London, where Henry would study painting under Augustus John.[51] Vanessa took a maternal interest in their plight. She resolved to help Nina find work and accommodation, describing Henry as 'a boy of 22 or thereabouts, knowing hardly any one in London, [he] doesn't know what to do at all'.[52]

Her search for rooms for the Friday Club resulted in the intrepid decision to rent a studio in Chelsea that was used for meetings and sublet to Henry during the day. 'Yesterday I had to meet Lamb at the studio we are going to take', she wrote to Margery. She delighted in what she considered to be outrageous behaviour, discussing Nina alone with him in a teashop in the King's Road: 'Lamb in his corduroys smoking a pipe – & I thought with joy of how shocked all my friends & relations would be if they could only come in & see us!'[53] Nina was invited to Gordon Square and 18 months later Vanessa met her again in Paris; by this time she was married to Henry but abandoned by him and looking after two of Augustus John's children.[54] Vanessa was intrigued by her and invited her back to Gordon Square to paint her and encourage further confidences: 'She is known in Paris as – could it be a "Lesbian!"' she wrote to Clive. 'Anyhow . . . she told me awful secret tales of how Henry Lamb performed an illegal operation upon her!' Nina had lost a baby soon after they were married.[55]

Vanessa cultivated an exceptional range of individuals through the Friday Club, from artists and models to bishops and politicians.[56] Virginia described the Club as 'our Bohemian dissipations' but it was also exemplary as a skilfully managed network.[57] Members paid a subscription to offset against costs and they could invite guests. Lytton's reservations were charmed away in January 1906 when he attended an intimate 'Gothic at home' and was persuaded to hear Desmond MacCarthy 'read a paper on "Art"' the following night. 'I talked the whole time to Vanessa,' he wrote to Leonard, 'who's exquisite in the real Gothic way'.[58] Only a handful of people, including Henry, were present at the Thursday evening, but the Friday Club attracted 'a vast collection of persons – nearly all artists or quasi artists, male and female'.[59] Lytton went with his sister Pippa and Duncan, with whom he was infatuated: 'Duncan hasn't been there before, and hardly knows any of the people, so it will be rather nice to watch him.'[60] This time the meeting 'was in Henry Lamb's studio in Chelsea – a large square room, with a great north sloping window'. He described MacCarthy's presentation as 'the vaguest maunder about "art" and "technique" and "surface" . . . but it served its purpose of rousing a fiery discussion'.[61] Vanessa drew on her family and their contacts to keep the appeal broad. Thoby gave a paper on 'The Decadence of Modern Art' and Lord Robert was invited 'to speak for 10 minutes . . . on any subject, except politics'.[62] Soon after she was married, Vanessa invited John Maynard Keynes, drawing him more closely into her circle with her well-practised tactic: 'Can you face another evening at the Friday Club & if so will you dine with us on Friday the 13th and come on to hear Clive's paper?'[63] Women were encouraged as speakers. Helen Verrall opened a discussion about ghosts and Marjorie Strachey gave a talk so contentious that Roger wrote accusing her that it was 'a direct attack upon himself'.[64] If the Friday Club did not take itself too seriously, it did fulfil an important role in forging connections. It was through Vanessa and the Friday Club that Roger became a modernist. 'I should immensely like to come and start a discussion at your Club,' he wrote to her in January 1910.[65] It was there that he encountered the progressive young artists who would help shift his focus as a critic and scholar away from the Italian Renaissance towards contemporary practice.

The Friday Club held annual exhibitions.[66] They provided a focus for Vanessa's painting and gave her some leverage with her fellow exhibitors. 'Nessa has done some really good pictures for the show', Virginia wrote to Violet before the second exhibition in June 1906, noting that 'Lord Bob . . . looks much better framed'.[67] The exhibitions gave her a degree of control over the display of her work. She gained experience and confidence in managing a loose affiliation of artists, hiring rooms and curating the selection and installation of works. Her Friday Club influenced the Saturday afternoon 'At Homes' which began in 1907 and culminated in the formation of the Camden Town Group. Unlike that all-male society, however, which organised only three annual exhibitions from 1911 before evolving into the London Group, the Friday Club was inclusive and enduring. It was not prescriptive as to style or subject matter and it welcomed the women artists with whom Vanessa had trained: 'everybodies [sic] pictures have been accepted,' Virginia wrote to Violet in May 1907, mentioning by name Margery (who was staying at Gordon Square) and Mary Creighton, who was 'to illuminate the world with four separate panes of glass'.[68]

Having established the Club, Vanessa was not defined by it. She handed over responsibility for its exhibitions to Essil Elmslie.[69] Their longevity, still attracting leading artists through the First World War and into the 1920s, is a testament to Vanessa's founding vision. They showcased experimental work including early woodcuts by Gwen Raverat, one of Vanessa's first designs for a screen and Mark Gertler's portraits.[70] Vanessa had reservations about David Bomberg's *Vision of Ezekiel* and 'very clever' paintings by C.R.W. Nevinson when they were shown in 1914, but they demonstrate the Club's continuing ability to attract new artists and to show striking and ambitious modern pictures.[71] Although the 1910 exhibition was already installed when she first saw it, and by this time she was married and pregnant with her second child, she described it to Clive as 'better than any other we have had'.[72] She singled out an early work by Gertler, who was still a student at the Slade, for particular praise and she admired Duncan's *Lemon Gatherers* so much that she bought it.[73]

Motherhood might have derailed Vanessa's career if she had been more happily married. Clive was a bon viveur and philanderer. Vanessa had rejected his first proposal emphatically, telling Margery, 'I was stupid not to see what was going to happen . . . I could no more marry him than I could fly'.[74] But he was persistent. The following year he proposed again, and although Vanessa enjoyed his friendship she wrote to Margery: 'I shall never marry unless I am as much in love as I have it in me to be'. In command of her own household, she already felt loved and needed by her siblings: 'I get all

the fun & none of the bother of married life as it is.'[75] She rejected
Clive in July with some ambiguity: 'if marriage were only a question
of being very good friends and of caring for things in the same way,
I could say yes at once', but she didn't feel for him 'what I imagine
one ought to feel for the person one marries'.[76] She set sail for Athens
with Violet and Virginia, meeting Thoby and Adrian at Olympia.
Adrian reported on their progress to Clive and his letters describe
Vanessa's sudden illness. The first doctor they consulted 'was a fool'
who turned out to be their landlord's brother. The next diagnosed
appendicitis. Unable to walk, she was carried to a carriage and then,
exhausted by an eight-mile drive, carried again 'in a long chair to a
small rowing boat, the chair was propped up in the boat and she was
rowed to our ship'. They sailed to Constantinople, where an English
doctor advised them to return home by the Orient Express in order
'to travel straight through'.[77]

Vanessa returned to 'a turmoil' at Gordon Square.[78] Thoby had
arrived home ahead of her and was in bed with a high temperature
and suspected pneumonia. Clive was anxious to visit them both but
Vanessa put him off, telling him that her doctor forbade it. She didn't
want to marry 'in the abstract', she wrote, and for the third time in the
space of a month she explained, concerned to be modern and rational
in her relationship with him, that she would reject him unequivocally
unless he left her alone: 'it seems to me that in every way it would be
best if you were to go away – I thought for a year.' She believed her
illness and exhaustion to be a consequence of nursing Virginia two
years earlier: 'it had to come sooner or later.' Rather pointedly she
suggested that Clive find 'some kind of work'.[79]

Thoby died of typhoid fever on 20 November, less than three weeks
after Vanessa's return. Virginia had nursed them both with Margery's
help. Clive had visited Thoby daily, reading to him as his condition
deteriorated. Virginia imagined looking Clive in the eye and telling
him 'your [sic] not good enough' for Vanessa, an opinion she shared
with Lytton.[80] The funeral was held two days after Thoby's death
and Clive remained at Gordon Square with Vanessa, who was still
too ill to leave the house. They were engaged to be married by the
end of the day. 'It's easy to imagine how it happened,' Lytton wrote
to Leonard, but 'not so easy to see how she can be happy . . . one
must hope for the best'.[81]

Throughout her career Vanessa created interiors and then painted them. *Apples: 46 Gordon Square* shows the first-floor drawing room at Gordon Square after her marriage (fig. 3.4). Within days of the funeral Virginia and Adrian had agreed to 'set up house together' and leave Gordon Square to Vanessa and Clive.[82] Even on her honeymoon a few months later Vanessa was planning alterations to the house. 'I have great ideas for the studio – mauve curtains with yellow linings is one of them', she wrote to Virginia.[83] She arranged for rooms to be cleared and building work to be carried out while they were away. Virginia and Adrian joined her and Clive in Paris, where they also met Duncan at the Louvre. 'He is clever & very nice', Vanessa wrote to Margery, '& I hope we shall see him in London quite often when he goes back there.' She planned to make a new start on her painting: 'I haven't really been in London for any length of time since last July & I haven't really done any work since then either. Now I mean to have models & work hard at painting some nudes & perhaps one or two portraits.' She expected Gordon Square to be 'in a great mess' when they returned but would 'enjoy putting this straight & settling how all the furniture is to go'. In the event, they returned to chaos: 'Workmen still in the house & all upside down.'[84]

Superficially, *Apples: 46 Gordon Square* is a painting of Vanessa's curtains. Their design obviates the need for a pelmet as a generous length of fabric above the rufflette tape folds forwards and terminates in a horizontal band of contrasting colour. Vanessa enjoyed a lifelong love of materials as a designer and maker, often setting to work with her sewing machine to experiment with strikingly original designs. The painting's restrained palette describes the play of winter sunlight through the curtain on the left and across its fore-edge, while that on the right remains in shadow. Colours are built up in thin layers, with warm highlights more thickly painted in short horizontal and diagonal dashes of yellow and white. Immediately outside, Vanessa streamlines and alters the corbel and balcony to the adjoining house to anchor the pattern of vertical accents that dominate this painting with a solid plane of painted stucco. The picture explores an interface between the interior world of 46 Gordon Square and the flatter, more abstracted treatment of the streetscape and square. Painted from a low vantage point and an oblique angle, the composition accentuates the physical barrier of balcony railings rather than adopting a commanding view out over the balustrade. The subject is a commentary on the constraints that Vanessa experienced as a woman artist, particularly on her travels when she was restricted to painting what she could see from her hotel window. It would become a recurrent theme. Three apples in the foreground are arranged not in a fruit bowl but on a blue and white serving dish that tilts towards the viewer. The upper edge of the dish and the green of the apples correspond with the vibrant lawn dissected by the line of a path at the top of the picture, setting up a restless tension between interior and exterior spaces. The composition's pattern of diagonals (the edges of table and dish, the

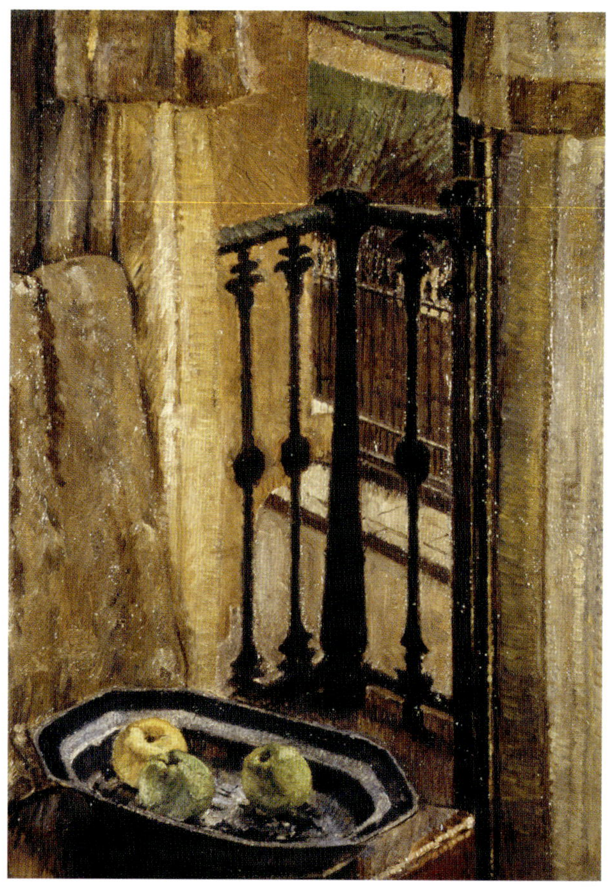

3.4. Vanessa Bell, *Apples: 46 Gordon Square*
undated, oil on canvas, 710 × 508 mm, on loan to The Charleston Trust

rails of the balcony, the curb between the street and pavement) is stabilised by the luminous vertical accents of the curtains and a quilt folded over a chair to one side.

The painting's understated modernity in subject matter and composition is difficult to date.[85] As early as 1905 Vanessa had seen paintings by Manet and Degas in Durand Ruel's Impressionist collection at the Grafton Galleries. She was alert to Impressionist paintings in Paris on her visits there and to interiors by Sickert and his followers. In October 1908 she wrote to Margery that she had been working on 'a still life which is perhaps rather ugly but well painted'. She was sitting for a portrait by Henry Lamb and, in discussions with him about painting technique, noted that he was 'using no black'. Vanessa, too, mixed other colours, 'blues, reds and greens – an expensive method' to create the rich brown of her balcony railings, avoiding black in *Apples: 46 Gordon Square*. Still focusing on her career as a portrait painter, she had just embarked on a portrait of Marjorie Strachey and she described its background of half tones and 'light coming in at the back on the wall' in her letter: 'I think my very careful still-life painting will come in usefully'.[86]

Vanessa's first child, Julian, was born in February 1908, almost exactly a year after her wedding. Two intimate portraits, rapidly sketched in the first months of his life, express her love for him. In the first, Julian's face emerges from an explosion of white paint, like the centre of a daisy surrounded by petals. The second portrait describes the vulnerability of the sleeping child and the artist's haste to capture his image (fig. 3.5). The colour is layered from a dark brown base coat with pink and paler flesh tones building up the image of head and face. A single curve of light brown paint articulates the smooth line from the outer edge of the baby's eye along his cheek to the nose, with a second curl of paint superimposed to outline the nostril. Cool tones of greenish grey shadow the baby's head and bold sweeps of white block in a sleeve and the squat form of his body, knees gathered up, beneath his robe. The painting shows Vanessa's mastery of colour and technique. She devoted a sketchbook to drawings of Julian, but her absorption in her new baby provoked a backlash.[87] Clive felt excluded and initiated an intimate interest in Virginia's writing that he hoped would culminate in an affair. Virginia, motivated by a more destructive jealousy and a complex desire to position herself within

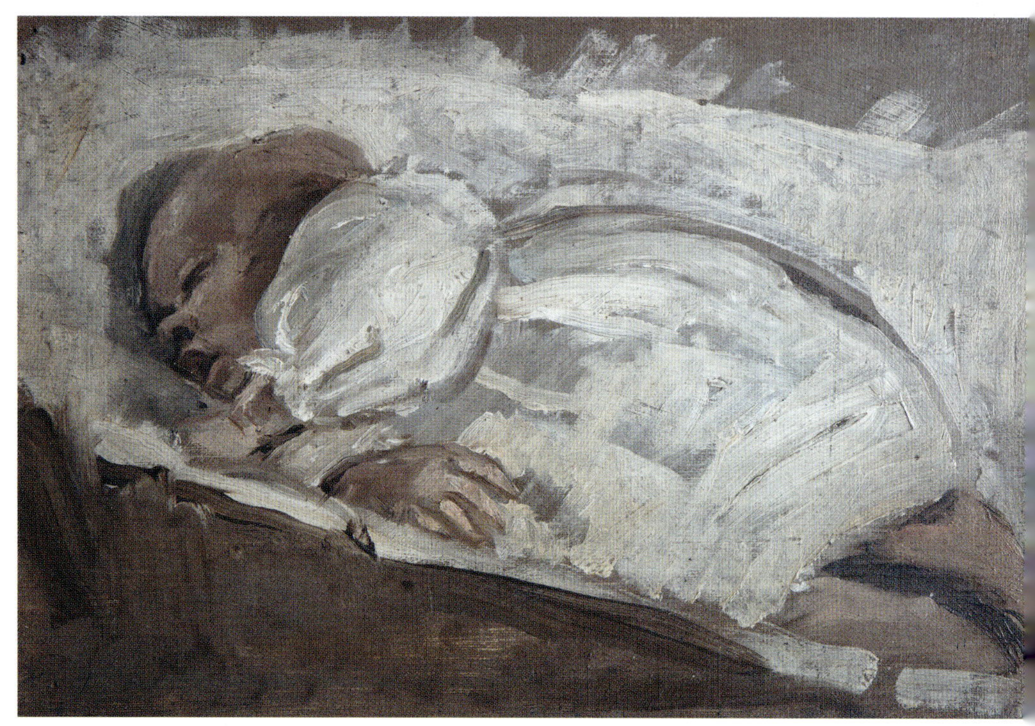

3.5. Vanessa Bell, *Julian Bell*
1908, oil on board, 160 × 215 mm, The Charleston Trust

her sister's marriage, encouraged his amorous correspondence. This betrayal, which resurfaced over several years, has been analysed and dissected by Bloomsbury biographers.[88] It scarred Vanessa's relationship with her sister and marked a turning point in her marriage. She renewed her professional resolve.

Vanessa employed a nurse and then a governess to help look after Julian and her subsequent children. This was usual for women of her social status. She was critical of Clive's family and their substantial country house at Seend in Wiltshire, finding the atmosphere there philistine and oppressive, but Julian regularly stayed with his grandparents for prolonged periods in the summer, at Easter and at Christmas. Vanessa looked after him there when his nurse took her holidays. The only local people at Seend whose company she enjoyed were the Raven-Hills, and she and Clive saw them frequently. At some point she understood that Mrs Raven-Hill had been Clive's first mistress and would be so again.[89] Clive's family, however, enabled Vanessa to travel and to focus on her work. 'Of course Julian's upbringing will be terrible,' she wrote to Margery from Paris, hoping that his grandparents would teach him good manners.[90] Reunited with him in London, she described her working day: 'I have now arranged to have him from 9.30 to 10.30 every morning, so that I can work for 3 hours after he goes. Then I have him for ½ an hour after lunch & ½ an hour after tea.'[91]

When she was first married, Vanessa wrote to Virginia that she painted Clive every morning. She showed with the Friday Club that June and submitted just one portrait to the Allied Artists Association's first exhibition at the Albert Hall. Paradoxically it was catalogued under Clive's name rather than her own.[92] The Allied Artists Association was modelled on the Salon des Indépendants in Paris, which Vanessa described as 'about the best show there, & so we live in hopes that the Albert Hall will be in London'. There was no selection committee: 'You pay a guinea & can send 5 works which all have to be hung', Vanessa wrote to Margery, making it 'the one place' where she and Sylvia (who submitted five works) could be confident of acceptance.[93] The exhibition promoted the theory that bad work was rejected by committees 'but that work that is inherently new runs a similar risk'.[94] Vanessa's *Portrait* hung alongside paintings by Robert Bevan and Harold Gilman but it was one of over 3,000 exhibits.

Her ambition in 1908 was to exhibit with the New English Art Club. The selection process was competitive and anonymous (at least in theory) but the Club was beginning to show more work by women.[95] While painting a new still life, *Iceland Poppies*, she wrote to Margery: 'I don't believe I shall ever have the courage to send it or anything else to the New English. I would if it weren't that one has to get two members to propose me.'[96] She used her network. Augustus John was one of the leading lights at the New English, as were Sickert, Sargent and Tonks. Vanessa and Clive acquired a major painting by John, *The Childhood of Pyramus*, for their newly decorated drawing room.[97] Writing to Margery that she was checking dates for the next exhibition, she added, 'we are asking the Rothensteins to dinner next week.'[98] Two years her junior, Albert Rothenstein had become a member of the New English in 1905 and was actively involved in the Friday Club. When she submitted *Iceland Poppies* and her portrait of Marjorie Strachey the following year she shared her insecurities with Margery, writing that she hadn't told Virginia or Sylvia: 'one always feels rather foolish when one's rejected'. She measured her progress against that of her contemporaries. Henry Lamb, she believed with some justification, would be 'sure of getting in', and she imagined Sylvia's portraits 'staring at me from the walls of the New English . . . while poor Marjorie Strachey will be languishing in Gordon Sq.'. In the event, her portrait of Marjorie was indeed rejected but *Iceland Poppies* was exhibited to critical acclaim.[99]

Although Vanessa resisted any narrative interpretation of her work, Frances Spalding has observed that a theme of 'three' emerged after Julian's birth, possibly reflecting triangular relationships within her marriage.[100] The fruit in *Apples: 46 Gordon Square* is an early example of this: two objects are painted close together, slightly separated and differentiated from a third. The flowers in *Iceland Poppies* are a more striking instance (fig. 3.6). Their elongated stems create a linear pattern in the foreground. A brilliant red flower, painted with great delicacy, is turned towards the viewer while two white flowers, one of which is cropped by the edge of the composition, are less open and turned away. Their ephemerality contrasts with the immutable three vessels above them: a porcelain bowl, a lidded French pharmacist's jar and a green medicine bottle stoppered with a cork. Duncan knew the painting as *Poppies and Poison* and the flowers may reference opiates.[101] Sloping bands of colour, uneven in depth, pattern the background and have a disorienting effect that is accentuated by a gestural handling of paint towards the left of the composition. It isn't clear how the objects are arranged and grounded in space. The silvery, greenish-grey palette contributes to a profound and deliberate impression of great stillness. Duncan described it as 'an exquisite still-life' when he reviewed the New English Art Club exhibition for the *Spectator*.[102] Sickert was so impressed by it that he wrote to Vanessa: 'I did not know that you were a painter.' Seeing her name in the catalogue, he wrote:

> I find that the little vase with two slain poppies stretched by it which we all admired & loved on the selecting jury is by you! . . . It's really worth writing to tell you because for once you get an absolutely unbiased opinion . . . I must say it is an agreeable emotion to find it is yours. 'Continuez'.[103]

The painting and its reception marked a turning point in Vanessa's career.

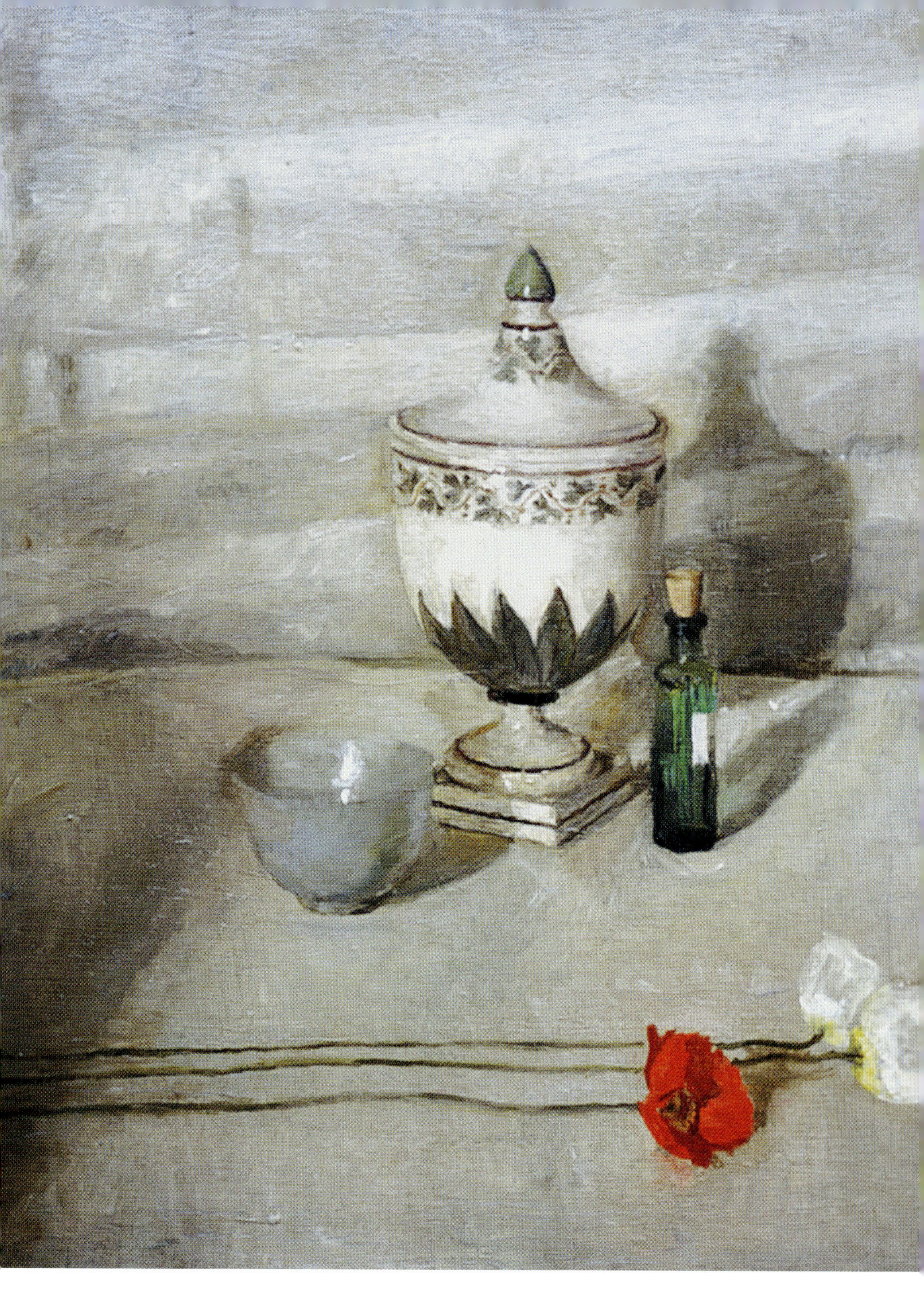

3.6. Vanessa Bell, *Iceland Poppies*

1908–9, oil on canvas, 540 × 450 mm, The Charleston Trust.
Acquired with the assistance of the National Lottery through the Heritage
Lottery Fund, the Art Fund and the Quentin Bell Commemoration Fund.

4

PLACE MAKING

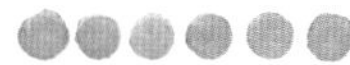

'Of course Duncan's model didn't turn up for our class this morning', Vanessa wrote to Clive, 'so we painted each other. I had to sit draped only in a sheet. The others were too cowardly or too prudish to take off more than a coat'.[1] Vanessa blurred the boundaries between studio and drawing room behaviours, using her status as an artist to disrupt. She persuaded her guests (men such as Oliver Strachey as well as his sister Marjorie) to undress and pose naked for sketches and photographs, building on the shared bohemian culture that she had nurtured at the Friday Club. As a 'place maker', the experimental environments that she created were another aspect of her work. They were essential to her practice as an innovator but they also encouraged her friends and family to engage directly with modernism. Just as the Friday Club included non-exhibiting members, Adrian and Saxon as well as Duncan were encouraged to paint that Sunday morning at Gordon Square in December 1910. The previous evening they'd watched one of the first performances of Strauss's *Salome* at the Royal Opera House (it was initially banned) and *Manet and the Post-Impressionists* was currently causing outrage at the Grafton Galleries.[2] Stripping down to a sheet was an act of radicalism.

Vanessa's close and creative relationship with Virginia throughout her life provided a foundation for the enduring collaborations that she formed with other artists. Virginia and Adrian created a separate household at 29 Fitzroy Square when Vanessa married Clive; they moved to 38 Brunswick Square in November 1911. These houses, separated from Gordon Square by a walk of less than 15 minutes, consolidated the Bloomsbury Group's identity with that area of London. Virginia and Adrian lived with Duncan, Maynard, Leonard and Gerald Shove. They were all single at the time, although Duncan and Maynard were lovers and then Adrian became Duncan's boyfriend. Leonard, one of Thoby's close Cambridge friends, married Virginia in 1912. Vanessa and Virginia's households operated in tandem. 'Thursday evenings' moved with Virginia and Adrian to Fitzroy Square and the proximity of Virginia's very different household provided Vanessa with an antidote to family life. After her marriage she made Gordon Square a place where sex and gay as well as straight relationships were openly discussed and celebrated. She was charged with initiating Roger into the bawdy talk there.[3] Her generous hospitality and her inclusivity made the house a centre for impromptu meetings and social gatherings as well as for painting and design.

In 1910, Vanessa was included in Roger's plans to secure paintings for *Manet and the Post-Impressionists* from artists, dealers and private collectors in Paris. Initially she had been intrigued and intimidated by him as a renowned authority on Italian art and a member of the New English Art Club. 'He was vaguely associated in my mind', she wrote, 'with other terrifying figures of about the same age.'[4] He was 12 years her senior. They had first met when she was seated next to him at a dinner hosted by Desmond MacCarthy around five years earlier. Feeling shy and nervous, she recalled, she prepared to be silent and was then astonished by the equality of their conversation: 'how could it be that I was able to say what I thought quite freely to one of these formidable painters and critics, even to contradict and dispute hotly.'[5] She was invited to his home in Hampstead where she met his wife, also a painter, and their children, but when she saw him again, waiting for the London train at Cambridge railway station, she wasn't sure that he would remember her. She introduced him to Clive. Roger had recently returned from a bruising appointment as curator of paintings at the Metropolitan Museum of Art in New York.[6] He knew his way around the dealers of London and Paris and had developed a detailed knowledge of recent French painting: 'talk began and continued unceasingly on the train'.[7] Vanessa invited him to speak at the Friday Club and when the Grafton Galleries asked him, in September 1910, to organise an exhibition for them at short notice, 'there had been a plan', Vanessa wrote, 'of my going with Clive, perhaps Duncan and Roger to choose pictures for the first Post-Impressionist Exhibition'.[8]

Vanessa's second child, Quentin, was born on 19 August 1910. Nevertheless she was planning her Paris wardrobe three weeks later. Virginia was recovering from a prolonged period of precarious mental health and Vanessa arranged to meet her, Clive, Saxon, Marjorie Strachey and others for a holiday at Studland (described in Chapter 5) before the trip. Quentin became seriously ill and Vanessa was left behind in lodgings with her family. She imagined Clive in Paris 'in that exciting atmosphere where people really seem to realise the existence of art'. She could picture Roger there, she wrote to him, but she was envious of Ottoline Morrell, whom Roger had also involved in selecting works for the show: 'I think Ottoline must be rather incongruous . . . She seems to me too essentially a part of Bloomsbury culture to mix well with Paris.'[9]

Manet and the Post-Impressionists had the effect of consolidating Bloomsbury's sense of its own identity as a group. It rallied in opposition to a storm of controversy and hostile reviews. 'On or about December 1910 human character changed', Virginia famously decreed.[10] In the world of painting, Vanessa observed, 'London knew little of Paris, incredibly little it seems now . . . It is impossible I think that any other single exhibition had so much effect as did that on the rising generation.' The New Gallery in Regent Street had offered 'glimpses', she wrote, of Cézanne and Van Gogh, but the effect of their work en masse, together with canonical exhibits by Manet, Gauguin and Matisse, was 'a sudden pointing to a possible path, a sudden liberation and encouragement to feel for oneself'. She described it as 'overwhelming'.[11]

'Post-Impressionism' became a byword for modernity among Bloomsbury's writers as well as its artists. At the start of 1911 Virginia rented a cottage in the Sussex village of Firle, where she could work and spend time away from London on her own terms. Vanessa had imagined getting rid of her servants and sharing a summer house with Virginia as early as 1907, when she was pregnant with Julian: 'We should be free to go & come as we liked & life would be very simple.'[12] The Arts and Crafts ideal of a modern, simple life in the country was well established and both sisters imagined a return to the long summers in Cornwall of their childhood. 'This is to be called Little Talland House, I believe', Vanessa wrote to Clive from Firle, 'but I call it Virginia's Villa.'[13] It immediately became a collaborative venture and a gathering place in Sussex for the Bloomsbury Group. Virginia described the cottage as 'inconceivably ugly' but it was 'done up in patches of post-impressionist colour'.[14] Vanessa described their first weekend together there, 'so hard at work, cooking our meals & making curtains . . . We have hardly had time to talk but sit & sew!' The curtains were 'violent orange' and hastily made. 'They are rather sketchy in consequence but full of emotion.' Vanessa was anxious to play a supportive role, rather than taking ownership of the project: 'I think it's really a good thing I came here as the Goat would have had a job to get it done by herself & it has been great fun', she wrote. ('Billy' and 'the Goat' were family nicknames for Virginia.) Vanessa commended her for finding an 'astonishingly comfortable' house in a beautiful rural village setting.[15]

Conversation Piece represents their 'patches of Post-Impressionist colour' in a boldly experimental painting (fig. 4.1). Purple and red as well as violent orange chair covers (made up for Virginia by a seamstress) are sketched in loosely. Years later, Vanessa wryly observed that British painters, responding to *Manet and the Post-Impressionists*, 'thought you could paint like Gauguin or Van Gogh by the simple process of putting a black line round everything' as she does here.[16] *Conversation Piece* is undated. The interior is that of Little Talland House but the three figures absorbed in conversation, Adrian, Leonard and Clive, are not known to have come together there. Vanessa's paintings are not always literal records of events. They were together at Asheham, however, at the beginning of March 1912, soon after Vanessa and Virginia leased that house as a joint project. Asheham was a large Regency house set in the South Downs close to Firle. It was a tangible instance of Vanessa's continuing support for Virginia after her marriage and their determination as sisters to create new spaces in which to live and work. The project coincided with Virginia's move to Brunswick Square and although Clive was unenthusiastic about Asheham, Virginia began negotiations for a lease in October 1911. They stayed at Little Talland with Adrian, cooking together and visiting Asheham, 'to take measurements so that we can have some idea for the decorations'.[17] Recurrences of

Virginia's mental illness confined her to bed for several periods in January and February 1912 and Vanessa wrote to her in the first days of March: 'We have just returned from Asheham where I hope you will think we did a great deal of work'. Virginia planned to visit a few days later so that Vanessa's account of laying down matting and putting up curtains was an encouragement to recovery. 'You'll find the dining room curtains half made. Don't try to finish them as they're wrong at present & must be altered before proceeded with', she wrote. 'Roger didn't come – so we were Clive, Duncan, Adrian, Leonard & myself . . . Clive & Adrian spent hours arguing with Leonard.'[18] In *Conversation Piece*, Adrian leans forwards intently in his purple armchair. Leonard sits opposite and the tilt of his right foot indicates an alert engagement in their discourse. The radical composition crops away Clive's upper body and he is identifiable

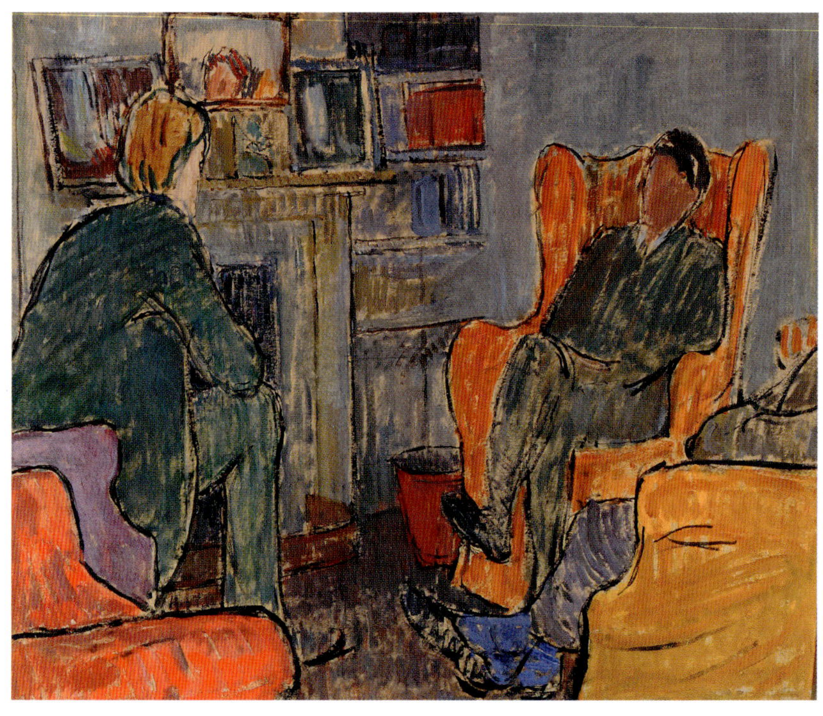

4.1. Vanessa Bell, *Conversation Piece*
1912, oil on board, 250 × 300 mm, University of Hull Art Collection

only by his bright blue socks and a reflection of his face in the mirror above the fireplace. Two months later, understanding the importance of *Conversation Piece* as an avant-garde painting, Vanessa chose to exhibit it in Paris.[19]

Sussex provided Vanessa with opportunities for intense periods of work and collaboration as friends and fellow artists were invited to stay. However, the most formative influence on her transition from *Iceland Poppies* to *Conversation Piece* was Roger. On a personal level she described his profound sympathy: 'he knew what it felt like to have one's baby ill.'[20] His wife, Helen, was institutionalised in 1910, giving him a particular insight into Vanessa's care for her sister. They shared a relatively informed interest in mental health. But Vanessa also described their alignment as artist critics and the experience of visiting *Manet and the Post-Impressionists* in his company. She was outspoken when she disagreed with his theories but she 'learnt to see many things', she recalled, 'through looking at them with him'.[21]

Roger joined Vanessa, Clive and their friend Harry Norton on a trip to Turkey in April 1911. Inspired by his energy, Vanessa was able to sketch outdoors with him and their friendship intensified. At the small town of Broussa she suffered a miscarriage and as Clive invariably found illness alarming (partly as a consequence of Thoby's death), it was Roger who nursed and cared for her there. She realised that she was in love with him and recuperated at his home, Durbins, in Guildford. For several years they were passionately and intimately involved in one another's lives. Roger's emotional maturity enabled Vanessa, perhaps for the first time since Stella's death, to relinquish control. They pushed one another to experiment: 'you & I are just beginning to find out what's in us', she wrote.[22] They painted together at Studland and Vanessa made arrangements for Roger to share her studio at Gordon Square and to stay overnight when he was in London on business or editing the *Burlington Magazine*.[23] She wrote that he had 'an extraordinary effect on other people's work. I always feel it when I'm with you'.[24]

Clive was jealous. 'If this had happened 3 years ago, when Clive was thinking only of Virginia, it might have been easy!'[25] Vanessa wrote. Instead, he became more amorous. When Vanessa thought she was pregnant again in October 1911 she wrote to Clive: 'it can only have happened that time a week ago when I thought I had made safe by washing. I know the stuff did go all over the place & of course I had to get upstairs, but it seems hardly possible . . . I know how wretched you will be.'[26] She gave Roger the letter to deliver by hand. Ten days later, not pregnant after all, she met up with Clive, Roger and Duncan in Paris and it was on this trip that she and Clive bought Picasso's *Pots et Citron*.[27] Her letters document the excitement of embarking on new projects and the strain of negotiating an honest relationship with Clive that accommodated her own sexual freedom. A seam of ambiguity, of knowing and not acknowledging, runs through Bloomsbury's affairs because the consequences of exposure would have been catastrophic, particularly for women and homosexuals in the Group. She warned Roger that if Clive were to 'get really angry past helping', she would have to submit to his wishes. 'I could have you to Asheham without Clive's knowing', she wrote, but the deceptions compromised her mental health.[28] Roger had described 'the mental effect' of her miscarriage as 'serious' in a letter to Ottoline at the time: 'What really alarms me is the state of mental terror which she gets into . . . as tho' everything were slipping away from her'.[29] Part of Fry's attraction was his empathy. He encouraged Vanessa to write to him about her symptoms and to see the pioneering psychiatrist Dr Maurice Craig.

Roger Fry was painted in January 1912 when they had a brief holiday alone together on the Isle of Wight (fig. 4.2). 'I did a sketch of Roger yesterday in Duncan's leopard manner with odd results but very like', Vanessa wrote, '& today R. is doing one of me. I've persuaded him to try the leopard technique too & he isn't at all happy in it, but is spotting away industriously in the hopes of getting at something in the end.'[30] They had seen pointillist paintings by Georges Seurat, Paul Signac and Henri-Edmond Cross in Paris and in *Manet and the Post-Impressionists*. Painting friends and family enabled Vanessa to experiment. The portrait captures Roger's concentration as an artist. Dashes of colour emanating from his head evoke his energy and in the background Vanessa introduced a phallus joke – a single cactus in a pot. While she was on holiday Virginia wrote to her in confidence that Leonard had proposed. 'It is quite true that Leonard is the only person I have ever seen whom I can imagine as the right husband for you,' she replied, 'but I also see that it's not the least necessary that you should marry at all'.[31]

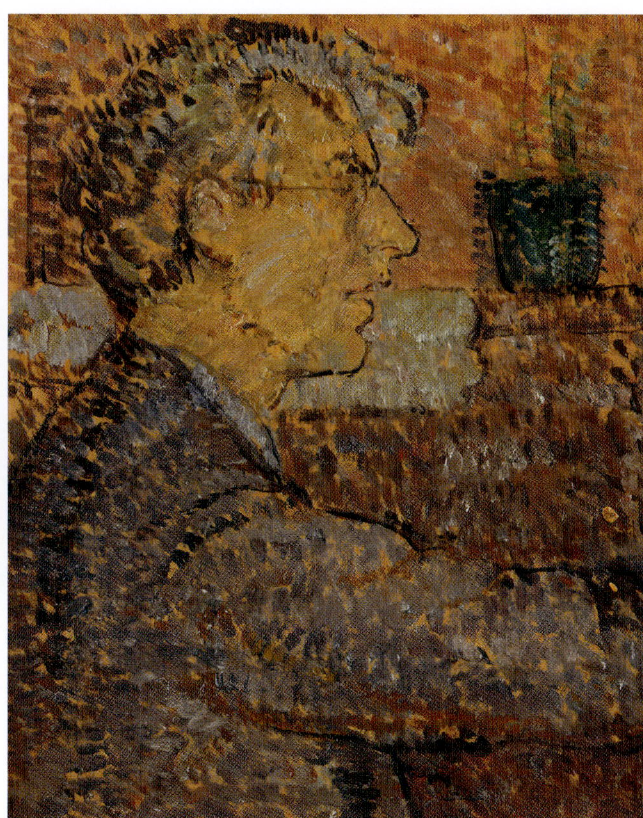

Virginia became the subject of a series of portraits in which Vanessa explored the limits of modern portraiture. These intimate paintings coincided with a period of extraordinary innovation as the sisters, now in their early thirties, challenged the orthodox expectations of women's lives. Virginia had been one of Vanessa's earliest models and she was often an unwilling sitter. Duncan recalled the need to work quickly when he painted her in Vanessa's studio at Gordon Square because 'she might just get up and walk out'.[32] Vanessa's portraits reflect the exceptionally close and complex relationship between the two women. They respond, in visual form, to Virginia's literary portraits of her. After Virginia's exploratory biography, written when Vanessa was pregnant with Julian, Vanessa painted her 'in her green & yellow dress against a dark blue background, life size or a very little under'. She wrote to Margery that 'the colour is rather beautiful &

it will be very interesting to do', but she was inhibited by Virginia's renowned beauty.[33] She felt nervous, she wrote, about 'doing her justice'.[34] The portraits of Virginia that she painted in 1911–12 are radical because their faces are obscured.

Virginia wrote disparagingly about the new focus on art theory and criticism that *Manet and the Post-Impressionists* aroused among her friends but she was keenly interested in the concept of Post-Impressionism and the processes of painting. She wrote a review of *The Post-Impressionists* by C. Lewis Hind and Vanessa took it to Paris to show Roger and Duncan in 1911. 'Roger says he likes it very much. It's just what he wanted to get said,' she wrote to her.[35] Two days later she described the 'great many gorgeous Cézannes' they had just seen, knowing that Virginia would understand her excitement.[36] Virginia was an informed sitter, contributing to Vanessa's incursions into modernism, and Vanessa, in turn, represented the inward-looking nature of her sister's brilliance. She and Roger sketched her together, leaning forwards with her hands clasped in front of her on a table, and the liveliness of Vanessa's image captures Virginia's thoughtful intelligence and her vulnerability.[37] Soon afterwards she painted her in the same winged armchair in which Leonard is seated in *Conversation Piece*, identifiable by its orange cover and the length of fabric protecting the chair back (fig. 4.3). The paintings are similar in palette and scale, and in the immediacy conveyed by the loose, vigorous handling of paint. Virginia is rarely passive in Vanessa's portraits but in this instance she was, perhaps, the butt of a family joke. Seven dashes of brown paint under her chin are more beard than shadow and the elongated formation of her hand may suggest a goat's hoof, playing on her nickname. If the painting was playful, however, it was also serious in intent. It references the sisters' familiarity with portraits by Cézanne and Matisse. According to Desmond MacCarthy, *Madame Cézanne in a Red Armchair* was one of the paintings that 'shocked London' in 1910 and Vanessa's portrait reconfigures its use of colour and the intensity of its cropped, asymmetrical composition.[38] She may have seen Cézanne's late portraits in Paris in which he also eradicated his subjects' features.[39]

The 'Post-Impressionist' orange armchair and Virginia's grey jacket with a dark green front band and cuffs are common components in a third portrait of her (fig. 4.4). Vanessa and Virginia both believed

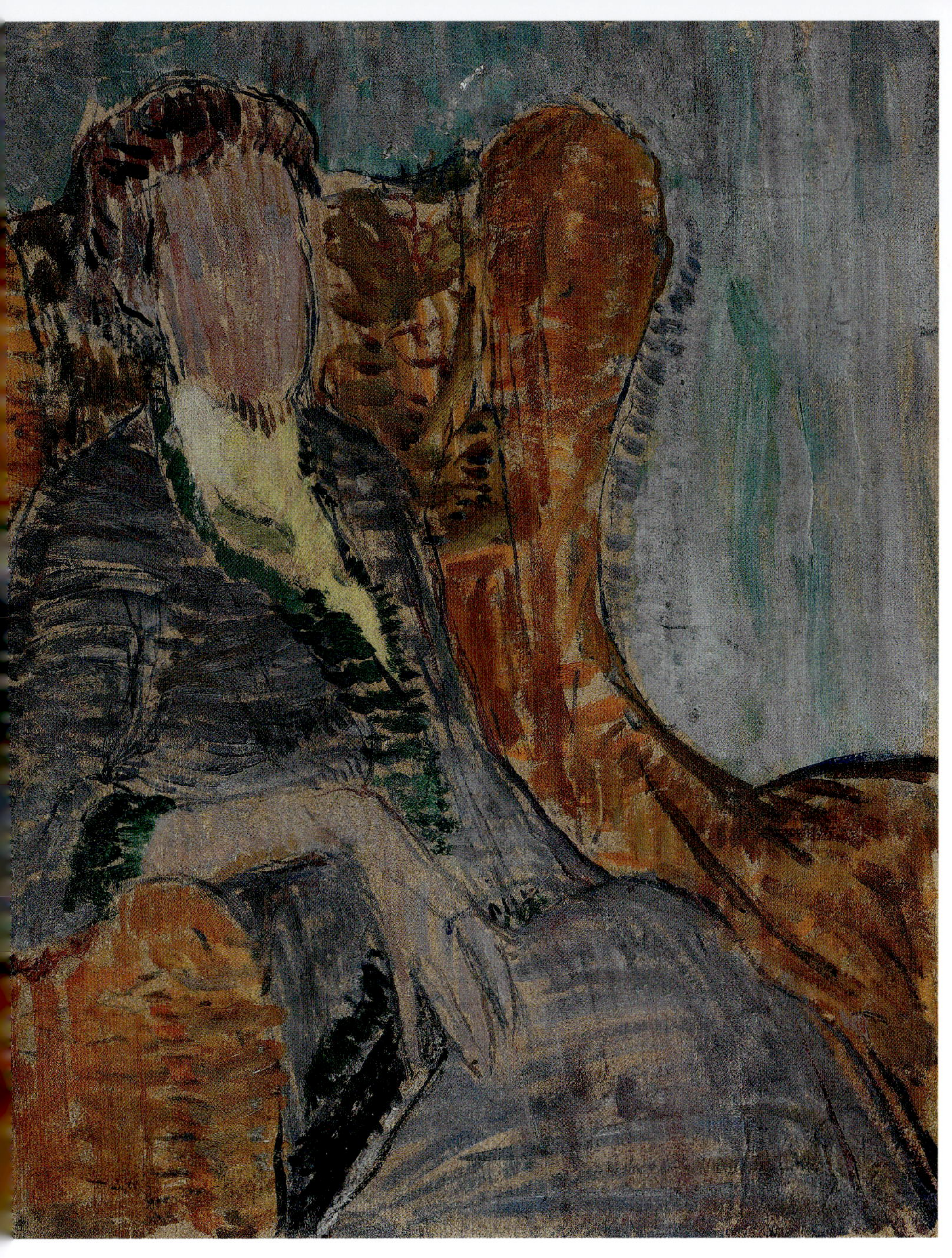

4.3. Vanessa Bell, *Virginia Woolf*

c.1912, oil on paperboard, 368 × 304 mm,
Smith College Museum of Art, Northampton, MA

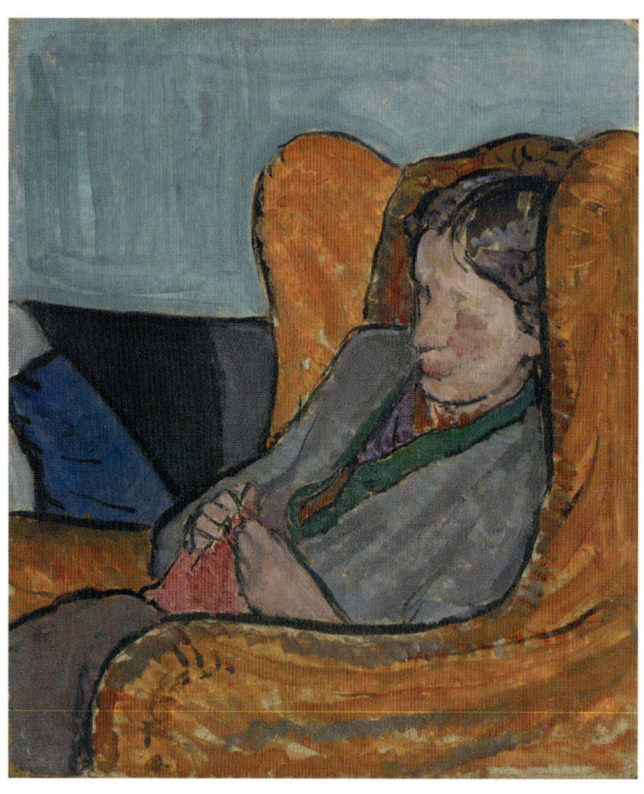

4.4. Vanessa Bell,
Virginia Woolf
1912, oil on board,
400 × 340 mm,
National Portrait
Gallery, London

in knitting and craftwork as well as the countryside as antidotes to mental illness. 'Knitting is the saving of life', Virginia wrote to Leonard.[40] In this painting she is absorbed in her work. Again her features are painted out and Vanessa's gestural handling of paint, zigzagging lines of pink over the eye, cheek and lips, is emotive. Frances Spalding has analysed these provocative, faceless portraits as an acknowledgement 'that even those we know well are never entirely present to us'. She describes the effect of obliterating the face as 'not one of anonymity but of intimate presence.'[41] Vanessa would have resisted biographical interpretations of her portraits but they are character studies as well as addressing the abstract subjects of thought and conversation. Primarily, they are formal explorations in paint and composition in which every component, as in the Cézanne portraits, contributes to the whole. The size and format of her portrait of Virginia knitting or crocheting, small and almost square, intensifies its intimacy. The striking colour and design demonstrate a resolved understanding of portraits by Cézanne and Van Gogh as well as *The*

Girl with Green Eyes by Matisse – one of the most talked-about portraits in *Manet and the Post-Impressionists*. Like Matisse, Vanessa considers the flat surface of her painting as an entity. She subdivides the background, blocking it out in an abstract pattern of grey and blue shapes to challenge perceptions of pictorial space.

Vanessa returned to Paris with Clive in April 1912 to help Roger install an exhibition of avant-garde paintings by British artists at the Galerie Barbazanges. She was one of ten artists, exhibiting alongside Frederick and Jessie Etchells, Helen Saunders, Wyndham Lewis, Spencer Gore, Charles Ginner and Charles Holmes as well as Duncan and Roger. 'The pictures altogether looked much better than I thought they would,' she wrote to Virginia, whom she imagined 'sitting in the sun at Asheham'.[42] She showed a representative collection of work including a design for a screen, a landscape and a still life. *Roger Fry* is likely to have been her *Portrait d'un Peintre* listed in the catalogue and *Au Bord de la Mer* may describe one of the Studland beach paintings discussed in the next chapter.[43] The exhibition gave her an opportunity to measure her own work against that of her British contemporaries. She travelled on to Bologna with Roger and Clive and was immediately struck down with measles: 'Oh God – to come to Italy & go to bed at once does seem damnable', she wrote to Duncan, but her creativity was undeterred: she invented the technique of paper mosaics, discussed in Chapter 5.[44] As soon as she was able, she painted outdoors with Roger. *Haystacks in Italy* consolidates the studies in colour and composition that she had explored in her portraits (fig. 4.5). Vanessa's distinctive palette, blending soft browns and pinks with burnt orange tones, is evident in the phallic, towering stack in the foreground and its conical counterpart. Pale blues and ochre yellows mirror the tones in Duncan's much larger *The Queen of Sheba*, exhibited at the Galerie Barbazanges. Her colours also relate to a shared admiration for Piero della Francesca.[45] She didn't accompany Clive to Arezzo but they talked about Piero's paintings there. 'I am green with envy,' she wrote to Duncan, recalling Piero's use of colour and his portraits in the Uffizi as 'the most amazing things almost I had ever seen . . . rather like some of your colour'.[46] *Haystacks* shows Vanessa engaging in a sophisticated visual dialogue with the artists and critics in her circle while drawing on the canon as well as contemporary paintings to originate her own style.

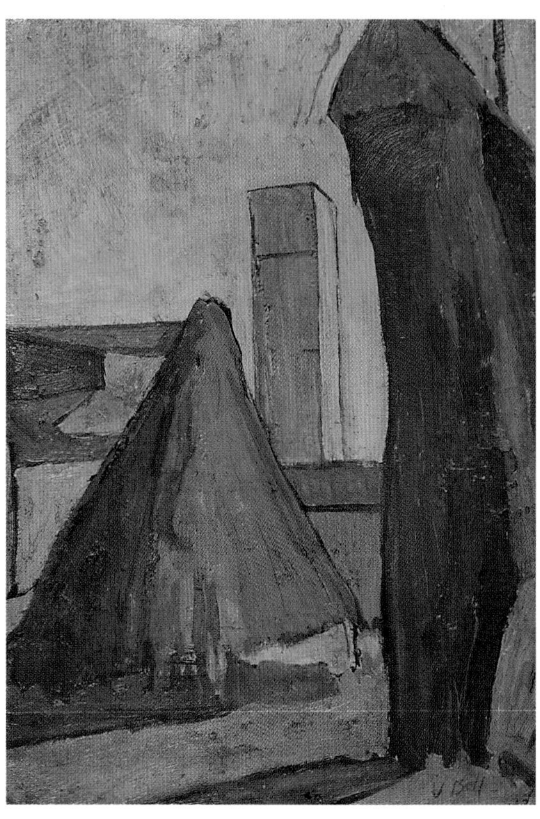

On her return, Vanessa invited artists to work with her at Asheham. In 1912 it was one of the places where she could build on the collaborative culture, the sense of a 'Bloomsbury family', which she and Virginia had initiated at Gordon Square. Although this was invisible labour, generating and enhancing connections between intellectual and aesthetic radicals from different disciplines, it was significant. It gave Vanessa and the women in her circle privileged access to partnerships from which they might otherwise have been excluded. It also established a basis for the professional relationships and creative processes that distinguished the Omega Workshops. Vanessa's invitations were strategic. 'Are you having a very good time with Doucet. How terrified I should be of painting with him', she wrote to Roger when he was in France with Henri Doucet. She then invited Doucet to Asheham.[47] She was envious of the London Borough Polytechnic murals, a commission Roger had secured for himself, Duncan, Frederick Etchells and others: 'some day', she wrote to him, 'perhaps you will give me a small finger, just my little finger, in some bit of decoration.'[48] She didn't invite Frederick and his sister Jessie Etchells to Asheham because she liked them – she found Frederick uncouth – but because she recognised his talent and his potential as a collaborator.[49] They were among the first of 'a constant stream' of visitors invited to Asheham that August and September while Virginia and Leonard were on their honeymoon.

Vanessa and Virginia's Sussex homes were close enough to London to attract friends and family but far enough away to be rural and remote. After travelling little more than an hour from London by train, Vanessa could walk or cycle from the nearest station, Lewes or Glynde, and luggage was collected by the milk cart and delivered in the morning. When they graduated from Little Talland to Asheham, however, Vanessa and Virginia exchanged a relatively new semi-detached cottage for a rambling old house in a state of disrepair. Leonard described Asheham as 'romantic, gentle, melancholy, lovely', but the plumbing was so antiquated that water had to be pumped by hand every morning and the lavatory was an earth closet outside.[50]

Roger was actively involved in helping Vanessa set the house up for the summer, transporting 'the most enormous quantity of luggage' and bringing in new furniture.[51] Her interior *Frederick and Jessie Etchells Painting* includes one of the curtains she had made literally days beforehand (fig. 4.6).[52] 'I'm very busy making curtains', she wrote to Clive.[53] Bright 'reddish orange . . . lined and bordered with mauve', they formed part of an arresting colour scheme that she described in a letter to Roger: 'They make the room look greener than before, & certainly are a lovely colour, but I can't tell quite what will happen till I get them up with their borders.'[54] *Frederick and Jessie Etchells Painting* reiterates Vanessa's progressive interest in colour and composition. The figures are faceless. Jessie's squat figure sits on the floor to paint and the accents of her white blouse and red stocking counterbalance the vertical form of her brother, standing at an easel. Outside, the garden features of terrace, lawn and flint wall are abstracted to bands of colour sandwiched between the vertical stripes of doorframe, green wall and curtain. The painting and *The Studio: Duncan Grant and Henri Doucet Painting at Asheham* show the artists working in a space stacked with canvases, some facing out and others turned to the wall.[55] They document an extraordinary assurance and originality as Vanessa laid claim to her inclusion and

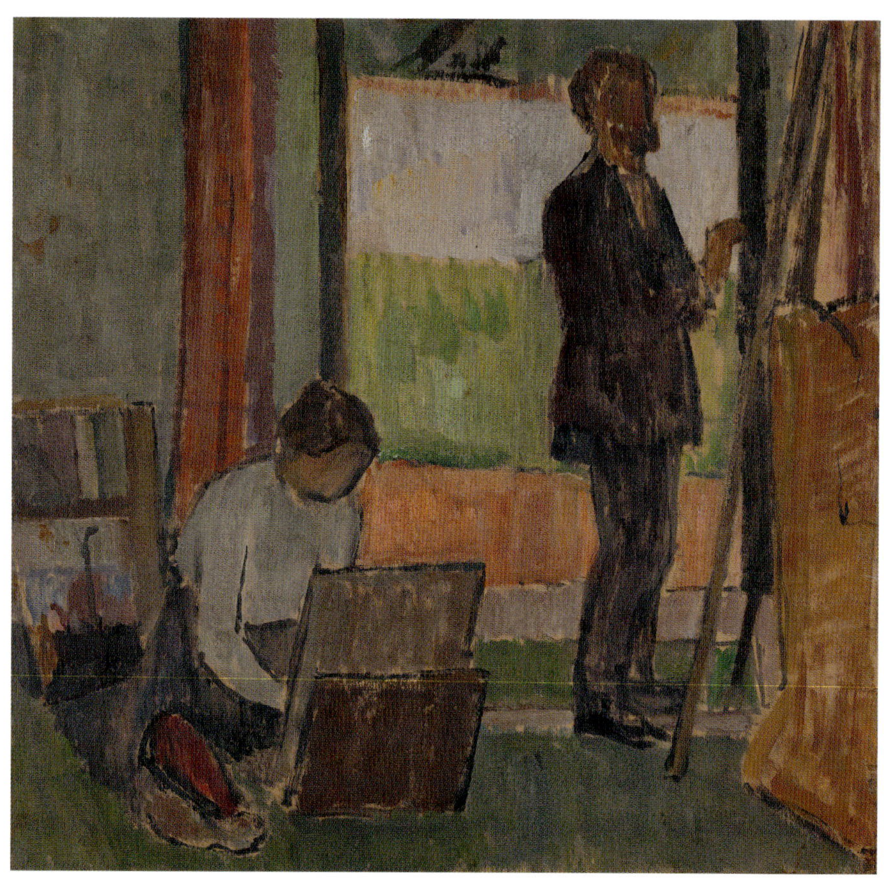

4.6. Vanessa Bell, *Frederick and Jessie Etchells Painting*
1912, oil on board, 511 × 530 mm, Tate, London

equality in the artistic circle that would form the Omega Workshops. Pressing further, for a collaboration through which the artists would work together on a single design and venture beyond painting, she worked with Roger in the days before Frederick and Jessie arrived on designs for a poster for the *Second Post-Impressionist Exhibition*. She described the process to Clive: 'He brought with him some designs of Duncan's for the Grafton poster, which he thought not very good for the purpose . . . so we spent the afternoon trying to do others'. Vanessa's design, 'a very fashionable woman looking in horror at the announcement of a 2nd P. I. exhibition', was discarded as 'too vulgar & I did another head'. All the designs were then sent to Duncan, 'to see if he can do something with them'. As soon as the Etchells had departed, Vanessa followed up with Roger: 'have you seen Duncan & what about the posters. Shall I do you one after all? I have some new ideas.'[56] The printed design, credited to Duncan, was probably finalised during his stay at Asheham in the ensuing days.[57]

Frederick and Jessie Etchells Painting and *The Studio: Duncan Grant and Henri Doucet Painting at Asheham* locate Vanessa in the vanguard of modernism. They describe her achievement in literally drawing the artists with whom she wanted to work into her own self-consciously designed domestic space. Christopher Reed has observed that Vanessa made her home 'a locus for a lifestyle associated with Post-Impressionism' and a 'site of female creativity'.[58] She challenged the urban focus and chauvinism of the Camden Town Group and other modernists. At 46 Gordon Square, Little Talland House and Asheham, she undermined gendered assumptions about painting, the decorative arts and domesticity. Impressively, she refused to become absorbed in the domestic responsibilities of hosting, prioritising her identity as an artist. 'I have done a good deal of painting here', she wrote to Margery from Asheham: 'It has been quite easy as other people have generally been painting too'.[59] Violet and Duncan arrived just as Frederick and Jessie left. She listed the subsequent guests for Virginia: 'Roger comes again next Sunday & Saxon & then Keynes, Sydney Waterlow, Molly, Oliver Strachey, Norton & perhaps others. I leave them all entirely alone & so it's quite easy.'[60] The house was so crowded, she wrote, that Duncan slept in the bathroom. 'The fact is this place is now a great success . . . so much so that they don't want to leave & everyone wants to come . . . It's certain that there never was such a house or such country for painters.'[61]

5

WOMEN AND CHILDREN

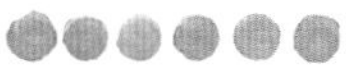

Women's bodies and maternity were important themes in Vanessa's early work, rooted in her own life-changing experiences of motherhood and miscarriage. Three iconic paintings, *Studland Beach*, *Women and Baby* and *Nursery Tea*, show how she asserted her originality as a modernist. Painted between *Manet and the Post-Impressionists* and the *Second Post-Impressionist Exhibition* in 1912 they confront representations of *baigneuses* and ordinary working women as modernist subjects. Vanessa is likely to have read Sickert's essay 'The Naked and the Nude' and seen his unflinching and controversial paintings of naked women exhibited initially in Paris and then in *The First Exhibition of the Camden Town Group* in June 1911.[1] She was party to discussions with Roger and Clive about 'significant form' and the emotive qualities of colour and composition. Visiting exhibitions and art dealers' showrooms with Roger and others, she was surrounded by critical theories relating to nudes by Manet, Cézanne, Gauguin, Denis, Picasso and Matisse. Roger was central to British interpretations of Cézanne's work. He wrote that all modernists derived, in some measure, 'from the great originator of the whole idea, Cézanne'.[2] He was actively engaged in the processing of Cézanne's legacy by contemporary artists, translating an essay by Maurice Denis on Cézanne for the *Burlington Magazine*, for example, that defended his anatomical distortions or 'deformations'.[3] Vanessa deliberately positioned her own work within a European canon, presenting an alternative, feminist perspective on female sexuality and fertility.

VANESSA BELL

88

In the long hot summer of 1911 when Vanessa stayed with Roger and then rented a cottage close to his home in Guildford, talk of paintings coincided with an acute awareness of her own body and those of others. She was recovering from her miscarriage and embarking on a passionate affair with Roger. He was preoccupied with the London Borough Polytechnic decorations. Duncan was working with him at the polytechnic on an innovative mural of male nudes, *Bathing*, and the two men would take the train back to Guildford together having spent the day painting: 'we went in boats at night', Vanessa recalled, and 'Roger and Duncan both bathed naked in the river'.[4] A serious mental and physical breakdown that summer restricted Vanessa's ability to paint. As she recovered she painted a series of beach scenes that challenged male-centric representations of women and their bodies. Culminating in *Studland Beach*, they describe the coexistence in her creative intelligence of complex historical, psychological, corporeal and artistic references.

Vanessa arranged four family holidays in Studland on the Dorset coast between 1909 and 1911, always including Virginia and often inviting friends to come and join them.[5] These seaside holidays when Julian and Quentin were babies evoked memories of Vanessa's childhood summers at Talland House. Like St Ives, Studland was popular with artists but it was much closer to London. Sylvia Milman had recommended 'charming lodgings' there. Vanessa could paint outdoors on the beach: 'I expected to see many Sladeites perched on the surrounding hills like myself,' she wrote to Virginia after a day trip to nearby Corfe, 'but luckily the season was too late for them & all have disappeared'.[6] Four paintings of Studland beach are currently known but there were others. Of these, the small scale and supports, board rather than canvas, distinguish *Figure on the Beach, Studland Bay* and *The Beach, Studland* as sketches, painted in situ.[7] The two remaining paintings, *Bathers* and *Studland Beach*, are larger and painted on canvas.[8] They develop complex and ambitious experiments in composition, suggesting that they were painted in Vanessa's lodgings or in her studio some time later. 'It's really very difficult to paint on the beach', Vanessa wrote to Roger. 'One can't get any composition & one's colour changes completely when one brings it in out of the sun.'[9] The freedom and immediacy of painting outdoors produced oil sketches that Vanessa would subsequently refine and distil.

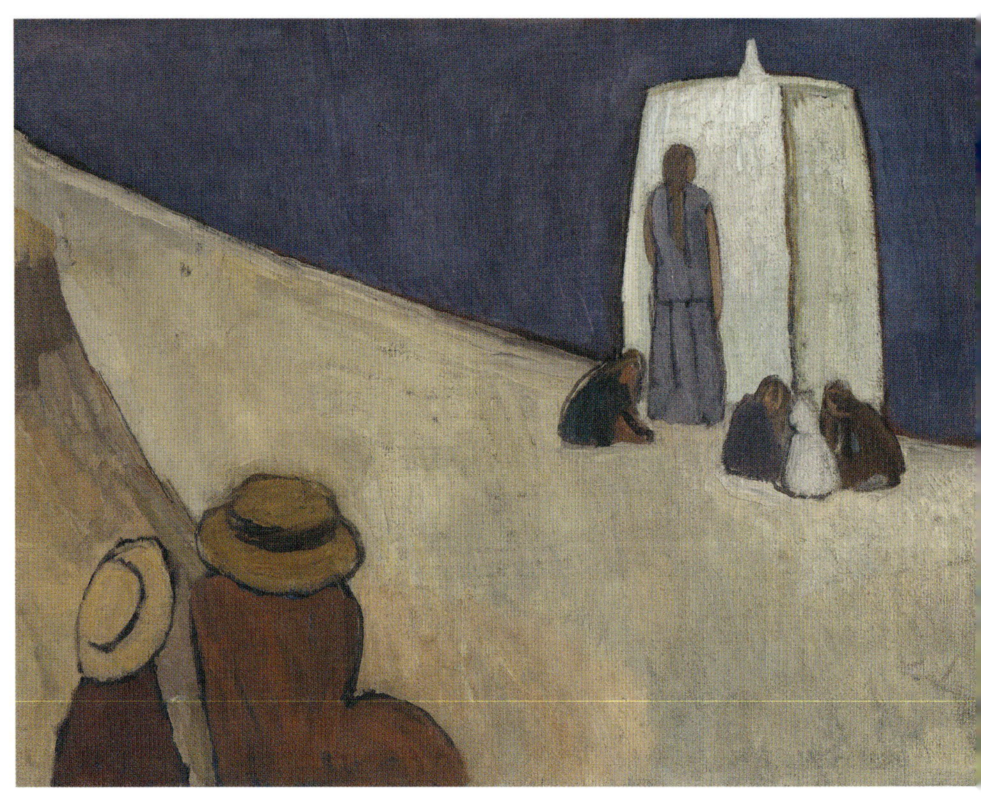

5.1. Vanessa Bell, *Studland Beach*
c.1912, oil on canvas, 762 × 1016 mm, Tate, London

Studland Beach is one of Vanessa's most iconic paintings (fig. 5.1). The ambiguity of its subject matter combined with its striking use of colour and composition have prompted analysis by leading art historians. It's easy to forget that Vanessa produced a multitude of studies and paintings that are lost and that paintings may have been substantially reworked or begun afresh later, so that surviving works may not relate directly to tantalising references in her letters. Paintings of Studland were not necessarily painted at Studland. *Studland Beach* is closely based on the in situ sketch, *The Beach, Studland* (fig. 5.2). It enlarges the dimensions of the oil on cardboard sketch by a factor of three, abstracting and replicating the main components of the composition. The deliberate layering of paint and its rich surface textures indicate that this was a studio painting. It is entirely different in scale and handling from, for example, *Frederick and Jessie Etchells Painting* (fig. 4.6), which was probably painted in a single session. A curved diagonal dissects the image into two parts with the intense blue of sea or sky above and the white and yellow tones of a beach below. The line is broken by the stylised form of a bathing tent at the boundary between sea and sand. Four children and a woman are clustered around it, counterbalanced, in the lower left corner, by a woman and child. All of the figures have their backs to the viewer. Lisa Tickner has noted that in the sketch the tent is 'flapping and festive' and the woman is in a pink dress, turned slightly with her hands raised to her hair.[10] Local by-laws insisted on proper changing facilities for the sake of propriety: 'No person shall bathe from the beach between the hours of 10 a.m. and 7 p.m. without using a tent or bathing machine.'[11] Three of the children in the study appear to be engaged in conversation and the fourth, a little distance away, is looking towards them.

One of the signals that the larger painting is no ordinary beach scene is the repositioning of the woman. She now resolutely faces the tent as if she could stare straight through it to the sea beyond. Her blockish form recalls the distortions of Cézanne's bathing nudes.[12] Clad in blue, it echoes the tent's contours, its monumentality and

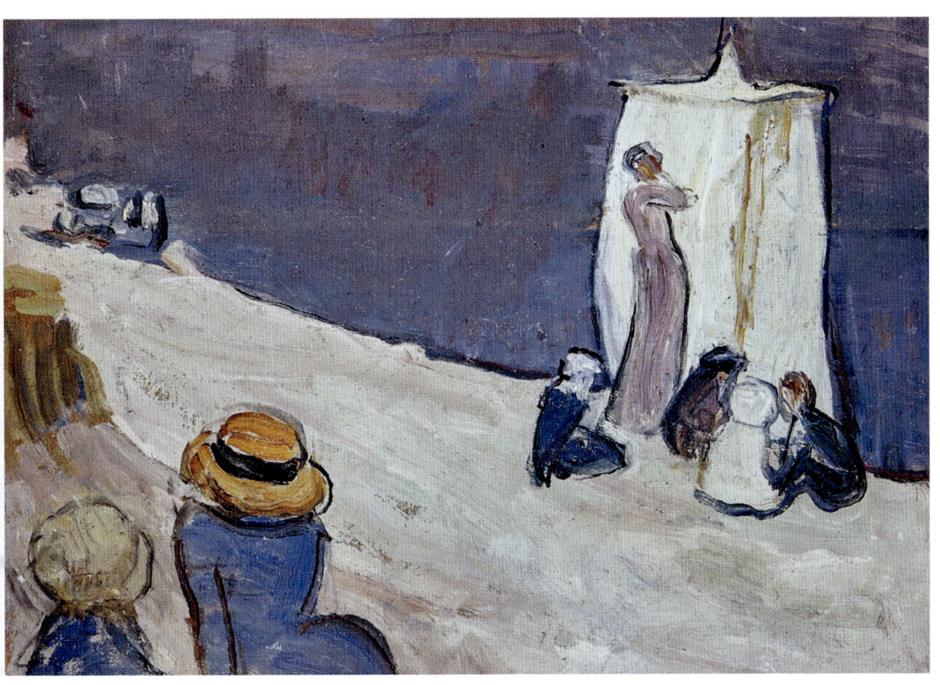

5.2. Vanessa Bell, *The Beach, Studland*
c.1912, oil on cardboard, 254 × 330 mm, photo © Sotheby's 2024

its stillness. The children are now huddled, looking down. The distinction between sea and sky has gone and the contour dividing the beach from the blue above has been raised within the composition and redefined with long, thick sweeps of paint, giving the beach a steep impenetrability. *Studland Beach* eliminates all extraneous detail. It is concentrated, too, in its handling of colour. The blue of the sea is layered in tones ranging from blue to lilac that complement the standing figure's dress. The dark reddish brown of the foreground figures resonates with the red under painting to the sea and this correlation between near and far is echoed in glimpses of blue showing through the figures' red coats and boaters. Tickner has observed that narrative readings of the painting contravene Vanessa's distaste for sentimentality but that it evokes a memory of her mother and her own familial position as the eldest of her three siblings.[13]

The painting references Renaissance images of the Madonna. Art historians have noted similarities between Piero della Francesca's *Madonna del Parto* and *Madonna della Misericordia* in the framing of the maternal figure in *Studland Beach*, enshrined within the outline of the tent with her children around her feet.[14] Blue, historically an expensive pigment, was often reserved for the robes of Madonnas and associated with spirituality. Roger's scholarly credentials were rooted in the Italian Renaissance and the painting reflects Vanessa's involvement with his critical theories. He was renowned for his ability to draw comparisons between art from different periods and cultures, and Vanessa shared his admiration for works by Piero and other artists. 'I am still overcome by thinking of that Giotto', she later wrote to him. 'My God, how divine, I see it does the whole thing . . . It also makes me feel how little one <u>can</u> analyse one's feelings before really great art. One is simply lifted into a different life & carried off in it.'[15]

Studland Beach is an exercise in the theory of significant form but it is more than that, as Tickner and Spalding have observed. It translates Vanessa's experience of matriarchy, memory and loss into a modernist statement. It codifies a challenge to the male gaze in representations of women and their communities that she had seen in *Manet and the Post-Impressionists*. The Studland paintings and the letters and photographs relating to them span three successive summers and describe a confluence of transformative experiences that shaped Vanessa's identity as a woman artist. They evidence a disjuncture between her own experiences of family, sex, pregnancy, birth and miscarriage and the progressive renderings of 'bathers' and 'maternity' by Cézanne, Gauguin and Denis that influenced her technique. *Studland Beach* may be understood as a repository through which Vanessa processed childhood memories and complex emotions that crystallised around Studland and its association with St Ives.

Vanessa's power as a matriarch and the inequalities of her position were polarised at Studland. It became a locus for conflicted maternal feelings for her new baby and for Virginia. After their first holiday there, when Virginia described Vanessa tucking her skirts up and wading into the sea with Julian, Vanessa and Clive returned to Studland with Virginia in the spring of 1910 to avert a crisis in Virginia's mental health. Already pregnant with Quentin, Vanessa then persuaded Virginia to take a rest cure in a nursing home in Twickenham. She shared her acute concerns with her: 'Now that I don't live with you it is impossible for me to be always badgering you & even if it does land you in a lunatic asylum or make you a permanent invalid I see that you must be left to your own devices.'[16] A few days later she booked Virginia's accommodation at Studland for September so that she could join her there as soon as she was on her feet again after the birth.[17]

Vanessa's commitment to her family was very different from Clive's. She was powerless to restrain him when he resumed his secretive correspondence with Virginia. The tone as well as the contents of Vanessa's letters indicate the nature of her relationships and in the early years of her marriage, uniquely, she demeaned herself to court Clive's favour: 'I think, by the way, that I might see the Goat's letter, even though I have seen her, mightn't I? It would amuse me – but not if you think I'd better not. Dolphin will subside if she's told she's naughty.'[18] Dolphin was one of her pet names.

Clive spent the weeks surrounding Quentin's birth at his parents' home with Julian, meeting up with Mrs Raven-Hill there: 'I hope you'll see your whore soon & get some amusing gossip out of her', Vanessa wrote to him.[19]

In the late stages of her pregnancy with Quentin, Vanessa compiled a photograph album. This was a period when she reflected on her family history.[20] 'I have spent most of my time arranging my family album . . . & have found the making of it a fascinating employment', she wrote to Virginia. 'I raked up endless family photographs & put them all in.' The first pages are dedicated to Stella and when Adrian visited they spent 'a happy afternoon' finding more photographs and reading aloud from one of Stella's diaries filled with her reforming voluntary work: 'days spent rushing all over London from Hampstead to Southwark, all by bus or underground, with never a pause. How she lived to be 28 I can't imagine', Vanessa wrote to Virginia.[21] Vanessa was 31 and, as Stella had been, still responsible for her siblings. When she photographed her friends and family on the beach at Studland a few weeks later the visual narratives she had constructed in her album pages were fresh in her mind. Photographs of Virginia and Adrian playing cricket in St Ives were sandwiched between memorial pages to her parents and to Thoby as well as Stella. Her Studland photographs were fixed into the album's later pages, consolidating mnemonic connections between St Ives and Studland, between her past and her adopted 'family' of Bloomsbury friends.[22]

The Studland photographs document Vanessa's centrality to the emerging Bloomsbury Group. They feature many of the friends who visited her in Gordon Square during her confinement. One album page shows Clive and Virginia with Julian, Saxon, Desmond, Molly and Marjorie Strachey. She is lying in the sand holding up a weekly newspaper, *Votes for Women*, to the camera.[23] Marjorie had argued with Clive about suffrage over dinner at Gordon Square a few weeks earlier. 'She was going off today to spend the summer suffrage campaigning. I asked her to come to Studland but she probably can't on account of suffrage', Vanessa wrote to Virginia in July.[24] Saxon, who was regularly at Gordon Square helping her choose names for the baby, was 'very much pleased at having been asked to Studland'.[25] Perhaps less welcome were Sydney and Alice Waterlow. Sydney had been in London for 'one of these Cambridge dinners' and described Alice's disapproval of a mutual friend because she 'hasn't enough maternal feeling' for her twins. 'I suppose the truth is', Vanessa wrote to Virginia, that she 'is a woman of some intelligence who apparently can be interested in her work as well as the twins.' They 'mean to take lodgings in Studland certainly if they can get them', she wrote.[26]

Her album pages for Studland are unusual because they include and name the servants in her party. Sophie Farrell, who was photographed by Gerald and Stella when she was cook for the Stephen family, was at Studland working for Virginia: 'She seems to intend spending most afternoons on the beach with Julian & is taking a tea-basket with her. I only hope the weather will allow of pic-nics', Vanessa wrote.[27] She wasn't included in the Studland pages but her presence would have reinforced family memories of St Ives. In the album, the 'Studland 1910' pages open with a photograph of 'Nurse Spoor' holding baby Quentin, taken at Gordon Square, next to an image of Julian with the children's nurse, Mabel Selwood. Vanessa's album pages were deliberately composed to narrate stories and it is significant that these photographs were arranged in a group above images of Vanessa and Julian in the sand, with Clive and Mabel seated on the grassy bank behind them.[28] The seaside and popular parks were modernist subjects for Impressionist and Post-Impressionist painters because working-class men and women achieved a degree of equality there, taking their leisure alongside wealthier people.[29] Art historians seeking to identify the figures in *Studland Beach* have proposed Mabel and Julian as the foreground figures in the painting.

Inequalities in Vanessa's relationship with Clive and the professional compromises and social isolation of motherhood were starkly apparent towards the end of the 1910 holiday when Vanessa weaned Quentin and he became seriously ill. She abandoned her plan to accompany Clive to Paris, where they were to have met Roger and others to select paintings for *Manet and the Post-Impressionists*, a task for which she was more qualified than Clive. Left behind with Virginia, the children and their servants, she wrote to him in Paris: 'I spent this morning looking after Claudian [her provisional name for Quentin] . . . & this afternoon we walked on the cliff. The sea is like the smoothest glass, but the sky is rather heavy.'[30] She described long conversations with Virginia about her relations with Lytton and Clive but mostly 'wandering reminiscences about our pasts'.[31] She arranged for her recent photographs to be developed, including images of Clive and Virginia together in their bathing suits, and sent them to him: 'The Goat and I are awful – she especially – & you are very curious.'[32]

No paintings can be dated with certainty to Vanessa's first holidays at Studland. She was painting there in 1910. Her 'beach at Studland' was rejected by the Friday Club that June and she was sketching at Corfe later in the summer but it was not until 1911 when she returned with Roger and her family that Studland became synonymous with radical new work.[33] By this time she was familiar with Post-Impressionist bathing scenes and was recovering from her breakdown, although she was still struggling with exhaustion and 'horrid sensations of unreality'. Between Guildford and Studland she spent nearly three weeks at Clive's family home in Seend, complaining to Roger: 'as I haven't done a stroke of work here I feel entitled to do something serious at Studland . . . some real serious work'.[34] She began by defying the local by-laws, taking nude photographs at the beach with Clive and Roger.[35] All three posed naked but these are not sunbathing snapshots. They were probably intended as reference material for paintings. In one, a tall sunflower has been propped up with stones and Vanessa poses next to it. She wears only a headscarf and a necklace and she holds a length of fabric draped across the backs of her legs.[36]

Vanessa and Roger painted together in the first days of the holiday when the photographs were taken. 'I've done no painting since you left but perhaps shall do a little on that lovely card this evening. You said such nice things to me about my sketch of you', Vanessa wrote to Roger when he returned to London and the *Burlington Magazine* for a few days.[37] 'I think perhaps I <u>did</u> do a little too much painting with you'.[38] She was experimenting, writing to Duncan for the recipe for casein, a tempera that he and Frederick were using: 'it would be rather good to put on cardboard for sketching here I think.'[39] She wrote that she was painting badly: 'I succeeded this morning in making my yesterday's failure still more of a failure & have given it up in despair.'[40] The holiday, too, was not an unparalleled success. When Marjorie joined them she was dismissive of Vanessa and Roger's paintings.[41] Lytton, when he visited, described the party as 'ghastly' and Clive as 'a corpse puffed up with worms and gases'. He described his 'inconceivable theories on art and life' as a consequence of Roger's influence.[42] Vanessa's mental health suffered. She was unable to paint for much of the holiday but in the last days before she returned to Gordon Square she was working again and filled with optimism. 'I've been trying this morning on the beach to paint your subject – the one with my colossal figure in the foreground', she wrote to Roger.[43] The letter suggests a degree of collaboration: 'your subject', 'my colossal figure'. Although she wrote that it was 'too difficult' and 'a failure',

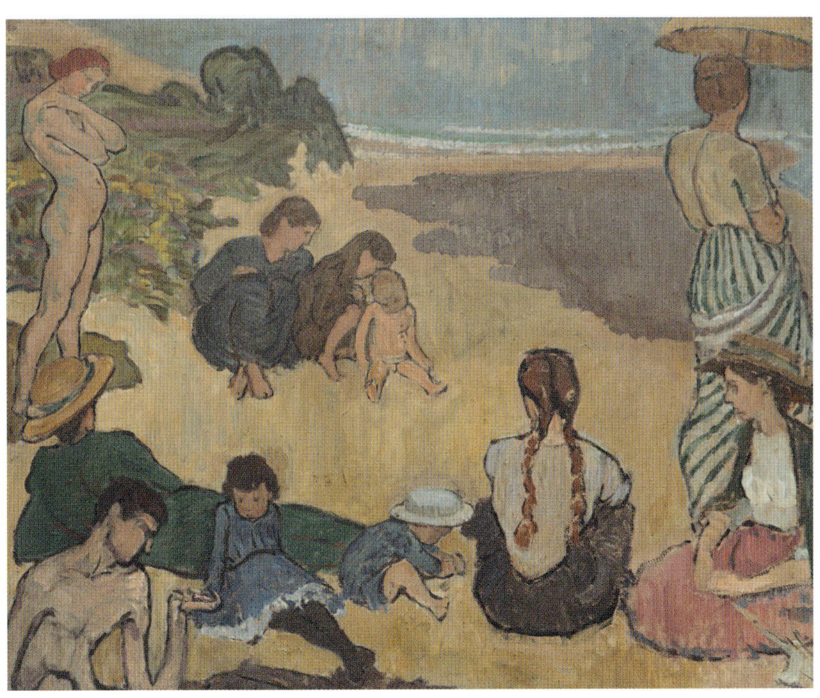

5.3. Vanessa Bell, *Bathers*

c.1911, oil on canvas, 762 × 1012 mm, private collection

she was already planning a 'painting party' for the following July: 'will you come?' she wrote to Duncan. 'We should sleep here & go out all day to paint . . . I believe it would lead to masterpieces.'[44] In the event, the painting party the following year was at Asheham.

Studland Beach and *Bathers* drew on the Studland sketches, photographs and experiences but they were also influenced by Vanessa's travels and a self-conscious determination to situate her work in the vanguard of European painting. She returned to London and, briefly, to the belief that she was pregnant either by Clive or Roger, before joining them and Duncan in Paris. During those few weeks she saw the London Borough Polytechnic murals, perhaps for the first time, and made a start on *Women and Baby*.[45] As soon as she arrived in Paris she and Clive bought the Picasso. 'Tomorrow when Roger and Duncan are here we shall see some pictures', she wrote to Virginia.[46] They spent the next morning 'looking for young geniuses at the autumn salon'.[47] 'The world of dealers was open to me now',

WOMEN AND CHILDREN

97

Vanessa later recalled. 'Roger had a way of making them disgorge things one wanted to see.'[48] Their shared interest in innovation, colour and composition and Roger's close visual analysis of paintings would have intensified Vanessa's assimilation of seminal Post-Impressionist works. She was certainly influenced by Cézanne and Denis, whose paintings Roger vigorously promoted.[49] He may have shown her photographs of Denis's radical nude, *Décor*, or taken her to see it.[50] In *Bathers* and *Studland Beach* she began to experiment with the ethereal, mythical qualities of Symbolist paintings such as *Ulysses and Calypso* and *Orpheus and Eurydice* by Denis that she had seen in *Manet and the Post-Impressionists*.[51] Emile Bernard's *Baigneuses à la vache rouge* may also have informed the composition of her *Bathers*.[52] The massing of foreground figures in both paintings and the central triangular group, apparently floating in the picture plane, invite comparisons.

The incongruity of naked and clothed figures of all ages, dissociated from one another, in Vanessa's *Bathers*, like the red cow on the beach in Bernard's *Baigneuses*, implies a mysterious narrative (fig. 5.3). The vertical accents of a naked woman covering her breasts and a standing woman in the foreground crisply attired in blue and white stripes may relate to the 'colossal figure' and the 'failure' in Vanessa's letters, but these could equally have referenced sketches for the painting or early versions of it. After her return to London, Vanessa wrote to Roger, 'I have been muddling away at my beach but I doubt it will ever come right.'[53] She may have been referring to *Bathers*, which was never entirely resolved as a composition, or *Studland Beach* or to another painting altogether. It is possible, however, that she exhibited *Studland Beach* as *Au Bord de la Mer* at the Galerie Barbazanges the following May in a determined effort to assert her position as a modernist.[54]

Women and Baby may also be interpreted as a psychologically charged, autobiographical painting through which Vanessa processed loss (fig. 5.4). It was painted over a prolonged period, overlapping with *Studland Beach* and *Nursery Tea*. Vanessa described it as 'my nativity' in a letter to Roger written immediately after her return to Gordon Square from Studland: 'Do you think when you come up tomorrow you could bring with you the drawing you did of me for my nativity? I want to set to work on the mother's figure &

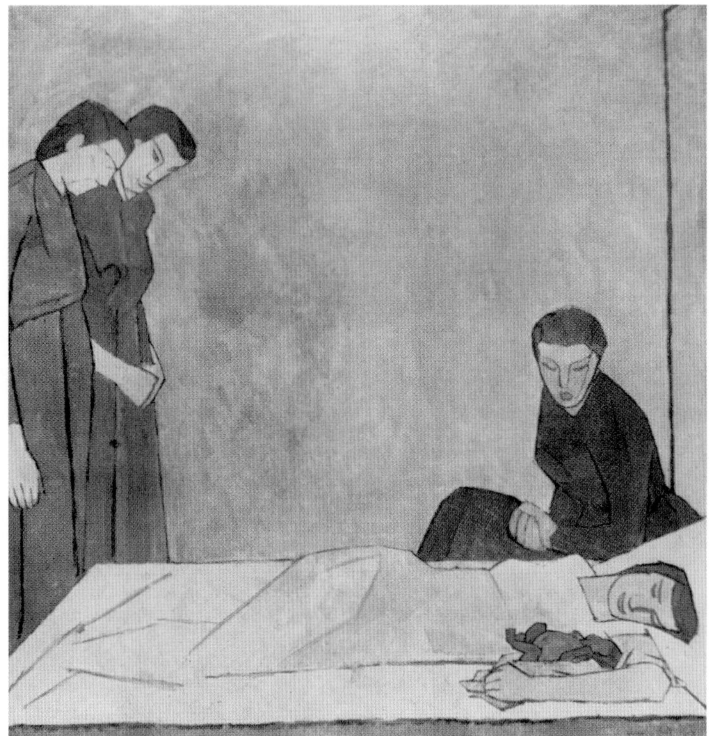

I expect that would help me.'[55] She understood the biblical connotations of her provisional title, writing ironically a year later, 'God was angry with me for what I said about my nativity'. She was punished, she wrote, by a wretched day working on it, 'painting & repainting & getting thoroughly depressed'.[56] *Women and Baby* was her most reductive and perhaps her largest painting (it was six feet square) when it was selected with that title for the survey exhibition *Twentieth Century Art* at the Whitechapel Art Gallery in 1914.[57] Now lost, it represented three women standing or seated around the bedside of a fourth reclining figure. She turns away from them to gaze at a disproportionately small baby, cushioned on a cloth in the crook of her arm. This and the painting's intense, dreamlike quality suggest that it was a reflection on miscarriage. While she was working on the painting Vanessa helped to install the *Second Post-Impressionist Exhibition* and it demonstrates a mature understanding of the works by Gauguin and Matisse she had seen over the past two years.[58]

Women and Baby confronts the eroticised 'primitive' images by Gauguin of nude and semi-nude Tahitian women in paintings such as *The Spirit of the Dead Watching*, *Tahitian Women Bathing* and *Maternité II*, exhibited in *Manet and the Post-Impressionists*.[59] Vanessa was consciously comparing her own work with that of Picasso when she returned to Gordon Square from Paris: 'I've got a most exciting idea in my head which has been itching there for some days, longing to come out & I shall probably try it tomorrow & it's not Picasso or anyone but Vanessa', she wrote to Roger.[60] A week later she was at Little Talland House with Virginia and Adrian, taking measurements for Asheham, and it was not until October 1912 when she had just helped Roger with the installation of the *Second Post-Impressionist Exhibition* that her letters describe work on 'my Nativity' again. She was in thrall to Matisse. The exhibition included iconic works such as *The Red Studio* and *Dance (1)* and Vanessa would paint the Large Gallery in which 16 of his paintings were hung together.[61] Roger took a holiday after the show was installed and Vanessa checked the colour proofs for the exhibition catalogue, writing to him: 'I am more interested in my Nativity which at present I still find absurdly exciting.'[62] She wrote that, because of its size, it would 'take a long time to work through each stage & the depressed stage is still to come. But as yet I'm still always altering such essential things that it keeps one alive.'[63] The depressed stage began a few days later: 'Yes, I do think it's empty. I suppose it really is. I don't believe there's enough design in it to carry it through. What a fool I was to embark on such a thing.' She included a sketch for the head of the seated figure: 'How is one to get form into heads & figures without saying more than one wants to about them?'[64] Two days later she was still 'pounding away at my Nativity', complaining that she would 'take a rest from it soon so as to get a fresh eye. I don't know what's happening, but it's slow work'.[65]

It was another year before Vanessa returned to *Women and Baby* in her letters to Roger and by this time they had co-founded the Omega Workshops with Duncan. Roger was negotiating to acquire the painting from Vanessa when she wrote in October 1913 that she was 'trying to liven [the painting] up a bit that seems to consist mostly in taking out all the features'. She had the confidence to dispute his opinions, writing that if he thought it 'spoilt' he could 'have the screen design instead & £10 too, which I say to myself to make myself free to spoil, as it's the only way to go on'.[66] The painting is signed and dated 1912 in a photograph that Roger used as the lead image for an article he wrote on Vanessa, published in *Vogue* in 1926.[67] He loaned it to the second Grafton Group exhibition and *Twentieth Century Art* in 1914 and the same version of the painting was photographed again installed at Fry's home, Durbins, for another *Vogue* article, 'A Possible Domestic Architecture', in 1918.[68] *Women and Baby* was favourably reviewed but Vanessa remained dissatisfied with it. She wrote to Duncan from Durbins soon after Christmas in 1914: 'I am working at the new picture of the women & baby which I hope Roger is beginning to prefer'. She'd rolled the new painting up and taken it with her because, she wrote, the old one 'makes me shiver to see on the wall but he's still very obstinate about it'.[69]

Following her miscarriage, Vanessa became increasingly interested in progressive design and mosaic. Needlepoint, or 'woolwork' as she called it, was part of her therapy. She was the only artist to exhibit a design for a screen alongside her paintings in Paris in May 1912 and when, having helped to install the exhibition, she became ill in Bologna, she tested the boundaries between art and decoration further, inventing the technique of making paper mosaics: 'I have been practising the art of paper-mosaic while lying in bed', she wrote to Duncan. 'Roger bought some lovely coloured paper & I have been sticking small squares onto cardboard. The result is divine. Extraordinary brilliance & great beauty of line & colour. We _must_ do some real mosaic.'[70] Cutting coloured paper into tiny rectangles and pasting them onto cardboard had therapeutic benefits similar to needlepoint. The mosaic could be made without mess, a little at a time in her hotel bedroom. In Italy, Vanessa was surrounded by decorative mosaics but her paper mosaic exploits the material qualities of this new medium and technique to innovate (fig. 5.5). Similarly, two years later she would experiment with collage to explore abstraction. Her mosaic represents two women and a child. A woman in blue kneeling before the child with her head bowed references the trope of the Madonna while conventional hierarchies are subverted by a standing figure reaching down to lift the infant. Her apron identifies her as a nurse. The design is sketched onto the cardboard and Vanessa uses her paper tesserae, variously cut into squares or rectangles and arranged in lines,

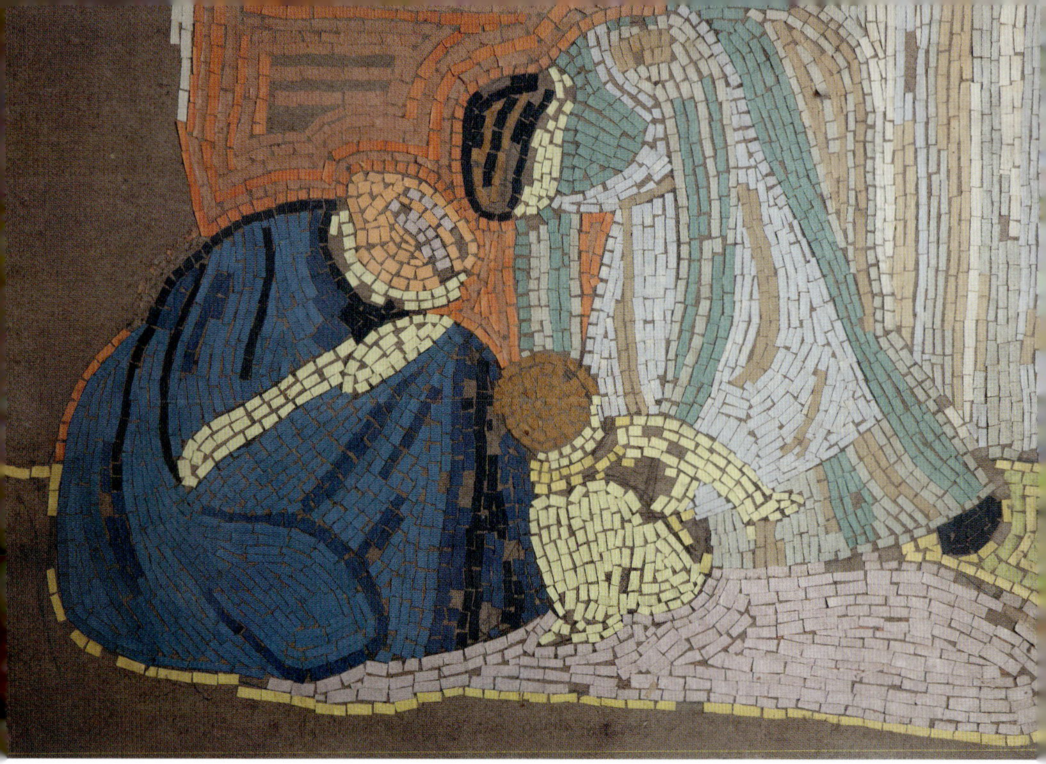

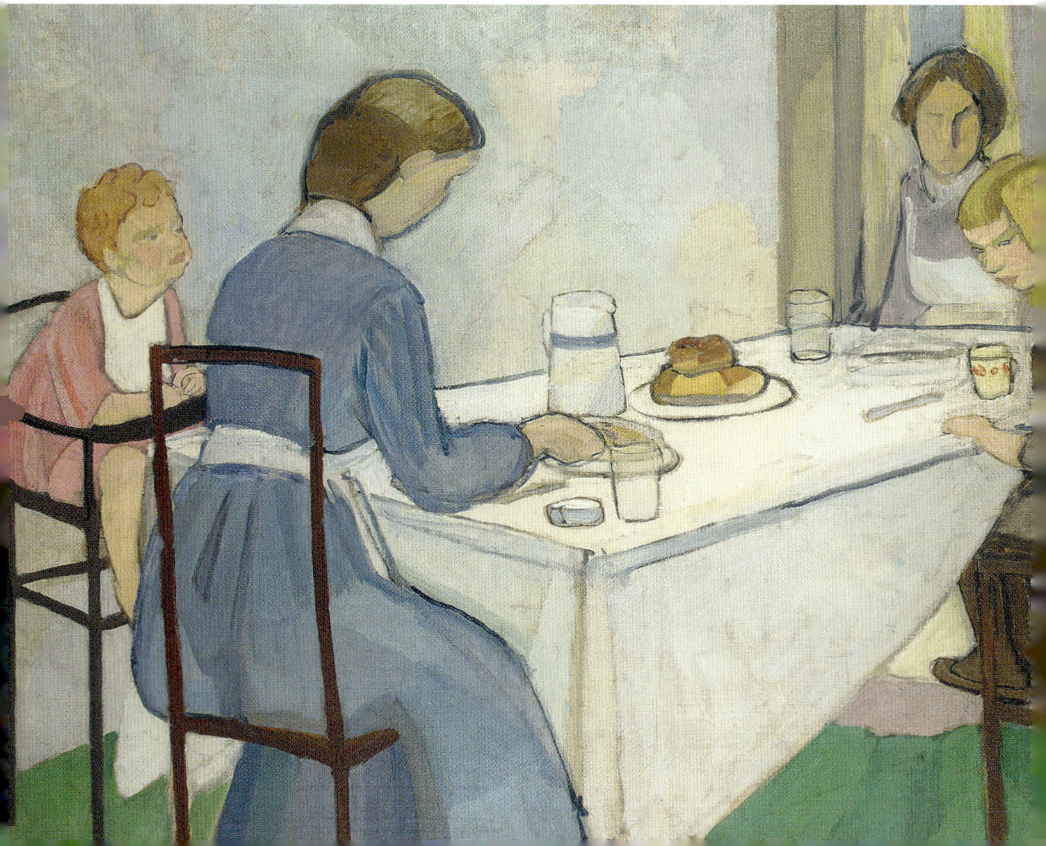

to articulate the image. The child's legs, for example, are formed in a single colour by the meticulous placing of paper pieces. Because Vanessa's letter dates the mosaic precisely it provides a snapshot of the bold pioneering originality of her work in May 1912.

Within weeks, Vanessa was back in Gordon Square and embarking on a more straightforward representation of the intimate lives of women and children. *Nursery Tea* develops her ideas in paint (fig. 5.6). She described the scene as 'rather comic' in a letter to Roger,

> but I am just in an exciting stage as I flatter myself that I am painting in an entirely new way (for me) . . . I am trying to paint as if I were mosaicing, not by painting in spots, but by considering the picture as patches, each of which has to be filled by one definite space of colour as one has to do with mosaic or woolwork, not allowing myself to brush the patches into each other.[71]

She was unafraid of failure and wrote that it was 'amusing' to see if this new technique might 'give one something of the life one seems to get with mosaic' even if it didn't succeed.[72] The painting is comparable in scale to *Studland Beach*. Like that image, it is structured around two distinct groups of figures pushed out towards the edges of the composition to create a disconcerting emptiness at the painting's centre. A woman and child are seated at either end of a long table. Again there is a restless dynamic: the eye flicks from one group to the other and the image is structured around emphatic diagonal lines, here articulated by the edges of the insubstantial table and its cloth. The tension is psychological as well as physical. The foreground figure has her back to the viewer and the table's sharp corner and stark lines, stretching away to the older child, exclude rather than invite participation. The figures do not make eye contact with one another or with the viewer. The younger child and furthest woman look to the older child who in turn looks away, towards the empty space at his side, intensifying an impression of social isolation. Little comfort is offered by the paucity of the meal and the empty glasses on the table. Vanessa was familiar with Dutch and French genre paintings of people eating and drinking and still lifes of tables laden with food. The cool blues and greens of her palette as well as her reductive treatment of this subject establish *Nursery Tea* in opposition to them. It lays down a challenge, too, to the conventions of motherhood as a subject.

Nursery Tea is self-consciously modern. It depicts the reality of family life for women of Vanessa's social standing and their servants. Nursery tea was one of the daily rituals from which Vanessa was excluded. It was served in the day nursery by the children's nurses, identified here by their white collars and aprons. The children resemble Quentin and Julian, who were nearly two and four in June 1912. Their respective nurses, Mabel and Florence Selwood, were 19 and 15. They were sisters, making this a painting of brothers and sisters with very different expectations of life.[73] There was a defined hierarchy and sometimes rivalry among servants and Vanessa was privy to the more formal nursery regimes at Durbins and at Seend. She helped look after her children there when their nurses were on holiday, writing to Virginia, 'I am left to wonder how anyone can ever be a nurse'.[74] Even on holidays at Studland there was a separate day nursery but Vanessa was thrown into greater proximity with her servants there.[75] She was interested in their lives and acutely aware of her dependence upon them in order to work, writing to Roger of Mabel, 'my happiness is largely in her hands'.[76] Mabel's elder sister Elsie had been Julian's first nurse but she fell in love with the postman at Studland and had to leave when she married him, so Florence took her place. The subject of servants dominates Vanessa's correspondence with Virginia. Both women were caught between feminist and socialist determinations to modernise and empower the lives of working women and the necessity of hiring help to maintain the standards that were expected of them as wives, mothers and hostesses.

Studland Beach, *Women and Baby* and *Nursery Tea* are radical reconfigurations of the ideation of maternity and bathing as subjects for art. They describe the beach as a space for reflection. They address the social and psychological isolation of women's lives and their interdependence. They explore absence and memory as modernist subjects. The class and gender inequalities that predetermined the everyday realities of Vanessa's days – and, as a consequence, her work – could be debated as political issues within Bloomsbury gatherings. The trauma of miscarriage and the childhood roots of mental illness, in contrast, could not. At Studland in 1910 Vanessa and Virginia had talked about her future prospects of marriage and motherhood as well as their shared history. Vanessa's return to London was delayed to accommodate Elsie's romance: 'I see that the nurses are anxious to make me stay as long as possible, I expect on account of the postman George', she wrote to Clive.[77] She was acutely aware of the dichotomy between marriage and motherhood, and maintaining a professional life. All three paintings re-envision the bonds between women. They complicate the idealisation of maternity in Renaissance Madonnas and its fetishisation by painters such as Gauguin. In *Studland Beach* and *Nursery Tea* the maternal figure is unavailable to her children. In *Women and Baby* the connection between mother and child is problematised by the baby's diminutive size. The paintings document Vanessa's prolonged relationships with subjects, and sometimes with a single painting, over periods of several years. They evidence connections between her paintings and her photographs and albums. Vanessa's use of a sketch by Roger for her 'nativity' epitomises the tactic of collaboration that would secure her acceptance as a progressive within the masculine domains of mural painters and the Camden Town Group. At Studland, Asheham and Gordon Square she embodied the role of matriarch for her Bloomsbury friends, many of whom were childless. She organised provisions and accommodation and she managed the servants. The detachment in these three paintings may in part be a consequence of the 'sensations of unreality' that were symptomatic of Vanessa's illness. It also demonstrates an objectivity and a determination to inject an alternative reality into the Post-Impressionist fictions with which she was surrounded.

6

OMEGA DESIGNS

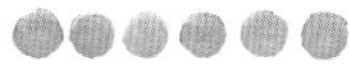

'I wonder what will happen if we get together this group of people in the autumn,' Vanessa wrote to Roger as early as August 1911 before their Studland holiday: 'You'll stir them all up to something quite new.'[1] She proposed the Studland 'painting party' to Duncan the following month. At Asheham she established her studio as a rural retreat where artists were invited to work and at Gordon Square she moved her studio downstairs to the drawing room, the grandest and historically the most sociable room in the house. 'Tomorrow they are going to begin moving our furniture here & I have been making preliminary moves of my canvases into the front room', she wrote to Roger in 1912. 'It will make a very good studio.'[2] Duncan and Roger were encouraged to work with her there as well as at Asheham. Vanessa achieved her ambitions, by necessity, through collaborations with influential men. The evolution of the Omega Workshops exemplified her discrete skills as an arts manager. She blazed a trail for modernist women through her strategies as well as her pioneering practice.

Vanessa's generosity was reciprocated. Duncan hired a model as soon as she returned from Italy and she painted with him at Brunswick Square: 'I am going tomorrow to paint a Spanish model he is having who sounds exciting. I wish you were going to be there', she wrote to Roger.[3] The next day she described the experience: 'Duncan's model has on a very lovely dress but she herself is rather old & painted. His room has got very dark with the tree I think. I'm longing to get to work properly & am going again to paint tomorrow'.[4] Duncan's room

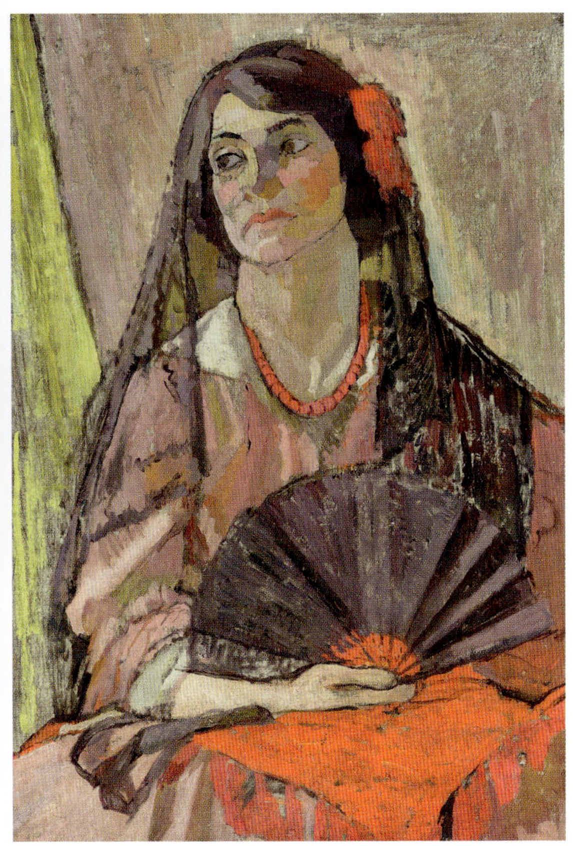

was on the ground floor of the shared house in Brunswick Square and was shaded in summer by a deciduous tree, making the light in Vanessa's new studio a preferable alternative. They went to the New English Art Club exhibition in the afternoon where the 'only decent painting', she wrote, was Sickert's portrait *Jacques-Emile Blanche*.[5] 'It makes everything else look too silly for words.'[6] It informed the subdued tonal range in her painting *The Spanish Lady*, and Vanessa's palette, combining the soft pinks of the model's dress, flesh tones and backdrop with scarlet, black and yellow, was experimental (fig. 6.1). It contrasts with the cool blues of *Nursery Tea* that was painted at the same time. Like Sickert, Vanessa set her figure within a shallow picture space with no foreground or perspective so that, unlike *Nursery Tea*, there are no compositional barriers between viewer and subject. The model's averted gaze and distracted expression contradict her exotic attributes: the black lace mantilla and fan, the scarlet accents of necklace and shawl and the flowers in her hair. They are a rebuke to the erotic othering of Hispanic cultures.

Vanessa sold the painting to the Contemporary Art Society later that summer. She used Gordon Square to store some of the paintings that had been shown at the Galerie Barbazanges after the exhibition toured to the National Museum of Wales. Two members of the Society, Charles Aitken (director of the Whitechapel Art Gallery) and Robert Ross, 'suddenly appeared to see the Duncans' she wrote to Clive. Charles and Roger were among the small group that had inaugurated the Contemporary Art Society at the home of Lady Ottoline and Philip Morrell three years earlier. They selected Duncan's *The Queen of Sheba*. 'Then Ross asked me how much I wanted for my Spanish lady', Vanessa wrote. 'I didn't know what to ask or whether he really wanted to buy it, but I thought I'd better stick to low prices, so I said £5.5.0 . . . Perhaps it will be an advertisement and help me to sell.'[7] She quoted £600 when he also expressed an interest in buying their Augustus John.[8]

Vanessa and Roger created professional opportunities for Clive. At the beginning of 1912 they planned a new magazine together: 'I believe that if the idea could be started, some of the money found, people got together & Clive asked to be editor it would be a new existence for him', Vanessa wrote to Roger.[9] The magazine didn't materialise but at Asheham later that year, less than a month before the opening of the *Second Post-Impressionist Exhibition* at the Grafton Galleries, she wrote to Virginia: 'Clive is now perfectly happy here . . . He has been given the complete control of the English section at the Grafton & is very busy getting pictures out of John etc.'[10] Again, the exhibition was organised by Roger and in his catalogue essay he described it as a sequel to *Manet and the Post-Impressionists*: 'although this year it is mainly the moderns, and not the masters that are represented'. Masterpieces by Cézanne, Gauguin and Van Gogh were included for reference purposes 'by the retrospective exhibition of Monsieur Druet's admirable photographs'. In 'the new movement in art', Roger wrote, 'it is not the object of these artists to exhibit their skill or proclaim their knowledge, but only to attempt to express by pictorial and plastic form certain spiritual experiences'.[11] Clive might have selected any of the paintings that Vanessa had shown in Paris, her portraits of Virginia or *Nursery Tea* for inclusion in the *Second*

Post-Impressionist Exhibition. Instead he banked on her credentials with the Contemporary Art Society that, Vanessa wryly observed, 'may have some effect on artistic snobs'.[12] He chose *The Spanish Lady* together with two still lifes and a landscape, *Asheham*.[13] 'I have four things at the Grafton which are quite ordinary & no one's ideas but my own', Vanessa wrote to her old friend Margery. She described the exhibition as 'even more of a success than it was two years ago . . . I am hoping to show you all the latest explosions & hear your sensible remarks . . . You must bring painting things & be prepared to work.'[14] Of the 242 works listed in the initial version of the catalogue only 12 were by women. Vanessa and Jessie Etchells were the only British women among the 44 artists represented and in total just six of these were women. The 'moderns', by implication, were almost exclusively men.

That Christmas Vanessa stayed at Gordon Square while Clive and the children spent the holiday, as usual, with his family at Seend. Virginia described her as 'more or less broken down': 'she never seems to have got rid of the effects of that miscarriage, and I don't see how she's ever going to in the midst of all the rush at Gordon Square.' It would be two years, Vanessa later recalled, before she was fully recovered.[15] 'I was getting into such a state of depression lying in my bedroom that something had to be done', she wrote to Clive. Roger came to stay and moved her bed into the studio 'where I get all the sun going & it is much more cheerful'. He took her into the square for fresh air every day and bought fabrics for her to choose from so that she could make a bag for Virginia and one for herself.[16] She reassured Clive: 'I do feel really convalescent.'[17] She and Duncan had been experimenting as designers together for some time. They had 'invented a new art, the art of covering boxes with a most beautiful lacquer of different colours & painted with figures', the previous year.[18] In November 1912 she spent an entire day 'doing designs with Duncan', complaining to Roger: 'His are so gay & lovely – mine rather dull & stupid . . . oh it's long since I've been so depressed by working with him'.[19] On Christmas Eve she and Roger painted boxes together: 'Roger has nearly painted two more boxes. I have begun one which I think I may give to Saxon.'[20] She gave a box to Clive and because he didn't like it she offered to exchange it for another: 'I'm very sorry the box is so bad', she wrote to him on Christmas Day: 'I am doing rather a nice one now I think, very simple, squares & circles.'[21] By this time Roger had drawn up a fundraising letter seeking investment in the Omega Workshops and sent a copy to Clive's father.[22] He, too, was unimpressed. Vanessa wrote again to Clive on Boxing Day, relaying to him Mr Bell's letter to Roger about the Omega proposal, 'saying that the project would have appealed to him very much if he had not been to the Grafton but that after going there he was afraid he could have nothing to do with it'. She added: 'I'm afraid that perhaps the box won't help matters! Is there any use sending another?'[23]

The Omega Workshops and the Grafton Group, a design studio at 33 Fitzroy Square in Bloomsbury and a new exhibition society, were devised in tandem. Both were co-founded by Vanessa with Roger and Duncan and applied the aesthetics of Post-Impressionism to the decorative arts. For Roger, Omega was rooted in a philosophical commitment to socialism and a determination to disrupt the effects of Victorian arts patronage. He rehearsed the guiding principles for the Workshops in an essay, 'Art and Socialism', that was first published in a collection edited by H.G. Wells in 1912. He demanded 'a freedom from restraint' for the modern artist: 'he cannot work to order.' Like William Morris, he expanded upon Ruskin's condemnation of mass-produced ornament and recommended that the artist's 'creative energy and delight in work' might infuse 'the work of the ordinary craftsman'.[24] He listed the 'objects of daily life – our chairs and tables, our carpets and pottery' that could benefit if artists were to work 'short hours' as designers to earn a basic income. These were the very objects that the Workshops would manufacture. By early December the theory was consolidated into a fundraising letter and then a prospectus, detailing the business arrangements and the Workshops' creative ambitions.[25] There would be a showroom and a studio where artists would work for up to three half-days a week for a fee of 30 shillings. Roger envisaged a European context for the Workshops, citing Paul Poiret's design school in Paris as a model. Poiret was a successful couturier, closely associated with the Galerie Barbazanges, who had established a decorative arts company the previous year.[26] Roger anticipated a 'mutual exchange of ideas and products' taking advantage of his experience of manufacturing designer textiles and other goods. 'I have also the promise of assistance from several young

French artists who have experience of such work', Roger wrote, perhaps with Henri Doucet in mind. Omega built upon the creative collaborations that Vanessa had fostered. Cooperation was 'a first necessity', Roger claimed, but the example he gave was the all-male 'group of artists who decorated the Borough Polytechnic'. These artists, he wrote, had already 'formed the habit of working together with mutual assistance instead of each insisting on the singularity of his personal gifts'.[27] The principle that designs would be anonymous was not established in either document.

Virginia described Roger as 'rampant' over the Christmas period: 'They're starting on furniture now – have you heard?' she wrote to Lytton, and she shared the artists' 'furious excitement' somewhat cynically with Violet: 'there's to be a shop and a warehouse next month.'[28] Their imaginations were not limited to furniture. Adrian and Duncan (who by this time had been a couple for over two years) visited Vanessa every day over Christmas and Vanessa described Duncan lying on the floor discussing 'how we are to turn my studio into a tropical forest with great red figures on the walls, a blue ceiling with birds of paradise floating from it (my idea), and curtains each one different'.[29] Within a year, she had translated this fantasy into one of three complete room settings, a nursery, for the Omega showrooms.

She spent the first six weeks of 1913 recuperating at Asheham. She stitched Duncan's needlepoint design for a chair seat, *Cat on a Cabbage*: 'I am working at Duncan's cats. It will need a genius to do them I see, but then – I have done nothing else much. My boxes disgust me too much to go on with them', she wrote to Roger.[30] She quickly recovered, writing to Virginia, 'I am much happier now I can do some painting. In fact I see that this would be the way of working. I have done more real work here in a few days than one often does in weeks in London.'[31] Roger and Duncan, as well as other friends and family, joined her and she returned to London, briefly, when the *Second Post-Impressionist Exhibition* was de-installed.[32] By early February she was planning a 'Bohemian dinner' to launch the Omega Workshops in July 'given by all the grateful young artists' to Roger. They would invite his 'aristocratic friends' and other potential patrons 'and after dinner we should repair to Fitzroy Sq., where would be seen decorated furniture, painted walls, etc.'. She joked that the aristocrats would be lured by drinking and dancing with artists into thinking they were 'really in the thick of things' and place their orders, but there were calculations underpinning the camaraderie: 'By the end of summer we should have a lot to show and orders could be delivered in the autumn.'[33] She was making underwear for Virginia and clothes for herself at Asheham and may have been hand-painting garments, experimenting with ideas based on those she had seen in Paris. 'I have been painting today – finishing my clothes', she wrote to Roger.[34]

She persuaded Clive that they should invest their own resources in the Workshops: 'Clive has decided today that we are to give you £100', she wrote to Roger. 'I'm not sure but I think he really wants to give it – & also to make a slight grievance of it!'[35] Clive was aggrieved, too, when the Omega Workshops was registered as a limited company and the shares were allocated to Vanessa as one of five original shareholders: 'As for your remarks about the money we lent to the O. I think they're a little uncalled for', she wrote to him. 'As I drew the cheques that were actually given to the company of course the receipt & share certificate were given to me.'[36] He was concerned, too, when Duncan and Frederick set to work decorating a table and screen before all the capital was in place.[37] They exemplified the artists needing to earn their livings that Roger hoped to support through the Workshops. 'Clive says he [Frederick] is coming to London on the understanding that you are going to begin using the money you have got for decoration at once & that there will therefore be paid work for him to do immediately', Vanessa wrote to Roger. She confessed her own reservations about Frederick: 'I am a little embittered as you may see by sitting in this room where I suffered so much in September. What a mess it all was with two palettes on the floor & that dog growling in corners & the eternal sex problem at all meals!' Frederick had brought his dog to Asheham and liked to talk to Vanessa about sex.[38] The embryonic Omega Workshops was not the only outlet, however, for painted screens and other applied arts.

Vanessa used the Friday Club to exhibit a design for a screen as early as February 1912 and she encouraged other women to join the Club. Jessie Etchells, Winifred Gill, Helen Saunders and Constance Lloyd were among ten women exhibiting as 'non-members' that February. The latter showed a screen together with fans and embroidered bags as well as pictures.[39] Sixty-five of the 125 works exhibited were by women. A row erupted soon after the show. 'They are all very much upset about it & longing for us to return', Vanessa wrote to Roger, 'though <u>you</u> are thought to be too definite & strong for the Club. I said however that Duncan & I could not return either with or without you'.[40] Her solidarity with Roger and Duncan resulted in a new exhibition society, the Grafton Group, which showcased artists from the Galerie Barbazanges exhibition and the *Second Post-Impressionist Exhibition*, several of whom were involved with the Omega Workshops. 'The name will be understood when I say that Mrs Bell, Mr Roger Fry, Mr Duncan Grant, Mr P. Wyndham Lewis, and Mr Frederick Etchells compose the society', one reviewer wrote. 'The society is Post-Impressionist'.[41]

The Grafton Group's first exhibition introduced the principle of anonymity that Omega would adopt. It set Vanessa on an equal footing with her male colleagues. Her founding position was irrefutable. She was boldly identified on the catalogue cover for its second exhibition: 'The Grafton Group. Vanessa Bell. Roger Fry. Duncan Grant'. The artists were listed in alphabetical order with no concessions to sexism.[42] There were only two exhibitions before the venture was terminated by the First World War. The first launched in March 1913 while the artists were creating stock for Omega and included Omega artist Cuthbert Hamilton as well as Thérèse Lessore, Spencer Gore and Christopher Nevinson. Reviewers insisted on identifying the artists for key works and the principle of anonymity was abandoned in the second exhibition in January of the following year. The Grafton Group consolidated and expanded the identity of a British contribution to European Post-Impressionism that embraced the decorative as well as the fine arts. Roger borrowed works by Wassily Kandinsky and Max Weber, and he loaned pictures by Picasso and Derain from his own collection to its exhibitions. The artists used photographs to contextualise their ambitions, representing recent work by Picasso, just as the *Second Post-Impressionist Exhibition* had used photographs. Sculpture by Henri Gaudier-Brzeska and screens by Vanessa, Duncan and Roger that would appear in the Omega showrooms were shown in a gallery setting. Vanessa exhibited *Women and Baby*, probably for the first time, with the Grafton Group and she raised her prices, bringing them more into line with those of Roger and Duncan.[43]

Textiles and screens were among the Omega Workshops' most prominent exhibits when it opened to the public in July 1913. Press

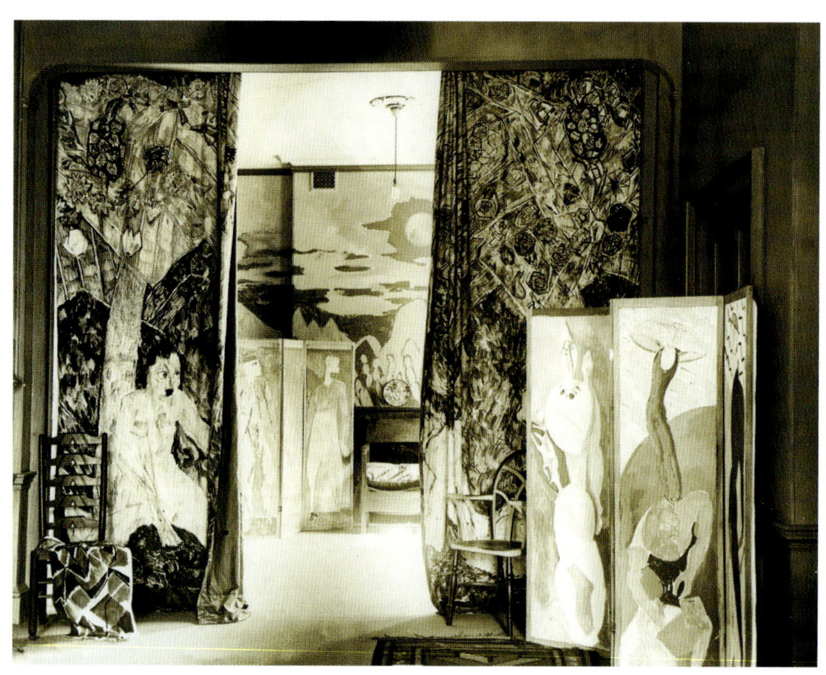

6.2. Unknown photographer, press photograph for the opening
of the Omega Workshops, 33 Fitzroy Square, London

1913, The Charleston Trust

photographs show a curtain attributed to Henri Doucet dividing the front and back showrooms and screens painted by Wyndham Lewis and Duncan Grant (fig. 6.2). Winifred Gill, who was employed by the Workshops, remembered Vanessa working almost full-time with Duncan and Roger in 'the all-out effort to get enough stuff ready for the opening'. She recalled footing a ladder for Henri as he decorated the back showroom. It was distempered 'a warm puce' and he used a stencil to make a pattern of 'sprays of leaves, each about eight feet long . . . I seem to remember a comb coming into the process.' She held the can of purple dye which he 'spattered all round' while snorting with rage because he thought she couldn't understand his French. She did understand, but 'I was much too shy to have uttered a word.'[44]

The Omega opened with six designs for printed linens, produced in France in several colourways.[45] Half of them, *Maud*, *White* and *Pamela*, are attributed to Vanessa and the remaining three, *Amenophis*,

Margery and *Mechtilde*, to Roger and Frederick. A drawing for a seventh design, apparently not put into production, is also by Vanessa (figs 6.3, 6.4). The linens were sold by the yard and made up into tunics, curtains, bedspreads and cushion covers. When Alice Mayes came into the showrooms during the War looking for 'something to make the room look bright for her husband coming home on leave' Winifred, on realising that she was married to David Bomberg, 'sold her some cushion covers cheap'.[46] The range of Vanessa's patterns, from the spare simplicity of *White* with its linear grids overlaid with blotches of colour to the lyrical, Futurist rhythms of her unpublished design, demonstrates her creative originality as a designer. She assimilated progressive influences such as those of Kandinsky and the Italian Futurists whose work she could have seen in an important exhibition at the Sackville Gallery in London.[47] 'Can't we paint stuffs etc. which <u>won't</u> be gay & pretty', she had written to Roger in the summer of 1912. Their Galerie Barbazanges exhibition had just returned from Wales and she was comparing their work unfavourably with that of Picasso, Derain and Matisse.[48] As preparations for the opening of Omega gathered momentum she wrote to Clive from Gordon Square that 'Roger arrived this morning from his aristocrats & has been hard at work on patterns ever since'.[49] A few days later she wrote that she was taking a break from pattern designing: 'Duncan has been trying to do a pattern but gets even more muddled than I do, in fact I don't think he'll ever master repeats.'[50] The clarity and vibrancy of her own designs make

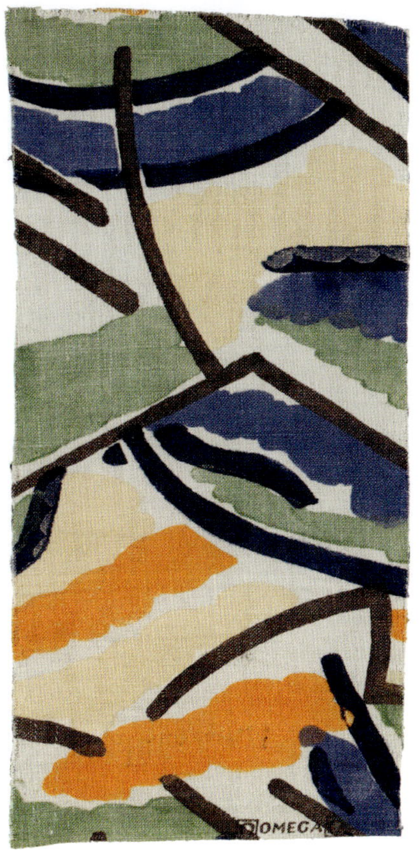

6.3. Vanessa Bell, *Pamela*
1913, printed linen, 200 × 405 mm,
Victoria and Albert Museum, London

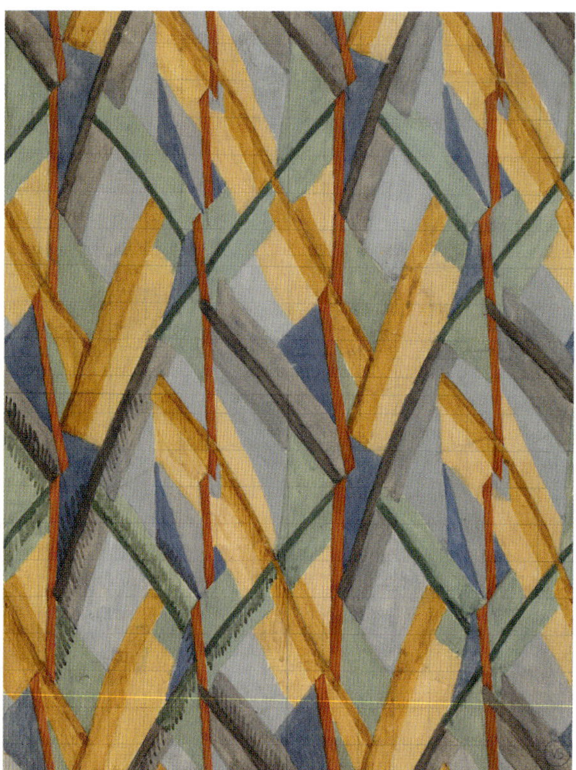

the art of putting a pattern into repeat (essential to textile design) seem effortless. Their appeal was immediately recognised: 'The fabrics scrawled over with an elaborate confusion of lines and spurted with colour, are fierce and fascinating', one reviewer wrote. 'They are an assault . . . upon the law and order of the average wall-paper, upon the rule of garlands and festoons, upon the sovereignty of the repeating pattern . . . they will spread more quickly than the Morris patterns of the "eighties".'[51] Vanessa's Omega textiles influenced her contemporaries and made a significant contribution to the history of design that is now widely acknowledged.[52]

As a director and shareholder, Vanessa could shape the Workshops' coherent aesthetic and its product range but her influence was understated. Roger was the primary investor and the Workshops' public face. She could not counter the habitual chauvinism of artists such as Henri, Wyndham and Frederick but she nevertheless achieved a degree of equality for the Workshops' women artists. Winifred and Nina Hamnett both exhibited with the Grafton Group. Winifred described a two-tier system, however, at the Workshops in which 'the bulk of the work really was done by Roger and Vanessa and Duncan' and she and Nina were part of a cohort of 'rank and file' women responsible for 'the rather boring routine jobs'.[53] They reproduced designs, filled in backgrounds, dyed fabrics, sewed, made jewellery and staffed the showrooms. 'Vanessa produced a Mrs Miles, who sat in the upstairs studio patiently doing cross-stitch'. She was married to the caretaker. Winifred described how needlepoint designs were transferred onto canvas by Omega artists 'in diluted oil paint which made them easy to work' and that Vanessa was 'our expert in this department' and would select the appropriate wools.[54] Winifred would stitch other artists' needlepoint designs for cushions, chair seats and backs but Omega's 'basic rule' of anonymity enabled her to work up her own designs too.[55]

'The important thing', Winifred recalled, 'was that everything produced was anonymous – it just went under the trade mark of Omega.' She listed the 'young up and coming artists' who designed for Omega and because she was interviewed by men when Omega's history was recorded it was men whom she named.[56] The Workshops sold signed pictures and small sculptures by David Bomberg, Roald Kristian, William Roberts and Henri Gaudier-Brzeska on commission. Its designers included Wyndham Lewis, Frederick Etchells, Paul Nash, Edward Wadsworth and Cuthbert Hamilton: 'they weren't given their orders as they would have been in any kind of business', Winifred recalled.[57] They came in to work 'when they wanted money' and could choose to produce a design or to paint or assemble products. Designs were stored in a portfolio, a 'Bank of Designs' that was drawn upon for orders and stock. 'Unsigned, it is now impossible to say by whom they were made, but that was the condition laid down. The idea being that purchasers might ask for work by known artists only, leaving other designs, perhaps quite as good or better, on our hands.'[58] For artists such as Winifred, Nina, Dora Carrington, Jessie Etchells and Christine Nash the system was a revelation. Their own designs and workmanship could be assessed entirely on merit. Subsequently, however, flattery and unconscious bias discriminated against the women. An example of this is the marquetry tray that Vanessa designed for Omega. Her abstract design was the most progressive of three inlaid trays that she designed with Duncan and

Gaudier-Brzeska. She singled out Duncan's tray for praise when they were delivered by the cabinetmaker, John Joseph Kallenborn, writing to Duncan: 'Your elephant tray has come back & is most lovely.'[59] Winifred wrote a history of Omega in a series of letters to Duncan more than 50 years later and flattered him again. She misremembered that when George Bernard Shaw, one of Omega's original investors, came into the showrooms with his wife they chose his elephant tray: 'I remarked that Roger Fry thought this was one of the best things we had done. "Then kindly tell him that I picked it out myself without any prompting from you," he said. "He always thinks I haven't any taste."'[60] In fact the tray that Shaw selected, still in the National Trust collection at Shaw's Corner, was the abstract design by Vanessa.[61]

Soon after the Omega Workshops' launch Vanessa became involved in a commission to design a 'Post-Impressionist room' for the *Daily Mail*'s *Ideal Home Exhibition*. 'I am looking forward to the Ideal Home', she wrote to Roger: 'I expect we shall turn out something lovely & make all the other rooms look silly!'[62] She had planned another 'painting party' at Asheham that summer but went camping first, with Roger, Duncan, Clive and other Bloomsbury friends.[63] 'I have just come back from the most amazing fresh air cure I have ever had in my life', she wrote to Virginia, and set to work immediately 'working at the O. painting a panel for the Ideal room' and decorating the nursery at Gordon Square.[64] She described the three large panels for the *Ideal Home* room to Clive: 'each of two dancing figures in reddish pink & green yellow'. The whole wall, she wrote, 'ought to be rather fine in colour' with red painted pilasters and an ochre surround. 'Duncan & I & Roger are each doing a panel. It's great fun working on a large scale.'[65]

Omega thrived on the publicity that exhibitions generated. The Bloomsbury artists had enjoyed the public outrage that greeted the Post-Impressionist exhibitions and the Workshops purposefully used exhibitions for marketing. Shaw had warned Roger that the showrooms, away from the main thoroughfare in a quiet London square and looking like 'an Orthopaedic Institute', would otherwise limit the Workshops' clientele to a clique.[66] Just before the *Ideal Home Exhibition* opened, Vanessa used her influence at Asheham to make Duncan paint one of a pair of canvases to hang outside the showrooms. 'I think unless I do one Duncan will never do his', she wrote to Roger (see fig. 0.3).[67] He stayed on with her there until the paintings were ready a week later and then returned to London to help Roger with the *Ideal Home* installation. Vanessa apologised that she would be menstruating and so couldn't help until the following Tuesday, 'which would give me one day wouldn't it before the show opens to touch up my panel'.[68] The huge paintings (Vanessa's was subsequently attributed to Duncan or Wyndham) were designed to resonate with the publicity from the *Ideal Home Exhibition* and to shock when they were hung above the entrance to the Workshops. Vanessa wrote that Marjorie Strachey 'thinks them hideous and that we shall be stopped by the police'.[69] Characteristically, she flattered Duncan and was deprecating about her own work when Roger collected them from Asheham: 'He said the only fault he had to find with them was that they looked as if they were advertisements for a dancing Academy', she wrote to Duncan. 'Otherwise he liked them very much – yours at any rate. He made the best of mine too, but I got to hate it so much that I long to destroy it.'[70]

Winifred believed that the 'anonymity which Roger and Vanessa and Duncan were quite happy under' at the Workshops became 'an intolerable burden' for Wyndham, Frederick, Edward Wadsworth and Cuthbert Hamilton.[71] They sent an acrimonious 'Round Robin' letter to Omega's supporters accusing Roger of appropriating the commission for the *Ideal Home Exhibition*. They claimed that Spencer Gore was first approached to decorate the room with Wyndham and that the Omega was simply to provide the furniture. Wyndham, they wrote, was told 'that no decorations of any sort were to be placed on the walls' and was affronted when he returned to the Omega from a holiday to find 'large mural decorations, destined for the Olympia exhibition, around the walls of the workroom'. The letter exposes their prejudices. It condemned Omega for 'Prettiness', 'despite the Post-What-Not fashionableness of its draperies'. 'This family party', it claimed, was 'compelled to call in as much modern talent as they could find, to do the rough and masculine work without which they knew their efforts would not rise above the level of a pleasant tea party'. All four artists signed the letter and resigned from 'this unfortunate institution'.[72] Frederick and Wyndham also left the Grafton Group.

Vanessa was in charge of the Workshops when the letter was issued. Roger was on holiday in France with Henri Doucet. Her response was mature and decisive. She consulted their Bloomsbury friends and enlisted their support before confronting the issue head on: 'D[uncan] and I decided that we had better see Etchells & try to get him to see that whether they were right or not they had behaved monstrously in writing this letter without first accusing you to your face', she wrote to Roger. She wrote again that Frederick had stood his ground when they met but was persuaded to provide 'a list of the people to whom they had sent their circular'.[73] She went to Olympia to talk to the *Daily Mail* agent: 'I gave him definite questions written out to be answered' and he provided written confirmation that the commission was given 'to Mr Roger Fry without any conditions as to the artists he would employ'.[74] By chance, Clive encountered Wyndham in Bond Street and Vanessa relayed their conversation to Roger:

> Lewis was very much disappointed that you had not rushed back from France at once! What they would really like would be an action for libel. It seems quite clear now that the best thing to do is nothing. It is quite evident that no one will believe anything they say & that they will be crushed more by silence than any reply.[75]

Wyndham's claims, nevertheless, were believed in some quarters and would damage Vanessa's career and Bloomsbury's historiography.[76] When the London Group was formed a few weeks later, amalgamating the Camden Town Group with other societies, Vanessa wrote to Roger: 'Lewis is a member & so is Duncan as I think all Camden Towners are.' New members were democratically elected: 'They proposed both you & me as members,' she wrote, 'but I gather one may be blackballed!'[77] She was excluded from the London Group until 1919.

The Omega room at the *Ideal Home Exhibition* exemplified the coherent style and collaborative spirit that Vanessa embodied and pioneered for the Omega Workshops (fig. 6.5). The large decorative panels that Wyndham had objected to were calculated to arrest attention for their subject matter and their aesthetic. Some visitors would have made a connection between their theme of dancers and the Matisse, *Dance (I)*, dramatically displayed at the *Second Post-Impressionist Exhibition*. Winifred recalled that their 'unconventional

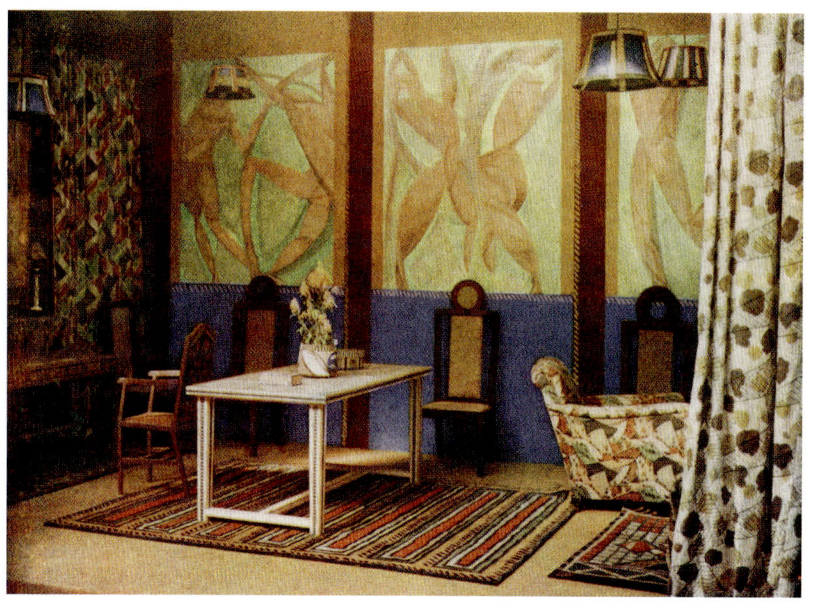

6.5. Omega Workshops, Post-Impressionist Room, Ideal Home Exhibition
1913, published in *Illustrated London News*, 25 October 1913

nudes called forth ribald comment' from those less visually literate.[78] Vanessa's designs were prominently featured in products that the public could order from the display as well as the painted panels. These included her lampshade designs, available in three sizes. Winifred described them as among the Workshops' best sellers. They were coloured in 'three shades of chrome yellow, with a background of deep blue and purple' and designed using 'straight lines only' to be easily reproduced.[79] Vanessa's linens, *Maud* and *White*, were made up into full-length curtains for the room. Nevertheless it was reviewed as 'a room designed by Roger Fry'.[80]

Curators and historians have unpicked the anonymity that benefited the Workshops' women designers and emerging talents. The central rug at the *Ideal Home Exhibition* was designed by Duncan, the table by Etchells and the dining chairs and armchair cover, *Amenophis*, by Roger. Vanessa's contribution to the Workshops was not limited, however, to the individual designs that can be attributed to her. Letters cannot document the collaborative spirit that she helped generate at the Omega studio in the spring and summer of 1913, or the concept that a design might encapsulate more than one creative intelligence. Her genuine commitment to design partnerships served as an inspiration to others. It earned her an exceptional professional status and public profile among the women artists of the avant-garde and it galvanised her ambition as a radical.

7

MODERN FIGURE STUDIES

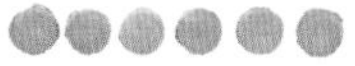

'I have done nothing lately', Vanessa wrote to Duncan at the end of 1913, '& am beginning to think the Omega has destroyed my faculties now that I have broken away from it.'[1] In fact the reverse was true. The Omega Workshops enabled Vanessa to dissolve boundaries between the fine and applied arts and operate in the liminal space between the two. The stylised figures and abstract patterns that she created for Omega decorations, often in the same studio as Duncan, Roger and others, transformed her creative practice. The Workshops gave her a measuring standard for her own work and a public platform where radical innovation was both a requisite and anonymous. In its first 12 months she was under constant pressure to create new designs, new stock, and to perpetuate the Workshops' anarchic identity through press campaigns and exhibitions. She explored new techniques, writing to Duncan before the press launch of a Post-Impressionist nursery which opened together with an Omega bedroom and sitting room at 33 Fitzroy Square in December 1913: 'we have been doing posters for the Omega show in coloured papers.'[2]

The nursery anticipated the work of Matisse in its use of paper cut-outs. Reviewing the room for the *Observer*, P.G. Konody described a sunset 'stuck on to the cornice' (fig. 7.1).[3] Clouds spilled over from the painted ceiling to the walls, and the crisp outline of trees and a mammoth elephant suggests that these were also painted and then pasted on. The room was a collaborative effort. Duncan designed jointed wooden animals, which were sold separately and lined up along a deep shelf.[4] A practical storage area underneath was concealed

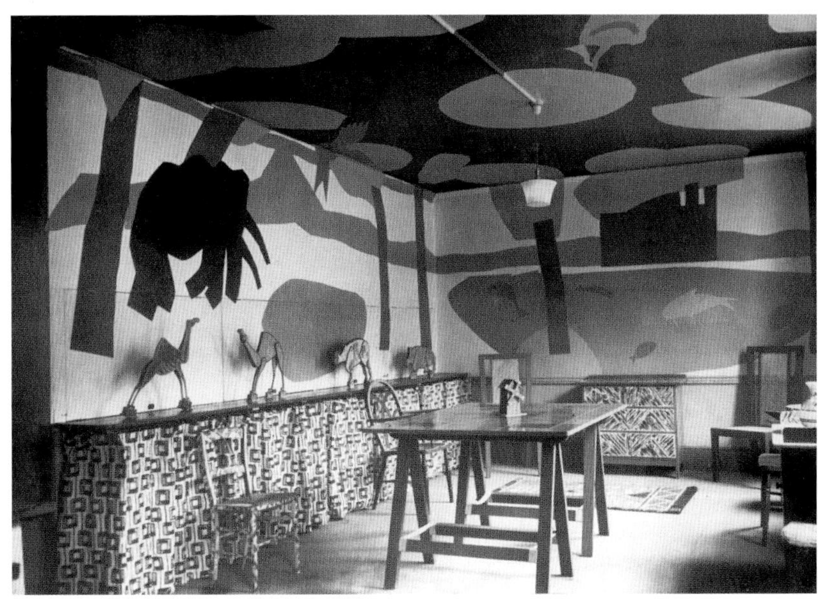

7.1. Omega Workshops, Model Nursery

December 1913, The Charleston Trust

behind one of the Omega Workshops' printed linens, *Mechtilde*, designed by Frederick. Konody credited Roger as its 'dominating influence' but the first iteration of the nursery was at Gordon Square. Vanessa designed it for Julian while she was at Seend in July 1913 and divided her time the following month between completing it and designs for the *Ideal Home Exhibition*. 'It is rather nice here with everyone away', she wrote to Virginia. 'I have finished painting the nursery which I believe is a most truthful portrait of Indian & African animal life.'[5] Julian's nursery showed 'lions stalking zebras & jaguars pouncing on deer'.[6] Vanessa worked with Winifred Gill on a second version for the Omega Workshops that November, complaining to Duncan that she had worked there nearly every day for a week but at least the nursery was finished and 'Winnie has found innumerable pieces of furniture for the dolls house which is a marvel of ingenuity.'[7]

Konody described the nursery as:

> the gay groves of Post-Impressionism . . . The floor is laid with brilliant yellow felt . . . The curtains are yellow also . . . A blue,

uneasy ribbon of colour is a range of mountains; a paler blue blob
is a pond and, unmistakably, on the stretch of yellow that may
be sand, is the black silhouette of a huge mammoth elephant.[8]

It would have appealed to affluent young mothers among the
Workshops' clientele, interested in the progressive theories about
art and creativity that Vanessa's first art teacher, Ebenezer Cooke,
espoused. 'Here, long before evil habits have been formed, the prat-
tling infant is to be led', Konody wrote. Nurseries had the added
advantage, as forays into playful and dramatic decoration, of being
private spaces, mostly out of sight.

There is only one known sculpture by Vanessa and it was another
product of Omega experiments. *Madonna and Child* traces the outline of a vulva with the woman's head, shrouded by her blue hooded
gown, in the place of a clitoris (fig. 7.2).[9] 'We went to the pottery,

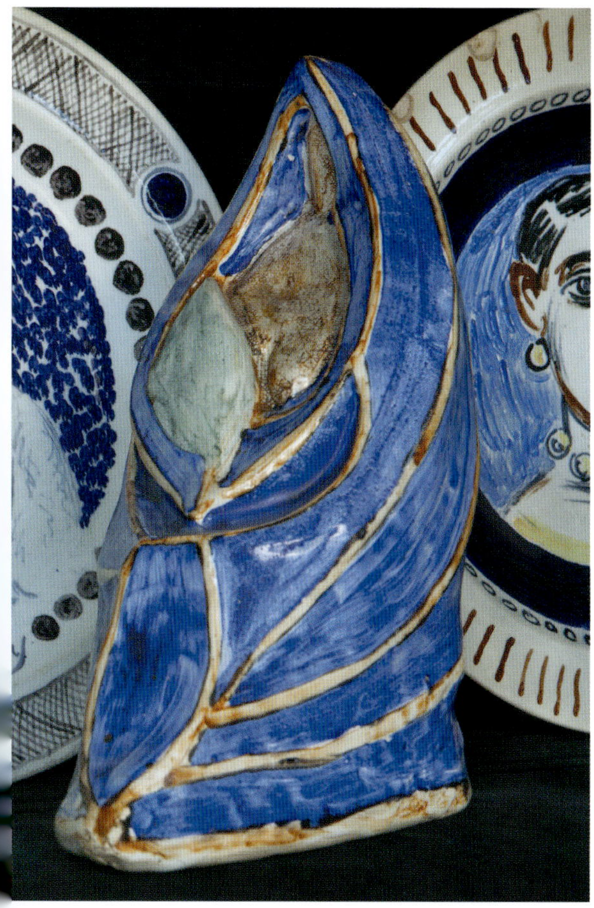

7.2. Vanessa Bell,
Madonna and Child

c.1913–14, glazed ceramic,
Omega Workshops, designed
and decorated by Vanessa
Bell, 225 × 190 × 115 mm,
The Charleston Trust

Adrian, Duncan and I', Vanessa wrote to Roger in late October 1913, and after spending the entire day producing '10 or 11 pots . . . Mr Schenck gave us some clay to bring home and said if we liked to model some figures he would cast them for us for a shilling or two and we could have them baked with the rest'. She had spent hours, she wrote, 'trying to model a figure, which of course is most exciting . . . I shall be curious to see what Duncan makes of his lump'.[10] The simple form of *Madonna and Child* may have been intended as a prototype ceramic sculpture that could be cast in an edition for the Workshops. Henri Gaudier-Brzeska had recently been introduced to the Omega by Nina Hamnett and showed his small sculptures there. He modelled a ceramic cat for Omega, probably using the clay that Schenck supplied, which was subsequently reproduced in a small press-moulded edition. Vanessa's *Madonna and Child* may have been a product of her first visit to the pottery at Mitcham or, like the Gaudier-Brzeska *Cat*, it may date from the following year.[11] However, her letter describes the fluidity and ambition of her creative imagination, envisaging ceramic sculpture for the Workshops, perhaps in response to Gaudier-Brzeska's arrival. Vanessa replicated the design for *Madonna and Child* from three dimensions to two in a painted tray, demonstrating her ability to translate a visual concept into different media.[12]

Of the three co-founders of Omega, it was Roger who proved most adept as a potter. Vanessa had organised the initial visit to the pottery at Mitcham and returned with him on several occasions. She was dismissive of advice that it required seven years to master the craft of potting and after her first visit she believed that having produced 'enough variety of shapes now' the 'old potter' could try to reproduce their dishes and bowls.[13] A few months later, however, she chose not to accompany Roger when he took one of the Workshops' patrons, Princess Mechtilde Lichnowsky, to Mitcham. 'I saw that now he has really managed to pot himself he wouldn't be able to stand letting me do it incompetently while he looked on', she explained to Duncan.[14] Nevertheless she persevered. Roger helped her to centre her pots when she returned to Mitcham with him in March 1914 and she described 'the feeling of the clay rising between one's fingers' in a letter to Duncan, 'like the keenest sexual joy!'.[15] Two weeks later she wrote: 'I have been working hard all today at pottery. Most of the pots are done but a good many tiles still remain'.[16] Vanessa decorated ceramics that were crafted by others throughout her career.

During 1913, as the Omega Workshops gathered momentum, Vanessa's identity as a matriarch shifted. Roger had provided Leonard with temporary employment as secretary to the *Second Post-Impressionist Exhibition* on his return from honeymoon, but as the exhibition drew to a close there was a rift between the Woolfs and their Bloomsbury family. While they were away Leonard had revealed to Virginia that, 'in a moment of rashness', Vanessa had read him letters from Walter Lamb as well as extracts from Virginia's letters, 'foreseeing possible events'. Walter had been one of Virginia's suitors.[17] Virginia felt betrayed and 'purposefully avoided Gordon Square' throughout the winter. When Vanessa was ill and joined her at Asheham in January 1913 it 'was too much for her. Out it all came'.[18] Vanessa was exasperated by Leonard's 'mischief making' and concerned to re-establish a close relationship with her sister while respecting Leonard's responsibilities as her new husband. She encouraged Virginia's desire to have a baby: 'by waiting a bit & being careful enough you could have one with very little risk', she wrote, and she questioned Leonard's reservations: 'I wonder why Leonard has gradually come to think child bearing so dangerous.'[19] Virginia had a breakdown in July 1913. Gerald Duckworth's publishing house had accepted her first novel, *The Voyage Out*, in April and Vanessa believed the 'entire cause' to be 'her worrying over what people will think of her novel . . . Oh God. I can't help being rather worried lest I ought to have done more,' she wrote to Roger, 'but after all one can't do much with married people.'[20] She embarked on a new relationship with Leonard, supporting him through Virginia's illnesses, steadfastly defending her sister from the prospect of incarceration and helping him to recruit nurses. She often accompanied them both on their visits to specialists. When Virginia attempted suicide in September 1913 Vanessa was summoned immediately and spent the night sitting up with her so that Leonard could sleep. 'How I do wish I could be of more use to you', she wrote to him.[21]

While Virginia was recuperating and Vanessa was preparing for the *Ideal Home Exhibition* she was also hoping to have another baby. She was still intimate with Clive but a letter to Roger implies that he was the intended father.[22] This radical affront to societal norms, anticipating her relationship with Duncan, was accompanied by house-hunting expeditions to the seaside with Adrian. 'I am rather inclined to try Studland country', she wrote to Roger. 'I hope you will know of other places . . . Will you house hunt with me?'[23] Nothing materialised but when Leonard gave her the manuscript for his second novel, *The Wise Virgins*, at the end of 1913 she baulked at its narrow representations of women and the breaches of trust it displayed. Vanessa was reconciled to Virginia's characterisation of her as the maternal Helen in *The Voyage Out*. She described the pleasure of working out who had inspired the characters in her sister's subsequent novels, a pastime shared by many of their friends. In *The Wise Virgins* Leonard idealised her as the older sister to the novel's heroine, a beautiful and brilliant painter, Camilla, unmistakably based on Virginia. His own character, also a painter, was passionately in love with the physically unresponsive Camilla and in competition for her affections with Arthur, a fictional version of Clive:

> Arthur Woodhouse tossed his fat, round little body and his little, round, fat mind from side to side . . . he was one of those men so small mentally and morally that anything which took place in his little mind or little soul naturally seemed to him to be one of the great convulsions of nature.[24]

The novel exposed tensions in the Woolfs' marriage and it laid bare the relentless, endemic anti-Semitism with which Leonard had to contend, even within Bloomsbury. His mother and sister, also portrayed in the novel, threatened a serious break with him if he published. 'I have been going on with Woolf's novel', Vanessa wrote to Roger on Christmas Day 1913: 'It is superficial & dull & somehow very commonplace & very badly written. But I may be prejudiced by the part I object to for other reasons . . . I shall certainly try to get him not to publish it.'[25] Virginia was protected from reading *The Wise Virgins* until three months after its publication in October 1914. When she did so, it preceded the worst of her mental breakdowns and the only one in which she rejected Leonard.[26]

Virginia spent the first months of 1914 recuperating at Asheham and when Leonard, exhausted by his responsibilities as her carer, went to stay with Lytton, Vanessa took turns with their friends Janet Case and Ka Cox to stay with her there. Lytton stoked the animosity between Leonard and Clive. 'Lytton gave Woolf a lot of Clive's letters to read', Vanessa wrote to Roger.

> In one of them Clive said that as soon as Virginia was well enough he meant to start an affair with her! According to him it was obviously not meant seriously which I should think must be true. But Woolf took it quite seriously & you can imagine the result![27]

Vanessa defended Clive but she continued to prioritise Virginia's wellbeing above 'our usual embroilments'. She went with Leonard and Virginia to see her psychiatrist, Dr Craig, who by this time was caring for Leonard as well as Virginia, and reported on their visit in a long letter to Roger: 'He said she wasn't in a state where she could possibly be certified & that she couldn't therefore be made to go into a home or have nurses. He thought there was a certain amount of risk of suicide but that it must run.'[28]

Clive's book *Art*, 'a complete theory of visual art', was also published in 1914. It promoted the concept of significant form: the 'lines and colours combined in a particular way, certain forms and relations of forms' that provoked an 'aesthetic emotion' and was 'the quality common to all works of art'. Significant form, Clive argued, could be found in 'the windows at Chartres, Mexican sculpture, a Persian bowl, Chinese carpets, Giotto's frescoes at Padua, and the masterpieces of Poussin, Piero della Francesca, and Cézanne'.[29] In his preface, written in November 1913, he acknowledged the 'conversations and discussions' with Roger that had 'tempered and burnished' his convictions. Duncan later recalled that 'when this sudden avalanche of new ideas about painting came along which had to be thrashed out', Vanessa was an active participant.[30] Her thinking was 'original and logical and she was a quick reasoner, never hesitating to put forward her views', David Garnett later recalled. 'Her mind and manners were not in the least masculine, yet she was the only woman that any of us knew who could join in the talk of a group of men and allow them to forget that she was a woman, forgetting it herself.'[31] Nevertheless, Vanessa was not named in Clive's text and her formative role in shaping his identity as a critic was unacknowledged: 'My wife has been good enough to read both the MS and proof of this book', he wrote; 'she has corrected some errors, and called attention to the more glaring offences against Christian charity.'[32]

The year 1914 began with the second Grafton Group exhibition and Vanessa shared its organisation with Roger. Again her labour was invisible. She ordered canvas to line the gallery walls at the Alpine Club: 'I suppose it might possibly be put up on the day before we hang if the gallery should be free then', she wrote to Roger. She was responsible for notifying Omega customers: 'I sent off the last of the cards this morning. I think there were about 315 so we ought to have a good many visitors'.[33] She shared Roger's conviction that French paintings should be included to create a European context – 'It sounds to me as if we'd got about the right amount of French pictures' – and after spending Christmas with Clive's family she returned to Gordon Square on 30 December in time for the installation.[34] But when Roger wrote to Charles Vildrac in Paris two days later, thanking him for the French pictures, he automatically took sole credit for hanging the show: 'The pictures have arrived safely and I have just hung them in the beautiful Alpine Club gallery.'[35] Vanessa's creative initiatives and the time-consuming work that underpinned her partnership with Roger, and with Clive and Duncan, were taken for granted, in keeping with the gender dynamics of the period.

Vanessa enjoyed the recognition that her work received when the second Grafton Group exhibition was favourably reviewed in *The Times* by Arthur Clutton-Brock: 'I believe that Clutton is acquiring me a reputation!' she wrote to Roger. He singled out *Women and Baby* – 'the figures of the mother and the woman bending over her are both beautiful and moving' – and described it as the best of Vanessa's paintings to date.[36] Claude Phillips, writing for the *Daily Telegraph*, described it as 'powerful and expressive' although he mistook the work for a decorative composition. Vanessa also exhibited a still life; a portrait of Molly MacCarthy; a painting inspired by the Brandon camp the previous summer, *Tents*; and two decorative works, a screen and a *Design for Screen*. Phillips praised the 'original rhythm and genuine charm' of *Tents*.[37] The artists were not anonymous, as they had been in the first Grafton Group exhibition, so the selection identified Vanessa with specific Omega products. In combination, *Tents*, *Design for a Screen* and the screen itself may also have illuminated the process through which she developed her design concepts from photographs and sketches to abstract patterns.

Camping at Brandon the previous summer with Bloomsbury friends and the sisters Noel, Margery, Brynhild and Daphne Olivier, Vanessa had produced sketches and photographs: 'not one is a failure,' she wrote to Clive. 'Some are amazingly good.'[38] She dedicated five pages of her photograph album to them.[39] After her return she designed a four-fold screen, now known as *Bathers in a Landscape* but initially titled *Tents and Figures* (fig. 7.3). It was closely based on her painting *Summer Camp* (fig. 7.4).[40] 'I don't see that it matters being realistic sketching. One can use it afterwards', Vanessa advised Roger.[41] The screen abstracts the vertical poles and diagonal outlines of tents in her painting and is populated with four green female nudes. It may have processed a memory of the Olivier sisters that Vanessa shared with Virginia: 'I don't think I have ever talked so much before in my life. I lectured them on life & morals & I only hope it did them good but the young are very crude & cruel aren't they?'[42] The screen

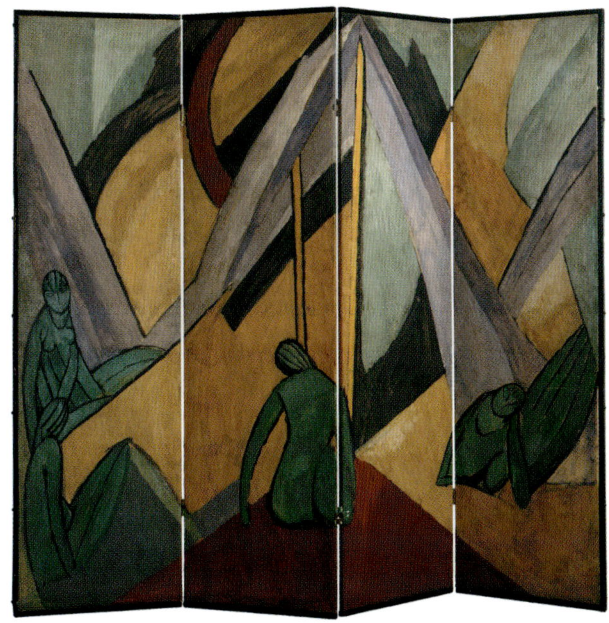

7.3. Vanessa Bell, *Bathers in a Landscape*

1913, Omega Workshops screen, distemper on paper mounted on canvas, painted softwood frame, 17784 × 523 × 18 mm, Victoria and Albert Museum, London

was probably designed and completed in time for the Grafton Group exhibition. A few months later Vanessa took her reductive design process a stage further in a fully abstract *Design for Omega Rug* (fig. 7.5).[43] It reiterated the colours in *Bathers in a Landscape* and accentuated the outline of tents and their poles in thick black lines. The structure of the screen panels is realised as a decorative element in a framing pattern of red and black verticals and horizontals.

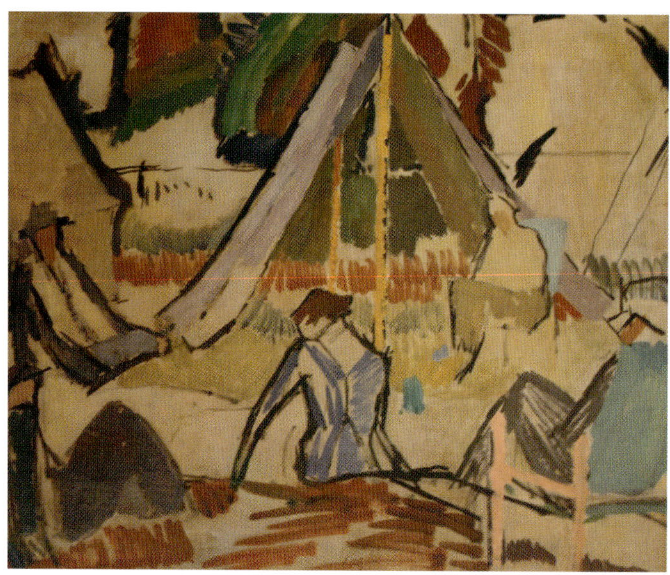

7.4. Vanessa Bell, *Summer Camp*

1913, oil on board, 787 × 838 mm, private collection

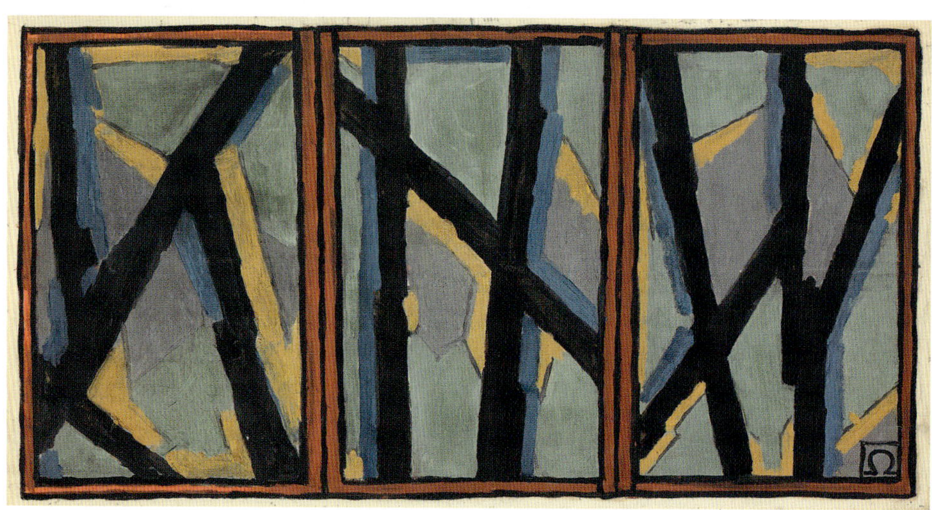

7.5. Vanessa Bell, Design for Omega Rug
1914, oil on paper, 305 × 605 mm, private collection

Vanessa spent less time at the Omega Workshops from 1914 but she continued to innovate in her designs for them.[44] She still deputised for Roger when he was away and contributed to stock and to the 'Bank of Designs'. Virginia described her at Asheham in February 'with several fans which she was painting, and rugs she was designing'.[45] She decorated parasols and an evening cloak and in March she wrote to Duncan that she was working on 'another screen, a twofold one which is always rather fun to do'.[46] *Design for a Folding Screen – Adam and Eve* responds to a common theme explored by the Omega artists (fig. 7.6). The showroom curtains, hand-painted for the opening, showed Adam and Eve in the Garden of Eden and a monumental *Adam and Eve* by Duncan, now lost, was one of the most contentious paintings in the second Grafton Group show.[47] In Vanessa's design, a powerful female figure wrenches the bow of a tree down while a second figure stoops awkwardly before her to collect the fruit. It subverts the parable of Eve's weakness. She stands with one foot sunk into brown earth and the other braced against an area of brighter yellow. Adam's feet are both in the earth and he reaches querulously towards the brightness. The stylised figures and branches are flattened and sketched in loosely while the landscape background is abstracted to a vivid pattern of yellow, blue and green. Vanessa photographed Marjorie Strachey and Molly MacCarthy posing naked in her studio as a source for this design and other paintings. The women emulate Mikhail Fokine's choreography for the Ballets Russes and although references to the ballet are sparse in Vanessa's correspondence the vogue for the Ballets Russes, which had taken London by storm from 1909, provided the Workshops and its clientele with a shared visual currency.[48] In one of the snapshots Molly stretches down towards the floor with her left arm extending upwards (fig. 7.7).[49] The line of the arms, the head and the back informed Vanessa's design but the gender of the bending figure in the screen is switched from female to male to represent Adam.

The taut composition and angular lines of *Design for a Folding Screen* are characteristic of Vanessa's decorative work and in the background to the photographs an immense canvas, pinned to her studio wall, also describes the originality and ambition of her painting at this time. Now known primarily from a study, it shows two monumental figures, one standing and facing forwards and the other seated, in profile, looking behind her (fig. 7.8).

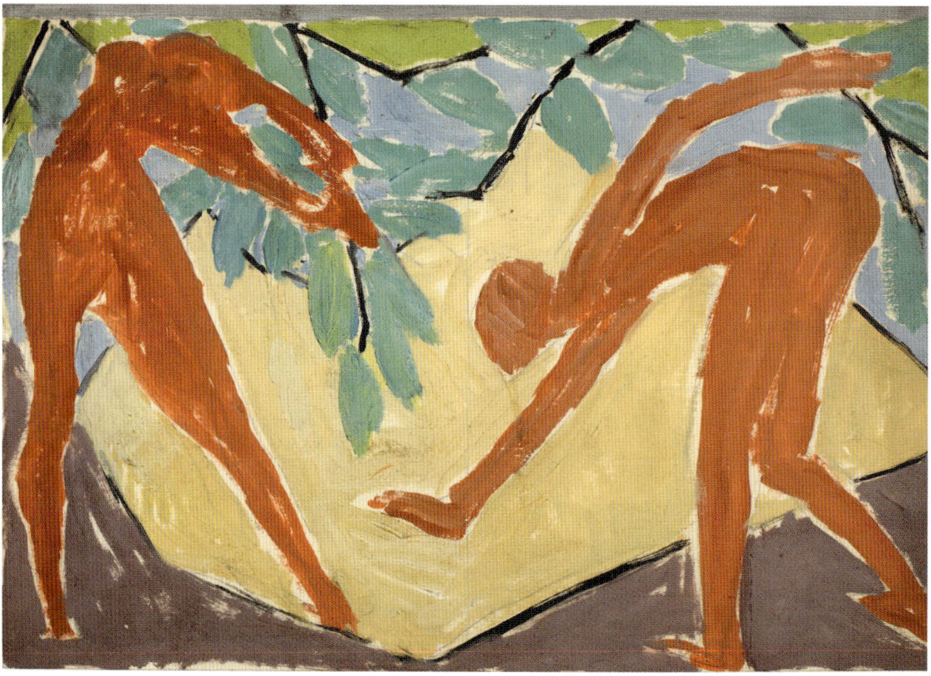

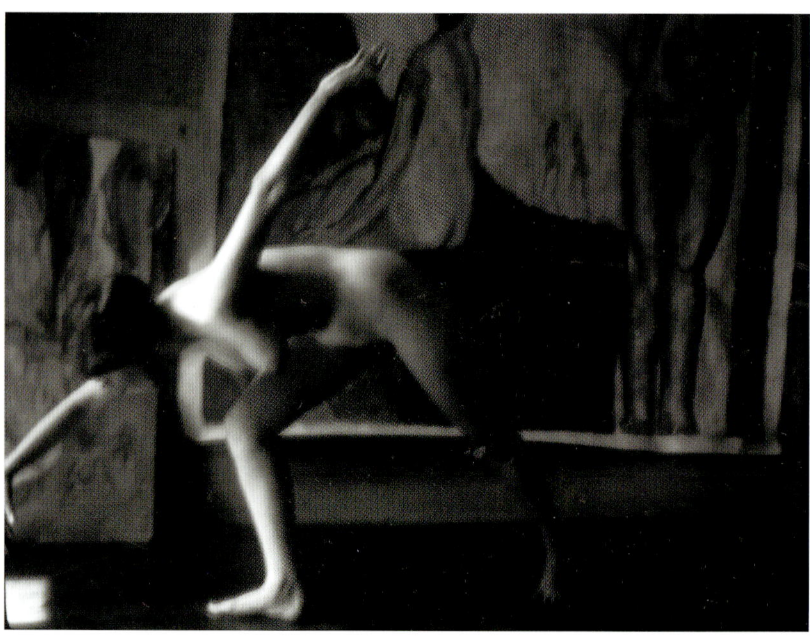

7.6. Vanessa Bell, *Design for a Folding Screen – Adam and Eve*

1913–14, oil, gouache and pencil on paper, 509 × 357 mm,
The Courtauld, London (Samuel Courtauld Trust)

7.7. Vanessa Bell, photograph of Molly MacCarthy posing
nude in the studio at 46 Gordon Square

1914, The Charleston Trust

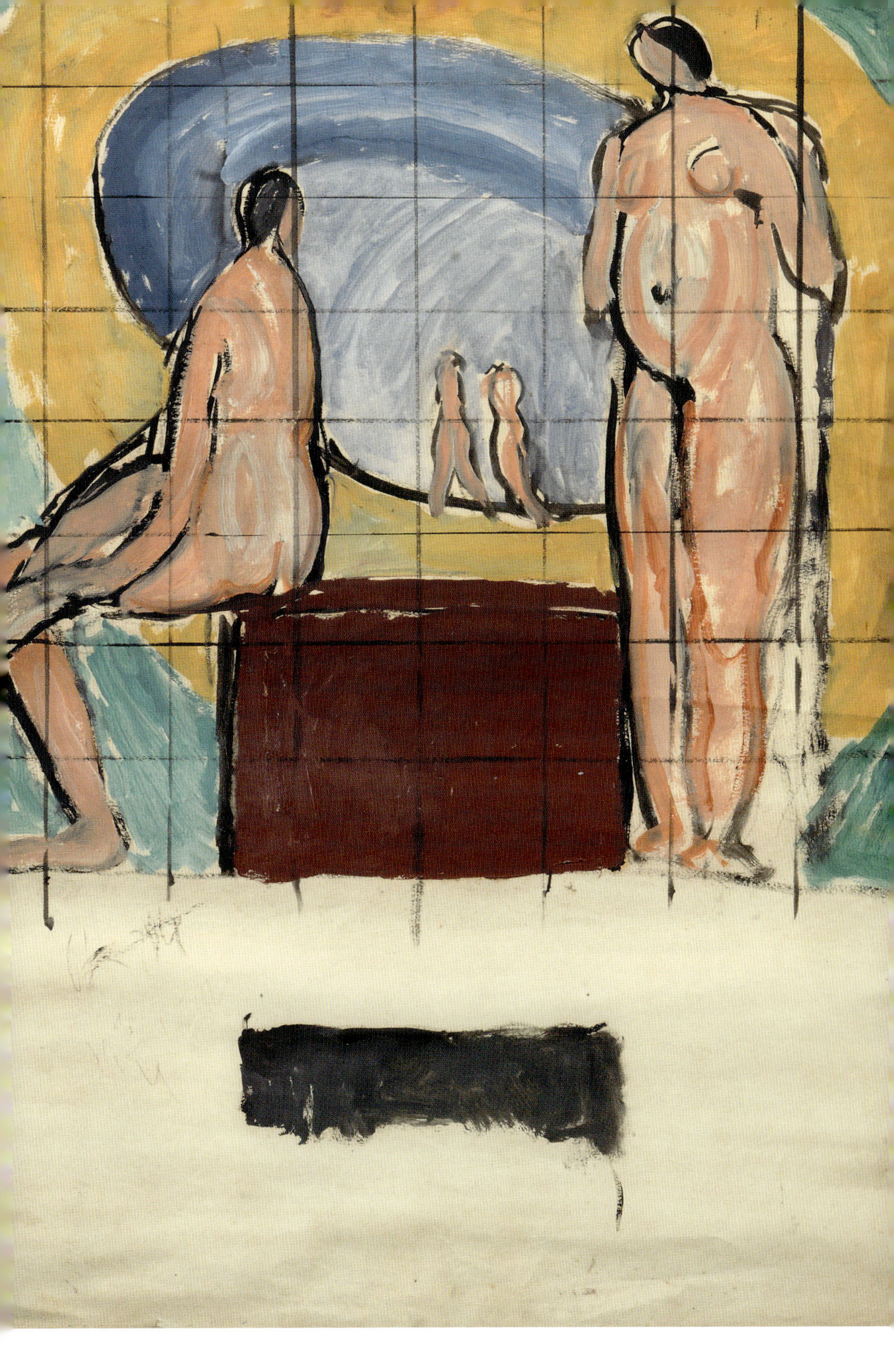

7.8. Vanessa Bell, Design for Fireplace Mural
c.1912, oil on paper, 763 × 558 mm, photo © Bonhams

The standing figure's enlarged belly is accentuated, suggesting pregnancy, and her hands are raised to her shoulders, appearing to draw back a cloak in order to reveal her form more fully. The seated figure turns away from the viewer towards a background in which two small figures walk or dance at the edge of a blue oval in a stylised landscape of blue, yellow and green. Like *Studland Beach* the study invites and frustrates narrative interpretations. The relationship of the figures to one another and to their background is psychologically charged. The seated woman's gaze, turning her back to the viewer, raises the possibility of a dream or memory and the looming egg motifs of the blue oval with its yellow surround echo the curve of the standing figure's belly. The painting may have been a reflection on fertility. The ellipses of oval and egg became a recurrent motif in Vanessa's work, explored again in *The Tub*, for example, which also challenged the distinction between painting and decoration.[50] The women in these paintings by Vanessa assimilate the influence of Cézanne and Matisse, of paintings such as *Le Luxe I* that she had seen at the *Second Post-Impressionist Exhibition*. They may be understood within a continuum of work in which she used the liminal space between painting and decoration to challenge the canon. They propose an alternative, empowered contribution to the themes of bathing, female fertility and sexuality.

The study, and the photographs that document its execution and display in Vanessa's studio, provide an insight into the lost works, the significant absences, which assessments of her importance must accommodate. There are nude photographs of Vanessa with Molly and Marjorie in her studio and these probably coincided with Clive's affair with Molly. They were not fixed into Vanessa's albums but were kept as loose snapshots that could be shared among the Bloomsbury artists and their friends.[51] Vanessa photographed Duncan naked and attempting a handstand on the South Downs, presumably as a source for the inverted male nude in his *Adam and Eve*. He may also have used her photographs for the experimental nudes that he painted in 1914 for which Molly and Marjorie were the models.[52] Vanessa's nude photographs describe the radical culture that prevailed at Gordon Square in the spring of 1914. They signal a rule-breaking liberation from conformity in her life as well as her art, and an element of solidarity between the women.

The pictures and letters that have been lost or destroyed, and the Omega Workshops' fragmentary records, make it impossible to measure the full extent of Vanessa's influence. Dora Carrington, for example, described 'Vanessa Bell's big picture of women' as 'so interesting' when she visited 'the Omega show' in November 1917 but no catalogue identifies the picture.[53] When Vanessa removed her own paintings and Duncan's from their London studios to the safety of Charleston at the outbreak of the Second World War she wrote that 'nude followed nude of every sex & colour' as the vans were unloaded. She didn't differentiate between Duncan's paintings and her own. At one moment, she wrote to him, two large paintings 'stood side by side, one representing Gumbo stark naked on a mossy bank, the other a young man – who? – I forget – also very stark naked – every colour of the rainbow – & the dolt arrived decently looking another way & placed in front of them an enormous picture of me lying on a sofa'.[54] Gumbo was their nickname for Marjorie Strachey and 'the dolt' an unkind name for Walter Higgens, who was married to Vanessa's housekeeper, Grace. The portrait of Vanessa lying on a sofa may have been Duncan's *Reclining Nude (Vanessa Bell)*, 1919, or his portrait of her clothed, *Vanessa Bell*, 1917, now in the National Portrait Gallery.[55]

Vanessa travelled to Paris with Molly in March 1914 to join Clive and Roger there for a few days. She visited Gertrude Stein, who took her to meet Picasso and Matisse in their respective studios. She saw more of their early work in the collection of Michael and Sarah Stein, including *Le Luxe I*, which had been loaned to the *Second Post-Impressionist Exhibition*, and she visited dealers including Picasso's dealer Daniel-Henry Kahnweiler and Ambroise Vollard. Within weeks of her return, she and Duncan were at Durbins with Roger, working together on a mosaic and a mural decoration of male and female nudes. These, too, may have been based on photographs that were subsequently lost.

From the beginning of their affair, Roger and Vanessa had discussed decorations. He had promised that they would 'design great walls to be done when you are well again', writing a few days later: 'You'll come and do my wall won't you. How shall I pay you for that?'[56] Vanessa's letters also reference designs.[57] The Omega prospectus claimed that its artists carried out 'wall decoration in tempera, in wax medium, or in mosaic'.[58] The *Ideal Home Exhibition* and the Post-Impressionist rooms at Fitzroy Square in December 1913 promoted this ambition but there was a paucity of clients bold enough to commission Omega interiors until Lady Hamilton, one of the Workshops' first shareholders, ordered decorations for her home at Hyde Park Gardens in March 1914. Vanessa designed a mosaic for her entrance hall, and a few weeks after it was commissioned she set about familiarising herself with the practicalities of mosaic work at Durbins.[59] The Bloomsbury artists and critics regarded Italian mosaics as precursors of European modernism: 'since the Byzantine primitives set their mosaics at Ravenna no artist in Europe has created forms of greater significance unless it be Cézanne', Clive enthused in *Art*.[60] However, Vanessa's ambition to mosaic a wall at Durbins, working in concert with Roger and Duncan, was thwarted: 'None of the mosaic has come', she wrote to Clive, and while they waited for a delivery of tesserae they worked together on the mural decoration in the entrance hall.[61] The Durbins mosaic patterned the wall of a summerhouse in the garden and when it proved too ambitious it was left (and remains) unfinished. The three nudes painted across the entrance hall wall facing the front door were more critical to the presentation of Durbins as an avant-garde home. Although the ideation of this mural was rooted in the first months of Vanessa and Roger's affair, stylistically it explored the Byzantine simplifications of form that they had seen in Ravenna and the anatomical distortions that all three artists admired in the work of Picasso and Matisse. The mural advanced the Omega Workshops' identity as a firm of decorators capable of interiors in the vanguard of modernism. It was photographed for an article by Roger in *Vogue*, 'A Possible Domestic Architecture', and when he sold Durbins in 1919 he boarded it over to protect it for posterity.[62]

Vanessa designed an overmantel at around this time with two androgynous figures standing above a simple fire surround (fig. 7.9). They each raise a hand as if in greeting to the other and their disproportionately small heads, capped with yellow hair, face one another in profile. Their massive bodies, painted in greys and greens and stripped of all detail, relate back to Vanessa's maternal figure in *Studland Beach*. The overmantel articulates a correlation between Vanessa's paintings and her decorative designs but the figures are

7.9. Vanessa Bell, Design for Overmantel
c.1912–13, oil on paper, 762 × 559 mm, Yale Center for British Art, New Haven, CT

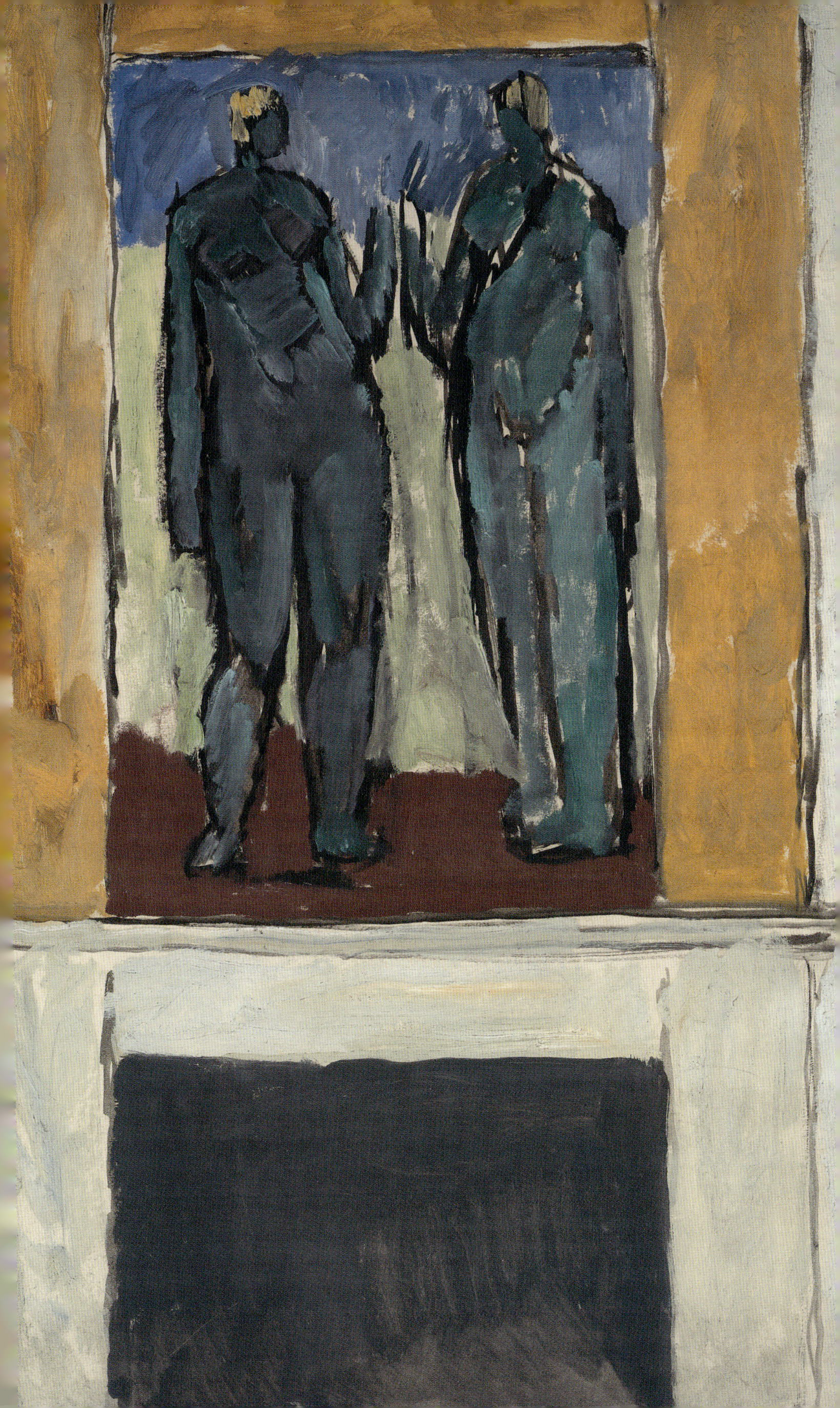

conceived as vertical elements within a composition in which colour and the materiality of the painted surface predominate. The bright contrast of the blue and yellow background establishes a flattening of the picture plane and the slabs of chrome yellow that frame the composition accentuate its purpose as a decorative scheme.

Vanessa was one of the most radical and widely represented artists in the important exhibition *Twentieth Century Art. A Review of Modern Movements* at the Whitechapel Art Gallery when it opened in May 1914. As well as her paintings, it showcased her work as a leading designer for the Omega Workshops. A substantial area of one of the galleries was dedicated to the Workshops and, although their products were displayed anonymously, Vanessa's designs would have been recognisable to many of her fellow artists. Her textiles were among 'Sixteen Pieces of Printed Linen on Walls' in an Omega-furnished bay and smaller items included trays, fans and parasols.[63] The display featured Omega ceramics including painted vases. Generic titles in the catalogue such as *Screen* and *Large Rug* reveal very little about the exhibits, making it impossible to assess the full extent of Vanessa's representation in *Twentieth Century Art* retrospectively. A large *Cartoon for Mosaic* was surely her design for Lady Hamilton's floor, however, and her rugs and screens would have been striking within the display.[64]

Gilbert Ramsay, director of the Whitechapel Art Gallery, curated the exhibition and selected a diverse range of paintings and sculpture by Wyndham Lewis, David Bomberg, Paul and John Nash, Mark Gertler, William Roberts, Jacob Epstein, Henri Gaudier-Brzeska, Thérèse Lessore, Harold Gilman and Stanley Spencer as well as Duncan, Roger and Vanessa. An older generation was represented by artists such as Walter Sickert and Augustus John. Aside from the Omega display, the exhibiting artists were named and Ramsay selected five pictures by Vanessa. Again, these are difficult to reconcile with extant works. He may have lifted *Women and Baby*, *Design for a Screen* and *Still Life,* framed and 'exhibition ready', directly from the second Grafton Group show that he would have seen a few months earlier. 'Three-quarters of the exhibits here are old friends (or enemies?)', Claude Phillips reported in the *Daily Telegraph*, 'and have been discussed by us in dealing with the recent exhibitions of the Grafton Group and the London Group'.[65] He described Vanessa's

Landscape and Figures as 'a composition reminiscent of Cézanne, and recalling also El Greco', but little more is known about this or her fifth picture, *The Girlhood of Thisbe*, beyond their titles.[66] She was one of only a handful of artists in the exhibition to be recognised for her decorative as well as her fine art. The inclusion of her *Design for a Screen* in the Upper Gallery next to her *Landscape and Figures* and other named pictures signifies the complex and interrelated nature of her work as an artist and designer. Her prominence would have encouraged the professional ambitions of women in her wider circle and other women artists more broadly. The exhibition demonstrated the breadth of her achievement, her versatility and her status as a modernist.

Vanessa's bold, abstract compositions for linens and rugs and her stylised designs for screens informed her figurative paintings. In *A Conversation* the details of her subject are pared back in the interests of significant form, as defined by Clive in *Art* (fig. 7.10). The painting reconceives the subject of three figures in conversation that Vanessa had initially addressed in 1911–12 but here the intense discussion takes place between three women. They are dressed in sombre tones, black, brown and olive green, which dominate the lower half of the canvas and provide a foil for their stylised faces. This lack of foreground detail invites the viewer into the compositional space and heightens the atmosphere of intrigue evoked by the women's body language and heads, drawn closely together. They are located within a curtained interior suggesting the dark confined space of a theatre box. Vanessa later described the painting to Virginia as '3 women talking with a flower bed seen out of the window behind' and suggested that it 'might also but not quite do as an illustration' for her short story *Kew Gardens*.[67] But she was aware of the theatre as a modernist subject and one that artists such as Renoir and Degas had explored as a commentary on the objectification of women. She would have seen Sickert's immense music-hall interiors at the Carfax Gallery in 1912 and Camden Town Group paintings such as Spencer Gore's *The Balcony at the Alhambra* representing three figures, two women wearing hats and a man, leaning over the edge of their balcony with a stylised view of the auditorium with its dark green upholstery and red carpet above their heads.[68] She acquired Jessie Etchells' *The Opera Box* after it was exhibited in *Twentieth Century Art*.[69] Beyond

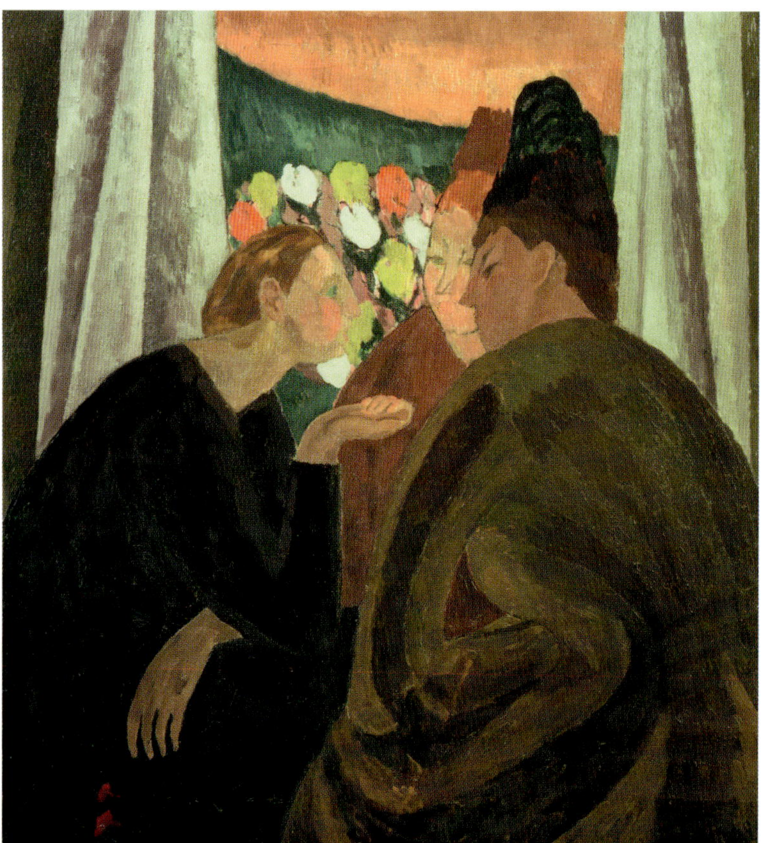

7.10. Vanessa Bell,
A Conversation
1913–16,
oil on canvas,
810 × 666 mm,
The Courtauld,
London (Samuel
Courtauld Trust)

the curtains in *A Conversation* the curved segment at the top of the painting suggests the line of an auditorium ceiling or balcony with brightly coloured bodies gathered below. These brilliant dashes of colour animate the space between the women's heads, and although they are correctly interpreted as flowers in a garden the painting may have originated as a theatre scene.

By locating her three women in a theatre box, unchaperoned and uninterested in the staging of displays, Vanessa would have deliberately positioned her own feminist vision within the self-referencing arenas of Impressionism and Post-Impressionism. Boxes at London's Royal Opera House were curtained and they were advertised in illustrated papers and magazines populated by glamorous women disporting themselves in clinging satin and lace evening dresses.[70] 'At the opera last night . . . Fashion was represented by Lady Cunard and Lady Randolph Churchill who sat with Rickets in a box', Mary

Hutchinson wrote to Vanessa in the summer of 1916 when she was reworking the painting.[71] She had begun *A Conversation* before the outbreak of the First World War but she wrote to Roger that she was 'going on with my old picture of the 3 women' while she was waiting for tribunal hearings that would determine Duncan's fate as a conscientious objector.[72] The dark camouflage colours of the women's clothes may date from this reworking and the painting's subtle, subversive references to popular and high culture may also have been a commentary on changes in clientele and behaviour at the opera. After the Royal Opera House was requisitioned as a furniture repository, Mary Hutchinson complained to Vanessa about 'the horror of the replete Jews' arriving late for a performance of *The Magic Flute* at the Aldwych Theatre. Instead of quietly watching the opera she described 'the scandal of the ladies in the boxes who spent the time when the scene was well-lighted in quizzing & joking about the people in the rest of the theatre'.[73]

Taking women's talk as a serious subject and the reduction of their dress and bodies to solid, compositional forms in *A Conversation* consolidated Vanessa's interest in the lives of women as modernist subjects. Like the Madonna and the female nudes discussed throughout this chapter, this large, ambitious painting challenged gender stereotypes and the objectification of women in paintings by men. It was this provocation that Virginia responded to, many years later, when she singled out *A Conversation* from the *London Group Retrospective Exhibition* of 1928 and asked Vanessa whether Roger would lend it to her 'for a week or so'.[74] Her comments illuminate the sisters' enduring complicity and mutual support as they forged their careers in the face of patriarchy. Virginia had forgotten, she wrote, 'the extreme brilliancy and flow and wit and ardour' of the painting.

> I think you are a most remarkable painter. But I maintain you are into the bargain, a satirist, a conveyer of impressions about human life: a short story writer of great wit and able to bring off a situation in a way that rouses my envy. I wonder if I could write the Three Women in prose.[75]

8

ABSTRACT COMPOSITIONS
AND MODERN PORTRAITS

Vanessa's abstract paintings and collages are pivotal works in the histories of European and British modernism. She was one of the first artists to create fully resolved abstracts before the outbreak of the First World War. Although the moment when she transferred her interest in abstract compositions from textiles and other decorative work to fine art is undocumented, she made a clear distinction between paintings and designs. Vanessa was acutely aware of contemporary developments in modernist circles. From her teens she had taken a critical interest in the exhibitions and visual culture of London, and as a traveller she analysed the work of artists she could learn from, from Tiepolo to Piero della Francesca. Her Grafton Group exhibitions included paintings and photographs of work by Kandinsky and Picasso and she helped create a culture at the Omega Workshops in which art theory and practice were avidly discussed. Winifred Gill provides a vivid recollection of Wyndham Lewis, wearing the first royal blue shirt she had ever seen and a black sombrero, sitting in the back studio there with his long legs stretched out in front of him alongside the central table as the other artists arrived: '"Been to the show?" he asked repeatedly. '"No, have you?" ". . . There this morning." "Oh, anything worth seeing?"' She described the 'portentous intake of breath' before he delivered his verdict in a rich deliberate speech: 'Very fine head by Brancusi'.[1]

Vanessa's letters to Roger, Clive and Duncan articulate an observational clarity and active engagement with contemporary practice, even when she disliked the artists. Within days of Wyndham libelling Roger and abandoning Omega she described his *Kermesse* as one of the best British paintings on show at the Doré Gallery: 'Lewis has that large dance which he had at the Albert Hall, but he's made it much better & I thought it good.'[2] The next Friday Club exhibition was condemned as 'utterly hopeless . . . There are a great many very bright, enthusiastic, lively young painters, all making experiments, but it seemed to me that they were all simply trying to be up to date'. The exceptions, she wrote to Duncan, were Nevinson and Bomberg, whose *Vision of Ezekiel* she found 'striking'.[3] Her extended social circle included museum directors, curators, critics, art dealers and collectors as well as her fellow artists and Bloomsbury 'family'. In April 1914, after meeting Gertrude Stein, Picasso and Matisse in Paris and before the opening of *Twentieth Century Art*, she hosted 'such an art-official dinner' at Gordon Square. Guests included the artist, critic and former keeper of the Tate Gallery D.S. MacColl, who had succeeded Claude Phillips as keeper of the Wallace Collection; his successor at Tate, Charles Aitken, who was formerly director of the Whitechapel Gallery; and 'the Campbell Dodders'. Campbell Dodgson had recently married Vanessa's fellow former student at the Royal Academy, Catherine Spooner. He was keeper of prints and drawings at the British Museum, a champion of women artists and would gift an important collection of prints to the British Museum, including the first works by Picasso that they would acquire. 'I don't shine in such society', Vanessa wrote to Roger, but the dinner highlights the interconnected nature of the London art world as a network and Vanessa's centrality to it.[4] Her influence as a 'connector' within modernist circles was profound. She was engaged in forming the critical theories that shaped modernist practice, and through her various fields of work, she was inseparable from the evolution of abstract art in Britain.

Grace Brockington has located Vanessa within an 'imagined community' of people associated with the international abstract movement, 'one held together by knowledge of one another's work and ideas, and by the virtual meeting places of galleries and publications'.[5] Vanessa would have seen the hugely influential *Exhibition of Works by the Italian Futurist Painters* when it arrived in London in March 1912 after its initial showing in Paris.[6] Work by Gino Severini and Luigi Russolo informed her textile designs for the Omega Workshops the following year. She travelled to Cologne with Roger and Clive that August with the sole purpose of seeing the international Sonderbund exhibition. There she saw Kandinsky's *Improvisation 21a* as well as drawings by Paul Klee and recent German Expressionist paintings.[7] 'The pictures were good but on the whole the show was disappointing', she wrote to Virginia.[8] Roger was selecting paintings for the *Second Post-Impressionist Exhibition* and their focus, as a consequence, was on familiar works by Cézanne and Van Gogh, but Kandinsky's philosophical treatise, *On the Spiritual in Art*, published in two editions in December 1911 and May 1912, would have been on their radar. When František Kupka's *Amphora: Fugue in Two Colours*, one of the earliest abstract paintings in Europe, was exhibited at the Salon d'Automne later that year, Vanessa would have heard about the press sensation it caused from Roger, even if she didn't see the painting at first hand.[9]

Roger's preface to the catalogue of the *Second Post-Impressionist Exhibition* summarises Bloomsbury's emerging theoretical position on the absence of referential content in painting. He describes 'a new movement in art' that reconsiders 'the very purpose and aim as well as the methods' of art 'to find a pictorial language appropriate to the sensibilities of the modern outlook'. The new aim of painting, he writes, is not to

> imitate form, but to create form; not to imitate life, but to find an equivalent for life . . . The logical extreme of such a method would undoubtedly be the attempt to give up all resemblance to natural form, and to create a purely abstract language of form – a visual music: and the later works of Picasso show this clearly enough.[10]

Leah Dickerman has described Picasso's photographs of paintings taken in his studio at Cadaqués from 1910 as more abstract, more 'difficult to decipher' than the finished paintings. On seeing these photographs, 'abstract in all but name', the art dealer Kahnweiler rejected the paintings as unfinished but he circulated Picasso's photographs to other artists, including Kandinsky, who described them as 'an auspicious sign of the enormous struggle toward the immaterial'.[11] For Vanessa and Duncan, the Picasso photographs included in their second Grafton Group exhibition together with his *Tête d'homme*, a painting recently acquired by Roger, were positioning statements. They located the exhibition and their own work within it in a modernist European context. They were also talismanic. Duncan later recalled making a careful copy of *Tête d'homme* and the influence of the Picasso on his *Interior at Gordon Square*, a Bloomsbury painting in the gateway between representation and abstraction.[12]

Vanessa's *Abstract Painting* was the culmination of three interconnected avenues of enquiry: her informed interest in the international abstract movement, developed through visits to exhibitions and art dealers and debated with Roger, Clive, Duncan and her wider circle; her experimental practice as a painter, often sharing studio spaces; and her work as a decorative designer (fig. 8.1). Her pioneering leadership as a designer of boldly original abstract patterns for the Omega Workshops can be charted with assurance. Her printed linens, discussed in Chapter 6, can be accurately dated to March and April 1913, coinciding with the first Grafton Group exhibition for which Roger had borrowed two abstract 'compositions' by Kandinsky. By October she was applying geometric abstract designs to lampshades, exhibited in the *Ideal Home Exhibition*. Her abstract design for an inlaid tray was produced in the autumn of 1913 and the following March, as described in Chapter 7, the commission from Lady Hamilton emboldened her to create some of the Workshops' most radical design statements in the form of her abstract rugs. Her example conditioned the visual consciousness of other Omega artists, including those who would assert their own, muscular identities as Vorticists. Her linens and lampshades, among the Workshops' most popular products, appealed to a forward-thinking clientele who patronised the Ballets Russes and exhibitions at the Grafton and Carfax galleries. Six years after she and Sylvia Milman had first exhibited with the Allied Artists Association at the Albert Hall, Vanessa's abstract linens and rugs dominated an Omega room setting at their 1914 exhibition.[13] The show overlapped with the final week of *Twentieth Century Art*, and modernist consumers, as well as practitioners, would have related the porosity between contemporary art and design in both shows to what Roger had termed 'the new movement in art'.[14]

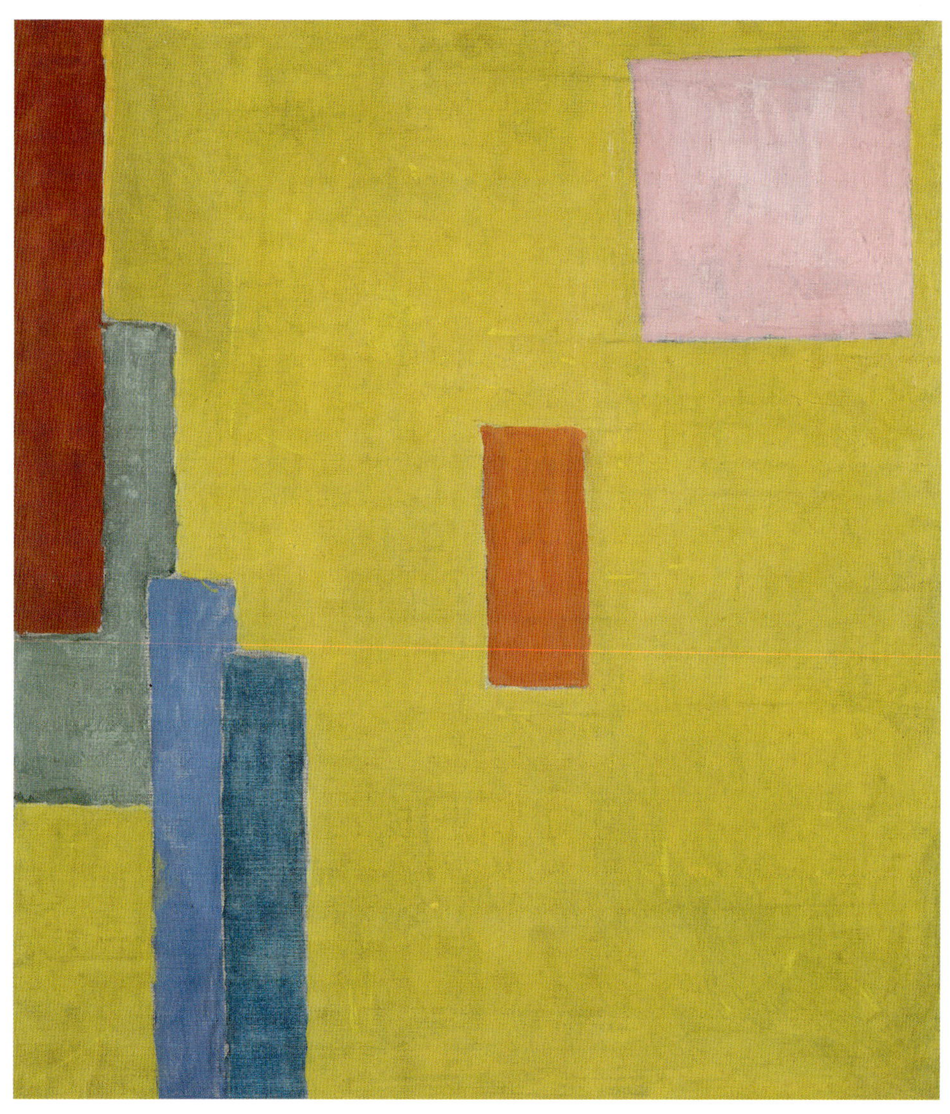

8.1. Vanessa Bell, *Abstract Painting*

c.1914, oil on canvas, 441 × 381 mm, Tate, London

Sequencing Vanessa's abstract paintings and collages is more complex. Duncan later claimed that he 'did not remember who was the first of the two of them to paint an abstract work' and that they had each produced 'a small number, not many' of abstracts.[15] One of these was Duncan's extraordinary *Abstract Kinetic Collage Painting with Sound*, which was begun in August 1914 when Vanessa wrote to Roger from Asheham, 'Duncan and I do nothing here but paint. He has started on a long painting which is meant to be rolled up after the manner of those Chinese paintings and seen by degrees. It is purely abstract . . . We talk of hardly anything but painting'.[16] Two abstract paintings and two collages by Vanessa are known to be extant. A third large abstract painting was owned by Roger and a fourth was at Gordon Square in June 1916.[17] All three Bloomsbury artists experimented with collage as well as painted abstracts, using the technique to enrich the surface qualities of their pictures and to problematise the conventions of pictorial space. Vanessa had experimented with paper cut-outs since her paper mosaic of 1912 and the collaged features in her Omega Workshops nursery.[18] She explored large-scale paper cut-outs as a technique in her fine art, too, writing to Roger in October 1915 that she was still working on the second version of *Women and Baby* and 'at my other large size picture & am now cutting the figures out in paper which I hope is an improvement'. This is likely to have been the standing and seated nudes discussed in Chapter 7. When she visited Picasso's studio with Roger and Clive in 1914 it was his collaged compositions as modernist provocations that struck her most forcibly: 'The whole studio seemed to be bristling with Picassos. All the bits of wood and frames had become like his pictures . . . One gets hardly any idea of them from the photographs, which often don't show what is picture and what isn't', she wrote to Duncan, referring to the prints they had included in the Grafton Group show. 'They are amazing arrangements of coloured papers and bits of wood which somehow do give me great satisfaction.'[19]

Her collage *Composition* draws on the simple geometry of the Omega rugs that she designed and exhibited immediately before and after her trip to Paris (fig. 8.2). The discipline of working with the warp and weft of textiles informed the composition of squares and rectangles. These are cut from painted paper and arranged with precision next to one another like pieces slotted into a puzzle or a mosaic. Vanessa was one of a handful of artists including Sophie Taeuber-Arp and Sonia Delaunay who combined textile design with abstract painting and in doing so, as Claudia Tobin has argued, absorbed the visual language of Middle Eastern textiles into the canon of modernism.[20] The quiet composure of her floating forms is

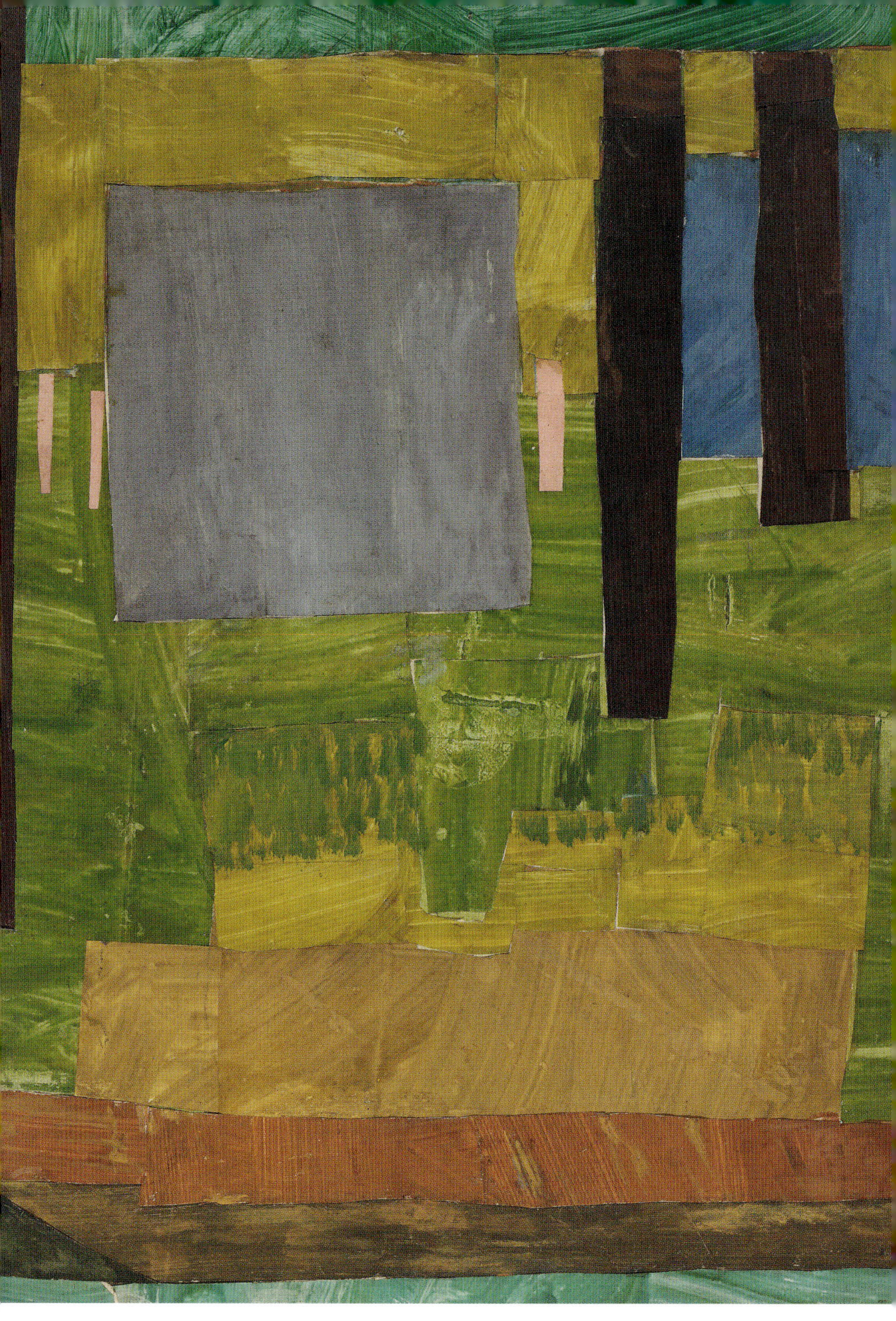

8.2. Vanessa Bell, *Composition*

*c.*1914, gouache, watercolour and coloured paper on cut-and-pasted paper, 551 × 437 mm,
Joan and Lester Avnet Collection, Museum of Modern Art, New York

remote from the fractured surfaces of Cubist paintings and collages. The picture's focus, an irregular grey square, is counterbalanced by four dark brown verticals. Two of these reinforce the edges of the picture while the smaller, much darker rectangles are arranged with their upper edges aligned but one, shorter than the other, plays with the concept of perspective and recession within the pictorial space. Between them, blue rectangles effectively recede within the composition. In a rare instance of papers overlapping, three narrow scraps of pale pink are laid on top of green papers to foreground the grey square that they flank. This inquisition into the illusory effects of colour within the picture space is wittily reinforced at the base of the composition by the physical layering of overlapping strips of blue, brown and burnt orange painted papers to create steps into the picture. The collage plays with the critical theory of significant form, taking painted surfaces as its vocabulary.

Vanessa used collage to make the gestural act of painting and composing works of art her subject matter. *Composition* is ground-breaking as a philosophical manifesto. It combines the distilled harmonies of Klee and Malevich with the bold spontaneity of American Abstract Expressionism. Gouache is used for its translucent materiality, articulating a tension between the largesse and directional flow of the brushstrokes on the fragments of paper and the scale of this carefully considered picture. Cut surfaces are painted over, bringing a rich texture and intentionality to the work of art.

Vanessa appears to have shared a supply of hand-painted papers with Duncan. They often worked together in her studios in Gordon Square and at Asheham. After Adrian married Karin Costelloe in October 1914, disrupting the household at Brunswick Square, Duncan took a room in 46 Gordon Square. He and Roger had studios nearby at 21 and 22 Fitzroy Street and Duncan had a fold-out bed in his studio. His account, many years later, of the chronology of events that led to his own collage, *Interior at Gordon Square*, describes his living and working arrangements with Vanessa.[21] He first painted a view through a doorway to Vanessa's first-floor studio at Gordon Square, working in situ. The painting, now in Tate's collection, abstracts the architectural forms of doorway and windows, a black sofa 'designed by Vanessa', and large canvases stacked against the wall. Having completed the painting, he told a Tate curator, he wanted to make a larger version and as the oil painting already existed he translated the design into a collage. 'The papers were cut from rolls already painted by the artist which he had available for various uses', the curator reported, and this had the added advantage of keeping 'each painted shape very definite and distinct', advancing the experiments that Duncan, Vanessa and Roger had made with mosaic.[22] There is a marked similarity between the green, grey, burgundy and burnt orange papers in Vanessa's *Composition* and in Duncan's collage, *Interior at Gordon Square*.

Hand-painted papers would become a feature of Omega Workshops interior design. The 1913 prospectus lists wall decorations 'in tempera, in wax medium, or in mosaic' but Vanessa expanded this range in a letter to Virginia as soon as she returned from Paris offering to paint blue wallpaper for her: 'Then you'll get a certain variety in the colour. I'll do that & send it to you.'[23] Three years later, Roger published a sketch for a geometric, abstract interior design pieced together using painted and block-printed papers. The design amplifies Vanessa's geometric abstracts and the accompanying article for *Colour* magazine describes the fluid transference of ideas and techniques among the Bloomsbury artists and between fine art and design. Roger promoted the 'infinitely greater richness and charm' of artists' papers. 'I have seen lately rooms done at almost no cost by artists in their own houses', he wrote, and he described the technique: 'the paper was first painted in size by artists quite roughly and rapidly, with no attempt to get a dead even surface . . . the whole surface has a play and vivacity which are essential to the effect of richness and solidity.'[24] He was probably describing Vanessa's recent decorations at Charleston.

Duncan's recollections about painting are invaluable to understandings of Bloomsbury's early history but the reliability of his dates and details is questionable. He found himself in the hot seat in the late 1960s and 1970s when a revival of interest in Bloomsbury and its art brought curators and art historians to his door. Vanessa had died in 1961 and Roger in 1934. Duncan was 84 when Tate acquired his *Interior at Gordon Square* and he was interviewed for the record. He was 91 when a Tate curator interviewed him again to document the acquisition of Vanessa's *Abstract Painting*. Although he was flattered by these attentions, 'Duncan was not particularly interested in history', one contemporary observer recalled. He was more concerned with his current work as a practising artist.[25] At around this time he was persuaded to sign and date pictures retrospectively. Signed works have a higher commercial value. Early drawings are signed in biro although they predate the invention of that pen and his collages *Interior at Gordon Square* and *Design for a Fire Screen Panel* are among the works with late signatures. Because he was uncertain about their chronology he dated them '*c.*1915' and '*c.*1916'.[26] Stylistically, *Interior with Gordon Square* is likely to have pre-dated Duncan's *Abstract Kinetic Collage* (which also uses strips of painted papers) and a range of sources document the completion of that work to the end of 1914.[27] His *Design for a Fire Screen Panel* includes strips of newspaper painted over with the date 1914 visible through the paint.[28] He may also have misremembered the provenance of the papers that he and Vanessa used for their collages. Imagining a race to abstraction or a purloining of papers between Vanessa and Duncan, however, would be to miss the point. What is interesting here is the proximity of their working practices, sharing materials and concepts about the nature and materiality of modernism in 1914.

Vanessa's abstract paintings coincided with a period of extraordinary candour and experiment in her personal life. Her insurgency as a modernist woman was inseparable from pioneering developments in her professional practice. She had discussed a desire for Duncan with Virginia in the spring of 1913 before the Omega Workshops opened, writing to her from Urbino during her travels with Clive, Roger and Duncan: 'My love was not repulsed. I fear it was not even noticed.'[29] By September 1914, when she and Duncan were working together at Asheham, she was falling out of love with Roger. The Omega Workshops, she wrote to him, 'did change things a good deal. It meant that I saw much more of you & in a very exasperating way.'[30] Adrian's marriage to Karin concluded his affair with Duncan and for Vanessa it may have encouraged an idea that homosexuality wasn't necessarily permanent. As her work with Duncan and her admiration for his art intensified, so too did their friendship. By the beginning of 1915 they were lovers. Duncan was almost exclusively homosexual and their relationship was soon complicated by his affair with the bisexual David Garnett, known as 'Bunny'. Roger, unable to cope with Vanessa's rejection of him in favour of Duncan, travelled to France, leaving Vanessa in charge of the Omega Workshops. Determined to be honest and rational, Vanessa wrote to him explaining her situation:

> I don't know how to describe the whole arrangement between
> the 3 of us. It is odd I suppose, but as far as the relations between
> me & Bunny go it is in a way simple. We should not see very
> much of each other I expect if it were not for Duncan. As it is
> we like each other very much. He is not the least in love with
> me, nor I with him. Duncan provides a curious meeting ground
> for us as we are both so intimate with him. I think B. is now not
> exactly in love with D. but he depends on him a great deal, &
> is very fond of him. At the same time I think he is really more
> attracted by women & generally has several flirtations on hand.[31]

It was too difficult to explain her relationship with Duncan in a letter, she wrote, except that their feeling for one another had changed very little.

Vanessa's insistence on alternative relationships within Bloomsbury extended to her continuing arrangements with Clive and his lovers, and a determination that she and Roger should maintain a close friendship. 'I wish I could in any way make things easier for you', she wrote to Roger, explaining that it was impossible 'as long as you want me to have sexual love for you because your wanting it can't help showing itself & then it prevents me from showing anything'.[32] They could be happy together, she believed, if he could be content with friendship: 'I should mind very much, dreadfully, if it all came to nothing between us. It would seem to me the most terrible waste. No, we must get at something.'[33] She was writing to him from Bosham, where Clive had taken a house so that they could spend the summer close to his latest lover, Mary Hutchinson. 'Clive & I are alone here now – the first time we have been so for years I believe.'[34] Vanessa accommodated Clive's lovers – literally – as a demonstration of her free-thinking radicalism, but there were practical advantages, too, in her doing so. Clive was invariably more cheerful in the company of his women friends and it pre-empted objections to her own lovers, who were limited to Roger and then Duncan.[35]

Mary was ten years younger than Vanessa and seven months pregnant when she first sat for her portrait to her and Duncan at Gordon Square in February 1915. 'On Friday we painted Mary', Vanessa wrote to Roger. 'Duncan got very desperate & began again which I think I ought to have done too but I didn't. It is a frightfully difficult arrangement for I'm bang in front of her & everything is very straight & simple & very delicate colour.' She wrote the letter while waiting for 'Duncan to appear' and for Mary to come downstairs for a second sitting: 'She slept here last night after our reading so she ought to be up soon.'[36] In opposition to the war, Bloomsbury had revived its play-reading society on Thursday evenings at 46 Gordon Square, and they had read *Antony and Cleopatra* the previous night. *Mary St John Hutchinson* is one of a series of portraits that assert Vanessa's position in the vanguard of modernism (fig. 8.3). As an opening gambit in the relationship between the two women it contests aesthetic as well as personal boundaries. Just as Vanessa had persuaded Molly to model for portraits and photographs she assumed a similar compliance, a shared interest in modernist principles, in her study of Mary (see fig. 0.1). Mary was already an Omega Workshops customer and a patron of the arts when she became involved with Clive. Duncan was her cousin and he had stayed with her and her husband, St John, at their home on the Sussex coast, Eleanor House in West Wittering, the previous summer.[37] The painting was not a commission, shifting the power dynamics between artist and sitter. It was painted in the home that Vanessa shared with Clive and Duncan, locating Mary as a Bloomsbury arriviste. It perpetuated a practice that Vanessa had cultivated in which she painted the same subject simultaneously with Duncan or Roger, or with the two of them together, consolidating the status of the artists as a formidable entity within the Bloomsbury Group and introducing an element of competition. Relieved of any obligation to flatter or present a likeness in these conditions, Vanessa produced her most daring portraits. They include *Lytton Strachey* painted at Asheham in 1913 and *David Garnett*.[38] They enabled her to scrutinise and subjugate her sitters.

Vanessa uses colour to dissolve the boundaries between her subject and the background to *Mary St John Hutchinson*. Mary is painted at close quarters, exactly as Vanessa described, 'bang in front' and 'very straight & simple'. The portrait expands on a *Profile of a Man* painted by Vanessa, addressing recent work by Rouault, in which a face is reduced to a minimal assemblage of features (fig. 8.4).[39] Two thick swipes of paint outline the nose and three dashes, two horizontal and one vertical, frame the mouth in *Profile of a Man*. It describes Vanessa's pleasure in the material textures of paint, the mark making

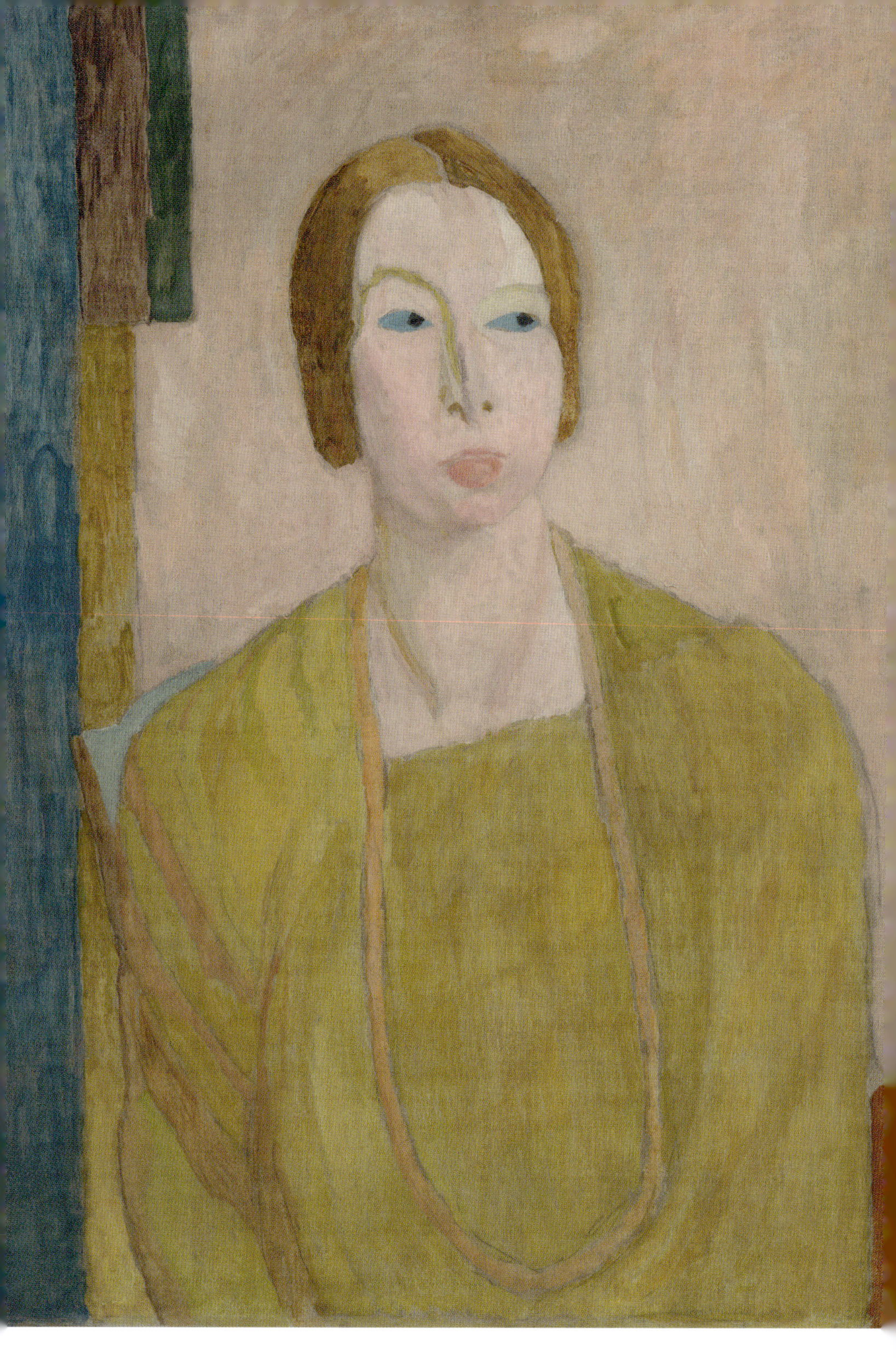

8.3. Vanessa Bell, *Portrait of Mary St John Hutchinson*
1915, oil on canvas, 790 × 550 mm, Rollins Museum of Art, Orlando, Florida

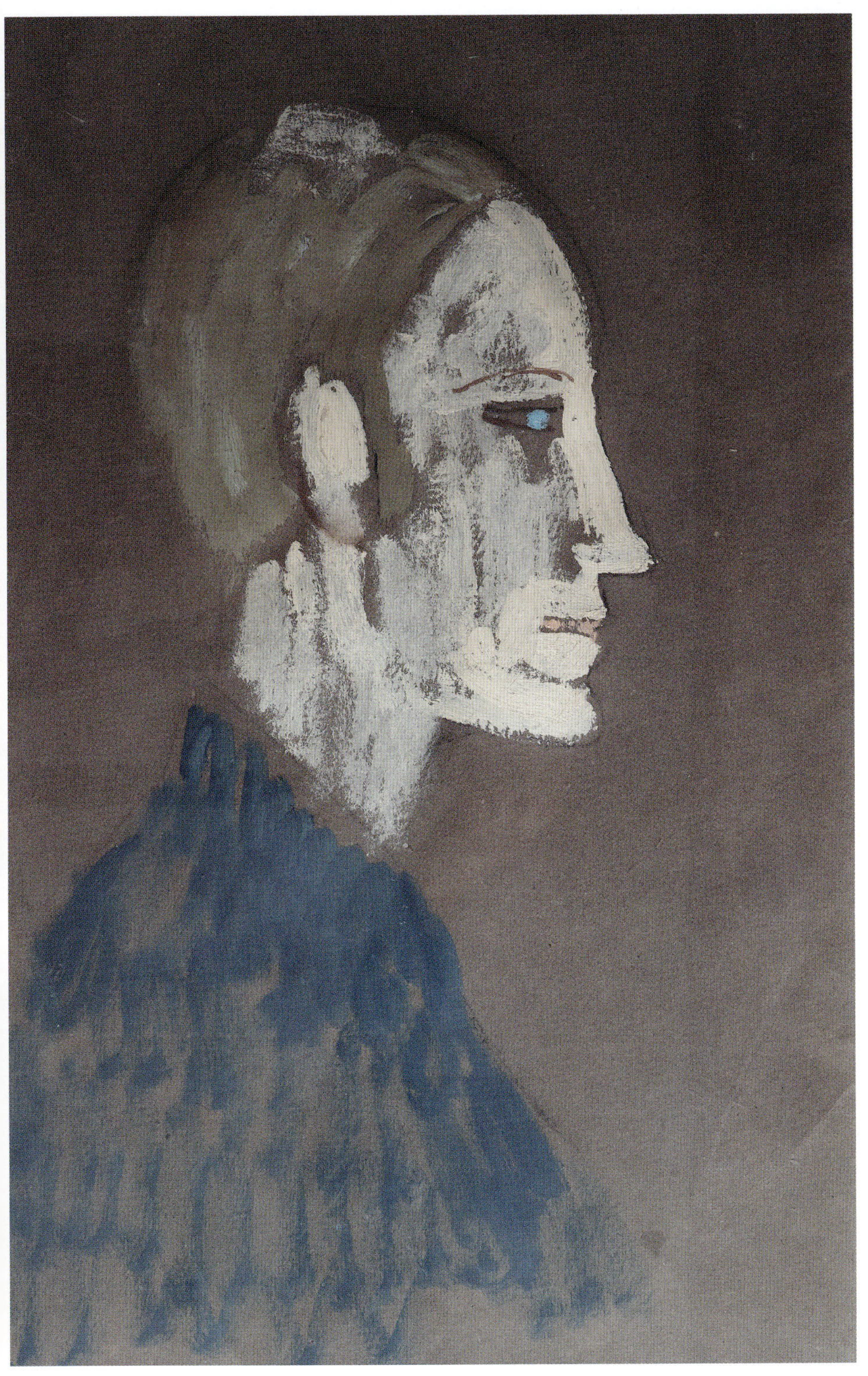

8.4. Vanessa Bell, *Profile of a Man*

undated, oil on brown paper, 533 × 304 mm, The Charleston Trust

and processes of painting. In both works the eyes are stylised and their whites darkened (the brown paper showing through that of the man), giving the faces a sinister quality. Pink, green and yellow brush marks across the face of *Mary Hutchinson* are repeated in her body and background, asserting the flatness of the picture plane and the reality of the portrait as a painted object.

Vanessa and Duncan painted Mary on several occasions and as an Omega patron she purchased their work and commissioned interiors from them. She owned an equally unflattering portrait by Vanessa with a pattern of Omega plates on a dresser behind her (fig. 8.5). She also owned the Omega plates and the painting was prominently displayed in her inner drawing room when it was photographed for *Vogue*.[40] The deliberation with which Vanessa constructed her portraits imbues their background details with significance. She and Duncan had studied the inclusion of works of art in the backgrounds to Post-Impressionist paintings such as *The Girl with Green Eyes* by Matisse and they purposefully paid homage or made jokes in their own settings. One portrait of Bunny by Duncan, for example, echoes the Matisse by locating a crotchy female nude just above his head, as if it is the subject of his imagination.[41] Vanessa situated Molly next to a window with a cushion and a colourful abstract behind her in a collage portrait (fig. 0.1), but the background to *Mary Hutchinson* is exceptional. There are four versions of the painting, two oils by Duncan (which describe his starting again) and two by Vanessa. These document her practice of replicating paintings to explore subtle variations in the palette, proportions and handling of paint: 'portraits are desperate work', she later noted. 'Always when one has to stop one thinks one sees how one could go on. Perhaps one ought then to do another from the original or do one very quickly from life.'[42]

One of the portraits of Mary Hutchinson, either by Duncan or, more likely, the first version by Vanessa, was hanging in Gordon Square by October 1915. Clive described it in a letter to Mary: 'Your portrait, which looks humourously [sic] and rather sly, over the back of my chair, seems to say "Yes", or, at any rate, "Try".'[43] Vanessa included it in her first solo exhibition at the Omega Workshops in 1916. 'You are for sale at seven guineas', Clive wrote to Mary, noting the title, 'Mrs H'.[44] This was almost certainly the version that

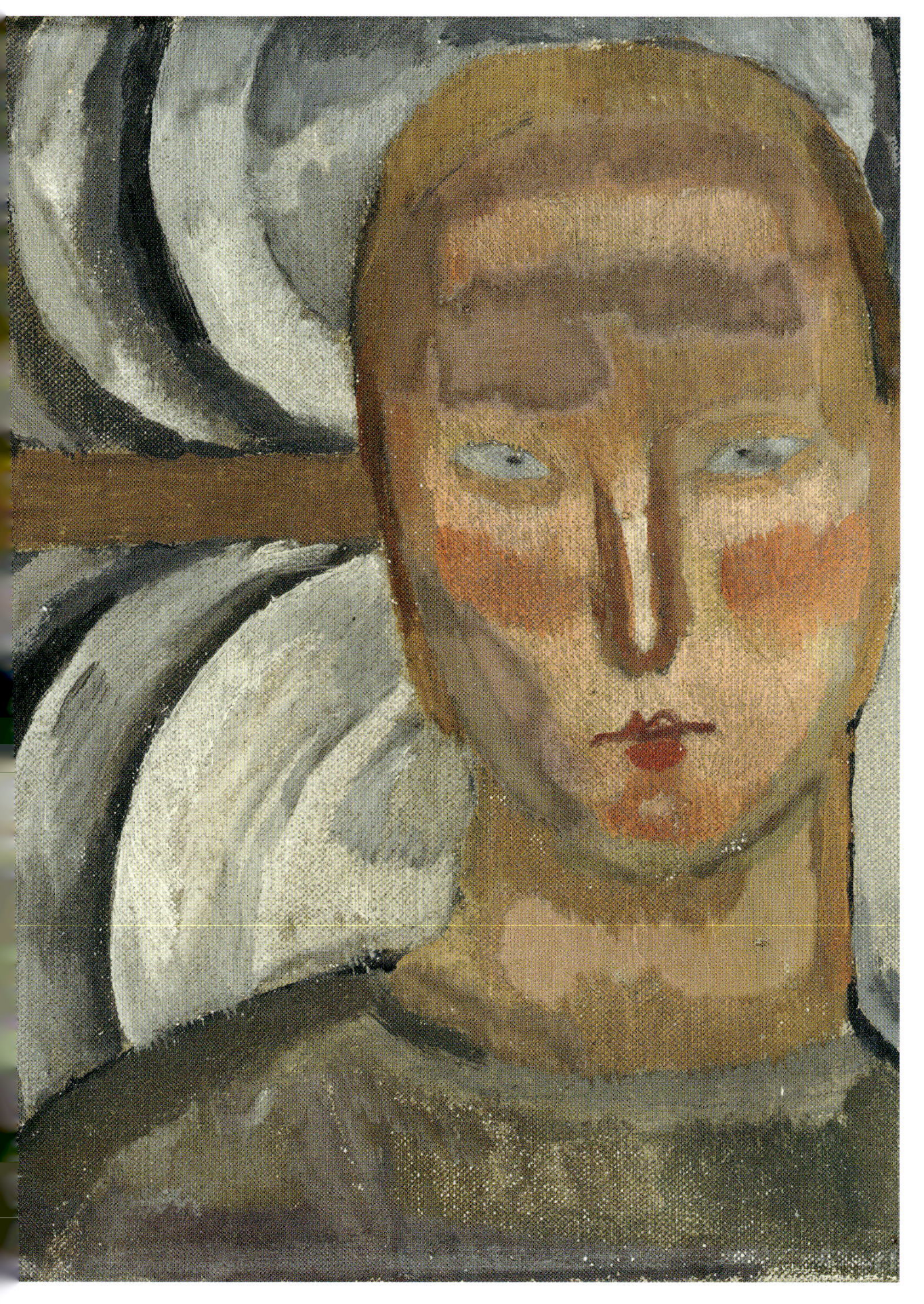

8.5. Vanessa Bell, *Study of a Woman*

c.1916– 17, oil on canvas, 294 × 230 mm, The Charleston Trust

Roger acquired and loaned to an exhibition, *The New Movement in Art*, which he organised for the Mansard Gallery the following year. Vanessa retained a second version, and when she was invited to show with the London Group in 1919, she revised it: 'It's perfectly hideous now and yet quite unmistakable', she wrote to Roger, perhaps describing the overpainting of green and blue highlights around the cheeks and chin, the brighter and fuller red lips that distinguish her two portraits (see fig. 0.2).[45] In all four oils Mary is seated in front of a large, abstract composition with elongated coloured rectangles set against a pink ground. This has been mistaken for a wall decoration or screen but its emphatic presence and flatness as a component part of the painting suggest that Vanessa posed Mary in front of one of her large abstract paintings. The clarity and simplicity of the geometric design are compatible with *Abstract Painting* and because *Mary Hutchinson* can be dated it helps to establish the chronology of Vanessa's earlier abstracts (figs 8.1 and 8.2).

In both her versions of the portrait and in *Abstract Painting* Vanessa presents a sequence of painted rectangles aligned against the edge of the canvas. The expanse of yellow in *Abstract Painting* is echoed in the open pink space of the painting behind Mary, and to the right of the figure, the inclusion of a blue rectangle reflects Vanessa's concern with the colour harmonics of abstract compositions. *Abstract Painting* is more focused and smaller in scale. The paint is thinly applied and ghost lines of canvas separate each block of colour, documenting Vanessa's precision as a painter. In doing so they contradict the impression of one form laid on top of another, of yellow as 'background'. The composition pivots around an isolated small orange-red rectangle towards the centre. A painted surface in miniature, it folds in warmer orange tones, and contrasts with the cool overlaying of pink against blue in the square above. Vanessa titled this work *Abstract Test for Chrome Yellow* in an inventory of paintings at Charleston in 1951.[46] It suggests a clinical application of her extraordinary sensitivity to the emotional and aesthetic effects of colour. The title could also imply that a subsequent abstract, *Chrome Yellow*, may be numbered among her lost works.

As a colourist, self-consciously exploring the processes of painting, the mark making of the brush and the texture and flatness of the picture surface, it would be surprising if Vanessa was unaware

of her contribution to modernist propositions about the nature of art. Clive wrote in *Art* 'that the representation of three-dimensional space is neither irrelevant nor essential to all art, and that every other sort of representation is irrelevant'.[47] Repeatedly throughout her career, Vanessa apologised that although she could be articulate in conversation she was not a writer: 'Well, I can't write art criticism but I wish we could talk', she wrote to Duncan.[48] She presented her arguments in paint. She recognised the value of her abstract paintings, storing them together with Duncan's work at Charleston: 'We have both been turning out a lot of old rolled up pictures from our stores here', she wrote to Roger in 1923. Their paintings had changed and improved, she hoped, over the past seven to ten years: 'there was a great deal of excitement about colour then', she wrote. 'I suppose it was the result of trying first to change everything into colour. It certainly made me inclined to destroy the solidity of objects, but I wonder whether now one couldn't get more of that sort of intensity of colour without losing solidity of objects and space.' Characteristically, it was Duncan's early works that she described as 'extraordinarily brilliant' and it was Duncan's abstracts that were exhibited.[49] In June 1915 he was invited to show with the Vorticists: 'he has sent two abstract pictures & a still life,' Vanessa told Roger.[50]

Vanessa's focus on purely abstract paintings and collage coincided with the months surrounding the outbreak of the First World War and a period of risk-taking in her personal as well as her professional life. It contributed to a momentum, begun in 1910 with *Manet and the Post-Impressionists*, to locate her own work in the vanguard of international modernism. The war made travel difficult and dangerous and it limited the flow of new paintings and exhibitions in and out of London, drawing British artists into the international abstract movement. The tragedy of war was brought home to Vanessa when two of her former Omega Workshops colleagues, Doucet and Gaudier-Brzeska, were killed at the front: 'It is too horrible . . . how terrible a waste that such a charming gentle creature should be killed', she wrote of Doucet.[51] Bloomsbury was vehemently pacifist, and although Vanessa didn't like Rupert Brooke it is significant that Duncan processed his grief following the death of his friend through an abstract collage, *In Memoriam: Rupert Brooke*.[52] Working closely, Vanessa and Duncan continued to explore abstraction alongside their portraits

and still lifes in 1915 and when they moved out of London to Wissett Lodge in 1916 Duncan wrote to her, 'if you <u>could</u> bring your big abstract well you know how much I should like it in my bedroom.'[53]

In the 1920s Vanessa described the courage required to embark on large paintings and their function in her practice: 'I think even if they come to no good it teaches me a good deal to try to push a big thing as far as one can.' Five-foot canvases qualified as large: 'I find it rather a good plan to have two – as when I've got rather stale with one I turn on to the other', she wrote to Roger. One of these in 1924 was 'the two nudes in your studio', indicating that Vanessa continued to replicate and rework paintings, now lost, that were formerly in Roger's collection. She described the confidence that his acquisitions gave her.[54] Reflecting on her painting around the outbreak of the war, when time and materials were still plentiful, she wrote: 'One began an astonishing number of large works which were never finished'.[55] She loaned one of her abstracts to Virginia, reassuring Roger, who owned the painting, that she could tear it from Virginia's wall at any moment, hang another in its place and return the abstract to him.[56] By the end of the war, however, Roger's enthusiasm for Vanessa's abstracts had waned. 'The only picture of yours which has gone thin on my hands is that big abstract business which I have in my studio & which doesn't mean anything to me now. All the rest have got better and better.'[57]

Vanessa's use of collage and her prominence as a designer under-mined the authority of her abstracts. Matthew Affron has noted that in the historiography of modernism these practices were downgraded in a gendered insistence on 'purity and specificity of medium'.[58] Her abstract paintings are also difficult to quantify. She included abstract settings in her 1915 portraits, discussed in the next chapter, and in still lifes such as *Omega Paper Flowers in a Bottle*.[59] Whether these represented paintings, screens or textiles or were conceived entirely in the interests of using colour to 'destroy the solidity of objects', they describe a fascination with non-figurative pattern that informed every aspect of her work. Abstract art was not widely appreciated at the time, even among the cognoscenti. When Duncan invited E.M. Forster, Bunny, Frieda and D.H Lawrence to tea at his studio in January 1915, he and Bunny unwound his abstract kinetic scroll for the assembled company. The following day Lawrence wrote to

Ottoline Morrell that he liked Duncan very much but: 'Tell him not to make silly experiments in the futuristic line with bits of colour on moving paper.'[60] Duncan recalled that Roger's response, too, to *Abstract Kinetic Collage* was less than encouraging.[61]

There was no such ambivalence in the value that Vanessa placed on Duncan's abstracts. She had a fight with Maynard over one of them. 'Do you remember an abstract painting by Duncan – very long & with pieces of wood on it? – He painted it in Fitzroy St. No. 22', she wrote to Roger. It had hung in the dining room at Gordon Square and then moved upstairs to Maynard's room after he took over the lease. 'Duncan gave it to me long ago, & when I moved I told M. it was mine', Vanessa recounted. Maynard believed that having lived with the collage for so many years it was certainly his, and when Vanessa insisted on its return he screwed it to the bathroom wall. She waited until he was on his honeymoon with Lydia Lopokova in 1925 before taking a screwdriver to 46 Gordon Square and carrying it away. 'I am now waiting in some fear to see how angry Maynard will be when he discovers it', she wrote to Roger.[62]

During and after the war Vanessa and Duncan's abstract works were uncelebrated. Duncan added figurative elements to one of his abstract collages a few years after its initial completion.[63] Some years after Vanessa's death a white spot was added to the exquisite balance of her *Abstract Painting*. It was carefully removed after the work was acquired by Tate.[64] Abstracts were not included in Roger's exhibition *The New Movement in Art* or lionised in the articles that Roger and Clive subsequently wrote. Vanessa's *Abstract Painting* prefigures the work of Mondrian in its quietude and seriousness of purpose. Unlike Mondrian, however, who was still pursuing Neo-Plasticism with the De Stijl movement and then the Abstraction-Création group into the 1930s, Vanessa lacked the intellectual and emotional support to continue with this pioneering vein in her paintings. In her decorations at Charleston and elsewhere, however, discussed in Chapters 10 and 13, abstract compositions were enlarged to cover door panels and fire surrounds. They were projected across entire walls that exploded the conventions of colour and technique and the boundaries between art and decoration.

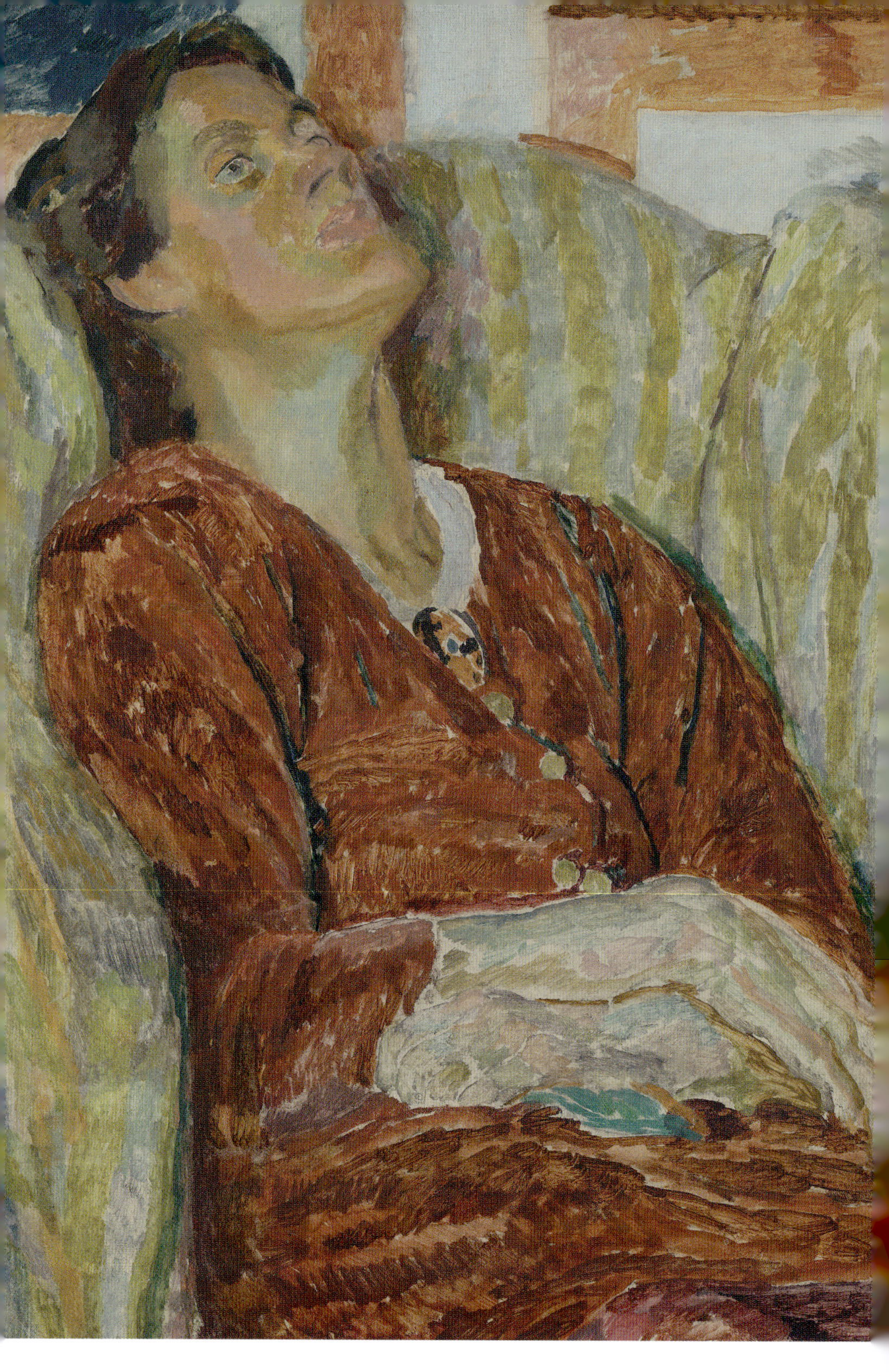

9.1. Duncan Grant, *At Eleanor: Vanessa Bell*

1915, oil on canvas, 760 × 556 mm, Yale Center for British Art, New Haven, CT

9

VANESSA BELL – DUNCAN GRANT

'I have been sitting to Duncan in a very easy position, which means that sooner or later I generally go to sleep. I haven't done a stroke of work myself unless you count dress making work.'[1] Vanessa was making up for late nights in London when she wrote to Roger in the spring of 1915 from Eleanor House in West Wittering, near Chichester. Mary and Jack Hutchinson had taken the house the previous year and Mary offered it to Duncan when she first sat for her portrait at Gordon Square, so that he could go away 'to paint quietly'. She may have understood that Vanessa would join him there.[2] 'Clive is quite happy with Mary & seems to be in no hurry to have me back', Vanessa wrote.[3] She was dismissive of Mary's taste: 'This is a small house done up rather in the New English Art Club style of decoration with spots & stripes & bright colours everywhere – very pretty for the most part with some lapses.' She went on to describe the large boathouse close by that Henry Tonks, one of Mary's close friends, used as a studio: 'all as neat as a new pin with his own pots & pans hanging up in shining layers & a few incredibly bad niggled sketches'.[4] Vanessa and Duncan were invited to use it while Tonks was engaged in war work but when it was cold and they were alone in the house Duncan painted Vanessa in the dining room and they used 'a very small back room' as a studio.[5]

Reclining in a yellow-and-white striped armchair, her hands folded across her lap, *At Eleanor: Vanessa Bell* captures the same intense inner vision that Vanessa's paintings of Virginia describe (fig. 9.1). She is wearing a red dress with prominent yellow buttons, almost certainly home-made to her own design, and an Omega Workshops brooch closes the white collar. Modelling was an extension of Vanessa's artistry. 'I see one ought always to do a certain amount of it', she wrote to Roger.[6] Duncan's paintings reveal his fascination with Vanessa Their relationship became a lifelong partnership and his portraits range from affectionate small studies of Vanessa wearing a headscarf and a sun hat, naked and pregnant with his daughter Angelica, through to a drawing of her on her deathbed. They painted one another painting, and Vanessa sat for large ambitious portraits designed in part for exhibition. *At Eleanor* was one of these. Duncan's portraits detail Vanessa's innovations as a dress designer, the radical interiors and garden settings in which they lived and worked together, and her fertility as the mother of his child, making these highly charged representations of her creativity as well as his. A regal portrait of Vanessa, painted after Virginia's suicide and acquired by Tate in 1943, within a year of its completion, is a poignant testament to Duncan's sense of her fragility as well as her potency.[7] Invariably her eyes are averted in these portraits and her expression is introspective, slightly melancholy. Vanessa had learned to offer this face up as a young Edwardian woman, for photographs by George Beresford, for example, but Duncan's paintings penetrate beyond the superficiality of her renowned beauty. His large portraits of her, many of which now represent them both in national collections, envision a mystery, something withheld or unknowable, underpinning a primal power.

Duncan's career trajectory ran parallel to that of Vanessa. They shared a visual vocabulary, often painting the same subjects simultaneously and exhibiting in the same shows. He was six years her junior and she singled him out as a rising talent and promoted his work from his first submission to the Friday Club in 1910. Their professional regard for one another was central to their enduring relationship. Few curators today, comparing the portraits of Lytton and Mary that Vanessa and Duncan painted shoulder to shoulder, would identify Duncan as the better painter.[8] Vanessa's portraits were more innovative and vibrant, more resolved as colour compositions, and yet it was Duncan who was heralded as 'the best English painter alive'.[9] Similarly their *Still Life (Triple Alliance)* and *Still Life, Asheham House*, painted soon after the outbreak of war in 1914, evidence Vanessa's more sophisticated interest in collage and simplification of form. She incorporated newspaper cuttings, maps of the German-French border and a cheque for five guineas that she had made out to herself and then cropped and painted over to form the body of a bottle.[10]

Duncan was well connected but he lacked Vanessa's financial security. He had boarded at the same preparatory school as Rupert Brooke and then lived with his cousins, the Stracheys, while attending St Paul's School in London as a day boy. Lady Strachey encouraged his ambition to be an artist. He attended Westminster School of Art before studying in Paris at Jacques-Emile Blanche's school, La Palette. Intense homosexual affairs with his cousin Lytton, Maynard Keynes and Adrian Stephen drew him into the Bloomsbury Group, and his living arrangements at Brunswick Square extended this close circle to include Leonard and Virginia. When the latter couple secretly became engaged in 1912 he was one of the few people with whom Vanessa could share the secret.

Vanessa measured her own work against Duncan's, and he in turn deferred to her judgement. Working together to produce paintings for exhibitions and designs for Omega, Vanessa was initially intimidated by Duncan's talent. She was analytical in her comparisons, describing their flower still lifes, painted at Asheham in the months before the *Second Post-Impressionist Exhibition*: 'Duncan's is very beautiful, I think, but I don't know how interesting. It started by being very cubic'. Her own work, she wrote to Roger after three days of painting, was 'a failure . . . simply dull'.[11] A few weeks later, painting a new arrangement of flowers together, she wrote that she was no longer 'much impeded by working with Duncan although of course I always think why didn't I see it like that? But as I have come to the conclusion that I didn't see it like that I no longer try to think I did.'[12] Their decorative designs were often indistinguishable, even to Duncan in his later years when museums sought to attribute their work. On occasion, when Vanessa judged her own decorations 'too boring for words' she still found it 'depressing to be brought into direct comparison with Duncan'.[13] But she was astute enough to understand that those very comparisons established her credentials as a modernist.

Her proximity to Duncan, often living and working with him, storing his work with hers in her studios, and the similarities in their work, opened doors for Vanessa. They countered prejudices against 'women painters'. In 1921, for example, Roger co-selected a *Nameless Exhibition of Modern British Painting* with Charles Sims of the Royal Academy and Tonks. The submissions were anonymous and he was delighted by Tonks's insistence that a painting by Vanessa, *The Visit*, should be prominently displayed:

> Your *Visit* occupies the centre of the wall facing one entering and visible all down the corridor . . . The amusing thing is that Tonks doesn't to this day know whom it's by. He's got you and D[uncan] exactly inverted and gave a little lecture on what a pity that women always imitated men.[14]

The joke became public in the last two weeks of the show when the artists' names were revealed. Roger advised Vanessa that it was 'bad for both of you' to produce such similar work but Vanessa argued that it was 'so economical to share models & as one uses the same studio it's difficult not to have the same objects in still lives'.[15]

In London and Paris Duncan was assimilated into patriarchal artistic structures and communities from his art school training at La Palette to the Camden Town Group. He was encouraged to produce large, daring paintings for exhibition that were endorsed by acquisitions and reviews. *The Queen of Sheba* was selected by Clive for the *Second Post-Impressionist Exhibition*, for example, and acquired by the Contemporary Art Society, which presented it to Tate in 1917. Rupert Brooke reviewed the exhibition, noting Duncan's 'genius' and the 'exquisite wit and invention' of the painting.[16] His work was consistently singled out in exhibition reviews, and as a consequence he was able to put his prices up, which in turn consolidated his reputation. Frank Rutter recalled that when he was first sent out to review an exhibition he asked a fellow journalist 'if he did not think art criticism was frightfully difficult, "Oh no", he replied smiling, "this is quite simple. You see", he explained, "the prices are printed in the catalogue"'.[17] The higher the price, the better the work of art. Throughout her career Vanessa regarded sales as a means of recouping the costs of organising exhibitions and providing essential income. She painted landscapes and still lifes that she knew would appeal to a wide market and she kept her prices low. Roger wrote to her before she exhibited with the London Group for the first time in 1919: 'As for the prices of your pictures D[uncan] and I agree you must put them up now', but at the end of the First World War, estimating their respective incomes from sales, he listed: Duncan £400; Nina Hamnett £250; himself £250; and Vanessa £200.[18] Vanessa's large, ambitious paintings could be exhibited without prices as loans from Roger's prestigious collection or anonymously, as in the case of *The Visit*. Duncan and other radicals such as Stanley Spencer and David Bomberg were less vulnerable to condemnation.

In the public domain, Vanessa's upbringing instilled in her an enduring semblance of passivity. Leonard recalled that when he first met her and Virginia in Thoby's rooms in Cambridge in 1902 'they weren't allowed to go to their brother's rooms without a chaperone . . . and they hardly spoke'.[19] Vanessa was 23. Duncan spent a year living in the attics of a hotel in Paris with fellow students when he was 21. 'I hadn't become acquainted with the Fauves or visited the Salon d'Automne at that time', he later recalled, but he'd been sent to meet Matisse in his studio when he was 17 and been introduced to Gertrude Stein. The comparison highlights a startling lack of parity in the ease and independence with which these two artists were able to operate early in their careers and subsequently. Inevitably, Vanessa internalised the prejudices that limited her career.

She used portraiture in her own practice to draw people more closely into her network. From Henry Lamb's first wife, Nina Forrest, to Omega clients such as Iris Tree, she invited women who interested her to sit for their portraits at Gordon Square and in the process became more intimate with them. When she modelled for Duncan it was a means of claiming his undivided attention, from the Sunday morning in December 1910 when she sat to him, Adrian and Saxon 'draped only in a sheet' to their first visit to Eleanor House when she subordinated her own painting in support of his.[20] The small number of paintings by Vanessa of Duncan relative to the substantial series of his portraits of her reflects the cultural conditioning that obliged women to serve as models to men. It manifests the complex power dynamics within their relationship.

Vanessa painted Duncan's back while he made a self-portrait. Almost half the canvas in *Duncan Grant in front of a Mirror* describes the bulk of his green jacket and Vanessa's nearness, painting

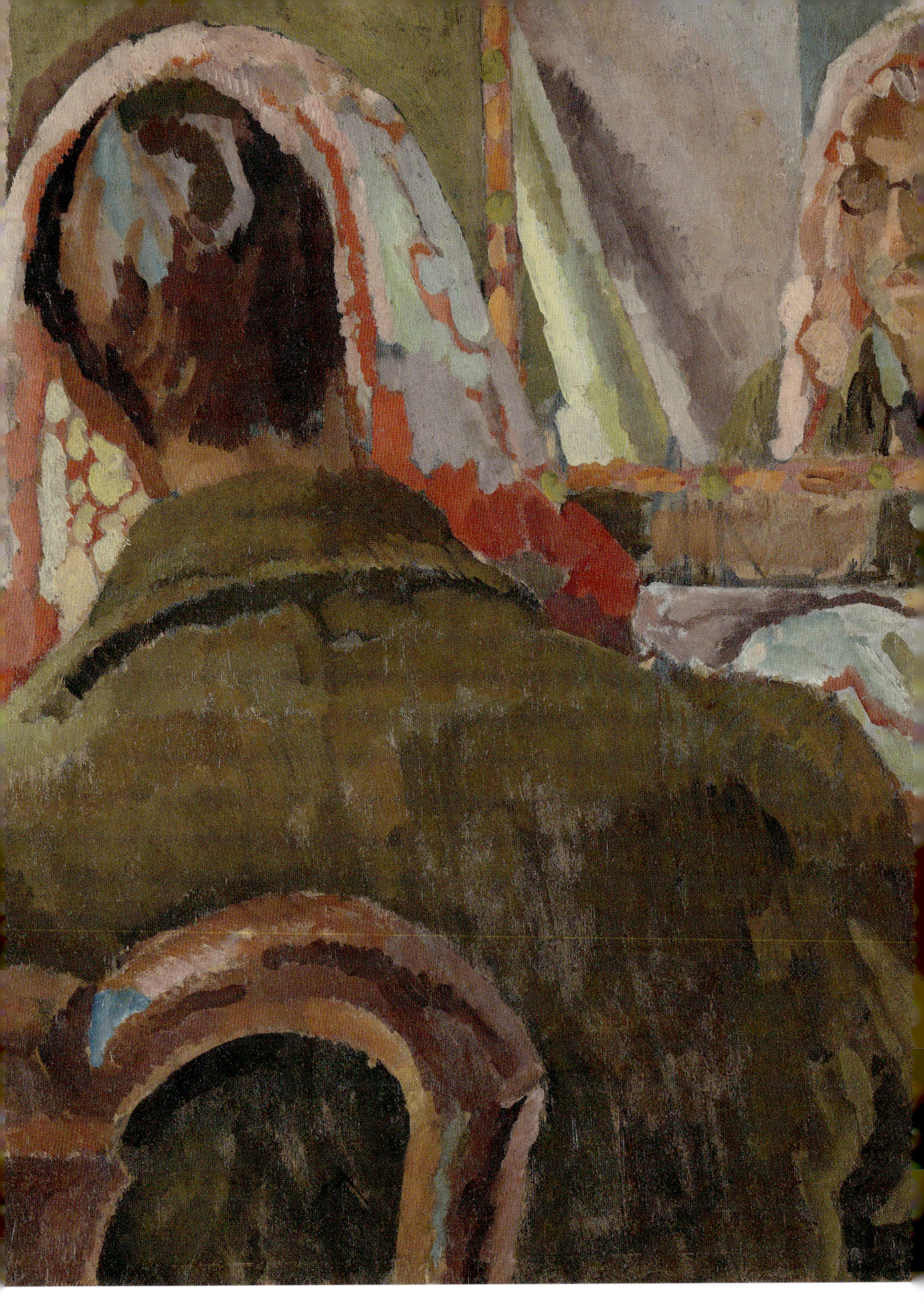

9.2. Vanessa Bell, *Duncan Grant in front of a Mirror*
c.1915–17, oil on plywood, 578 × 476 mm, Metropolitan Museum of Art, New York

immediately behind him (fig. 9.2).[21] An illusion of depth is deliberately constructed by linking the curved chair back in the foreground, with its bright blue and pink impasto highlights, to the pinks in Duncan's reflection in the top right corner of the composition. The portrait explores the textures of paint as well as colour: the curve of pink around the top of the head, echoed in the head covering in the mirror, draws the eye into the picture's depth and reveals the double nature of this portrait, the back and front of a head captured in a single image. Vanessa was familiar with conventions in the art-historical canon that deployed mirrors to represent the artist at work, but here the denial of her presence is reiterated. Duncan's gaze in the mirror is directed at himself and his own painting is glimpsed below the mirror. Vanessa describes the play of light on a yellow curtain, reflected in the mirror and casting a shadow on the pink wall at the back of the room, behind her. Duncan's head covering, a colourful fabric draped like a tea towel around his face, is a study in microcosm. Illuminated by sunlight from the window to the left of his head, the same colours are dulled by shade to the right. The portrait is a subtle evocation of the intimacy of two painters, sitting next to the window, one behind the other, to share the natural light in this small room and to paint together.

Vanessa Bell Painting is one of several oil studies by Duncan of Vanessa at work with her back to him (fig. 9.3).[22] It describes her method, seated on a distinctive Arts and Crafts corner chair with a foot resting on the rail of a second chair that serves as a makeshift easel. The larger scale of the portrait and Duncan's distance from his subject are consequences of the spaciousness of Tonks's studio, and the subject of the still life that Vanessa is painting is one of his 'pots and pans hanging up in shining layers'. The empty vessel reiterates the recurrent theme of pools and ovoid forms in her paintings. Beneath her hand, which is raised in the act of painting, Duncan wittily located his own signature at the base of her canvas. Vanessa divided her time between West Wittering and London in 1915 in denial of the war. 'It is very nice and peaceful with no front door & no telephones & no one expected to dinner', she wrote to Clive, adding that she was sleeping alone: 'No little Grant has yet had a chance to come into existence.'[23] Bloomsbury friends were invited for intensely sociable weekends and as Vanessa's circle expanded to include Mary and her

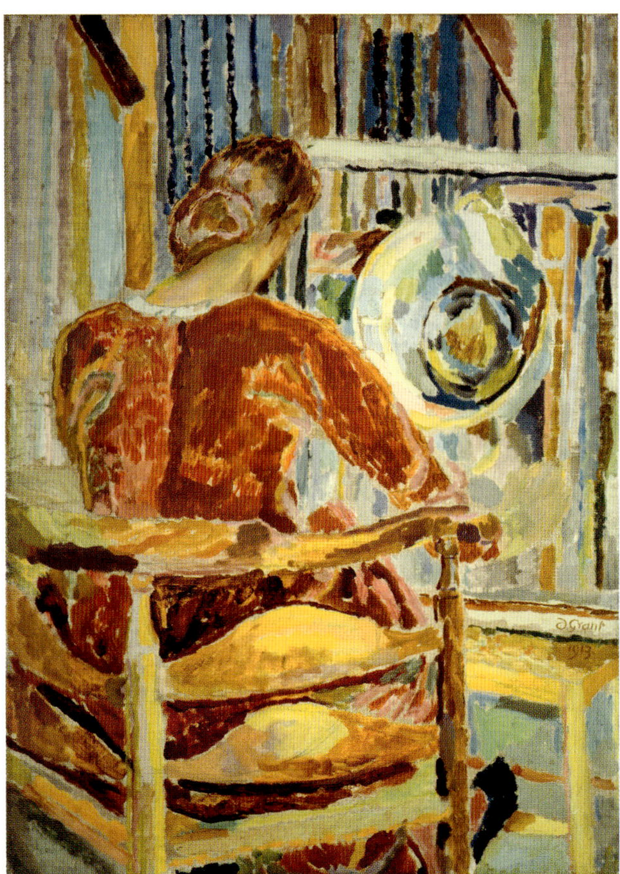

9.3. Duncan Grant,
Vanessa Bell Painting
1915 (incorrectly dated 1913),
oil on canvas, 762 × 559 mm,
National Galleries of Scotland

more fashionable associates she conceived the idea of designing a dress collection for the Omega Workshops.

The scope of Vanessa's work as a dress designer can be pieced together from fragments of evidence: her painted portraits, photographs and letters. It coincided with a re-envisioning of women and their roles in society during the First World War. In April 1915 Vanessa took control of Omega while Roger joined his sister Margery to work for the Quaker War Victims' Relief Fund in France. The Workshops had offered hand-painted evening cloaks and gowns for an elite market since its inception, and tunics made up in the distinctive linens that Vanessa, Roger and Frederick designed. They dyed their own fabrics and the extraordinary pea green of Mary's loose-fitting top in Vanessa's first portrait of her, together with the long string of yellow beads, identified her as an Omega customer and a modernist. Characteristically, Vanessa couched her business proposal in unassuming terms as an arrangement among friends when she wrote to Roger from Eleanor House proposing a designer dress collection for the Workshops. She had completed her own new dress between sittings for Duncan and was making one for Marjorie Strachey. Ottoline Morrell, she wrote, was also anxious to commission a dress. She had offered to host 'a sort of dress parade' in her drawing room where she, Marjorie, the actress Marie Beerbohm and her daughter Iris Tree could model Vanessa's designs for an assembled party. Initially, Vanessa suggested that they might use Ottoline's dressmaker to produce 'dresses that would use the fashions and yet not be like dressmaker's dresses'.[24]

Vanessa worked hard to negotiate a professional basis for this new strand of Omega business. Batik and block-printed fabrics were dyed and hand-printed on the premises at 33 Fitzroy Square using bold and unorthodox colours that outraged even Liberty of London customers. Winifred Gill recalled that colour was 'the most revolutionary thing' about Omega and when she tried to buy emerald silk at Liberty during the war 'the shopwalker was greatly shocked: He said "Emerald, Madam, is a colour we never stock."'[25] Vanessa insisted that her scheme would only work if a dressmaker were employed to be on hand at the Workshops. Customers could then select from 'specimen dresses' and a range of textiles with professional assistance and come in for fittings as their orders were made up.[26] Roger and the Workshops manager, Mr Robinson, were reluctant to commit to salaried staff but Vanessa ingeniously recruited Joy Brown, who was due to leave her employment at Durbins where she looked after Roger's daughter, Pamela. Vanessa knew her from the Brandon camping holiday.[27] 'I believe Miss Joy with a little more training would be just what we want', she wrote to Roger.[28] She arrived at an agreement with the philanthropist Hilary Douglas Pepler that Joy should be trained and employed in the dressmaking team at his Hampshire House Workshops but 'spend her afternoons at the Omega ready to see people or fit them'. Omega would pay her a commission and be invoiced by the Hampshire House Workshops for the dresses that she made. 'We should risk nothing as we only pay when we have an order', Vanessa reasoned.[29] Her collection was launched with a short exhibition at the Omega Workshops, opening on 10 June 1915. At least five 'specimen dresses' were produced, including a dress for Iris Tree and the one that Vanessa had intended to make for Marjorie, described as 'a red dress, tight as a glove to the bottom & then fan tailed'.[30]

Vanessa's life was complicated in the two months between pitching her idea for a dress collection and its realisation. Roger was desolate in France, jeopardising the future of the Omega Workshops. Bunny moved into the boathouse studio with Duncan. 'I suppose I ought to feel de trop,' she wrote to Clive, and when Mary planned to return to Eleanor House for the summer with her husband and new baby Vanessa was tasked with finding alternative accommodation nearby.[31] 'I don't quite know how we shall manage,' she wrote to Roger, describing a nearby cottage, 'as the rooms are small and we can only just squeeze in. The children and Mabel in one room, I in another and Clive in a caravan in the garden!'[32] More alarmingly, Virginia's first novel was finally published in March 1915 and she suffered an acute breakdown. She was violent, attacking one of her three nurses, and Leonard feared that he would be driven to follow her doctor's advice that she be admitted into an asylum. 'He won't do anything without seeing me first', Vanessa wrote, before returning to London two weeks before her show.[33]

Vanessa was confined to bed with exhaustion by Dr Craig before the dress exhibition opened. Duncan stayed with her at Gordon Square and took care of Omega business, while Vanessa managed the final arrangements for finishing dresses and taking orders remotely. 'Miss Joy is hard at work & all is getting ready & D. is looking after them. I hope if orders come in after the show I shall be able to help with them', she wrote to Roger.[34] Lady Christabel MacLaren ordered a coat in one of Omega's most expensive fabrics: 'Bright red & yellow. What <u>will</u> she look like.'[35] Mary promised to buy a dress, Vanessa ordered two for herself and Omega had not lost its capacity to shock the following year when Karin Stephen visited Virginia: 'My God what colours you are responsible for!' she wrote to Vanessa. 'Karins clothes almost wrenched my eyes from their sockets – a skirt barred with reds and yellows of the vilest kind, and a pea green blouse on top, with a gaudy handkerchief on her head, supposed to be the very boldest taste.'[36]

While she was ill, Vanessa wrote to Roger, 'I lie & read & think of the pictures I mean to paint.'[37] As she recovered, she constructed artificial flowers out of stiffened and painted tarlatan. These exotic,

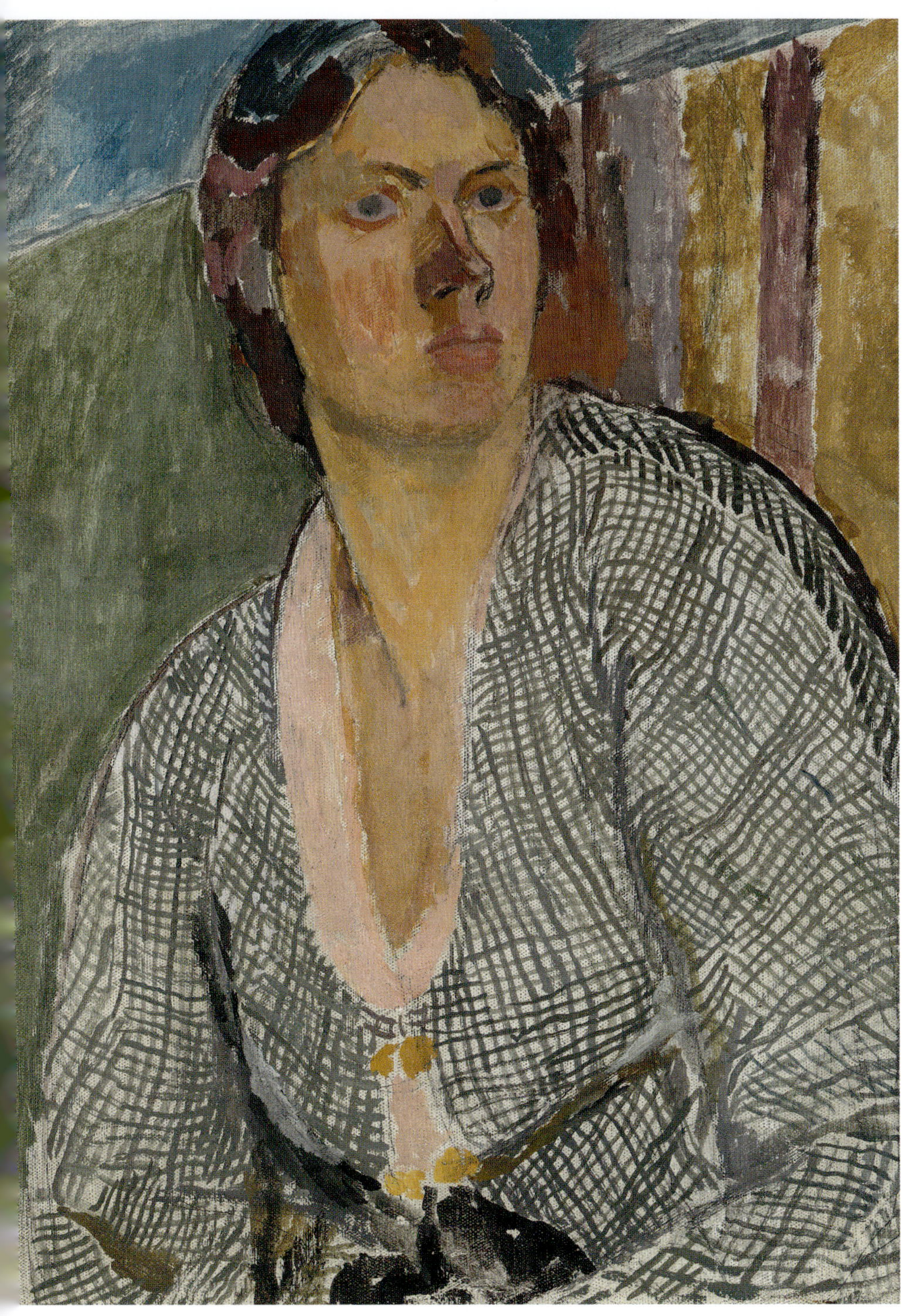

9.4. Vanessa Bell, *Self-Portrait*

c.1915, oil on canvas laid on panel, 638 × 459 mm, Yale Center for British Art, New Haven, CT

sculptural objects, which Winifred and Duncan also produced, extended her experiments in abstraction into three dimensions. They became Omega Workshops signature products and bestsellers. Like the printed linens, they were striking and affordable, making modernity wearable as a buttonhole, or brightening a room as an arrangement in a vase.[38] Roger recognised the erotic connotations of Vanessa's flowers, referencing male and female genitalia: 'I want some quite monstrous orchid-like flowers', he wrote to her: 'They should be phallic and funeste but rather by implication than any direct statement'.[39] They were the subject of still lifes by all the Bloomsbury artists and, like Vanessa's most radical dresses, their appeal was enduring. Mary was still wearing a red ankle-length Omega dress, patterned with large abstract shapes, when her baby was old enough to walk with her to school.[40] Two vases of Omega flowers were prominently displayed on a vivid blue painted table in the drawing room of Osbert and Sacheverell Sitwell beneath a painting by C.R. Nevinson when it was photographed for *Vogue* in 1924.[41] Vanessa's dress collection, however, was designed to be practical as well as distinctive and she painted it in a series of carefully constructed portraits of Omega's educated and independent customers. *Iris Tree*, *Helen Dudley*, the portraits of Mary and a self-portrait document Omega waistcoats, tops and the empire line dresses that Vanessa designed.[42] In all of these portraits the backgrounds are abstract. *Self-Portrait* describes a chequered, drop-shoulder dress with yellow buttons fastened over a pink top with a shawl collar (fig. 9.4). Vanessa's collection obviated the need for restrictive corsets and the portrait exaggerates her bulk. The face and figure are distorted; the nose reflects the influence of Picasso's *Demoiselles d'Avignon*. Above the outline of her left shoulder, which is reinforced with a thick line of paint, passages of chrome yellow and elongated rectangles recall her *Abstract Painting*. Her portraits experiment with colour, composition and form and yet they posit the individuality of their subjects. No concessions are made to feminine beauty. *Self-Portrait* is cropped so that the figure fills the frame, contributing to the effect of assertive power and vitality.

In February 1916 Vanessa staged her first solo exhibition in a room at the Omega Workshops. 'I haven't done any painting here beyond beginning a water colour', she wrote to Roger from Asheham, 'but I have been making some artificial flowers. I thought I must show some with my pictures.'[43] No catalogue is known to survive and a single review in *The Times* offers little insight into the content of the exhibition. Judith Collins has suggested that Vanessa included Omega flowers to inform interpretations of her recent paintings such as *Still Life on Corner of a Mantelpiece*, a bold, abstracted arrangement of Omega flowers and boxes that she painted side by side with Duncan, and *Omega Paper Flowers in a Bottle*.[44] The artificial flowers helped visitors to read these innovative paintings. Vanessa had focused on portraits, still lifes, abstract paintings and collages since the last important exhibition of her work in *Twentieth Century Art* before the outbreak of the war. She may have exhibited these at the Omega Workshops in a combination that illuminated the coherence of her vision as a modernist. *Mary St John Hutchinson* (fig. 8.3) was one of the paintings in the show, and if Vanessa's abstract compositions and still lifes with abstract backgrounds were also exhibited, they would have resonated as a coherent enquiry into the nature of painting.[45] A review in *The Times* was anonymous but the author, probably Clutton-Brock, was familiar with Vanessa's earlier work. In the same column, a memorial exhibition of work by Spencer Gore at the Carfax Gallery was favourably reviewed: 'Mr Sickert, in his preface to the catalogue, calls him a child of the French impressionists . . . The exhibition convinces us that he had thoroughly found himself only in the last two or three years of his life.' Vanessa, by comparison, had lost her way: 'Nothing in the exhibition seems to us as good as her *Nativity* . . . she is painting pictures as she thinks they ought to be painted rather than as she would naturally paint them.' Her work, more radical and experimental than anything Gore ever produced, raised questions, the reviewer wrote, 'about their method: and to most people, of course, the method will seem merely an absurd scribbling with paint'. The review criticised Vanessa for 'aiming too much at beauty, a beauty not of the objects represented, but of calligraphy in paint or of abstract design'. It implied that her work was derivative – and the Vorticists (with Duncan) had exhibited abstracts the previous year – concluding with a note of condescension: 'perhaps Mrs Bell will pass through these experiments to a more direct expression of herself.'[46]

Vanessa's professional achievements and her disregard for normative relationships provided a beacon for Virginia as she recovered and regained her confidence following the publication of *The Voyage Out*. She visited the exhibition and addressed the criticisms in *The Times* in a letter (now lost) to Vanessa. 'I'm very much pleased by your compliments', Vanessa replied.

> I think in some ways pictures ought to be able to please people who are sensitive to art in general, as you are. You might not be able to criticize in detail but I want you to feel something – so I'm glad you do. I have a great respect for your judgement as to whether a thing is genuine or not.[47]

Roger had been staying with Virginia and, now complaining that he was easily bored by pictures, loaned her two works from his collection. One of these may have been the large abstract by Vanessa, discussed in Chapter 8. 'I'm very glad you should have the picture if you like it,' Vanessa wryly noted, 'but if you get tired of it you can change it for another.'[48]

Duncan was offered his first solo exhibition at the end of the war. It was held at the prestigious Carfax Gallery in Old Bond Street in February 1920. Both he and Vanessa, by this time, had retreated from abstraction, keeping pace with a renewed interest in the 'solidity of objects and space' combined with 'intensity of colour' that they admired in recent work by Picasso, Matisse and others.[49] They had moved together with Bunny to Suffolk, and then to Charleston in East Sussex in 1916 so that the two men could work on the land as conscientious objectors. Vanessa modelled for Duncan when she was pregnant with his child in their first summer there (fig. 9.5). She lost the baby and became pregnant again the following year. The painting, now in the National Portrait Gallery, shows her reclining in a vibrant turquoise interior with marbled window shutters and red curtains.[50] She is wearing one of the dresses and waistcoats that she designed and on the mantel behind her a single oriental poppy in an Omega Workshops vase references the garden that she was making at Charleston. Duncan's work as an agricultural labourer limited the time and energy that he could devote to painting. Vanessa's work became focused on establishing her household in a remote farmhouse with no electricity, a water supply that had to be pumped every morning, rationed food, coal shortages and a seismic shift in

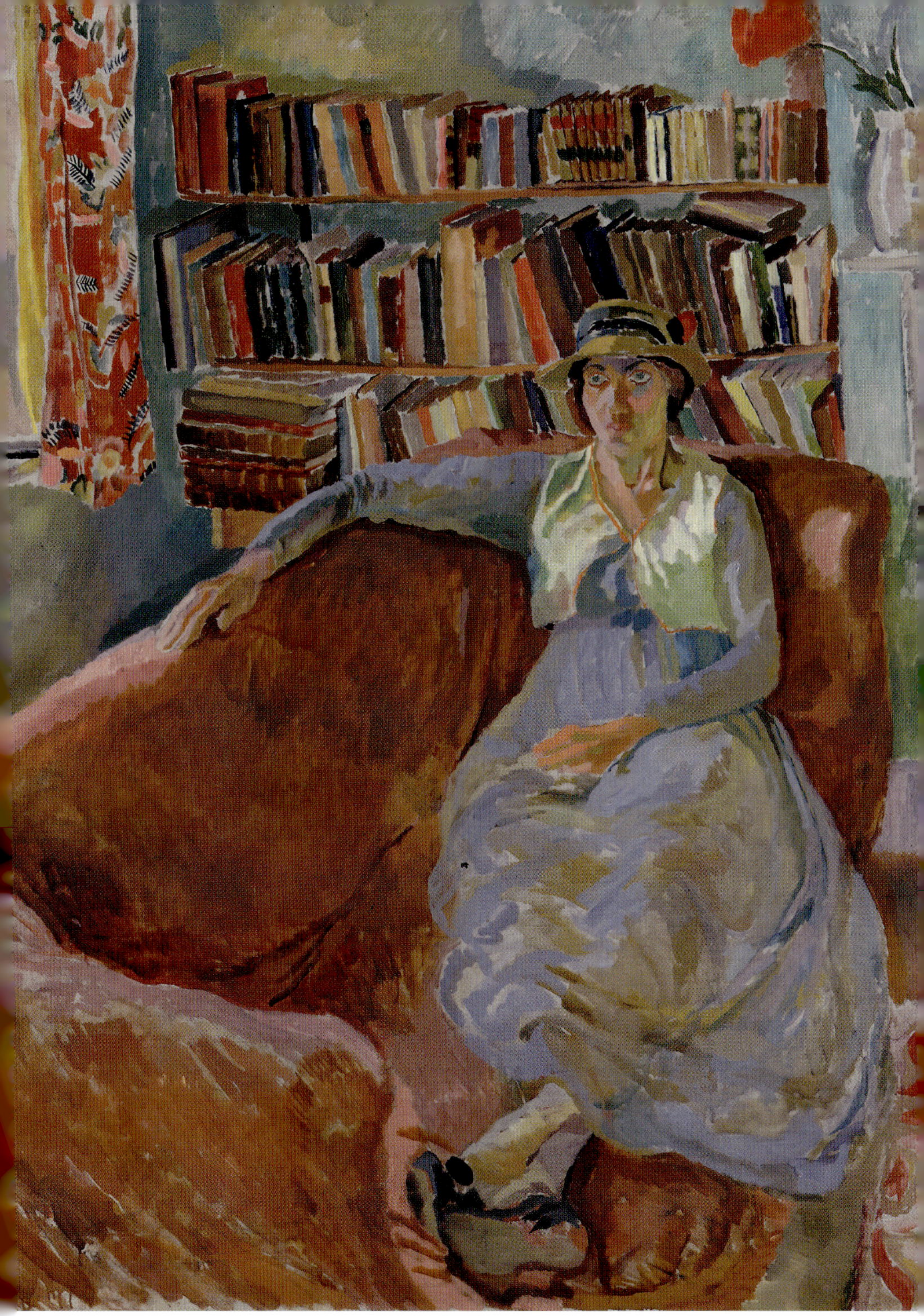

9.5. Duncan Grant, *Vanessa Bell*

1917, oil on canvas, 1270 × 1016 mm, National Portrait Gallery, London

the labour relations between employers and the servants necessary for the smooth running of such a house. It was so cold in their first winter at Charleston that the water froze over in the wash basins. Vanessa's third child, Angelica, was born there on Christmas Day 1918 and Vanessa modelled for Duncan, now a father, throughout the following year as he assembled a body of work for his show. Three of the 31 paintings in his breakthrough exhibition were recognisably of Vanessa. She is seated, holding a rose loosely between her fingers in a reference to Tudor dynastic portraits, in his definitive *Vanessa Bell*, now also in the National Portrait Gallery.[51] One of the most expensive paintings in the show at 50 guineas, it concludes a series of large portraits that he made of her wearing this red dress, made to her own design. In *The Room with a View* (30 guineas) she is viewed through an open door, reclining in a garden chair, and in *Venus and Adonis* she is cast in the role of goddess.[52]

Sales and substantial reviews in *The Times*, the *Telegraph*, the *Athenaeum* and the *New Statesman* rewarded Duncan's 'great talent' and marked a turning point in the disparity between the two artists' reputations. Twenty-four of the paintings sold for a total of £855. 'No one can look at his *Room with a View* without seeing that he is a born painter, one whose very paint makes beauty', *The Times* enthused.[53] Clive was unrestrained in the *Athenaeum*, describing the 'sensibility, power and intelligence' necessary to achieve significant form. No British painter since Gainsborough and Constable until Duncan, he wrote, had this 'possibility of greatness in them'.[54] Roger countered critical comments in *The Times* and the *Telegraph* by describing the new paintings as an intense effort by Duncan 'to push his art further – to amplify, solidify, and deepen the expression of his vision'. He described *Venus and Adonis* as 'one of the most strikingly original and poetical inventions that Mr Grant has ever created'.[55] Roger would have known the classical myth in which Venus was transformed by the gods into a tree and gave birth, nine months later, to Adonis, who was famed for his beauty. The irony, however, was lost on Duncan.[56]

10

CHARLESTON

●●●●●●

'I am rather astonished on coming here again to find how much energy we spent on this place,' Vanessa wrote to Duncan in 1921: 'how many tables and chairs and doors we painted and how many colour schemes we invented. Considering what a struggle it was to exist here at all, I can't think how we had so much surplus energy.'[1] Vanessa had arrived at Charleston five years earlier with her two sons, Mabel (who would become the children's governess), a cook and Henry the dog, to create a refuge from the war where she could live with Duncan and Bunny. The two men set out every morning at 7.30 to work on a nearby farm where, as agricultural labourers and conscientious objectors, they were exempt from conscription. Vanessa's first years at Charleston are essential to Bloomsbury's wartime narrative but she continued to work on the house, redecorate its rooms, rearrange their contents and make structural additions for the next three decades. She created an extraordinary setting there, where she could focus on her work and Bloomsbury would continue to gather. Virginia described her and Duncan, living and working together in 1930: 'As for Nessa & Duncan I am persuaded that nothing can be now destructive of that easy relationship, because it is based on Bohemianism.'[2]

Charleston is a remote farmhouse in the Sussex Downs enclosed on two sides by high garden walls. Although it is little more than an hour from London by train and it is now a house museum, it retains an atmosphere of privacy and peaceful isolation. 'The war', Vanessa wrote to Roger, 'seems to have destroyed the social world as we knew it'.[3] It polarised opinions, alienating Bloomsbury as a circle of pacifists and consolidating their sense of identity as a group of dissidents. Vanessa's financial security was jeopardised when Clive wrote a pamphlet, *Peace at Once*, which opened a rift with his family, but the chaos of war also precipitated radical change. It presented Vanessa and Clive with an opportunity to formalise their separate living arrangements. He joined Ottoline and Philip Morrell's more comfortable household of conscientious objectors at Garsington Manor near Oxford and made regular visits to Charleston with Mary. Charleston fulfilled Vanessa's long-standing desire to live in the country. Even before conscription was introduced she had imagined a house 'not too far from London, say near Lewes', where she could live with the children, while keeping a room each for herself and Clive in town.[4] 'Clive has now seriously agreed', she wrote to Roger, 'provided I undertake it all.'[5]

Vanessa became increasingly concerned about conscription after her exhibition in 1916. Duncan faced tribunal hearings that threatened to send him to the front or to prison. 'I'm already getting petrified within', she wrote to him.[6] She volunteered for the National Council for Civil Liberties and rallied their friends in support of his case. She rented Wissett Lodge in Suffolk and Maynard contributed to the costs so that Duncan, with Bunny in tow, could work there as a fruit farmer on a small estate formerly owned by one of his aunts.[7] They reasoned that it would strengthen their case for exemption if they were already farming. 'I must go and see what it's like and what is wanted before taking the children there', Vanessa wrote to Ottoline just weeks before she moved in.[8] Maynard was employed by the Treasury and he used his authority, taking the stand at an appeal tribunal, to support Duncan's case for exemption. Duncan and Bunny were permitted to take work as conscientious objectors on condition that they find an alternative to the family-owned fruit farm and Vanessa immediately wrote to Virginia from Wissett, asking for her help.

Virginia and Leonard – who, like Clive, was exempt from active service on medical grounds – divided their time between Asheham and Hogarth House in Richmond during the war.[9] 'I wish you'd leave Wissett and take Charleston', Virginia had urged Vanessa as soon as she moved to Suffolk: 'Leonard went over it, and says it's a most delightful house . . . and 4 miles from us, so you wouldn't be badgered by us.' She described the 'large rooms, and one room with big windows fit for a studio'. The house, she wrote, needed doing up, the wallpapers were awful and the garden 'run wild' but Vanessa, she wrote, 'could make it lovely'.[10] 'I think I may try to come to Lewes & prospect', Vanessa wrote to her after the Central Tribunal. Duncan and Bunny were busy harvesting on a farm near Wissett and Maynard had agreed to take over the lease at Gordon Square. 'He will move in at the end of this month & I shall come up a few days before to get the house straight for him.'[11] Initially Vanessa intended 'keeping rooms for the children & one for myself, which would be a very cheap arrangement for us, almost as good as letting the house', but it was settled instead that Clive should have a room in Gordon Square as his London base. Vanessa was drawn to Charleston because of its proximity to London and to Virginia. She planned to 'take the house & run it' for Duncan and Bunny.[12]

Her letters outline the work involved. Most farmers were prejudiced against conscientious objectors so she made the case that Duncan and Bunny would work hard for low wages: 'they would work seriously . . . & not be fine gentlemen.'[13] She took the train to Lewes to meet local farmers at the market, and having found work for the two men at New House Farm she made a second visit to meet the tenant farmer at Charleston, Mr Stacey, and view the house. 'I have just returned from Charleston which I have taken – all but the signing of the Lease', she wrote to Duncan. She sketched the house and described the surrounding landscape to him: 'one is overcome by the extraordinary peace & beauty of this place. The colour is too amazing now, all very warm, most lovely browns & warm greys & reds & with the chalk everywhere giving that odd kind of softness.'[14] There was a walled garden, an orchard and a pond in front of the house. 'The rooms are very light & of good proportions'. They were papered 'with rather horrid but quite new papers, so Mr S. wouldn't do them again naturally'.

> The paint too was quite good but harmless colours – mostly white or green. I said I should probably white or colour wash many of the walls & he said he didn't mind what I did – but of course he'll only pay for what is necessary.

She was obliged to meet his wife over lunch at their home in Firle:

> Mrs & I hated each other instinctively & she revealed to me the present state of mind of the British nation & why we want to go on with the war & why mothers like their sons to be killed – all hers of course are at the front.[15]

In the 1960s Quentin interviewed Duncan and compared the technique that they used to decorate Wissett with the drip paintings of Jackson Pollock: 'when I see his work it always reminds me strongly of what you and Vanessa used to do when I was six years old, all over the walls at Wissett', he said. Making a deliberate use of accident, they 'simply let the paint run down or splash'.[16] The decorations served as a prelude to Charleston. Vanessa and Duncan experimented at Wissett in defiance against the precarity of their situation, awaiting tribunals.[17] They made curtains and covers, dyed with coloured inks. Vanessa was already hoping to have a child with Duncan and they took a reproduction of the *Visitation* by Fra Angelico and enlarged it 'about 10 times as big' directly onto her bedroom wall.[18] She wrote to Roger that it was 'neither myself nor Fra Angelico & I'm rather desperate about it', but the process enabled her 'to understand pictures in a way one can't otherwise'.[19] Roger sent her photographs of work by Giotto to copy and the following year she and Duncan contributed to an *Exhibition of Copies and Translations* at the Omega.[20]

Vanessa established a studio in the top of a barn at Wissett where she started a large interior with figures, probably *The Visit* that she exhibited in the *Nameless Exhibition*. She resumed work on her painting *A Conversation* and she painted Bunny there, 'but he can only sit for a short time on Sundays', she wrote to Roger.[21] When it was too cold she painted in the house. The constant uncertainty, however, never being able to plan 'for more than a week or two at a time', was oppressive and made it difficult, she wrote, 'to think freely' and focus on her work.[22] Her decorations at Wissett were a substitute for easel painting which, she later wrote, 'seems to me the only real cure for unhappiness, [as] at least one gets to another world. I cannot do it when I am actually worried . . . but for other pains I think it is the only relief.'[23] She and Duncan were obliged to scrape and wash away 'every particle' of their decorations before they

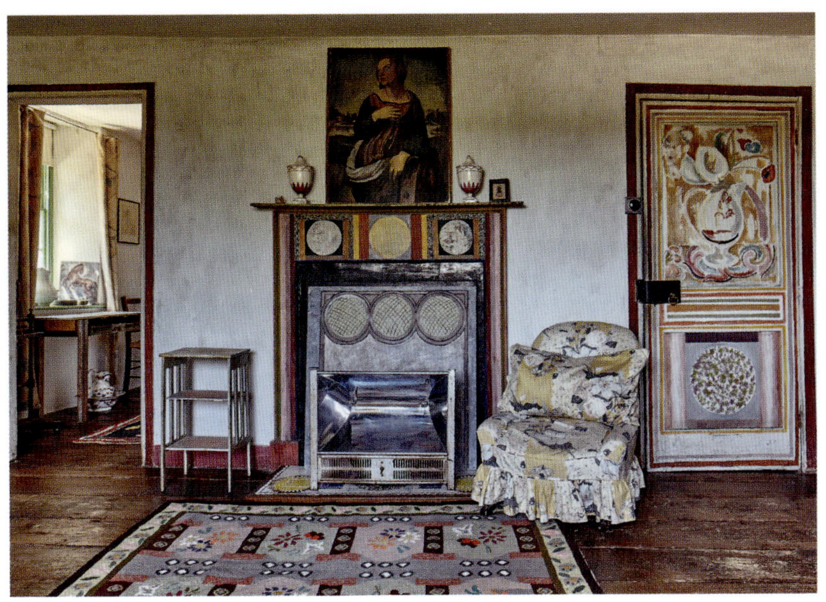

10.1. Vanessa Bell, decorated doors and fire surround, Duncan Grant's bedroom
Charleston, 1918, The Charleston Trust

moved out of Wissett, but Vanessa was undeterred.[24] She embarked on the transformation of Charleston into an artists' home almost as soon as they arrived.

The painted doors and fire surrounds at Charleston reference Monet's decorations for the art dealer Paul Durand-Ruel in his Paris apartment. Vanessa composed her decorative schemes with deliberation. She planned the chimney wall of Duncan's bedroom as a coherent composition, describing its central fireplace and two flanking doors as 'rather an amusing whole' in a letter to Roger. 'I'm not doing anything very startling – only pots of flowers and marbled circles', but her account and an accompanying sketch describe signature elements that would become characteristic of her interiors.[25] The 'marbled circles' in the lower door panels, set within painted frames, echo the abstract painted apron to the fireplace and would be repeated throughout the house (fig. 10.1). Vanessa ran a line of dark burgundy through the skirting, the door architraves and the pilasters to the fireplace to bind the interior architecture together. Flower still lifes in the upper door panels distinguish this as one of her most ebullient designs but

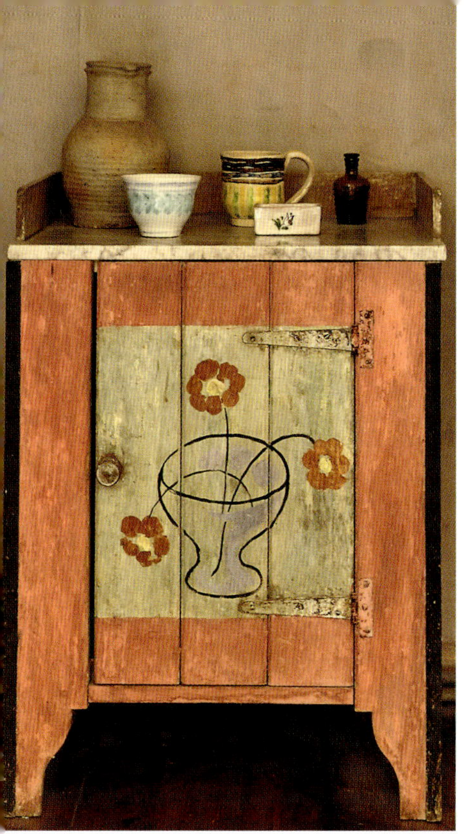

they were not drawn from life. Their tulips, daisies, poppies and arum lilies do not bloom in February. At least one of the panels was a copy of a still life by Duncan, paying homage to his work.[26]

Vanessa made a studio in another of the first-floor bedrooms and focused on making the house habitable in their first winter at Charleston. Remarkably, when Bunny wrote his memoir (and by this time Vanessa was his mother-in-law), he recalled only 'a room . . . for Duncan to paint in'. He was acutely aware that Vanessa was supporting him but he barely recognised her independence and status as an artist. 'In his schemes Duncan was always seconded by Vanessa', he wrote. 'One after another the rooms were decorated and altered almost out of recognition . . . Duncan painted many of the doors with pictures'.[27] Duncan did paint the doors to the schoolroom and to Vanessa's bedroom but he was exhausted by farm work five days a week and every Saturday morning for their first months at Charleston, until ill-health reduced his hours as a labourer.[28] Vanessa's correspondence describes her leading role in creating the unique aesthetic in the house. 'I hope to carry out the idea I have always had of bedrooms with the minimum of furniture,' she wrote to Roger, 'but it's odd how it creeps on one, even here one finds chests of drawers in the house unexpectedly.'[29] She rescued fabrics from the basement at the Omega Workshops. She organised vans and carts to bring furniture from Asheham and London: 'When I got home I found the hall again chock full of your furniture', she wrote to Duncan from Gordon Square.[30] She bought second-hand furniture in Lewes that they could paint and persuaded Barbara Bagenal to drive her to the Caledonian Market to buy cheap rugs.

A Victorian washstand with a marble top, painted pink and then decorated, is characteristic of her bold originality (fig. 10.2). Three flowers in a glass are outlined against a contrasting green square. Hinges to the cupboard door are incorporated into the design and the corner edges are accentuated with thin black lines. In other furniture, such as a tall cupboard that originally contained a fold-out bed and probably came from Duncan's studio, Vanessa developed her interest in purely abstract, geometric designs (fig. 10.3).[31] Four chrome yellow discs fill each of the cupboard's panels, floating against a dark burgundy ground. The two styles were combined in the window embrasure to the sitting room at the front of the house, now 'Clive Bell's Study' but initially a schoolroom. The shutters are patterned with an abstract, rectilinear design while simple, stylised flowers ornament the panels below.

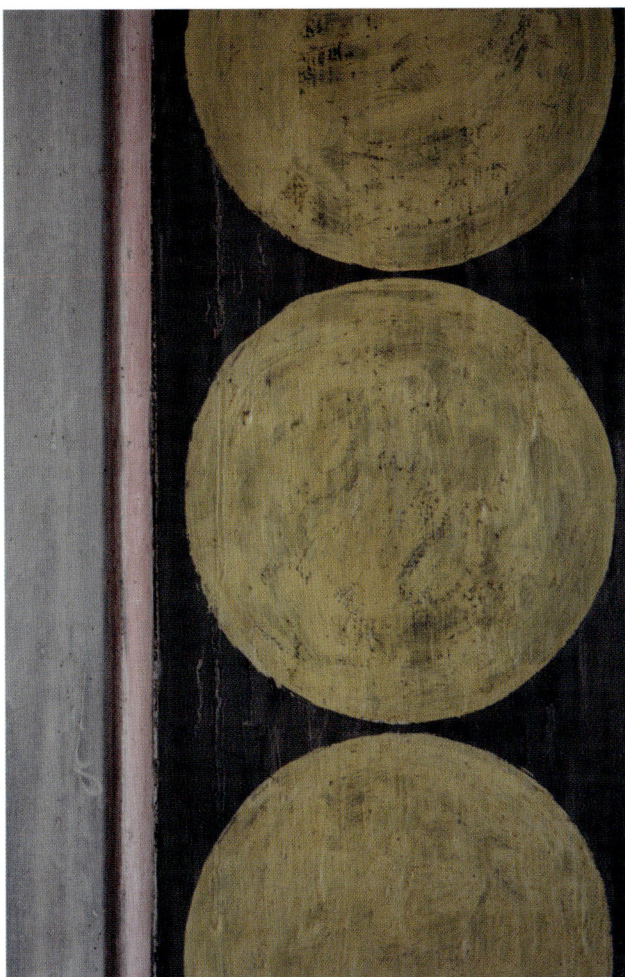

10.3. Vanessa Bell, cupboard, detail

c.1890, painted wood, manufactured to contain a folding bed by the Folding Brass Bed Company, decorated by Vanessa Bell c.1917, 2190 × 910 × 320 mm, The Charleston Trust

Vanessa prioritised the rooms that the children would use but in the first exceptionally cold winter at Charleston she was also pragmatic: 'the cold is simply appalling . . . I sat & shivered, painting as long as I could stand it all last week, then had a warm at the fire', she wrote to Roger. 'The only thing to do is to paint the mantel-pieces so I have done the one in the studio'.[32] A lexicon of design components evolved alongside a distinctive Charleston palette so that, as rooms were completed or partially redecorated, they retained a harmonious coherence. Vanessa painted or repainted the fireplace in the school room in 1925–6 after she had negotiated the renewal of Charleston's lease. The window embrasure to Duncan's bedroom was painted at around the same time. In both instances the familiar motifs of marbled circles chimed with the earlier decorations. The extraordinary combination of warm, cocoa browns, rose pinks and greys that first appeared in the window shutters reflects the autumn landscape hues that Vanessa had described to Duncan when she initially committed to Charleston. They were combined with chrome yellow, burnt orange and burgundy throughout the house. The palette, and Vanessa's handling of paint, was entirely original and without precedent.

The bedrock around Charleston is chalk and this, too, found form in Charleston's painted surfaces. Vanessa distempered the walls mixing whiting (or chalk), size (probably rabbit-skin glue) and pigment to achieve a soft, velvety texture on walls that, like the bloom on a blueberry, rubs away to the touch. The Omega Workshops had been a melting pot for experimental techniques. Dyes were mixed there and the smell of size, made from parchment waste rather than rabbit skin, permeated the studio. Vanessa mixed her own paint at Charleston. She combined the glue with water and heated it to form a liquid. A creamy paste was made separately by adding water to the chalk powder, and as soon as they were ready the two mixtures were combined and pigments were added. Distemper has a relatively short shelf life. It must be used within a couple of days of mixing before it goes off and begins to smell of foul sweaty feet. A traditional material, it was considered inferior to more modern and 'hygienic' wallpapers by 1916 but it was cheap and covered well, and because it was quick-drying it had the advantage that colours could be layered as pigments were added to the mix. Vanessa's experiments with distemper broke all the rules of decorating before the war. A professional finish was even in tone and showed no brush marks. Having applied her base coat Vanessa added more pigment to the mix and painted it on boldly, diluting it so that the paint would blend and run. She produced a sketch for a wall for an unknown interior, writing that she could make the colour warmer: 'I could make it much better colour in carrying it out . . . getting in a lot of slightly different in between tones would make it better, which one can't do in a small sketch.'[33] Distemper was water-soluble and so it could also be washed off with a wet rag and the range of colours that could be achieved was limited only by the availability of powdered pigments. For Vanessa's purposes, obliterating the wallpapers at Charleston and creating innovative colour combinations, it was ideal. Her colour-washed walls were also unprecedented as a decorative finish.

Charleston's interiors were immediately influential and they have continued to inspire generations of designers. Roger alluded to them in his 1917 article for *Colour* and, painting the walls to his new studio two years later when he left Durbins, he emulated the variegated surfaces that Vanessa had invented.[34] The decorations at Charleston were not designed for longevity. Vanessa had taken a short lease to see her through the war, and just as she reworked her paintings and painted over old canvases, she always prioritised the immediate effect she wanted to achieve over preservation. The turquoise walls in Duncan's portrait of her, made early in the summer of 1917, provide a rare insight into her first radical colour schemes at Charleston (see fig. 9.5). They were redecorated with silver-grey distemper, stencilled with a paisley pattern and overpainted by hand with white flowers in the 1940s. Angelica recalled that her mother, by this time in her sixties, mixed up great bowls of paint. 'She didn't mind how much of a mess she made'.[35] It is significant, however, that when Clive settled at Charleston for the duration of the Second World War the original decorations were retained in the suite of first-floor rooms that he was given. These included the first-floor studio, Vanessa's former bedroom and an adjoining bathroom. Vanessa and Duncan had distempered the walls to her bedroom black. Tall burnt orange rectangles accentuate the corners of the room. Duncan had painted her bed with a radical collage representing Morpheus, the god of sleep, and above and below the window he painted a cockerel and a portrait of Henry the dog. He painted the door panels with baskets of fruit and attenuated figures supporting baskets on their heads. They referenced *Lemon Gatherers*, the painting Vanessa had bought from him at the beginning of their relationship when it was shown at the Friday Club.[36] Clive brought his bookshelves from London (where they had been painted for him by Vanessa and Duncan) and they filled the former bedroom, but the distempered walls and Duncan's door panels were not redecorated for Clive. The main studio at Charleston, too, was largely unchanged when Duncan died, more than half a century after it was created.

Roger designed the studio as an extension after Charleston's lease was renewed in 1925. Between the wars the house was used for weekends and holidays and Vanessa initially set up a temporary studio in an ex-army hut at the bottom of the garden which they called 'Les Misérables': 'I've had a skylight put in & white-washed it & it now makes a very good studio with a good north light & heaps of room for 2 or even 3 painters', she wrote to Roger.[37] It was quiet and separate from the house but in their absence it was vandalised and the new skylight smashed with stones.[38] 'I go on trying to work in the studio but the rain comes through & one has to dodge it & the wind nearly blows it down', she wrote to Roger.[39] It was almost impossible, she wrote, to paint outdoors: 'it blew a gale & the sun went in & out & there were showers & I don't see how anyone ever paints out of doors in England at any rate.'[40] She negotiated a new seven-year lease for Charleston with the Firle Estate and obtained estimates for building and repairs. As wartime restrictions lifted she could employ builders and professional decorators again. 'The studio is not quite finished but they say they will have finished by tomorrow', she wrote to Roger in August 1925. 'They are now putting on a second coat of pale grey paint . . . The light I think is very good & of a lovely quality . . . I am longing to begin working in it.'[41] The following year she wrote to Duncan, 'I can't start household decorations as I have discovered I have no brushes. Do you think you could possibly go to Jones & get a large house painter's brush & a smaller brush, such as we used at Mary's & bring them on Saturday?'[42] Duncan painted the fire surround in the studio with semi-nude boys leaning casually on a high table. Goldfish swim in a painted vessel between them and they support the mantel above with their raised arms, referencing Greek caryatids (fig. 10.4).[43] The overmantel was patterned with a composition of rectangles and squares flanking a central niche. This was designed

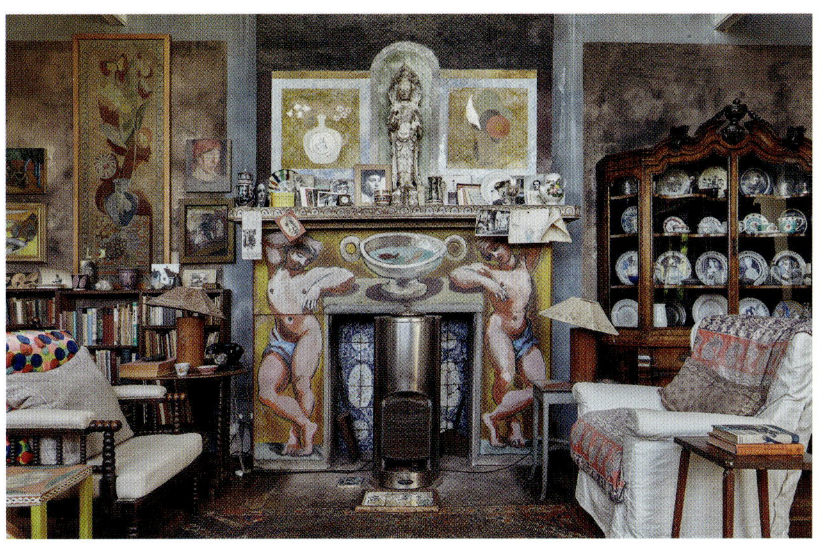

to frame a plaster cast of a sixth-century Buddha. Roger had owned the original and had copies made before he sold it, including one that came to Charleston. As professional decorators, Vanessa and Duncan would highlight their clients' art collections with painted backdrops.

They didn't bother to finish areas of wall that would be hidden behind their own paintings and bookshelves.[44] A pale rectangle above the door in the adjoining wall between the studio and the main body of the house indicates that the location of paintings was carefully planned as part of the decorative scheme. When the painting was removed it revealed the layering of colours. The doorway below was framed by painted roundels and vertical strips of dark grey divide the pink passage of distemper from vast rectangles of brown. Despite the freedom and unpredictability of the colour-washing technique, the grey verticals are not simply painted on top. Each component part of the composition is painted directly onto the pale grey walls so that the colours do not bleed through. Narrow seams of pale grey may be glimpsed between the blocks of pink, grey and brown just as ghost lines of canvas show through Vanessa's *Abstract Painting* (see fig. 8.1). The studio leaked almost from the outset and water damage, preserved as part of the integrity of the interior when it was restored, complicates the aesthetic of the original painted surfaces. Nevertheless, brown, grey, pink and pea green walls in the studio offer an insight into the dramatic colour combinations, the surface textures and the sophistication of Vanessa and Duncan's work as decorators.

Angelica and Quentin were actively involved in the restoration of Charleston after Duncan's death in 1978. By this time the house, still rented rather than owned, was dilapidated and many of its painted surfaces and textiles were beyond repair. Angelica mixed the distemper for freshly plastered walls and Quentin urged conservators to abandon their painstaking approach and be vigorous in their brushwork as they created facsimile effects in the studio.[45] In other rooms, painted wallpapers were removed for conservation and then reinstated in an extraordinarily complex and skilled operation.[46] The stencilled papers in the garden room, the dining room and the spare room at Charleston are substantially original and they preserve Vanessa's later decorative schemes, working collaboratively with Duncan and with her grown-up children.

Charleston provided a vehicle for Vanessa and Duncan to experiment with techniques and products that they developed as professional designers and decorators. When they first moved there Vanessa repurposed curtains and covers from Wissett and London. 'I had better wait & see what we can do with the curtains we already have, & get stuffs in Lewes perhaps', she wrote to Duncan.[47] Her *View of the Pond at Charleston*, painted in the first-floor studio, includes the window frame and her red curtains in that room, contrasting with the green and orange paintwork of walls and sill (see fig. 11.2).[48] The same fabric, lined with yellow, appears in Duncan's portrait of her in the sitting room directly below (see fig. 9.5). Vanessa painted curtains, writing to Duncan: 'Our curtains have returned exquisitely clean & smooth, only some of the watercolour parts slightly effaced.'[49] In the 1930s she incorporated the printed fabrics that she and Duncan designed for Allan Walton (discussed in Chapter 12) into the interiors. An archive photograph of the studio shows an armchair covered with two fabrics that Duncan designed in 1931, *Grapes* and a pelmet pattern used here for the upholstery skirt.[50] In Duncan's bedroom, Vanessa complemented the printed curtains he designed, *Little Urn*, and the painted arches of the window embrasure below with an

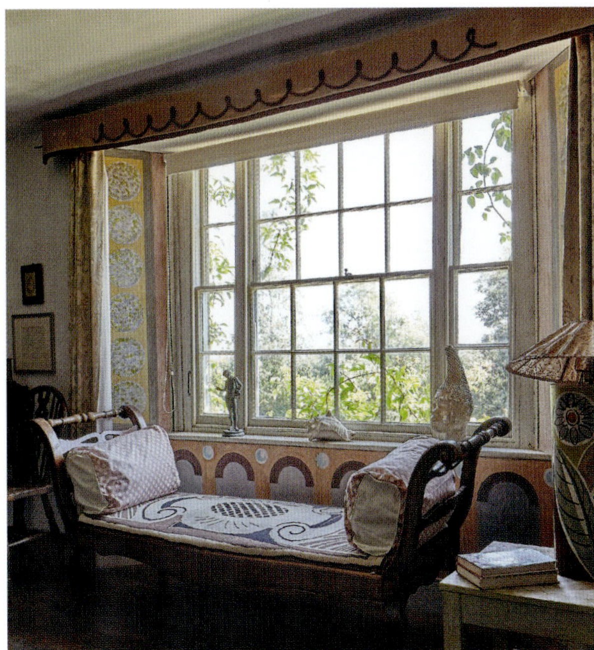

10.5. Vanessa Bell and Duncan Grant, window embrasure including pelmet, Duncan Grant's bedroom

Charleston, The Charleston Trust

extraordinary pelmet. She made loops out of soft woollen rope to complete the assemblage of patterns (fig. 10.5).[51]

From the outset, Vanessa established a household at Charleston that was exploratory and alternative. 'It will be an odd life, won't it', she wrote to Roger when she first moved in, 'but it seems to me it ought to be a good one for painting.'[52] She was hospitable, creating a refuge from the pressures of London and from both world wars for her family and friends, but the mornings were ringfenced for work. Visitors were encouraged to bring work with them or entertain themselves while Vanessa and Duncan painted. Virginia noted that she could cycle over from Asheham in under an hour but she often stayed. 'Yesterday it rained all day, so I sat in', she wrote in her diary in November 1917. She wrote a review for the *Times Literary Supplement* in the morning, 'sitting in the studio after luncheon'.

> Duncan painted a table, & Nessa copied a Giotto . . . I like the
> feeling that she gives of a whole nature in use. In working order,
> I mean; living practically, not an amateur, as Duncan & Bunny
> both to some extent are of course.[53]

It was Vanessa's responsibilities, she believed, that gave her this authority. Maynard was a frequent visitor, bringing news of the war and his Treasury papers. Bunny recalled that he 'breakfasted in bed and spent the morning working. He liked tearing up papers after he had dealt with them, and all his life prided himself on having filled his wastepaper basket before lunch.'[54] In 1919 he wrote *The Economic Consequences of Peace* at Charleston. The writers in the circle read from their manuscripts in the evenings, and as the end of hostilities made it possible for him to dedicate his time to painting, Duncan assembled a substantial body of new work in 'Les Misérables' and the first-floor studio for his solo exhibition at the Carfax Gallery.

Throughout the war, Vanessa's letters describe the unseen work of recruiting and managing servants, without whom there could be no childcare, no food prepared and cooked on the range, no beds made and bedding laundered, no fires and oil lamps lit. There was no fridge or freezer, no electricity at Charleston until the 1930s, and the house wasn't connected to a mains water supply until 1942. The social isolation and hardship of country life were not attractive to London servants and women left domestic service in droves for the independence and status of jobs vacated by men during the war. Charleston's many visitors, nevertheless, expected standards to be maintained. Vanessa speculated that Lytton would 'come & stay as soon as he thinks it will be comfortable enough'.[55] She upset Mary Hutchinson when her governess Mabel Selwood's sister, Trissie, left Mary's employment to join her as the cook at Charleston: 'It is the greatest relief having Trissie & knowing that after I give orders in the morning I needn't think about food again till it appears', Vanessa wrote to Roger. 'I can hardly believe in it yet & keep thinking I must go & see about something & remembering I needn't.' Mary, however, wrote to Vanessa that she was now 'going to bed for a month from exhaustion'.[56] Even in the 1940s, when Vanessa's household at Charleston was well established with a housekeeper, Grace Higgens, and daily help from Mrs Stevens, she described the obstacles to painting her *Nativity* for Berwick Church:

> I was driven distracted first by Grace who came in to ask what she should bake when I thought all had been as clear as a pike-staff, then Mrs S who wanted a bit of rag as a bandage, then

again because she thought I ought to pay the washing book –
I was so infuriated that I seriously considered locking the door
& telling them both I cannot be interrupted.[57]

She shared her frustrations and anxieties with Virginia, who understood their political as well as their personal consequences. Vanessa
was resourceful. Stephen family money gave her a degree of financial
autonomy but she depended upon the discreet support that Maynard
provided, taking on the lease of Gordon Square and contributing to the
running costs at Charleston.[58] Her letters are peppered with financial
calculations that a wealthier woman would not trouble with. 'I am
now fascinated by trying to housekeep economically', she wrote to
Virginia, while managing on 12 shillings a head, 'including washing
& oil & everything except coal'.[59] She bred chickens, ducks and
rabbits for the table and she kept pigs.[60] She took in Amber Blanco
White's two children to offset the costs of home-schooling Julian
and Quentin, supplementing Mabel's lessons herself with elementary
music and French classes. Amber was one of Clive's girlfriends and
worked for the Ministry of Munitions.[61]

Vanessa's letters describe Charleston's enduring importance for her
as a modernist home. Her work as a hostess and home-maker was
essential to Bloomsbury's evolution as a group. The 'sister houses'
of Charleston and Asheham, and then of Charleston and Monk's
House when Virginia and Leonard moved to Rodmell, perpetuated
the attractions of two households working together in tandem that
Vanessa and Virginia had established in London. The letters evidence
the practical and organisational skills that Virginia admired: 'I see
I shan't have time to do any house painting before Clive arrives on
Friday', Vanessa wrote to Duncan in the summer of 1928. 'Can you
bring the silver paper with you? I see we must do something over the
drawing room fireplace as the paper is now peeling off. Also I think
I must soon try to fetch the tile table – it would be so useful here.'[62]
They describe her passion for gardening and her sensual pleasure in
the colours and scents of the walled garden.

Bloomsbury photographs and paintings record Charleston as an
idyllic setting where the Group gathered in deckchairs or reclined in
a hammock by the pond. This was an outcome of Vanessa's labour.
Charleston was large enough to accommodate complex relationships

and in 1939 a new extension created a combined bedroom and bathroom on the ground floor for Vanessa and an attic studio, providing her with privacy and space where she could grieve after Julian was killed in the Spanish Civil War. The bedroom, with French doors opening directly into the garden, was unorthodox. Vanessa rejected the twentieth-century ideal of separate bathrooms and scribbled out a wall on the architect's drawing so that she could take her bath in her bedroom, as she had done as a child. Her disregard for conventions encouraged the ground-breaking ideas and aesthetics that developed through conversations, painting and writing at Charleston but her letters are also evocative, describing her own pleasure in the place as a seductive mnemonic invitation. 'It has been simply delicious here lately, hot sun, cloudless sky, no wind . . . We work in the studio & in the garden & see no one', she wrote to Roger. 'I admit I can't imagine a much more perfect existence. I hope I don't seem foolish?'[63]

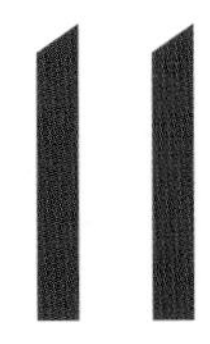

STILL LIFE

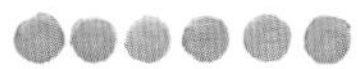

Vanessa achieved a lifelong ambition to take a studio in Paris for a month in 1922. She described the small room, one of a pair 'with a good north light' at the top of a house, to Margery Snowdon. 'We have been working quite hard. The first time I have ever really been able to do more than sketch in Paris though I have always wanted to'. She was completing a body of work for a one-woman exhibition at the Independent Gallery in London. Together with Duncan and her three children she had spent the previous autumn and early winter painting in the South of France before she was obliged to return to London and settle the children in their respective schools. 'So having them all disposed of I returned here to a gay bachelor life', she wrote to Margery. Her letter makes light of the complexity of life as a painter and working mother. Duncan, she wrote, had found the studio for her, adjacent to his own. 'I now know quite a lot of people here, mostly painters or people who are interested in painting'. She was 'seeing lots & lots of pictures, going to the painters' studios', and they in turn, she wrote, 'which is sometimes very alarming', were visiting her studio. Characteristically, she described the benefits for Duncan that were equally applicable to herself.

> I am very glad . . . that Duncan's work should be seen here. No one knows much about it as he has shown very little here, but this time he had a lot of work he had done in the south & I think it has been very good for him to get appreciation & criticism from painters whom he himself admires.[1]

Leaving Charleston for the South of France marked a deliberate transition in Vanessa's work, just as her earlier moves to Gordon Square, Asheham and Charleston had provided fresh perspectives. Although she remained friends with Margery and with Sylvia Milman, and she urged Margery to come and paint with her in Paris 'if you ever screwed yourself up to it', her work and her lifestyle were now very different from theirs. When Margery visited her in London 'she was the same as ever & insisted upon my going to the Royal Academy with her', she complained to Virginia.[2] Her letters differentiate her from most of the women she had studied with. 'Are you surprised to see this address?' she wrote to Margery from St Tropez.

> I myself really felt very much astonished when I found myself aboard the boat from Newhaven to Dieppe with 3 children & 2 English girls, Nellie & Grace, myself the only person able to speak a word of French & everyone in a state of wild excitement, bound for Paris & the south of France.[3]

Grace Higgens was only 19 at the time and would work for Vanessa and Duncan for over 50 years. The letters set out the practicalities and the affordability of Vanessa's life: the French cook who came with the shopping every morning to make lunch for them and the 'ex-nun, perfectly rotund and with a beard which she cuts with scissors', who taught the children French.[4] Roger wrote to Virginia that Vanessa was 'completely absorbed by domesticity whenever she isn't painting. She is such a virtuous mother and how she ever manages to do anything else, considering how much she looks after her family, I can't conceive. She is, as a matter of fact, painting very well.'[5]

Vanessa and Duncan had joined Roger in St Tropez for the light. She was immediately seduced by the landscape and the climate: 'it's still possible on most days to paint out of doors from 9 till 3.30 or 4', she wrote in December, enabling her to paint landscapes, 'which I have hardly ever done before'. Seventeen of the twenty-seven paintings and six drawings that she exhibited in her solo exhibition were landscapes. St Tropez, she wrote to Margery, was 'one of the regular painters' haunts'. 'I wish you were here . . . Not only is it so wonderful to paint but somehow the public attitude towards painting is so different from what it is in England that one can't help being

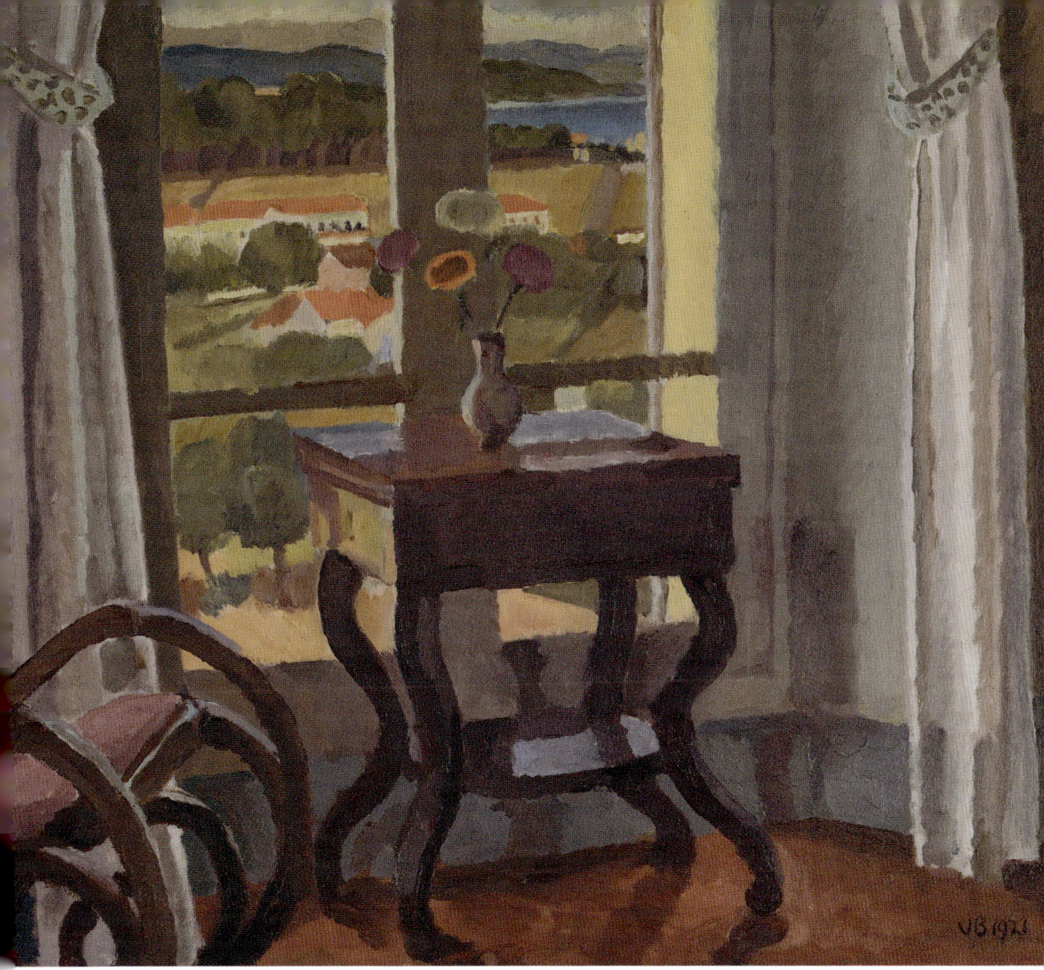

11.1. Vanessa Bell, *Interior with a Table*
1921, oil on canvas, 540 × 641 mm, Tate, London

much more encouraged to work seriously.'[6] Painting alongside Roger had always given her the confidence to work outside and in Paris she painted with Duncan. 'The colour is unlike anything in the north . . . every detail is colour', she wrote: 'never a muddy indefinite grey as in England'. One of the paintings she exhibited was *Vineyard in Winter*: 'now that the vines are bare one gets the warm colour of the earth', she wrote to Margery, and to Maynard she wrote that she was 'almost forced to be a landscape painter entirely' because of the climate.[7] There were also financial incentives. With Maynard's encouragement, Vanessa and Duncan were determined to earn their livings as painters after the war and when Percy Moore Turner, an art dealer who had worked in Paris and dealt mainly in French Impressionist and Post-Impressionist works, established his Independent Gallery in London in 1920 they were among the first to exhibit with him. They had shared an exhibition with Robert Lotiron in November 1920 and while they were in St Tropez Turner wrote to Duncan that he had sold more of his paintings and was taking orders. He was 'clamouring for more landscapes by him', Vanessa wrote.[8]

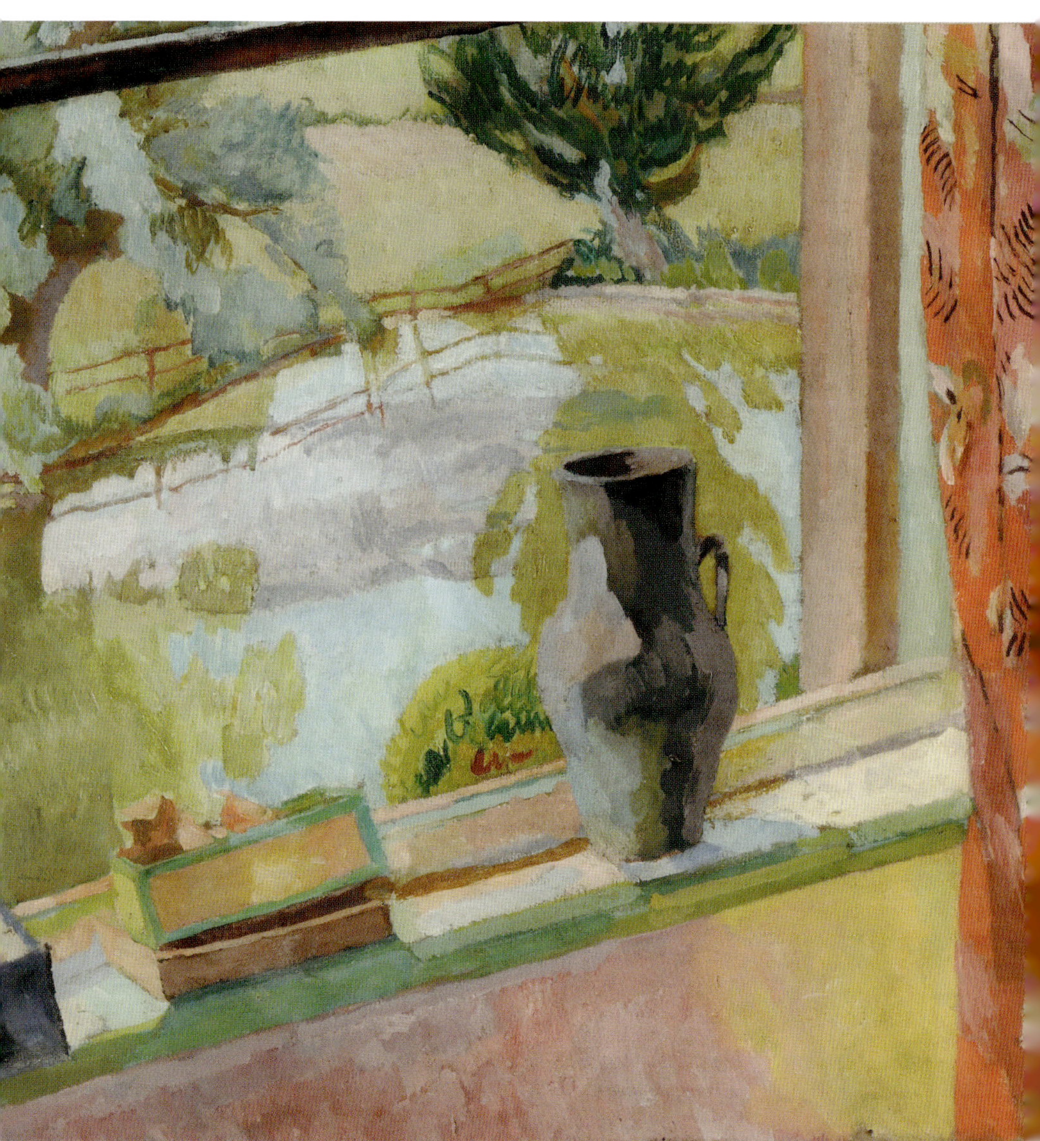

11.2. Vanessa Bell, *View of the Pond at Charleston*

c.1919, oil on canvas, 798 × 840 mm, Sheffield Museums Trust

Interior with a Table is likely to have been shown as *The Window* in her solo exhibition (fig. 11.1). It expands upon a theme that began with *Apples: 46 Gordon Square* combining an interior as distilled as a still life painting with a landscape viewed through a closed window (see fig. 3.4). The subject suited Vanessa's method as a painter. Duncan described the deliberation with which she applied paint to canvas. Landscapes such as *The Pond at Charleston* were painted from the controlled conditions of her first-floor studio there, and in *View of the Pond at Charleston* the window with its still life of an Omega box and vase on the sill, and its interior decoration, are integral to the composition (fig. 11.2).[9] It was convenient to paint indoors in inclement weather but Vanessa also felt compelled not to draw attention to herself as a woman painter. She had written to Margery before embarking on one of her earliest expeditions, to Greece in 1906, that if she was able to paint 'it will have to be generally from my bedroom window, after our fashion of old, for I expect that a Greek crowd would be even worse than a French one'.[10] The window represents a boundary or barrier between the interior constraints and decorum of women's lives and the world beyond. In *View of the Pond at Charleston*, perhaps significantly, the studio sash window is raised and the vibrant red curtain blows in the breeze. *Interior with a Table* is smaller, not least because the French paintings had to be packed and transported back to London. Vanessa had recently seen an exhibition of Dutch paintings in Paris: 'The Vermeers are simply amazing', she wrote to Roger. She admired *Girl with a Pearl Earring* and 'a wonderful landscape as fresh as if it had just been painted with houses with dark blue roofs'.[11] *Interior with a Table* assimilates the intensity and stillness of Vermeer's painting. It is darker and more condensed in tone and composition than *View of the Pond at Charleston*. Vanessa's use of colour is more saturated, and rather than using colour to dissolve form she was increasingly concerned with what Roger termed 'plasticity'. The rhythm of table legs and the curved frame of the armchair accentuate the solidity and depth of the interior with its sparse arrangement of flowers on a table and the long view to the coast beyond.

Soon after they arrived in St Tropez Vanessa wrote to Maynard that, perhaps following Roger's advice after the *Nameless Exhibition*, she and Duncan were 'both at work on several canvases but we have made a vow not to see each other's work for a month'.[12] It was a relief, she wrote to Maynard, when Roger left: 'his paintings get on one's nerves' and made him 'out of sympathy with both Duncan's and mine – although he gives one criticisms at every point notwithstanding. I think Duncan found it depressing'.[13] In a letter to Clive she described 'painful moments when I have been simply driven into a corner about his painting' and she urged Clive to be as appreciative about Roger's work as possible when he saw him.[14] Roger was out of sympathy too, with Clive. 'He hasn't much personal judgement and he is a terrible snob', he wrote to Jean Marchand on his return to London. Rather than truly understanding art, Roger observed that Clive 'collects hearsay and remarks from other artists, etc. He has no rudder; he simply floats in the currents of avant-garde opinion'. Roger admired Clive's influence as a journalist: 'he writes with such assurance that the world of snobs listens to him greedily.' But his criticisms, he wrote, 'have done me more harm than all the others'.[15] Clive had been invited to work in America when Vanessa moved to St Tropez. He had developed friendships with Picasso and Derain when they stayed in London, working on designs for Diaghilev and Massine's ballets. Vanessa had returned to Paris and to Picasso's studio in 1920 and again in May 1921 when she found Clive installed at the Hôtel de Londres, drinking every night with Derain 'and a lot of others' until the early hours of the morning. 'But they never mention painting, which makes it less interesting than it might be', she wrote.[16]

St Tropez and the Paris studio were the culmination of a determined effort, on Vanessa's part, to re-establish herself within a vibrant modernist culture. Paris in the 1920s was the epicentre of modernism. Throughout the war she had maintained her support for the Omega Workshops. She revived the dress collection in 1917, injecting a fresh and coherent design aesthetic and handing over responsibility for its management and development to Faith Henderson, a young graduate from Newnham College. It remained a profitable concern, even when Omega was losing money more generally, and it perpetuated the Omega 'brand', identifying its affluent and influential women clients, in particular, with modernism.[17] Vanessa and Duncan contributed to small group exhibitions that Roger organised for the Workshops and to *The New Movement in Art*, an exhibition drawing extensively on his own collection that was first shown in Birmingham and then at Heal's on the Tottenham Court Road in the new Mansard Gallery. Before the exhibition moved to London Vanessa was delighted to sell a landscape painted at Bosham, close to Eleanor House, to Michael Sadler who was building an important collection and then a second painting, her collage now known as *Triple Alliance*. 'The only thing', she wrote to Duncan, 'is that Sadler is often unable to pay'.[18] At the Mansard Gallery she was represented by seven still lifes and again exhibited her portrait of Mary, which by now was in Roger's collection.

The absence of 'purely abstract' paintings was particularly noted in a review of an *Exhibition of Modern Paintings and Drawings at the Omega Workshops* the following year. Vanessa's still life, *Paper Flowers*, was praised for its 'valuable qualities, especially of colour, peculiar to the rare work that may be classified as essentially feminine'. The Workshops remained 'a focus for certain artists who take a leading part in the development of the modern movement in London', the reviewer wrote.[19] It enabled Vanessa to exhibit regularly and its group exhibitions now included work by Sickert, Gertler, Hamnett and Edward McKnight Kauffer. However, Vanessa renewed her engagement with a broader European avant-garde when she began to paint again a few months after Angelica's birth and the end of the war.

Vanessa rented a friend's flat in Regent Square for a year: 'I mean to furnish it in April if I can & let it from May to October when I intend to come there myself with the children for the winter', she wrote to Roger from Charleston, enquiring about his furniture suppliers for the Omega Workshops.[20] She sublet the flat to Derain and met him and Picasso while they were in London. She attended the London premiere of the ballet *Parade* in November 1919 and when she wrote to Clive, enthusiastically describing it, he read her letter aloud to Picasso, Erik Satie and Jean Cocteau with whom he was having lunch in Paris: 'It had an immense success; & Picasso showed himself a good deal touched.'[21] By this time London was cold, wet and dark and the Regent Square flat was proving too small for larger canvases. 'It's practically impossible to paint on account of the light & quite impossible with only one room for myself & the children when they don't go to school for any reason', Vanessa wrote to Roger.[22] She was imagining a new life in Paris or the South of France with Duncan, Roger, Clive and the children: 'we might make a kind of colony', she wrote to Roger. 'I am quite serious about this'.[23] In Paris, she wrote,

'one would have the chance now of knowing all the best painters &
I think there can be no doubt one would be more likely to do one's
best there'.[24] She and Duncan entertained their friend Charles Vildrac
when he came to London and agreed with him that, together with
Roger, they 'would have a show together in his shop' in Paris.[25]

Vanessa returned to Paris with Duncan in the spring of 1920
after his exhibition at the Carfax Gallery. They were en route to
Rome where they spent a month with Maynard. 'After 6 years of
England . . . one had got to think it impossible the war would ever
come to an end or that one would ever get abroad again', she wrote
to Roger. 'So many things that have to be repressed in one seem to
expand and develop when one gets into France'.[26] She wrote that he
would think her absurd to be painting still lifes in a studio in Rome:
'But you know even in a studio the colour is quite different from
England.'[27] On their way through Paris they had chosen frames for
their exhibition with Vildrac: 'I'm afraid you had a lot of bother as
usual over arranging about everything', she replied to Roger from
Rome when he described the exhibition to her.[28] They stayed with
the Berensons at I Tatti in Florence before returning to Paris on their
way home. She and Duncan visited Picasso in his studio: 'He showed
us quantities of his latest work and things he is actually at work on,
nearly all more or less abstract designs . . . Some were amazingly
beautiful.' They were also shown 'an astonishing painting of 2 nudes,
most elaborately finished and rounder and more definite than any
Ingres, fearfully good, I thought'.[29]

Vanessa had hoped to rent Charleston to an old family friend,
Madge Vaughan, for five guineas a week while she was in Italy.
However, Madge visited the house and wrote to Vanessa from
Charleston that she had heard 'sordid gossip' there, presumably about
Angelica's illegitimacy which, she wrote, 'gnaws at my poor heart'
and made it impossible for her to holiday there with her headmaster
husband and their two sons.[30] Her letter and Vanessa's reply articulate
the considerable risks of social ostracism and disgrace that Vanessa
perpetually negotiated because of her life choices. 'I was half amused
& half furious', she replied.

> Why on earth should my moral character have anything to do
> with the question of your taking Charleston . . . As for the gossip

about me, as to which of course I have not been left in ignorance,
I must admit that it seems to me almost incredibly impertinent
of you to ask me to satisfy your curiosity about it.[31]

Madge shared their correspondence with a mutual friend. 'I cannot help admiring her, & her great strength of mind and character, though I do not think her right', she wrote, urging Madge to cling to her Christian values: 'she must realise that if you felt she were leading a life of which you totally disapproved . . . this surely was a good reason for you refusing to take her house'.[32] Perhaps as a consequence of this exchange, Vanessa painted a large family group of her three children at Charleston with Clive 'as père de famille!' *Clive Bell and Family* was completed in 1924.[33]

Vanessa and Duncan were committed to the classicism, and the return to representation, of contemporary painting in Paris when they visited again in May 1921. They dined with Derain, Braque and Satie and Vanessa wrote to Roger that a Picasso show was one of the most exciting things she had seen. She described the crowd at the private view and Picasso's recent paintings: 'two large female figures . . . a huge thing, seemed to me splendid'.[34] She was intrigued, too, by the independent lives of women artists in Paris. She and Duncan had lunch with Constance Lloyd, a friend of Gwen John's, and they visited the Omega artist Dolores Courtney at her new apartment. Paris reignited Vanessa's ambition to take a studio there, and when her French friends advised her that studios were almost impossible to find she followed their recommendation to take a place near St Tropez, where she rented la Maison Blanche from the Vildracs. It was large enough to accommodate her family as well as Duncan and by now she had rooms at 50 Gordon Square that she let to cover the cost.[35]

After three months spent painting in St Tropez Vanessa hoped to meet Clive in Paris so that he could take the children back to London in January 1922. When cleaning and packing up la Maison Blanche, however, she still hadn't heard whether he was going to America: 'He hasn't said a word to me about his plans except that he doesn't mean to come to Paris', she wrote to Roger.[36] She travelled back to London with the three children and as each of them in turn then caught influenza, 'instead of being able to despatch them to school I had to stay & look after them', she wrote to Margery, costing her

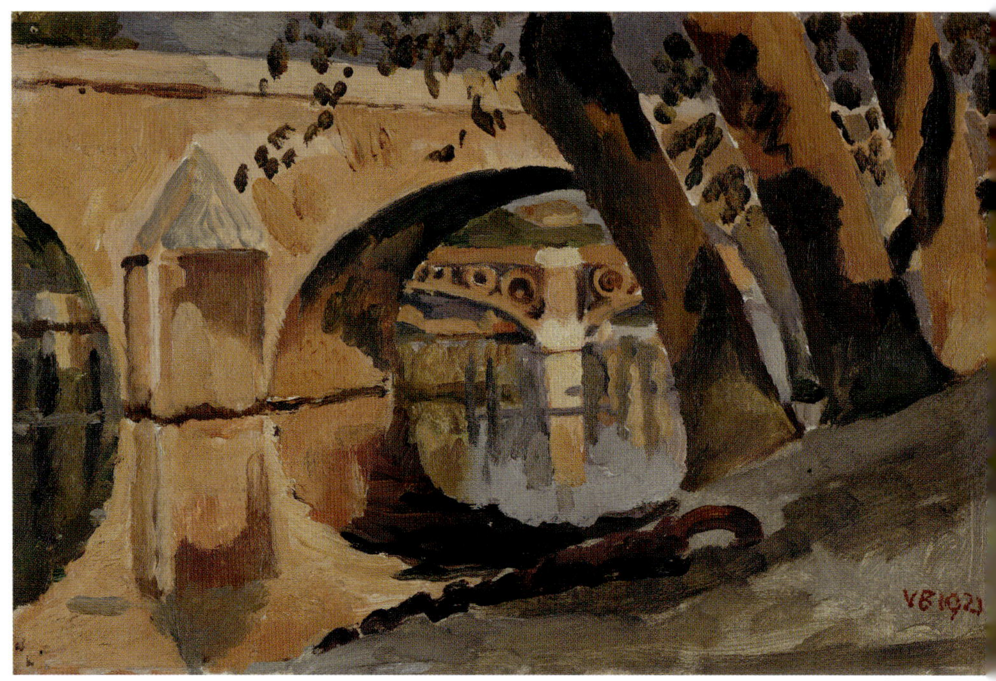

11.3. Vanessa Bell, *On the Seine*

1921, oil on canvas, 270 × 460 mm, Fitzwilliam Museum, Cambridge

a month of valuable painting time in the run-up to her exhibition.[37] She returned to Paris when Angelica was well enough to stay with Clive's family: 'I suddenly felt that unless I came at once I should certainly be kept again'.[38]

Vanessa had painted *On the Seine* (fig. 11.3), *Le Pont Neuf*, *Pont Royal* and the *Quay des Orfèvres* the previous spring in Paris with Vermeer's *View of Delft* in her mind's eye and they were all included in her exhibition.[39] In her Paris studio in February 1922 she focused on still lifes. A creative seam of still life paintings runs through her practice from *Iceland Poppies* to the canvases she produced in the attic studio at Charleston at the end of her life. The genre provided a respite from relentless visitors and collaborations in London and at Charleston: 'the railway station that is family life downstairs'.[40] Painting 'a quiet little still life', she wrote to Roger, was 'the greatest relief after theatrical hurry-skurry. It's extraordinary to find that one can spend as long as one likes over what one's doing & that it doesn't matter what anyone else thinks of it.'[41] Still lifes enabled her to focus on new directions in painting and collage but they also catered to the demands of an established commercial market, and Vanessa equated sales with success. Seven of the paintings in her exhibition at the Independent Gallery were still lifes and although she wrote to Roger, 'I'm determined to do nothing on purpose for my own show', Turner subjected her to a charm offensive in the lead-up to the exhibition. He wrote to her 'full of compliments about my pictures', which took the form, she cynically observed to Roger, 'also of buying one', and he paid her and Duncan a visit in Paris: 'He looked at all Duncan's things & mine & never said a word.'[42]

Still Life at a Window is likely to have been the *Still Life* listed in Vanessa's exhibition catalogue (fig. 11.4).[43] She had painted objects on a window ledge in Rome as well as at Charleston, but here the solid form of an undecorated

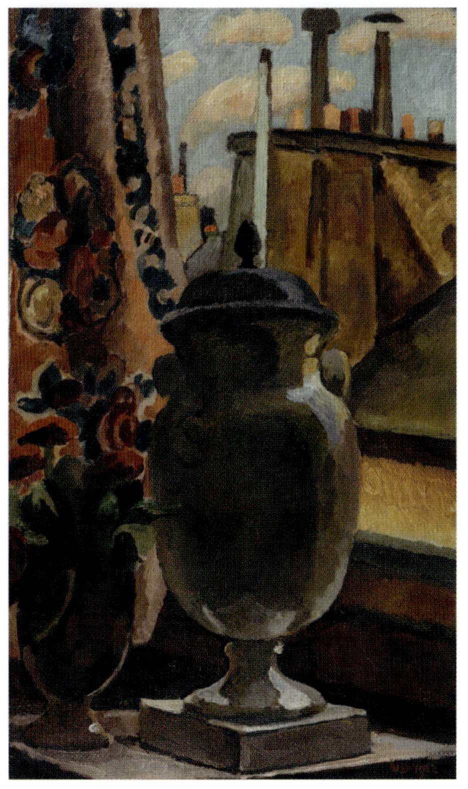

11.4. Vanessa Bell, *Still Life at a Window*
1922, oil on canvas, 598 × 357 mm,
The Courtauld, London (Samuel Courtauld Trust)

porcelain urn is emphatically located in the centre of the composition, almost filling the foreground. Subtle variations in colour define the roundness of its reflective surface. Vanessa contrasts the straight diagonal lines of the table, the plinth, the windowframe and the roofs and chimneys of the urban scene beyond as foils to the vessel's rotundity. A smaller vase of flowers and the gaiety of a pink floral patterned curtain catching the light accentuate the darker solemnity and presence of the urn. Painted within four years of the end of the war in a city that had suffered devastating losses, the still life perpetuates a long tradition of flower paintings as memento mori. Vildrac had told Vanessa 'stories about the war which made it seem more real than anything else I had heard', she wrote.[44] The size and form of the vessel are those of a funerary urn.

Vanessa's letters from Paris describe the company she was keeping and the paintings that impressed her. She proposed a 'scheme for an Omega in Paris', visited Picasso at his studio again and perhaps pointedly described his 'abstractions in stripes & lines' to Roger, who had been ambivalent about Picasso's abstracts when he reviewed his exhibition at the Leicester Galleries in London.[45] She spent time with Nina Hamnett, met Matthew Smith, saw an exhibition of new works by Matisse, 'many of which as usual simply bowl one over', and admired pictures by Modigliani, Rouault and Derain, as well as Renoir, Cézanne, Courbet, Delacroix and Ingres.[46] Although she didn't write about her own paintings she was stimulated by the artists in her circle and their reciprocal visits to one another's studios. She described the sculptor Marcel Gimond, a former pupil of Maillol's, looking at her paintings by the light of an oil lamp and engaging in an argument about art that lasted for three hours.[47] 'We went to see Segonzac one day & saw all his latest things', she wrote to Roger. The French artist André Dunoyer de Segonzac visited Vanessa and Duncan's studios the following day. 'I am glad to say that though he thinks there are superficial likenesses due to working together he also thinks me & Duncan fundamentally quite different! . . . You see how terrified I am of the usual female fate.'[48]

Vanessa packed up her paintings in March 1922, 'a large packet of boards, done up with wooden boards at each side, & a roll of unstretched canvases', and returned to 50 Gordon Square.[49] She was relieved, when she reviewed her work, 'to find that I have quite 30 pictures that I could show'. She was hard at work, she wrote to Roger, 'doing one or two things from sketches & generally trying to finish beginnings for my show'. Imagining the exhibition as an entity, she was concerned that it 'may be rather monotonous, mostly landscapes or still lives'. Although she reiterated her conviction that it was 'fatal to feel bound to do things on purpose to show', she wrote to Roger that she was hiring a model to paint a nude that 'may be showable'.[50] Matisse's new nudes had particularly impressed her in Paris. Ambiguous titles in her exhibition catalogue make it difficult to identify extant paintings with certainty but three figure paintings are listed: *Portrait of Monsieur Simon Bussy*, *Portrait of Mrs X.* and *Portrait of Mrs M.* (fig. 11.5), all of which were portraits rather than nudes.[51] Vanessa was more relaxed now about inviting other artists

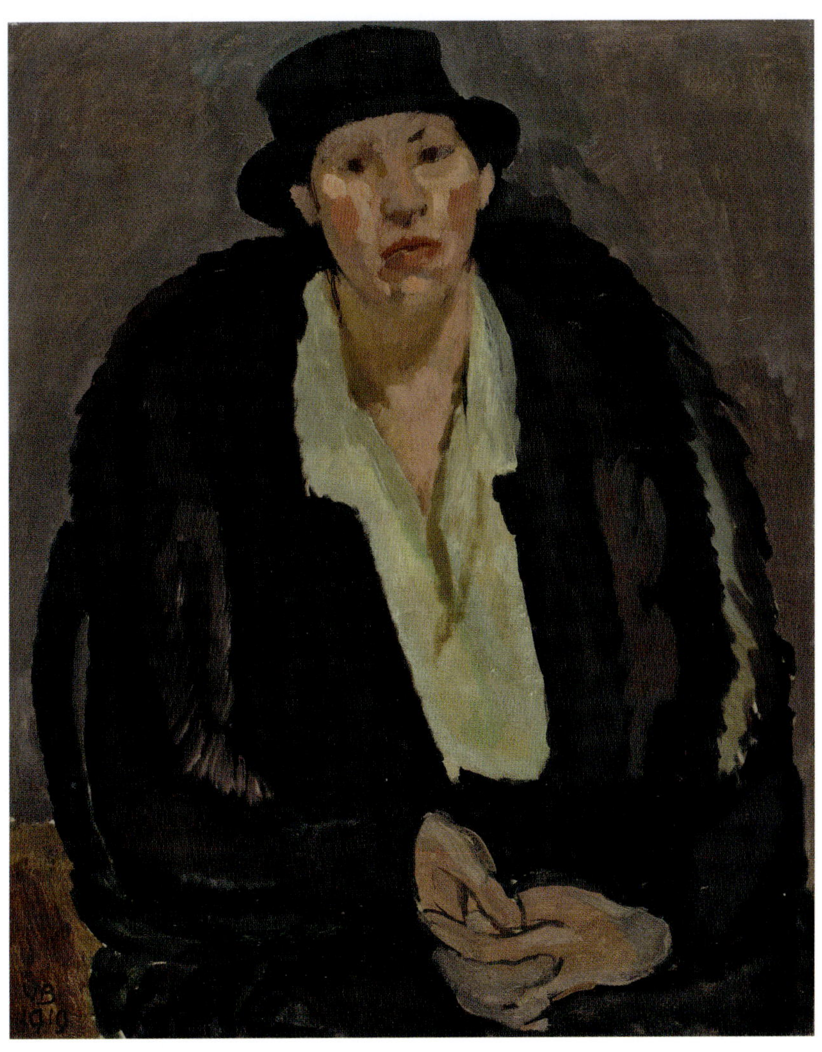

11.5. Vanessa Bell, *Portrait of Mrs M.*
1919, oil on canvas, 682 × 568 mm, Fitzwilliam Museum, Cambridge

into her studio at 50 Gordon Square. Sickert visited her there on a Sunday morning ten days before her exhibition opened. He was in 'tremendous spirits', she wrote to Clive, 'shouting & singing & looking very well & young'. Vanessa was a regular visitor to Maynard's establishment at 46 Gordon Square, which, she wrote, was always full, with bells ringing all day and telegrams arriving even at night.

She entertained Sickert and Thérèse Lessore for lunch there a few days later and Sickert stayed until late afternoon, 'lecturing me on the advantages of painting from drawings'.[52]

Vanessa's exhibition was critically acclaimed and commercially successful. 'I am astonished that I have already sold 7 pictures & drawings, so at any rate I shan't be out of pocket over it. Turner is very much pleased', she wrote to Clive immediately after the opening (which he missed).[53] 'Vanessa Bell', Sickert wrote in a lengthy review for the *Burlington Magazine*, 'has been from the first a painter. Instinct and intelligence and a certain scholarly tact have made of her a good painter. The medium bends beneath her like a horse that knows its rider.' Generous illustrations of *The Seine*, *Portrait of Mrs M.* and *The Frozen Pond* showed the breadth of her work and Sickert drew particular attention to the latter landscape, a view from the Charleston studio: 'the full resources of the medium in all its beauty have been called into requisition in a manner which is nothing less than masterly.' *Portrait of Mrs M.*, he wrote, did not belong to the 'both-eyes, both-ears, both-hands and both-feet school' of portraiture characterised by Thomas Brock's statue of Henry Irving installed outside the National Portrait Gallery. 'Something happens under accomplished fingers, when guided by passion, which makes of the painter a conduit for strange insights greater than, and outside himself.'[54] The portrait was of Doctor Marie Moralt, a friend of Noel Olivier's and an Omega patron who had come to the rescue soon after Angelica was born and prescribed a change of diet that effectively saved the baby's life. Vanessa described her as 'rather a find, as she's certainly sensible and quite easy to say anything to, which is more than most doctors are'.[55] She stayed on at Charleston and returned for a Sunday the following May, when Vanessa and Duncan began to paint her. 'She's simply wonderful to paint', Vanessa wrote to Roger.[56] *Portrait of Mrs M.* is a relatively large work, and when Vanessa and Duncan painted her again it was in Roger's London studio in December 1919 after Vanessa had moved to Regent Square. 'She has only sat twice yet & it's been pitch dark (as it always is) both times', Vanessa wrote.[57] In scale and approach, 'bang in front' with Duncan painting at her side, it is comparable with *Mrs St John Hutchinson* (fig. 0.2). Vanessa was reworking that portrait for the London Group exhibition at around the same time.[58] Here the

background is neutral, however, and the figure of Marie Moralt fills the picture. Although it was not a new portrait, Roger described it as 'perhaps the most brilliant thing in the whole exhibition'. In his perceptive review for the *New Statesman* he observed 'how little the human figure makes its appearance in Vanessa Bell's work; her rooms are empty and her landscapes lonely. This suits, I expect, her habitual mood of grave but joyous contemplation.'[59] Her portraits, he noted, were 'rather detached and external, but these figures are singularly alive and coherent in gesture and expression'. He applauded their 'great power of characterisation'.

The exhibition was distinctively French in content, aligning Vanessa with European modernism. The three Parisian bridges, the views of St Tropez, even a still life, *Aubergines and Onions*, denoted a cosmopolitanism that was exotic and alien to most Londoners in the 1920s. Roger wrote that Vanessa was unequalled among contemporary English artists as a colourist. He described her colour as 'extraordinarily distinguished', highlighting its resonance and harmony in the views of the Pont Neuf:

> There are nothing but a few tones of warm grey and ochre lights, but how luminous and gay the result is . . . She never puts in a touch of merely non-committal or nondescript colour. However apparently neutral or unimportant a tone of grey shadow may appear, its pitch is as exactly found as if it were a piece of brilliant local colour.

Vanessa's salient quality, he concluded, was the purity and 'extreme honesty' of her painting. 'She follows her own vision unhesitatingly and confidingly, without troubling at all whither it may lead her.' He addressed the comparisons between Vanessa and Duncan's painting that she feared would continue to attract prejudice against her as a woman and denigrate her work as derivative:

> She has worked much with Duncan Grant, who is distinguished for the charm and elegance of his 'handwriting'. Her 'handwriting' though it is always distinguished, is not elegant. It is slower, more deliberate, less exhilarating . . . She has, in fact, entirely avoided a mistake . . . She knows that 'handling' and quality of

paint are only really beautiful when they come unconsciously in the process of trying to express an idea.

Roger's thoughtful and generous review describes the depth of understanding and encouragement of Vanessa's work that underpinned his professional and personal relationship with her, even when she was less enthusiastic about his own painting. He concluded that 'the feeling of grave, untroubled serenity and happiness, which is the dominant mood of the exhibition, comes from the singular honesty and purity with which she accepts and expresses her vision'. The exhibition was proof, he wrote, of 'how high a place Vanessa Bell is entitled to in contemporary English art'. His opinion was shared by significant collectors, Frank Hindley Smith and Samuel Courtauld, both advised by Percy Turner. They acquired *Portrait of Mrs M.*, *Interior with a Table*, *On the Seine*, *Le Pont Neuf* and *Still Life at a Window* for their collections.[60]

Vanessa had finally been admitted to the London Group in 1919. She became a driving force alongside Roger and Duncan within that artists' collective and increasingly, through the 1920s, she asserted her position as part of the arts establishment.

12

DECORATIVE DESIGNS

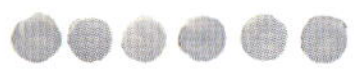

Vanessa's influence as the co-founder of a design partnership with Duncan in the 1920s has barely been recognised. She was an essential practitioner in a history of British design that links the Omega Workshops with the industrial demands of *Britain Can Make It* (an exhibition promoting modern product design and innovation) and the Festival of Britain. After the closure of Omega in 1919 Vanessa developed a flourishing practice that included the design of furniture, ceramics and textiles. Her product designs and her interiors (discussed in the next chapter) flattened the classical forms emerging in her still lifes and expanded her interest in abstraction.[1] Her distinctive book jackets for the Hogarth Press made her sister's novels conspicuous and, working collaboratively with Duncan, the pathway she continued to forge as an artist designer created opportunities for younger artists such as Graham Sutherland, Barbara Hepworth and Ben Nicholson. She was at the forefront of artists designing for industry.

Vanessa's commercial partnership with Duncan made a virtue of the similarities between their styles and it played to their strengths as natural collaborators. As a consequence historians have bypassed their designs because work that cannot be attributed to a single artist is problematic. The partnership served as a decoy, normalising Vanessa and Duncan's living and working arrangements. Clive's family didn't visit Charleston and was unaware that Vanessa and Clive lived apart.[2] When his older brother, Cory, visited them in the South of France Clive ensured that he was also staying with Vanessa at the time. She

described her relief when they departed within days of one another. 'Do you know how people do sometimes take a pleasure in their own power of making conversation?' she wrote to Roger; 'the worst part was dinner in the evenings with Sabine, when Clive drank a good deal of brandy & carried on such elaborate flirtations in French with her that one was simply on tenterhooks as to what he'd say next.'[3] Sabine was employed to help with the children. Vanessa stitched designs by Duncan at Clive's family home in Seend, describing the semblance of ordinary domesticity to Virginia: 'After dinner we sit in the library. I read & cross-stitch. Mrs Bell knits. Mr Bell sleeps & reads the paper.'[4]

Vanessa was the only woman designer in an ambitious exhibition, *Modern Designs in Needlework*, in Percy Moore Turner's Independent Gallery in 1925. 'Mrs Bell and Mr Grant being born decorators . . . have probably produced in this single exhibition more good textile designs than have been produced in England during the present century', Robert Tatlock wrote in the *Burlington Magazine*. He analysed Vanessa's 'return to the fold' from abstraction and her continuing importance as a pioneering figure in the decorative arts.[5] He discussed her work in the context of a 'new school' of designers that included Raoul Dufy and Phyllis Barron. By 1920 Vanessa had a reputation as one of 'the most distinguished and . . . most prominent members of the London Group'.[6] Tatlock described her as 'the most important woman painter in Europe'.[7] Like the majority of British critics, including Clive and Roger, he regarded abstraction as 'a good training' rather than a watershed for modernism. 'In Paris, abstract painting is still much in evidence . . . In English art exhibitions, even in those of the London group, it is practically dead.' Abstract painting, he wrote, was 'simply a composition without a subject', and its principal benefit was to contemporary design: 'some erstwhile abstract painters have discovered ways of applying the principles they mastered to other crafts than that of oil painting.' He described Vanessa's understanding of abstraction as 'the decorative element' underpinning both her paintings and her designs.[8] 'We see at once that the same mind in the same mood conceived both.'[9]

The exhibition perpetuated Vanessa's conviction that artists should design and decorate objects for everyday use. Following Arts and Crafts principles, the catalogue lists the embroiderer as well as

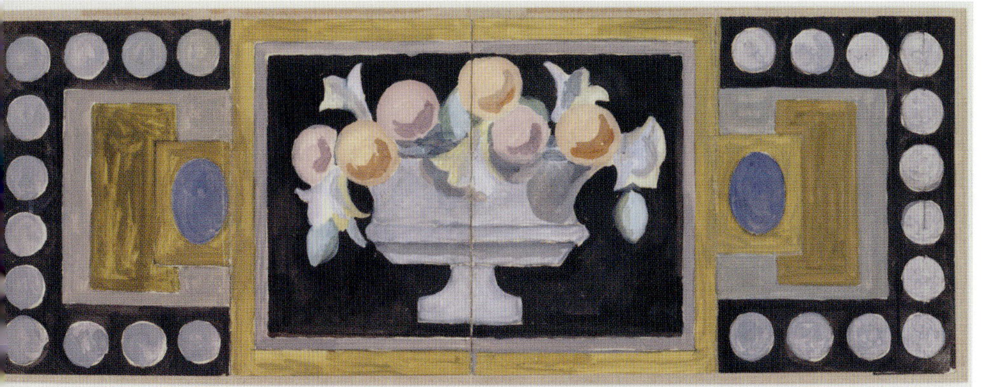

12.1 Vanessa Bell, design for an embroidered stool

c.1925, gouache on paper, 279 × 791 mm, Yale Center for British Art, New Haven, CT

the designer for each piece. All but one were women, articulating another of the hierarchies with which Vanessa had to contend. She designed four of the exhibits but stitched only one, a panel designed by Duncan. Vanessa and Roger were averse to the moral philosophy and the aesthetics of the Arts and Crafts movement and the exhibition aligned more closely with her interest in design collectives and designing for industry. Her fender stool (fig. 12.1) was one of three 'modern designs' selected from *Modern Designs in Needlework* by the British Institute of Industrial Art for a display at the Victoria and Albert Museum a few months later, where it was 'shown in striking contrast with reproductions of old work . . . the organisers of the exhibition had in view the desirability of bringing technicians into touch with modern artists' designs.'[10]

Vanessa had written to Roger from Paris in 1922 about an unexecuted plan she and Duncan were developing with the painter Edward Wolfe to find a new patron for 'an Omega in Paris'. They had someone in mind, Brandon Davies, to finance the business and manage it. 'I said I knew you would take no responsibility & wouldn't want to be much involved', she wrote to Roger, 'but I thought you would consent to do some things such as pottery & that you would help with criticism & would choose artists to work for it.'[11] She wrote to Roger again 'on business' after the needlepoint exhibition, 'to ask you whether you know or can find out how Dufy is employed by the manufacturers . . . Courtauld seems to be thinking of getting us to do some designs for woven stuffs & wants to know how the French employ artists & do the same thing here.'[12] Samuel Courtauld was an important collector and textile manufacturer and in 1925 he joined Maynard and two other guarantors to found the London Artists' Association. Vanessa was one of the founder members.

The London Artists' Association was one of Maynard's first experiments in arts funding, and like the Omega, it was designed to provide artists with a guaranteed income. It organised exhibitions and the salaries of its artists were offset against sales. 'Mr Bernard Adeney, Mr Keith Baynes, Miss [sic] Vanessa Bell, Mr Roger Fry, Mr Duncan Grant, and Mr F. J. Porter, painters, and Mr Frank Dobson, sculptor, appear as the "London Artists' Association," *The Times* announced when their inaugural exhibition opened at the Leicester Galleries in May 1926.[13] All seven artists continued their membership of the London Group and they were soon joined by Edward Wolfe and others. Vanessa measured the success of the first exhibition in terms of sales, which totalled over £1,600. She was assertive in the professional advice that she gave to Maynard: 'Today Duncan & I had to go & have a business talk with Maynard', she wrote to Roger.

> I think he'll pay the artists quarterly in future, at least the guar-
> anteed amount, & possibly also any extra earnings up to date . . .
> I find the only way to deal with him if one wants to make him
> do something is not to listen to a word he says, to let him talk,
> keeping one's attention carefully fixed on one's own ideas, &
> then repeat them regardless of anything he may have said, until
> after several repetitions he may agree or disagree.[14]

The following year Vanessa was given one of the Association's first solo shows.

The London Artists' Association, like the Friday Club, the Grafton Group and the Omega Workshops, afforded Vanessa the freedom to experiment and to exhibit designs as well as recent paintings. 'I suddenly took to the use of the palette knife,' she wrote to Duncan in the summer of 1925. 'I'd always looked askance at it before & been unable to manipulate it at all. I now feel as if I'd never want a brush again'.[15] She exhibited paintings using this new technique in her solo exhibition. 'To a person brought up on smooth painting . . . the frankness of the brushwork may be disconcerting at first', a reviewer wrote, 'but when the eye gets used to the scale of handling, and it is seen how honestly the strokes contribute to the character of the forms produced, what was a hindrance becomes a help to appreciation.'[16] Virginia sent Vanessa her press cuttings to Cassis in the South of France where Duncan had been taken ill and she had rushed to join him. 'I'm afraid, as far as I've heard, my show is a failure as to sales', Vanessa replied, 'it was a humble affair, only a few sketches collected hurriedly at the last moment from last summer's sketches', but she encouraged Virginia to share her thoughts about the show.[17] 'I'm rather nervous about criticising your pictures', Virginia replied, deconstructing them as if they were texts: 'All your pictures are built up of flying phrases. This is to me a very exciting and congenial stage. They have an air of complete spontaneity.' She was intrigued, seduced and satisfied, she wrote, by Vanessa's use of colour. 'I think we are now at the same point; both mistresses of our medium as never before: both therefore confronted with entirely new problems of structure.'[18] Two months later Vanessa would attempt an equally candid and profoundly supportive response to Virginia's latest novel, *To the Lighthouse*.

Vanessa used her influence within the London Artists' Association and the London Group to broaden the scope of their exhibitions, proposing that they include design. She often prioritised her work with Duncan on the design and decoration of interiors and in December 1925, working in the new studio at Charleston, her focus was the design of carpets and textiles: 'I intend at present to work entirely at designs for stuffs and carpets', she wrote to Duncan. 'I hope you'll do some too or else I fear they'll think us very unpractical. Has anything been heard of Kauffer?'[19] She wrote again the following week that her carpet design had become 'hideous and rather like a Wadsworth . . . I must do another.'[20] She had three carpets 'ready to send' and was working exclusively on textiles, she wrote to Duncan, repeating her encouragement that he, too, should focus on design: 'I feel unless one really gives up a week or two to it one will never get any done.'[21] The carpets and fabrics may have been for one of their interior commissions or a consequence of her association with Samuel Courtauld or with Allan Walton, who had joined the London Group that year.

Vanessa also suggested to Duncan that they send designs for decorative panels rather than paintings to the London Group. They were under pressure to produce new work for an exhibition that the London Artists' Association would tour to Berlin and New York, and as they had designs on approval with Mary Hutchinson at her home in Hammersmith Vanessa wrote: 'Would it be a good plan to consult Porter about the decorations?' (Frederick Porter was vice-president of the London Group.) 'I'm rather in favour of removing them from Mary's house anyhow as they've had quite long enough to make up their minds – the things will get dirty & torn'. Exhibiting the decorations, she argued, 'would save a picture for other purposes'.[22] Their two watercolour caryatid designs were both catalogued under Duncan's name but when Clive reviewed the London Group exhibition for *Vogue* they were separately attributed to Vanessa and to Duncan. 'Of the three outstanding works' in the show, he wrote, 'two are the big cartoons for a decoration by Duncan Grant and Vanessa Bell. These dominate the gallery'.[23]

Vanessa was fashionable in the 1920s. British *Vogue* featured her interiors and designs as well as a substantial article, 'The Work of a Woman Painter: Vanessa Bell', by Roger.[24] 'Modern English Decoration. Some Examples of the Interesting Work of Duncan Grant and Vanessa Bell', also in *Vogue*, summarised their pre-war work for Omega 'under the leadership of Roger Fry' before focusing on more recent designs by 'the firm of Grant and Bell'. 'They can turn their versatile hands to anything, from the complete scheme of decoration down to the last detail of a room, to the painting of a bowl, a tile, a screen or a cushion, the designing of a carpet or a chair-cover', the journalist enthused. Photographs included one of their interiors for Mary showing how Vanessa and Duncan's designs could incorporate her eclectic collection of furniture, rugs and modern paintings. They were 'deliberately fanciful, carefully capricious. On the walls are pictures by Matisse and Derain, Dufy and Mary Laurencin, but holding these together, framing them, and keeping them on terms are the decorations arranged by Duncan Grant and Vanessa Bell.'[25] It was the decorative panel designs for this house that the London Group included in its exhibition.

The lead images for the *Vogue* article were of the sitting room that Vanessa and Duncan designed for Virginia and Leonard at 52

Tavistock Square in Bloomsbury. Under the editorship of Dorothy Todd and her partner, the fashion editor Madge Garland, British *Vogue* introduced its readers to the homes and faces of celebrated modernists. Todd cultivated the Bloomsbury Group, regarding the avant-garde as integral to the fashionable world in London and Paris. The article describes Virginia as 'the brilliant author of *Jacob's Room* and *The Voyage Out*'. There was an edge of competition between Virginia and Vanessa in the 1920s. They had found a way to work together as professionals, however, as soon as the Hogarth Press was founded in 1917. They created a distinctive brand for the Press, reiterating the clearly distinguished areas of expertise and mutual support that had formed the basis of their sisterhood since childhood. 'It will be very exciting when you actually set up your press', Vanessa wrote to Virginia. 'Tell me if you want us to do any marbled papers for you.'[26] When Virginia asked her for a woodcut that could be used as a cover for a range of titles, simply by changing the lettering, she replied:

> I can do a design if you like but I have another suggestion to make as I think you'd get very tired of always using the same cover. Why not have marbled covers done with the same mixture of paint & paste with which the Omega does their printed papers? . . . I don't see why they should be at all expensive as marbling is very quick work. If done with the same mixture it would be as permanent as printing.

She suggested that a different colour scheme be used for each book and that the title and author be printed onto 'stick on labels'.[27] The first edition of *Kew Gardens* is characteristic of this early branding and the label bears Vanessa's name beneath that of her sister as the author of its woodcut illustrations.[28]

Just as Virginia and Leonard learned the mechanics of printing, Vanessa (together with Roger and Duncan) taught herself to make woodcuts. She found the cutting difficult while she was pregnant with Angelica. 'The bother is that one has to use a certain amount of force & stoop over the block a good deal to cut at all deeply', she wrote to Virginia. 'I rather doubt if I shall be able to do many more till after the baby is born.'[29] The discipline of cutting encouraged her to simplify her designs. She produced two woodcuts, *Nude* and *Dahlias*, for a book of *Original Woodcuts by Various Artists* that the Hogarth Press originally planned to publish, though concerns over print quality and creative control led the Omega to produce the volume (fig. 12.2). The reductive power of Vanessa's prints, balancing the negative, cut-away areas of white against black shadows and outlines, demonstrates her natural facility as a graphic artist. *Nude* adapts the composition of her recent painting *The Tub*, compressing the design and drawing the nude figure into the foreground. A rhythm of curves runs through the composition from the flowers in the background to the fluid line of the woman's hip and calf.

Vanessa designed the colophon for the Hogarth Press and a succession of strikingly original and experimental book jackets for her sister. The cover for *Monday or Tuesday*, published in 1921, is uncompromising in its modernity as an abstract design.[30] It is predominantly black, expressing the technical challenges of block cutting with its white, uneven lettering and central motif. The volume included four full-page illustrations by Vanessa.

Correspondence between Virginia and Vanessa 'on business' was often laced with humour. 'Would you have the great kindness to accept a small commission from me – to wit £1.1.–' Virginia wrote to Vanessa from Monk's House. 'We have got some new dining room chairs, and I find embroidery so soothing to the head that I want to work a cushion while I am here.'[31] In 1929 she wrote again 'to Bell.

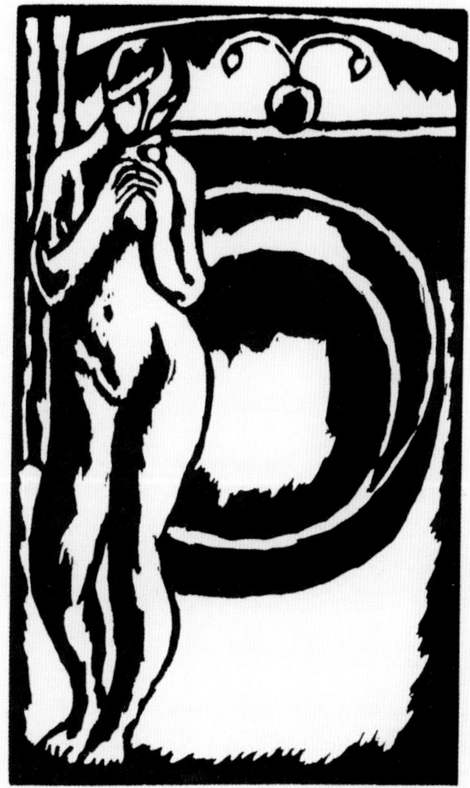

12.2. Vanessa Bell, *Nude* 1918, published in *Original Woodcuts by Various Artists* (London: Omega Workshops, 1918), The Charleston Trust

Decorator', requesting an estimate for a painted dinner table, two bouquets of artificial flowers and 'Have you got one of those tile tables? If so what price? or could you make one? . . . and please quote best terms.'[32] Vanessa suggested that she pay only the material costs when she ordered a painted table and chairs, cushions, lampshades, a mirror, six plates and a decorated bowl: 'One gets all the benefits of *The Lighthouse* or *Orlando* for a few shillings – or even free', she wrote to Virginia, 'so why shouldn't you get some benefits such as they are out of me?'[33] Virginia insisted on paying full price because, she wrote, 'if you gave me the things, then we could never ask you to do us furniture again . . . and there are other things I want.' She encouraged Vanessa, describing a set of chairs, now at Monk's House, that her sister had designed and painted: 'I get pleasure of at least three sorts every day: comfort; aesthetic; snob. Everyone who comes throws up their hands – says where do you get these lovely things? . . . I don't deny that in aesthetics, about chairs and covers, I am so wholly snobbish I am ashamed.'[34]

Vanessa designed furniture as well as decorating it, and the simple table, now at Monk's House, was constructed to her design.[35] At Charleston a circular, drop-leaf table with a detachable leg, set aside when one of the leaves was not extended, is also likely to have been Vanessa's work.[36] Her painted surfaces were not impromptu. She designed her decorations on paper for needlepoint as well as furniture, enabling her to carry out the work herself or in partnership with Duncan: 'We have finished the dining room table & got it with great difficulty into the dining room where I think it is a great success', she wrote to Roger from Charleston. 'At any rate there is room for people round it & food on it.'[37] When the painted surface became worn by use she produced a new design and repainted it (fig. 12.3).

The range of products that Virginia ordered in the spring of 1929, reiterating the list that *Vogue* had outlined nearly five years earlier, offers a rare insight into 'the firm of Grant and Bell'. It benefited from Bloomsbury's increasingly fashionable status as the novels and biographies of Virginia and Lytton, the political theories of Maynard and Leonard, and the art criticism of Roger and Clive gained traction. 'Two of the most famous of the Bloomsbury "set," Duncan Grant and Vanessa Bell, have been making chairs, tables, firescreens and radiator covers', Marianne Mayfayre noted in a column on spring

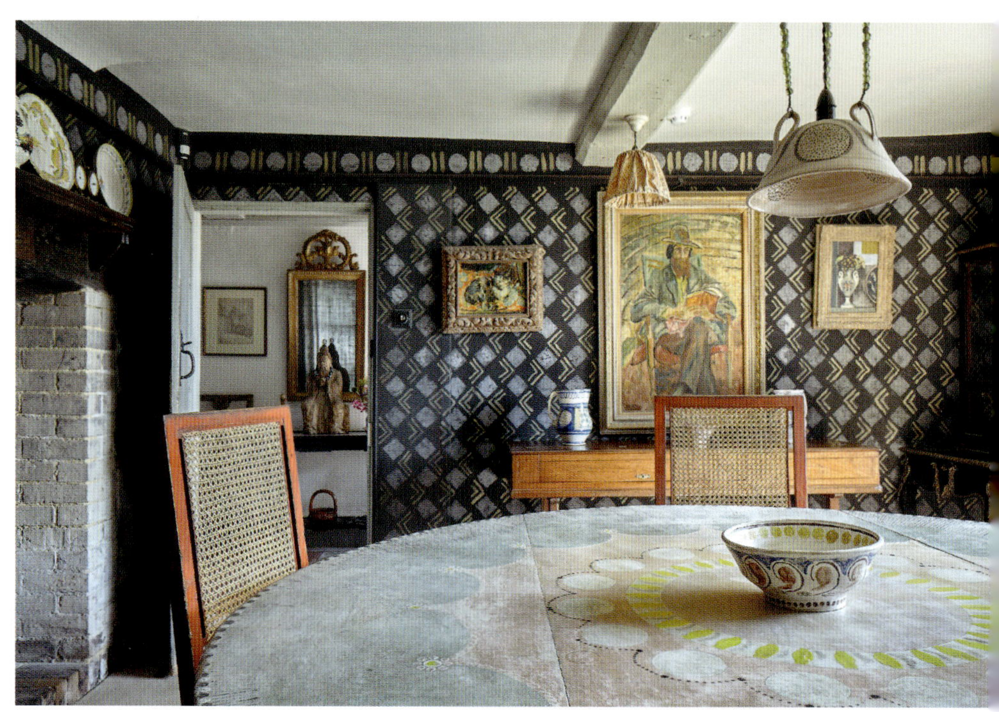

12.3. Vanessa Bell, circular painted table

c.1933, detail, painted wood, 705 × 1990 mm, diameter, The Charleston Trust.
Surface decoration repainted to a new design c.1952.

fashions for the *Daily Telegraph*. She named Rosamond Lehmann and Virginia as celebrity owners of low, square tables, with tops 'composed of thirty-six tiles, baked, painted with metalline paints, and then baked again and cemented in . . . one by Duncan Grant and one by Vanessa Bell'.[38]

The artists issued a typed circular in 1926 inviting orders for painted tiles that could be used for bathrooms and fireplaces.[39] One such panel of nine tiles was exhibited at the V&A 'under the auspices of the British Institute of Industrial Art'. It is conspicuously signed and dated 'Vanessa Bell 1926' (fig. 12.4).[40] It shows her sophistication as a decorator and the enduring influence of Matisse on her work. The subject, three nude bathers, recalls her earlier engagement with the *baigneuses* of Cézanne and Matisse and reasserts Vanessa's self-fashioning as a European modernist. By the 1920s Vanessa was renowned as a colourist and even with a restricted palette her juxtaposition of colours is striking. Thick blue and yellow lines, articulated against the

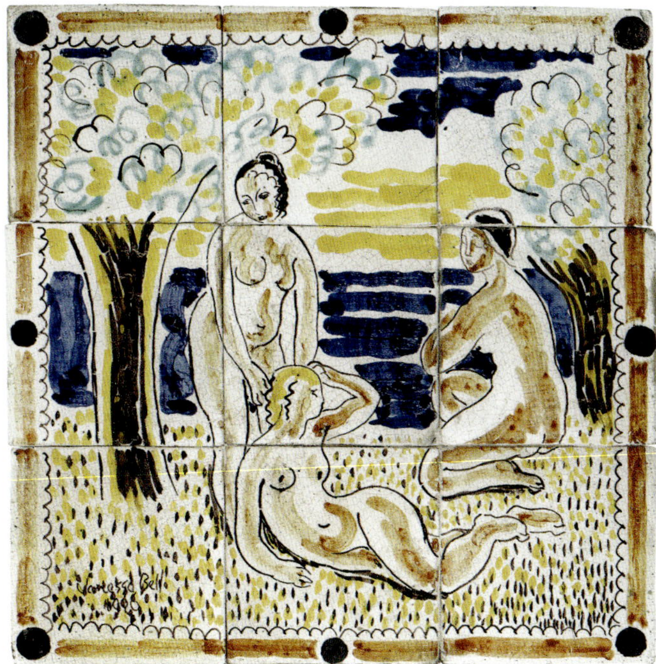

12.4. Vanessa Bell, tile panel

1926, tin-glazed earthenware, painted, 460 × 460 mm, Victoria and Albert Museum, London

white ground of the tiles, evoke the heat of the Mediterranean. Brown and yellow are sparingly used to highlight the contours of the three figures, but here Vanessa also demonstrates her mastery of drawing. Throughout the composition a playful and exquisitely sensitive use of line, more often associated with Duncan's designs than Vanessa's, outlines figures, trees, foliage and the composition's decorative frame. The panel has the immediacy of a watercolour sketch and yet every mark is considered. The directional use of brushwork – vertical for tree trunks and grass, horizontal for water – and the abstract framing device of circles connected by long sweeping strokes of brown complete the deceptively simple composition. The panel and its initial display positioned Vanessa in the vanguard of artists promoted by the British Institute of Industrial Art and the V&A. It justifies her reputation in the 1920s as a designer.

Vanessa was an early initiator of a movement to encourage manufacturers and contemporary artists to collaborate and so improve industrial design. This would be championed by individual critics such as Herbert Read and Nikolaus Pevsner, by institutions including the

British Institute of Industrial Art with its exhibitions at the V&A and by the *Studio* magazine. An exhibition of *Decorative Work, Stage and Other Designs* at the Goupil Gallery promoted the concept in January 1930. 'An increasing number of people nowadays are complaining of the difficulty of finding good designs in the ordinary objects of house furnishing, such as fabrics for curtains and chair covers, carpets, pottery &c.', the *Daily Telegraph* noted. The reviewer described 'attractive designs for wall decorations, panels and tiles' by Vanessa in the exhibition alongside rugs and fabrics designed by Marion Dorn, Enid Marx, Phyllis Barron, Edward McKnight Kauffer and others: 'there is much here that is really excellent', the reviewer concluded, hoping that 'seeing examples of their work will encourage the public, and, more important still, the great manufacturing firms, to make use of it'.[41] Paul Nash noted that artists as well as manufacturers were reluctant to diversify. 'In England', he wrote, 'it is still considered, by some artists, rather undignified to do anything but paint'.

> In France, for whatever reason, even the most eminent painters practise versatility; obviously not from necessity, as some others must, to boil the pot, but, it would seem, out of pure enjoyment. Picasso, Matisse and Derain have all illustrated books and made scenes for the stage, Leger [sic] designs rugs, Dufy textiles and wallpapers, Lurçat almost everything in applied art.[42]

The following year the London Artists' Association staged an important exhibition at the Cooling Galleries that launched a new range of fabrics designed by its members and manufactured by Allan Walton Ltd. Allan had been a member of the London Group since 1925, and like Vanessa and Duncan, he was an accomplished designer as well as a painter. He had designed the interior for Boulestin's Restaurant Français in Leicester Square that year and he was establishing a reputation as an interior designer. Initially (and briefly) he had trained to become an architect before attending the Slade and other art schools. He was on the executive committee for the *London Group Retrospective Exhibition* with Roger and Edward Wolfe in 1928 and his cover design for its catalogue was clearly influenced by Vanessa. His family background was in textiles. John Walton of Glossop's finishing works was established by the mid-nineteenth century and it

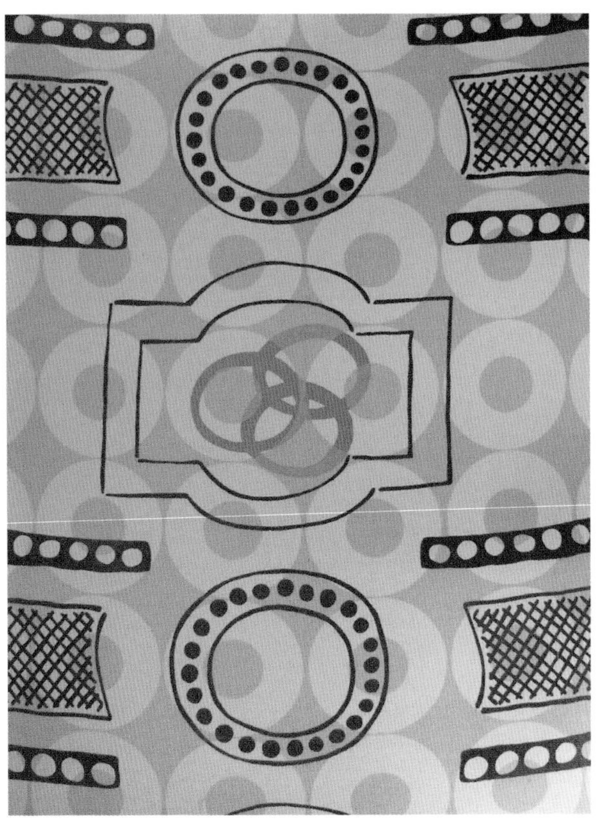

12.5. Vanessa Bell, *Abstract*
c.1931, furnishing fabric, The Charleston Trust

was described in the 1950s as 'among the most modern and efficient in the world'.[43] Finishing fabrics included bleaching, dyeing and printing. Allan and his brother Roger, who had left school to work in the family business after their father's death, established their own independent company specialising in designer fabrics in 1931. Their printing process was 'new and secret, enabling short lengths of the material to be sold without a loss'. This, Cyril Connolly explained in the *Architectural Review*, made it 'less necessary to play down to the public, experiments can be made, designs tried out without the risk of failure'.[44]

Connolly described the London Artists' Association exhibition as 'a noble and successful experiment, but not a daring one'. 'Vanessa Bell's squares and circles alone', he wrote, 'redeem the feathery splodges'.[45] Vanessa's design for Allan Walton Ltd, *Abstract*, also made a striking impression on a reviewer for *The Times*: 'Mrs Bell has produced an ingenious design of three intersecting rings and other geometrical forms constructed of black spots' (fig. 12.5). The two reviewers disagreed over other exhibits at the Cooling Galleries. *The Times* praised ceramics by Vanessa and Duncan: 'their decorations are both of great originality and skilfully adapted to the forms of the pots'.[46] Connolly dismissed them as 'disappointing . . . the coloured ones inevitably suggested the cover of another bad novel from a certain Press.' He compared the exhibition with a show of paintings by the London Group at Agnews Gallery. 'The most striking fact to emerge is the astonishing progress of Vanessa Bell', he wrote, describing her work as 'the most enlightened at the Cooling Galleries'. 'The importance of the exhibition is that it promises a closer alliance between artist and manufacturer'.[47]

Three of the new Allan Walton textiles were shown again a few months later at the Zwemmer Gallery in a *Room and Book* exhibition. It coincided with a publication with the same name by Paul Nash.[48] He reviewed the exhibition for the *Listener*: 'Mr Walton is a painter and it is to painters rather than to craftsmen that he has applied for textile designs', he wrote. 'Duncan Grant, Vanessa Bell, Keith Baynes and Bernard Adeney form the nucleus of his experiment. That experiment has been completely successful within the limits imposed, and its range is now being extended.' Other designers included Frank Dobson, H.J. Bull, Noel Gifford, Cedric Morris and Walton himself. His intention was to gradually enlist more artists to make his range representative of 'contemporary expression'.[49] Nash explained the reasons for Walton's success: 'He first made certain of an appropriate and economical material and secured a block cutter able to *interpret*, instead of copy, the vagaries of a painter's technique. He then explained the limitations of the process to his fellow workers and encouraged them to do what they pleased.' Prices ranged from *9s. 9d.* to *19s. 9d.* a yard (Omega linens had started at *2s. 9d.*), depending on the fabric and the number of colours in the design. Walton described a traditional linen as his preferred fabric: 'it is durable, it has high quality of surface, and it takes the colour well', but the patterns were also printed onto spun satin and a cotton and rayon mix.[50] Vanessa and Duncan's designs were not selected for *Room and Book* but the exhibition describes an important transition, as the new printed textiles were shown alongside work by a younger generation of modernists. They included Henry Moore, Barbara Hepworth, Ben Nicholson and Serge Chermayeff. Gordon Russell furniture and Best & Lloyd lamps in the exhibition heralded the austere simplicity that would become synonymous with the International Style of modernism. There was also a place in this aesthetic for textile designers Phyllis Barron, Dorothy Larcher and Enid Marx, women who perpetuated techniques used by the Omega Workshops of engraving their own blocks and dyeing and printing their fabrics by hand.

Vanessa's sharply original *Abstract* (fig. 12.5) was sold at Fortnum & Mason's new contemporary decoration department and at Heal's. It was featured again in the *Architectural Review* when Cyril Connolly wrote a sardonic review of 'A Music Room Decorated, Furnished and Painted by Vanessa Bell and Duncan Grant' at the Lefevre Galleries. He described it as 'a climax in the work of these artists' and the article is generously illustrated, showing the linen curtains and covers designed by Duncan for Allan Walton in a room setting filled with painted furniture, ceramics, wall panels and rugs designed by the two artists. Virginia underwrote the costs of the exhibition and many of the exhibits found permanent homes at Monk's House and Charleston, but the concept of a music room, extravagantly decorated for 'one of our remaining merchant princes', was incompatible with the direction of modernism in the inter-war years when radical new houses and apartments were streamlined and compact. Connolly concluded that the exhibition was primarily of interest to 'the connoisseur who enjoys discriminating between the work of the two painters, one so much better than the other'.[51]

Vanessa was devastated in September 1934 by the sudden death of Roger Fry. The following month her designs were featured in another collaborative venture between artists and industry and Fry's absence from these schemes is notable. 'It has taken nearly two years to organize this display', a reviewer wrote of *Modern Art for the Table*, a selling exhibition at Harrods.[52] The project was conceived by the sales manager for Foley China, Thomas Acland Fennemore, as well as Graham Sutherland and his friend Milner Gray, one of the founder members of the Society of Industrial Artists. Vanessa was on the initial list of artists who were selected because their names were synonymous with modernity in the public imagination. Others included the Unit One group, and as the project expanded to an industrial scale a total of 28 artists became involved. They were each paid £10 per design plus royalties to decorate tea services manufactured by Foley and Wilkinson using standard china blanks. The project was not a commercial success – Clarice Cliff wrote that it was the closest thing to a flop she had ever been associated with – though she recalled: 'It undoubtedly changed the trend of thought in design throughout the pottery district', and it was cited in Pevsner's influential survey a few years later, *An Enquiry into Industrial Art in England*.[53] Vanessa's glassware as well as her tea service were included in the exhibition. 'It seems to me cut glass designing should be the most severe of all the arts', she wrote to Duncan. 'It depends simply upon proportion – one has nothing else to rely on.'[54] Vanessa and Duncan were commissioned, too, to decorate dinner services for Clarice Cliff's *Bizarre* range, manufactured by Wilkinson's. Vanessa's strikingly simple blue and white plates, jug and tureen were included in an *Exhibition of British Art in Industry* at the Royal Academy in 1935, where she also showed a printed linen in a display of Walton textiles (fig. 12.6).[55] Allan Walton, Herbert Read and Kenneth Clark (who had recently been appointed director of the National Gallery and surveyor of the king's pictures) were three of the speakers who gave lectures to accompany the show.

If Vanessa's product designs distinguished her work from that of Duncan and located her in the vanguard of a younger generation of artists making their services available to industry she was also capable, as Hana Leaper and Christopher Reed have discussed, of taking a more quizzical and ironic approach to commissions. The Harrods project coincided with a unique *Famous Women Dinner Service* comprising around 140 pieces that Vanessa and Duncan decorated for Kenneth and Jane Clark.[56] 'We had great difficulty in choosing some sort of general idea for the service', Vanessa wrote to Roger, 'we thought there ought to be some sort of connecting subject. At last we decided to do portraits of celebrated females – it ought to please the feminists – of all times!'[57] Their styles are almost indistinguishable in a set of 50 plates representing celebrated queens, performers, authors

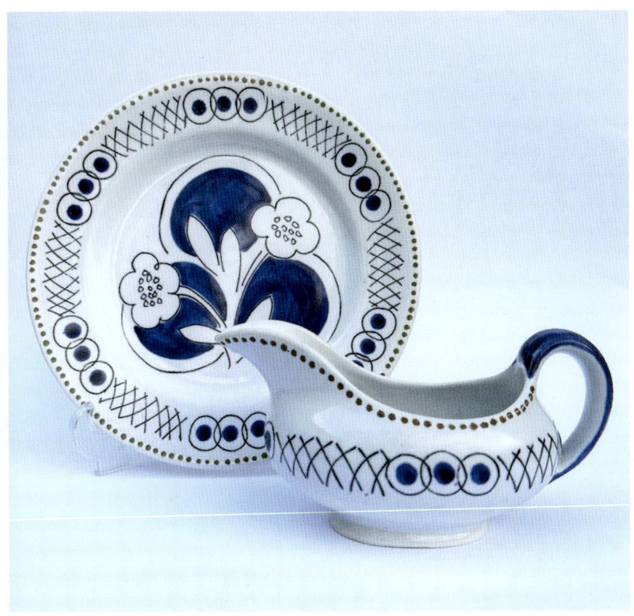

and beauties. They include portraits of Vanessa and of Duncan, the only honorary woman in the service. Vanessa complained that 'the K. Clarks suddenly appeared today to see their service & now we've got to give a party on Thursday to show it to people before it goes to them'.[58] She was practised, however, in promoting her work. When Virginia 'suddenly offered' to write a foreword for the catalogue to her 1930 solo exhibition with the London Artists' Association she dutifully went to tea with her to 'listen to her preface which made me rather uncomfortable, it's such an advertisement but I suppose that's what such things should be'.[59]

Vanessa's importance and her influence as a modernist designer did not usurp her focus on painting. Her solo exhibitions with the London Artists' Association in 1930 and 1934 were exclusively of paintings. Virginia wrote catalogue forewords for both of them. 'That a woman should hold a show of pictures in Bond Street,' she wrote in 1930, less than six months after the publication of *A Room of One's Own*: 'But Mrs Bell has a certain reputation it cannot be denied.' She contextualised her sister as a woman painter: 'Berthe Morisot, Marie Laurencin, Vanessa Bell – such is the stereotyped phrase which comes to mind when her name is mentioned', and she quoted a critic who described her as 'the most considerable painter of her own sex now alive'. Virginia toyed with the issues of gender that had plagued her own career as well as her sister's:

> One says, Anyhow Mrs Bell is a woman; and then half way round the room one says, But she may be a man. One says, She is interested in children; one has to add, But she is equally interested in rocks. One asks, Does she show any special knowledge of clothes? One replies, Stark nakedness seems to please her as well . . . Is she – for our patience is becoming exhausted – not a woman at all, but a mixture of Goddess and peasant, treading the clouds with her feet and with her hands shelling peas?[60]

She described the serene and ordered world that the exhibition evoked, the absence of narrative content in her sister's paintings and, following the dictates of significant form, their emotional charge.

Vanessa sent a copy of the catalogue to Clive (who again missed the exhibition). She played down its importance in her letter to him, describing instead Eddy Sackville-West's reaction when he 'came in to see a portrait of himself I am showing & nearly died of his proximity to a fat female nude'.[61] Writing to Duncan, she rejoiced that Virginia's support had made her 'a best seller . . . I have sold 12 pictures so far, amounting to 330 guineas, far more than I've ever done before'. She named the buyers who were almost literally fighting over her pictures but she also interrogated a review by Charles Marriott in *The Times*. 'Not for a long time have we seen such a sudden jump forward as that made by Mrs Vanessa Bell in her recent paintings,' he wrote, 'and the reason for the jump is evident. Mrs Bell has decided to paint unguardedly'. He quoted extensively from Virginia's foreword, demonstrating its influence, but questioned whether Vanessa was painting 'a bit above the scale for which she is prepared by knowledge'.[62] 'Please tell me if you think Marriott is right in his criticisms', Vanessa wrote to Duncan, 'but if one never tried to do what one can't, I don't think one would ever do what one can, if you know what I mean.'[63]

13

INTERIOR WORLDS

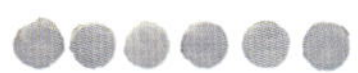

> Charleston in its heyday . . . [was] an enchanted place – a place
> of such potent individuality that whenever I stayed there I came
> away grateful to it, as it were, for giving me so much pleasure,
> so many rich and varied visual sensations, such *talk*, such an
> awareness that lives were being intensely and purposefully led
> there – for being *itself* in fact.[1]

In her description of Charleston, which she visited from the 1920s, Frances Partridge named Vanessa as the creator of its unique atmosphere and aesthetic. For Vanessa's granddaughter, Henrietta, it was synonymous with her personality: 'the essence of the house, this dichotomy between liberty and order, stemmed directly from her.'[2]

Vanessa and Duncan designed interiors for friends and family who were familiar with Charleston or their rooms in London. These operated as satellite spaces, reflecting the radical values, and enabling the disinhibited commitment to life and work, which were characteristic of Bloomsbury. The ephemeral interior worlds that Vanessa created with Duncan are important, as Christopher Reed has brilliantly demonstrated, as signifiers of Bloomsbury's identity as an influential subculture.[3]

Vanessa's experimental use of colour and surface texture to create these sensory interiors can only be imagined. It is inadequately recorded in black-and-white photographs and brief accounts, but for her clients it was her most daring quality. A few weeks after Mary and Clive saw the sitting room at Charleston with its turquoise colour-washed walls Vanessa painted River House in Hammersmith for Mary with apricot distemper. 'Duncan & I think of coming up to do Mary's room on Saturday week & working at it all Sunday. Could you have us then?' she wrote to Virginia in June 1917.[4] Hogarth House, Virginia's home in Richmond, was half an hour from River House by Underground.

Vanessa and Duncan began the room together and when he returned to Charleston in time for farm labouring on Monday morning Vanessa carried on with the painting. 'I worked hard all today & in the end had only done the walls . . . I had to wash off the grey paint from the experimental wall & had to make some more apricot paint & give it two coats'. She described the messiness of the process: 'I had to redo most of the big wall as the trickles showed so much, & then all had to be touched up at the edges'. Mary, she wrote, had looked into the room after they had left on Sunday evening and 'professed not to mind the mess at all . . . I had her with me all the afternoon & we had a long talk.' Vanessa wrote that she hoped to paint the mantelpiece, windows and door with an oil-based paint the following day 'but I see I may not. God knows when I shall return.'[5] River House was featured in *Vogue* with black-and-white photographs showing Mary's bedroom, drawing room, inner drawing room and study, all decorated over a period of 18 months. The walls were divided into bands of colour, above and below cornice and dado rails, and the article describes the extraordinary colour schemes. Mary's bedroom was 'black and warm apricot' with a yellow bed. In the drawing room, too, the walls were apricot with 'greenish yellow' architraves, and the study had 'walls of lemon yellow, and a deep frieze reddish ochre in colour'.[6]

Both Mary and Maynard were Bloomsbury clients who repeatedly commissioned interiors from Vanessa and Duncan and acquired their paintings and furniture. *Vogue* illustrated an Omega table, tray, textiles and ceramics as well as Mary's bedstead, *Nude with Poppies*, which Vanessa had painted for her the previous year.[7] Vanessa and Duncan had decorated rooms at Eleanor House and their work evolved through the River House rooms. 'I don't think we shall do Mary's other room just yet', Vanessa wrote to Virginia, 'perhaps not till she goes away, when we could possibly live in her house undisturbed which would be an advantage.'[8] They developed techniques

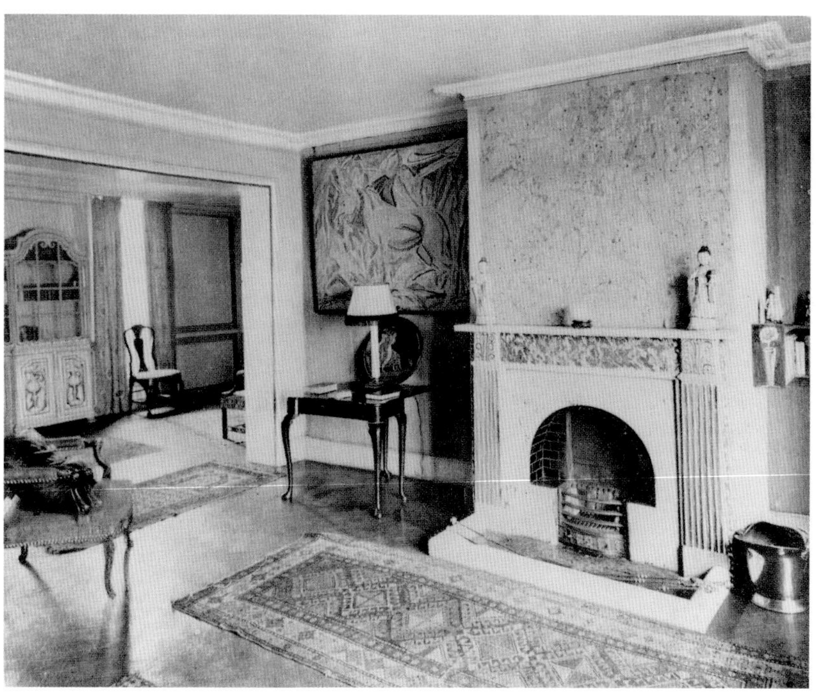

13.1. Vanessa Bell and Duncan Grant, drawing room at River House, Hammersmith, 1918–19, photograph from *Vogue*, early February 1919. The photograph shows the écriture wallpaper, painted fire surround, cabinet and the end of a painted bookshelf. Duncan's painted *Trojan Women* tray and *The Ass* are displayed to the left of the chimneybreast.

to reduce the amount of time that they worked on site and to confine the paint runs and spillages that their methods necessitated to their own studios: 'do you think you could get some white wall paper [sic] to marble for River House?' Vanessa wrote to Duncan. 'We really ought to do that.'⁹ The 'marbled' paper, based on their experiments at Wissett, was a radical innovation (see p. 184). It was a modernist riff on the traditional decorating technique of painting surfaces to resemble marble. Prefiguring the action painting of the 1950s, paint was spattered and dripped onto the paper, making visible the physical act of painting. At River House it was featured in the drawing room within a painted frame of cobalt blue to pattern the chimneybreast, the visual focus of the room (fig. 13.1). The paper was described as 'écriture' and featured in subsequent issues of *Vogue*. Similar papers were created for a frieze at 52 Tavistock Square and alcoves in Angus Davidson's Bloomsbury rooms: 'The narrow frieze round the top of the wall is in an amusing wall-paper made simply by an *écriture* of brush-strokes in subdued violet on a white and lemon yellow ground', *Vogue* reported. The magazine described the paper in the dining room alcove to Angus's room as 'of the same kind . . . except in that this case the *écriture* is of deep blue and pale grey, bespattered with red spots, on a white ground. The method sounds odd and rather haphazard, but the result is enchanting, and gives a slightly Chinese effect.' All of the work, they reassured their readers, was carried out by Vanessa and Duncan 'with their own hands, in their large studio' and was distinguished by its 'charming, lively, and extremely original colour'.[10]

Roger complained that Mary should have commissioned her rooms through the Omega Workshops and that by working for her directly Vanessa and Duncan imperilled the business. 'I want to help & not hinder the Omega & so does Duncan', Vanessa replied, 'we should both be quite ready to work through it' – but she reasoned that Duncan could now earn much more from the sale of his paintings than from working for the Workshops 'at a low rate . . . he hasn't had any work from the Omega or hardly any for the last two years'.[11] By the summer of 1917 Roger was already uncertain of the Omega's viability: 'we don't know yet whether the Omega will survive. I should like to kill it, personally', he wrote to Vanessa, but he was anxious that she and Duncan should not be seen as 'a rival firm'.[12] Vanessa's practice as a decorator was firmly rooted in her experience at the Workshops but by 1917 she was disassociating her work from that of Roger. When he took her to see a flat he had recently decorated and furnished she was 'so overcome with horror on first entering that I didn't know how to conceal it', she wrote to Duncan. It was 'simply chock full' of Omega furniture. 'It seemed to me to be full also of colours which didn't make colour, & to be thin & shiny in quality.'[13]

Vanessa and Duncan redecorated the first-floor drawing room and several other rooms at 46 Gordon Square for Maynard in a style that contrasts with this crowded interior and reflects Vanessa's initial intention to use furniture sparingly at Charleston. Maynard's biographer was struck by the interior's 'assertion of modernity' when he first met him in the drawing room in 1922. 'The room itself made a strong impression. It seemed empty, devoid of the usual ornaments and appendages, in a style that was rapidly to come into fashion but was strange to me'. The room was simply furnished with the small table at which they would have lunch, 'exceedingly comfortable' armchairs and two 'very modern' pictures. The effect, he wrote, was to provide 'a slightly exciting background' to Keynes as a public figure.[14] Vanessa and Duncan prepared carpet designs and colour palettes for Maynard (fig. 13.2). She wrote to Roger that the commission included painted panels for the large folding doors in her former studio and Keynes wrote to his mother that when it was finished his drawing room would be 'the flashiest room in London'.[15]

The door panels must have been painted at Charleston because Vanessa planned to take them to Gordon Square with Duncan when he could take time away from his farm work and 'put them up there & paint the doors round them'. She had also promised 'to choose new covers, etc. for the room. I expect we shall be there about a week',

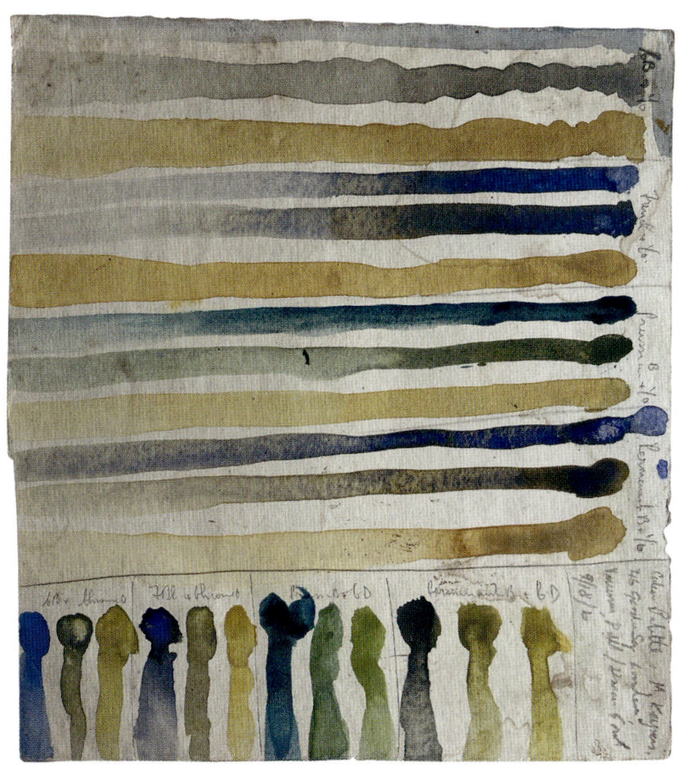

13.2. Vanessa Bell and Duncan Grant, colour palette for M. Keynes. 46 Gordon Square
1918, watercolour and pencil on paper, 174 × 189 mm, private collection

she wrote to Roger.[16] A few weeks later, however, when she was six months pregnant, Vanessa feared she was having another miscarriage. Duncan had gone to London ahead of her. 'I imagine you following in Lytton's footsteps, being asked to the houses of the great . . . I know when I come I shall find you established as a mascot to the Russian Ballet', she wrote, telling him in the same letter that she had fallen on the stairs at Charleston.[17] She wrote again from Durbins: 'You needn't be alarmed or worried about me when you read this as though I've had rather a fright there is every sign of things being all right now . . . there was some, but very little bleeding going on', and the doctor had been called.[18] The letter illuminates her reluctance to ask Duncan for support or to restrict his social and professional life. It also describes the complex alternative network of roles and relationships that had developed around her.

> Roger suggested your coming here for a day or a night but I don't think you ought to interrupt your time in London . . . I know what a bore it would be giving up some of your short time. As things are you can go on using R's studio.

She was alone with Roger when the doctor visited but Clive, she wrote, had 'saved my reputation' by arriving at Durbins with Mary. 'The worst of it is that I shan't be able I suppose to work at the panels or go to the ballet or anything'. Instead she reconciled herself to sending the panels to Gordon Square with Clive and Mary and lying on the sofa in the drawing room.[19] Duncan described her in a letter to Bunny, giving advice from the sofa while he began to paint the room. Maynard hired a horse and carriage to take her shopping. 'Roger came to lunch and Virginia and the two Sitwells came to tea', Duncan wrote. The following evening Vanessa was conveyed in her barouche to *Scheherazade* and then on to a fancy-dress party in Chelsea hosted by the Sitwells.[20]

Vogue featured the double doors to the drawing room at 46 Gordon Square with their painted panels surrounded by darker-coloured walls. The upper panels were painted as curtained windows through which a scene based on Vanessa's *View of the Pond at Charleston* (see fig. 11.2) was revealed and the second panel depicted Vanessa herself, viewed from behind with her hands raised to her hair as if checking her appearance in a small mirror.[21] The scheme asserted her prevailing influence at Gordon Square and the profound connection between Keynes's life in London and Sussex. He and Clive entertained extensively at 46 Gordon Square. They hosted parties for Picasso there the following year, making this a modernist setting where progressive dancers, musicians, artists, authors, critics, patrons and the political elite would congregate. Vanessa herself hosted London Group committee meetings at 46 Gordon Square after she moved back there for a period in 1922.[22]

Maynard's close friendship with Vanessa and Duncan underpinned his patronage, and as their reputations transitioned from avant-garde to fashionable decorators he too became an establishment figure. Anticipating their travels to Paris, Rome and Florence together in 1920, Vanessa and Duncan painted cupboard doors for Maynard's bedroom, wittily identifying themselves as Europeans in defiance against the xenophobia that still raged in Britain after the war.[23] Again, the upper panels are framed by painted curtains, as if the scenes are viewed through a hotel window or set on a stage. Four cities, London, Paris, Rome and Constantinople, are represented in the upper door panels and their characteristic breakfasts are pictured in still lifes in the panels below. Converting the hut nicknamed 'Les Misérables' into a large studio at Charleston enabled Vanessa and Duncan to work together on larger decorative panels. As soon as it was whitewashed Vanessa wrote to Roger describing a new scheme for Maynard's rooms at King's College, Cambridge: 'The hut makes a splendid studio, & there are 8 divisions all along one side which just take the panels, so it's a perfect place to do them in.'[24] Duncan had decorated Maynard's sitting room in Cambridge a decade earlier with a homoerotic circle of dancing nudes flanked by paintings of fruit pickers inspired by Piero della Francesca. The new scheme, carried out at Charleston over two consecutive summers, reconceived Vanessa and Duncan's homage to the Italian Renaissance, inspired by their recent travels with Maynard and, as Richard Shone has observed, by reproductions in the *Burlington Magazine*.[25]

Vogue produced a lavishly illustrated feature: 'An Economist and Modern Art. The Cambridge Rooms of Mr Keynes', describing the room as 'perhaps the most successful that has been carried out in England during this century'. The magazine described the eight

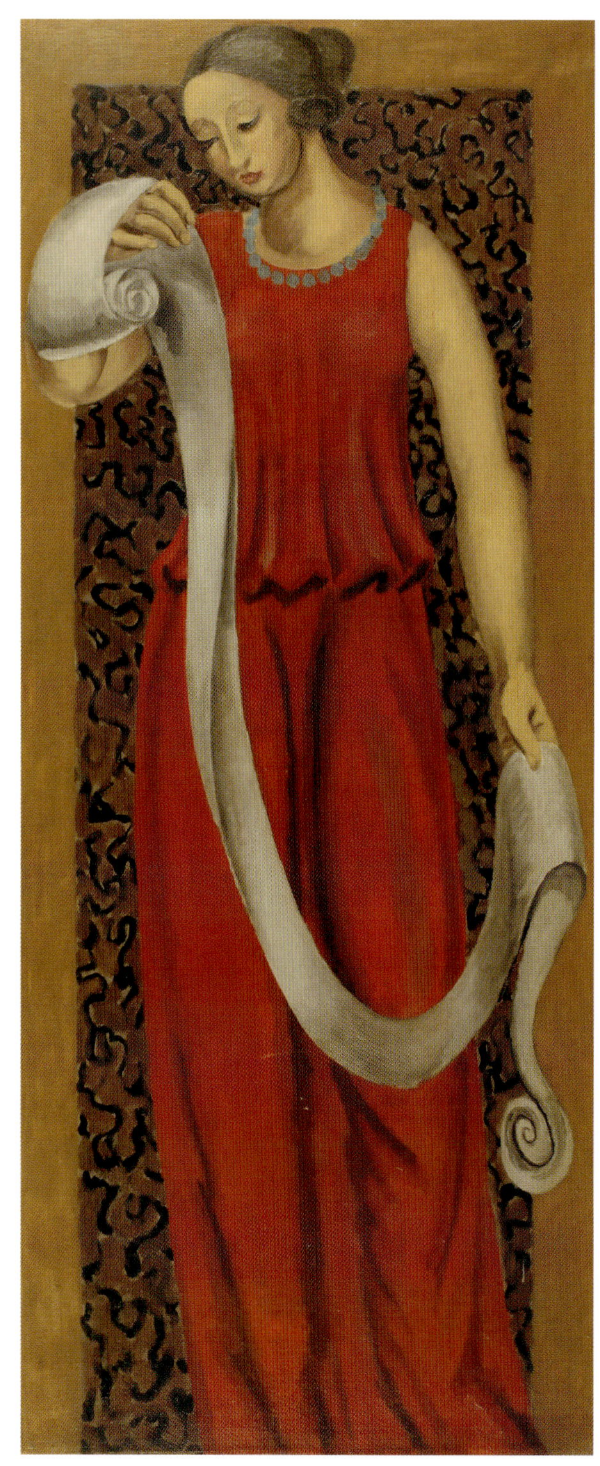

13.3. Vanessa Bell, *History*

1921, oil on canvas, decoration for John Maynard Keynes,
Webb Court, King's College, Cambridge

allegorical figures representing the arts and sciences, 'painted by Vanessa Bell and Duncan Grant, whose collaboration in decorative work is proving highly successful'.[26] Vanessa's panels are almost indistinguishable from those of Duncan. Initial pencil sketches by both artists show that the clothed female figures and naked males were divided equally between them, with Vanessa painting the four nearly life-sized figures on one side of a tall bookshelf and Duncan the four on the other side (figs 13.3 and 13.4).[27] 'I have tried to sketch some of the figures I have been doing for you, but I only have room for 3', Vanessa wrote to Roger. 'They are supposed to represent law, science, history, etc. though you mightn't think it – in fact we're always changing their arts & sciences.' Characteristically she focused on colour: 'The backgrounds are marbled . . . They have yellow Ochre bands round & the male figures are nude, mostly in pure Naples yellow. The females have dull green, vermilion, Prussian blue and white dresses. There's very little other colour & it's all rather

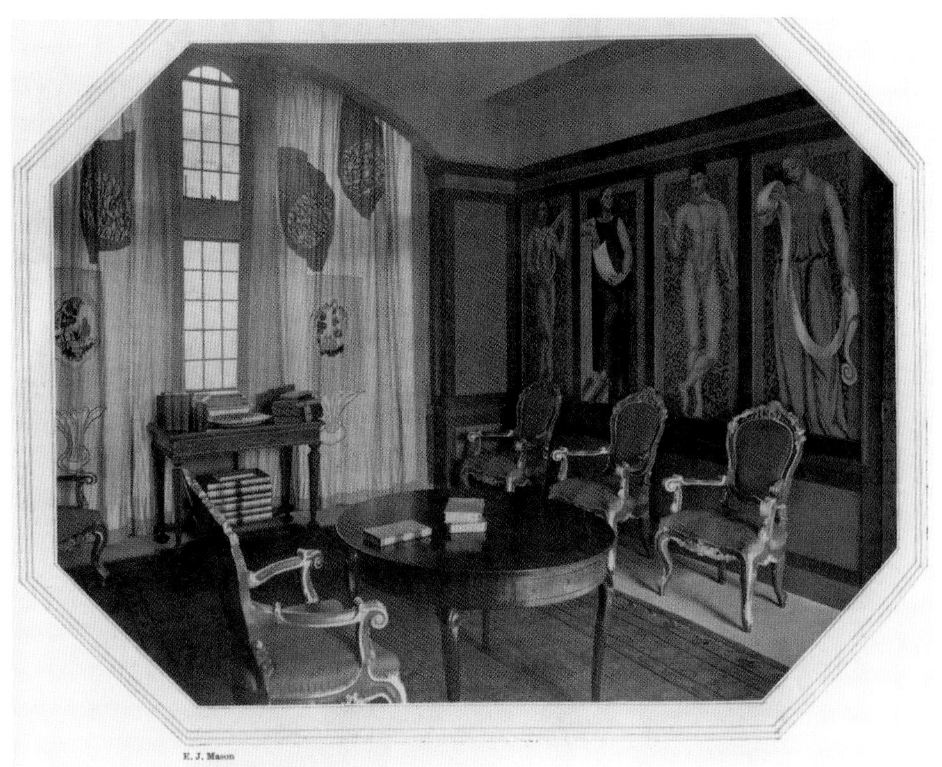

13.4. Vanessa Bell and Duncan Grant, decorations for John Maynard Keynes, Webb Court, King's College, Cambridge

Photograph from *Vogue*, early March 1925

severe I think.'[28] They produced studies exploring alternative poses and attributes for the figures, and as Keynes was staying with them at Charleston while the work was in progress he was easily consulted.[29] Vanessa's final versions of 'History' in a vermilion gown holding the classical attribute of a scroll, 'Law' and the nude male figure of 'Science' conform to the sketches in her letter to Roger, and so can be identified as her work. Her second male nude is more ambiguous as a muse. The inset photographs in *Vogue* show Duncan's panels but the article does not distinguish between the two artists' work or separately attribute the extraordinary floor-to-ceiling curtains that dress the windows at both ends of the room. These are characteristic of Vanessa's curtains at Gordon Square, Asheham and Charleston in their combination of fabrics to contrast the fore-edges and hems with the main body of the curtains. They introduced painted and appliquéd patterns. She painted directly onto linen, writing to Roger, 'We have prepared a lot of the Barker linen & it seems very nice to paint on.'[30] The curtains include circles painted with *écriture* set within darker, abstract forms and other painted passages, making them unique among window dressings of the period.

Vanessa's invisible labour in making the curtains is not recorded, but given their originality and the frequent references to curtain making in letters throughout her life they are likely to have been substantially made if not entirely created by her. The Cambridge project provides a broader insight into her unacknowledged labour in the partnership with Duncan. The initial studies for the panels were set aside for a year and when Vanessa returned to Charleston in 1921 and found that the skylight to Les Misérables had been smashed, she set about clearing away the broken glass. She tidied and unpacked the house: 'I have spent the morning getting the studio in order & haven't done any painting yet', she wrote to Duncan. 'When you come we must prepare a lot of canvas but I can't very well do it till you bring stretchers & tin tacks.'[31] Vanessa often stretched Duncan's canvases as well as her own. She had plans to establish 'a communal kitchen' in Bloomsbury, 'like a college kitchen, sending out meals to several houses', to reduce the need for cooks and kitchens. Clive and Maynard, she correctly predicted, would reject the proposal but 'I consider it one of the ideas that will be universally accepted in 10 years time.'[32] She managed all of the childcare and schooling arrangements. As Vanessa was one of a 'multi-parent family', Quentin recalled, 'most of the work and stress fell upon' her, and although Maynard volunteered to take over the housekeeping while he was at Charleston, 'he soon saw that was absurd' and abandoned the idea, Vanessa wrote to Duncan.[33]

In scale and subject the Cambridge room was compatible with public commissions. Reed has analysed its sober monumentality and art historical references within the context of Bloomsbury's renewed interest in Renaissance painting and Maynard's requirement for respectability as a leading economist and academic. It may have been designed to counter rumours about his homosexuality that Duncan's earlier scheme would have encouraged.[34] It established a new standard in Duncan and Vanessa's post-war work as decorators, and like 52 Tavistock Square, it had a currency as a 'Bloomsbury room' because of the renown of its owner: 'Mr Maynard Keynes . . . is the best known living economist', *Vogue* enthused. The article describes a symbiotic relationship between Maynard and the artists: 'Mr Keynes is also a well known and discriminating admirer of modern painting. He owns pictures by Cézanne, Seurat, Matisse and Derain; he was one of the first to recognise Mr Grant's talent, and owns several of his best works.' His patronage, *Vogue* concluded, 'may be said to have restored a tradition that has been lost to our Universities since the Renaissance'.[35]

Vanessa divided her time between Bloomsbury, Charleston and the South of France in the 1920s and 1930s. She created distinctive environments for her friends and family in all three centres. 'I foresee a migration to the south,' she wrote to Virginia in 1927.

> I only hope all our friends won't follow as they have to Bloomsbury, but it's very probable. In five years time I see us with Stracheys, Mortimers, Davidsons & all the rest, bobbing in & out of each others & our houses in France or Italy or the South Sea Islands if we decide on them . . . & I daresay even the Keynes will settle at one's door.[36]

Maynard had married the Russian ballerina Lydia Lopokova in 1925, against Vanessa's advice, and although her relationship with Lydia had initially been friendly and the couple took a house close to

Charleston at Tilton, the marriage caused a rift between Maynard and his Bloomsbury friends. Vanessa and Duncan had decorated rooms for Angus Davidson and Raymond Mortimer who, as Reed has documented, were drawn to Bloomsbury for its permissive acceptance of homosexuality, its outrageous gossip and its parties. Angus had been one of Duncan's boyfriends and the rooms at 3 Heathcote Street off Mecklenburgh Square that Vanessa and Duncan painted for him were shared, over a period of time, with his brother Douglas, Dadie Rylands and John Lehmann, all of whom were familiar figures within the Bloomsbury circle. Raymond was involved in long-term relationships with the writer Francis Birrell, who established a bookshop with Bunny, and with the diplomat Harold Nicolson, who was married to Vita Sackville-West. He threw a party to celebrate the completion of his Bloomsbury room at 6 Endsleigh Place (off Gordon Square), celebrating its dramatic potential to serve as a stage. The 'Amusing Style' of Vanessa and Duncan's interiors, as Reed has demonstrated, was a conspicuous indicator of queer culture.

Vanessa and Duncan's interiors were photographed and published in style surveys as well as professional and popular magazines. Vanessa was sympathetic when Dorothy Todd was ousted from British *Vogue* because she was changing the character of the magazine but also because she and Madge Garland were open and progressive in their attitude to what we would now term LGBTQ issues. Vanessa thought little of her work as a critic, however, writing to Duncan from Charleston:

> Clive brought with him Todd's article in the *Studio*. I haven't read it but I'm sure it's quite dotty & the reproductions for the most part look nothing. I suppose rooms are very difficult to photograph. I think the poor woman is completely at sea as to which of us, you & I, have done which, but it makes little difference.[37]

Many of the photographs were used again with the same attributions when Dorothy and Raymond published *The New Interior Decoration*, further complicating understandings of Vanessa's individual work within the firm of Grant and Bell. The book cast their work within an international context. Vanessa had to write to *Vogue* on Dorothy's behalf requesting photographs, 'as neither she nor

Raymond seem to be on speaking terms with *Vogue*'.[38] By this time Vanessa had established a home at La Bergère in Cassis and Raymond and Clive stayed with her and Duncan there before the book was published. Raymond adopted Clive's theory of significant form and credited him 'above all' for his influence on the text.[39] 'As always after the departure of a visitor the relief is very great', Vanessa wrote to Virginia, complaining that Raymond's presence had them 'all dizzily trying to talk in the style of . . . one of the ladies who writes for *Vogue* or the *Tatler*'.[40] She didn't recognise the critical theory that located her designs within a new direction for modernism alongside Bauhaus furniture and interiors by Mies van der Rohe and Le Corbusier.

The New Interior Decoration emphasised the influence of contemporary painting on British design: 'the English school, above all the others illustrated in this book, is a decorative school of painters.' It commended Vanessa and Duncan's designs because, unlike modern European architects, they worked with historic buildings: 'Most of us are obliged to live in Georgian, Victorian, or Edwardian houses'. The book reproduced a random selection of photographs of interiors and textiles by Vanessa and Duncan, complemented by a chapter on 'practical methods' for readers hoping to emulate their effects. Colour-washed walls are described and, the authors wrote, 'strips of different coloured papers can even be cut out and pasted up to form a design'. Vanessa and Duncan's decorative panels at 52 Tavistock Square are commended for their practicality because they were painted on canvas, framed and 'attached to the walls so that they may be removed to another house if necessary'. Clive's apartment at 50 Gordon Square, also decorated by Vanessa and Duncan, is illustrated and admired for his eclectic collection, which included a painting by Braque, hung above the fireplace against a rectangle of dark distemper surrounded by painted circle motifs.[41]

Raymond began to write for the *Architectural Review* in 1930, but his liberal values were increasingly incompatible with the reductive definition of modernism that the *Review* promoted. In a special issue dedicated entirely to modernism in English interior design the *Architectural Review* challenged Harrods and other retailers to abandon reproduction furniture and interiors in favour of original designs by leading 'artists of repute'.[42] It launched a competition for the design of a living room and a dining room, promising that the winning schemes would be manufactured and exhibited by Waring & Gillow. Vanessa was not optimistic. 'This morning I hoped to paint quietly but . . . then the editor of the *Architectural Review* rang up & wants to come & see me about an article on modern decoration', she wrote to Duncan. 'I daresay it's useless & absurd.'[43] Vanessa and Duncan's products and interiors were featured in two consecutive articles in the special issue: 'Electric' by Raymond and an influential survey of British interior design, '1830–1930 Still Going Strong: A Guide to the Recent History of Interior Decoration', by John Betjeman.[44] The magazine locates them as a coherent presence within a comprehensive array of contemporary designers.

Betjeman's text, however, disdained the decorative style that Vanessa, Duncan and Roger had pioneered. He disparaged the brightly coloured curtains and cushions of what he describes as:

> the 'awf'lly modern' period of decoration, started in 1920 and known as 'jazz' . . . chairs and sideboards are painted blue and yellow. The lampshade is made at home. A million women set to on every 'work' there is. With fingers busy at last, after long emancipation, they do 'batik-work' . . . 'lampshade work' and any other 'work' that can be devised. The harm they have done is terrific, for now the truly simple efforts of Le Corbusier and Dufy are hardly appreciated.

For Betjeman, who would become assistant editor at the *Architectural Review* a few months later, and for the architectural historians such as Pevsner who followed his lead, Le Corbusier, Mies van der Rohe and Walter Gropius personified the modern movement. They traced the British origins of their style back to the unadorned simplicity of Arts and Crafts architects such as C.F.A. Voysey and Charles Rennie Mackintosh, whose designs, Betjeman wrote, 'cleared many chairs of pads and frills' and 'showed up the ridiculousness of overmantels'. Bloomsbury design, which amplified the creative vision of the painter rather than that of the architect and encouraged the work of women and amateur practitioners, would be relegated by this historiography of modernism. Nevertheless, Vanessa's competition entry was published and awarded third place in the *Review*.[45]

The figurative elements within Vanessa's decorative schemes expanded the distilled monumentality of her post-war paintings. When Virginia encouraged her to be even more ambitious after her 1927 solo exhibition she replied that 'the large works you require are slowly being produced', citing the caryatid cartoon that she had exhibited with the London Group the previous year.[46] Vanessa and Duncan's interiors also intensified their ability to produce work that was indistinguishable. Raymond recalled, when he detached the canvas panels from his Bloomsbury room and donated them to the V&A, that Duncan had painted the still lifes above the doors and Vanessa *A Garden Scene* between them but they were designed as a coherent entity (figs 13.5 and 13.6).[47]

Vanessa acquired a ten-year lease for La Bergère in the South of France in 1928 and she took a studio adjoining Duncan's at 8 Fitzroy Street. The moves consolidated nearly a decade of makeshift arrangements in London and Cassis. 'You will be surprised to hear that we are actually here, installed, eating off a table, sitting on chairs, sleeping in beds, with . . . all the absolute necessities of life & some of the luxuries', she wrote to Virginia from La Bergère. 'How it has happened I can't quite understand.' She had negotiated the lease and the transformation of 'a tumble down shell of a house' into 'a very gay, cheerful pretty little cottage' with a large first-floor studio for Duncan and a smaller one for herself 'added on to one side'. She conjured up an idyllic life in France, even in February: 'Angelica goes off to school on her donkey at 9 o'clock with Grace. Elise comes for the morning & cooks lunch & does our shopping. Duncan & I paint, each in our own studio or even out of doors.'[48] It came at a cost, however: 'I seem to be spending far more than I've got as usual on keeping 3 houses going', she wrote to Virginia.[49] She had sublet her rooms at 37 Gordon Square to Ka Cox, writing to Virginia: 'Ka raves about the curtains in her letters to me!'[50] Charleston was rented out to Raymond and Francis Birrell in the summer of 1929 and initially she hoped that Raymond might also rent La Bergère when she was not using it.[51] She let it to the artists Dick Wyndham and Tristram Hillier the following year, and to the young painter and theatre designer Robert Medley and his partner, the dancer Rupert Doone.[52] Robert described it, isolated among the vineyards, as perfect and private in every respect. They were joined by Diaghilev's assistant, Alexandrine

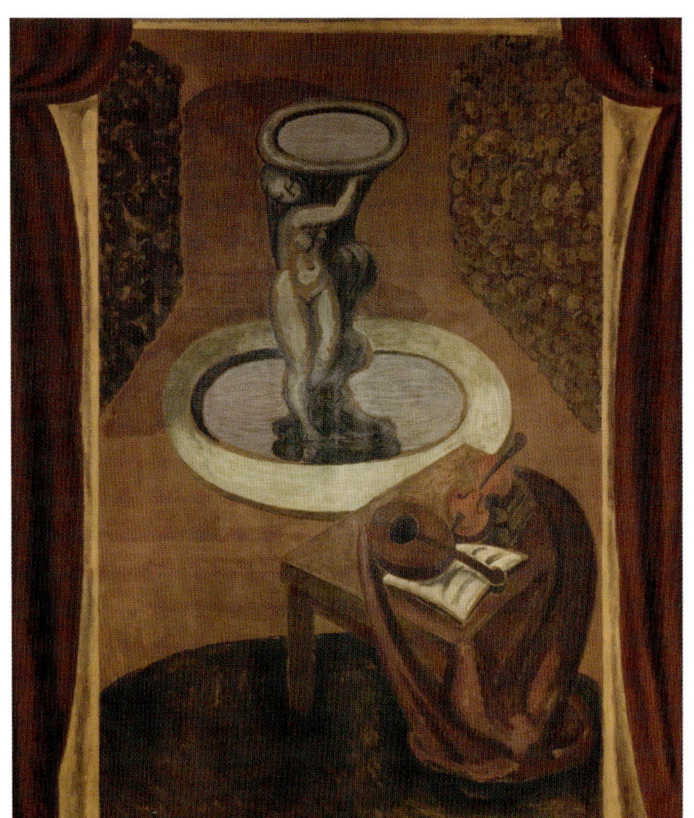

13.5. Vanessa Bell,
A Garden Scene

1925, oil on canvas,
2630 × 2244 mm,
Victoria and Albert
Museum, London

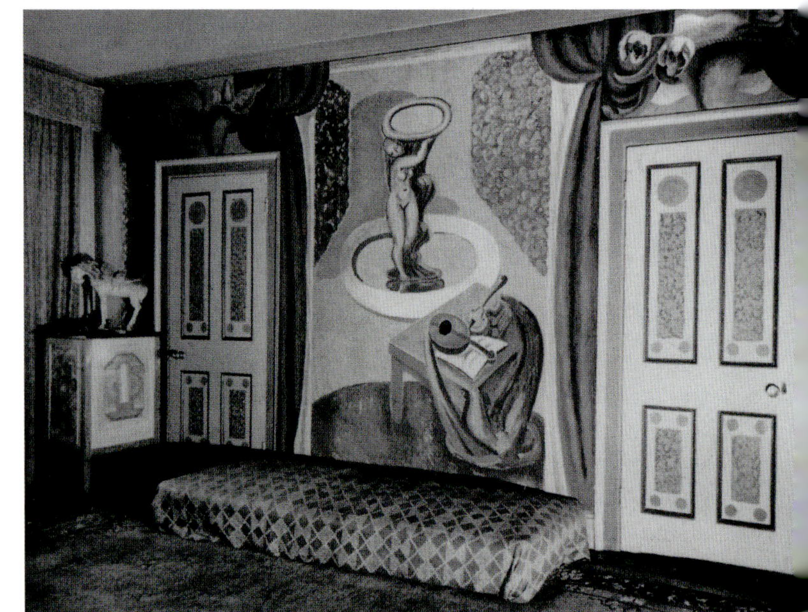

13.6. Vanessa Bell
and Duncan Grant,
a sitting-room in
the Bloomsbury
flat of Raymond
Mortimer

Published in
*Architectural
Review*,
1 May 1930

Troussevitch: 'there began a relationship that required no explanations and that was warm and hopeful. Elise, Vanessa's servant, came out every morning to look after us, and the sun shone.' More friends were invited. 'It was the first time in our lives that we were able to entertain in a fitting manner.'[53] Subletting 37 Gordon Square had brought Vanessa into conflict with the freeholder, the Bedford Estate, however, and all of this had to be managed remotely. 'I sometimes feel so harried that I think I must simply give it up', she wrote to Virginia. Quentin and Julian were grown up but as long as Angelica was living at home, she wrote, she needed 'a decent house to live in & can't just pig it in a studio which I feel will be my ultimate fate'.[54]

Pigging it was indeed her fate as soon as Angelica was sent to school. She sold the lease to 37 Gordon Square and arranged for Grace to have a room at Clive's apartment at 50 Gordon Square when she was in London. She rigged up a curtain dividing her studio from her living space at 8 Fitzroy Street: 'It will be odd perhaps but I believe it may save my reason', she wrote to Duncan.[55] Her letters, after he embarked on a serious relationship with George Bergen that excluded her completely, describe the intimacy of their partnership. 'It seems very odd not to have you next door & to have no morning tea', she wrote to him from Fitzroy Street.[56] The letters articulate her feelings about his other boyfriends, who she welcomed into her homes and became friends with: 'the fact that I don't know George at all & don't know if he's the kind of person who ever can live quietly near you & see us both & work & be happy with you makes it much harder for me.'[57] Their adjoining studios and professional partnership gave Vanessa easy access to the male and homosexual networks that Duncan enjoyed: 'as I was washing my hands in my back room suddenly Raymond looked in at the window. He was on his way to see you', she wrote to him. 'I don't mind being alone – you sometimes seem to think I do but I think its more seeing people without you I mind'. She took refuge in work: 'It is the only thing to do.'[58] Duncan's affair coincided with her solo exhibition at the Cooling Galleries in 1930 and she described the success of the show and her ongoing work in terms that describe the deep understanding between these two independent painters. She had hired models, she wrote, for a large composition of nudes and had managed a commission to decorate a room for the artist and society hostess Ethel Sands and her partner Nan Hudson at their home near Oxford. Vanessa and Duncan had painted murals at Ethel and Nan's French chateau three years earlier, but by now they were able to delegate the painting to Robert Medley as their assistant.

> Much against my will I had to set out for Ethel's . . . Robert has done most of it quite well, but I suspect we shall have to work on some of the details ourselves. No one ever seems to understand them . . . But he had done all the measuring out & the painting was very neat I thought. I suppose one really ought to be there when the colours are mixed.[59]

Vanessa's letters describe the integration of her work as a decorator and her priorities as a painter within the richly textured fabric of her family life. Writing to Duncan, she recounts sharing a Black model to paint nudes with Roger, making studio visits to see the sculptors Stephen Tomlin and Frank Dobson and visiting John Joseph Kallenborn to see tables designed for one of their commissions. Even before the *Architectural Review* initiative she and Duncan had begun to produce designs for a room that they hoped John Lewis would promote 'as part of a general scheme for employing artists in decorative work. I don't know if it will come off but it has added to the general business of life', she wrote.[60]

The small tiled tables made by Kallenborn completed an elaborate interior for the poet Dorothy Wellesley at her country estate, Penns-in-the-Rocks near Groombridge in Sussex. Vanessa and Duncan had produced preliminary drawings, pastels and huge canvas panels for the scheme at La Bergère the previous summer.[61] They filled the studios. 'We spent Friday afternoon and Saturday putting final touches – or rather, penultimate touches – to the room', Vanessa wrote to Quentin. 'On Saturday the guests arrived, Ethel Sands, Leigh Ashton, Hugh Walpole, Vita. We had a champagne dinner and everyone had to admire the room and say as many times as they could how lovely, beautiful, marvellous it was.' The interiors included a hexagonal table and cane-backed chairs as well as curtains that glittered with silk and sequins. 'I had to work about 14 hours a day at the curtains for the last few days and am thankful it's over', Vanessa wrote, describing the whole effect as 'very luminous and atmospheric'.[62]

The elite interior at Penns-in-the-Rocks with its playful, Baroque painted panels and furniture was published in *The Studio* in the summer of 1930. Madge Garland described it as 'a room of outstanding beauty, rich in colour, harmonious in design . . . a complete example of their decorative work'.[63] It was a precursor to the music room that Vanessa and Duncan staged as an exhibition at the Lefevre Galleries the following year, catering to the tastes and grandiose settings of Bloomsbury's aristocratic and society patrons. But the design and execution of these two elaborate interiors coincided with Vanessa and Duncan's unexecuted room for John Lewis and their industrial designs for Allan Walton fabrics and tableware for Clarice Cliff.

As a partnership, Vanessa and Duncan gave Bloomsbury and its wider circle a distinctive aesthetic identity. Their designs were published as aspirational and fashionable statements but they also appealed directly to a readership that understood and identified with Bloomsbury's broader incursions into modernism: with the writings of Virginia, Lytton and Maynard. They manifested the creative and intellectual challenges to sexual and political orthodoxies that the Bloomsbury Group represented in the 1920s and 1930s. The design partnership was integral to Vanessa and Duncan's practice as artists and to their private living arrangements, but its significance to the history of design has not attracted the same attention as the Omega Workshops that it superseded. The firm of Grant and Bell was more successful than Omega in securing interior and commercial design commissions and its lifespan was more than double that of the Omega. It expanded Vanessa's influence as a place maker, creating strikingly original and sensuous environments in which alternative ideologies and relationships could be explored. Through to the 1950s Vanessa often made paintings of rooms when they were completed, or painted them into the background of a portrait or a still life. These interior views are the antithesis to the hard lines and neutral colours of modernist interiors promoted by the *Architectural Review*. Paintings such as *Interior with Duncan Grant* and *Interior Scene with Clive Bell and Duncan Grant Drinking Wine* describe the warmth and informality of her spaces, populated by loved ones.[64] They respond to modernist domestic scenes painted by Matisse and they encapsulate Virginia's theory that interiors are redolent with the memories and personalities of the past. The firm of Grant and Bell challenged the very precepts of modernism and its boundaries.

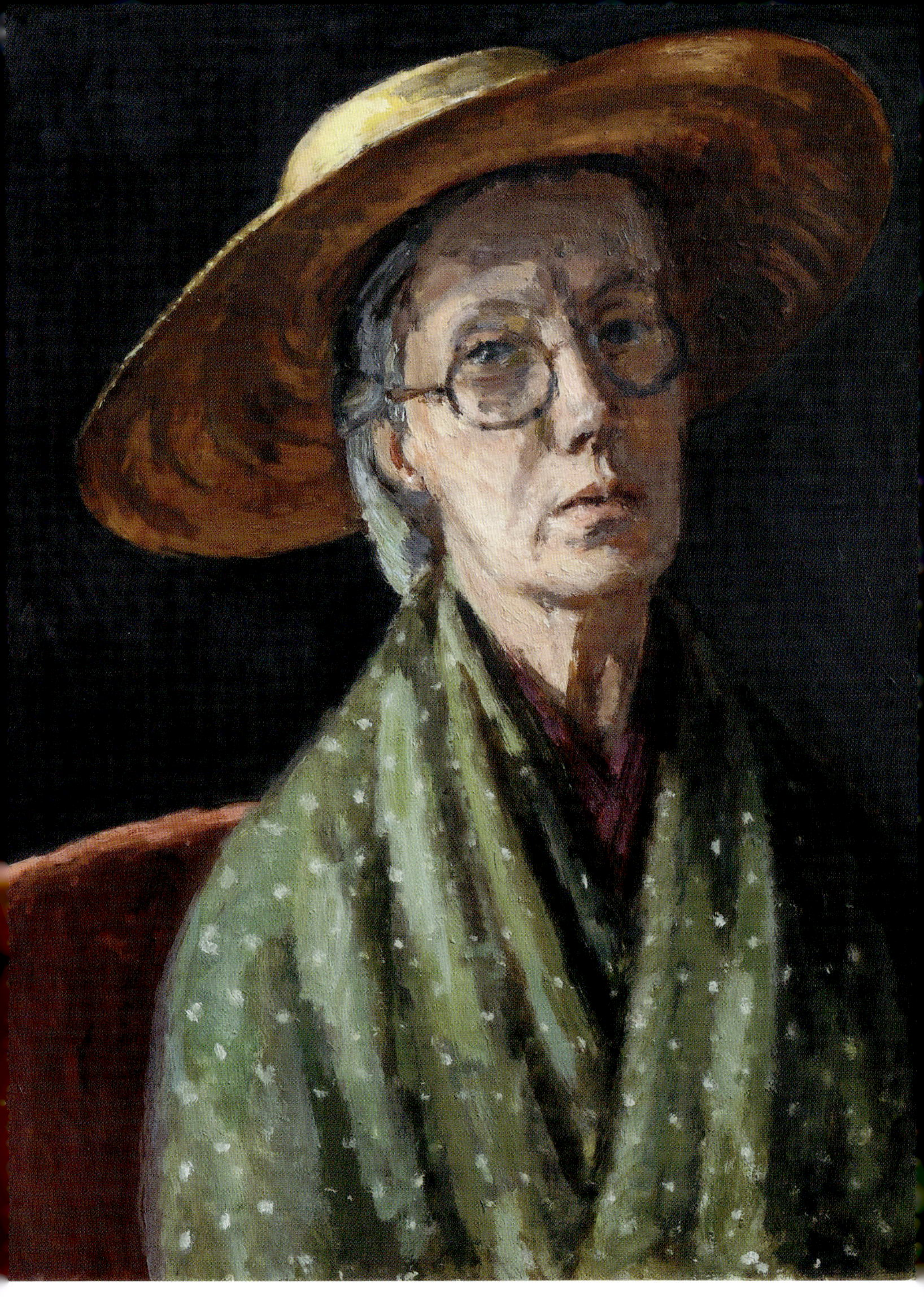

14.1. Vanessa Bell, *Self-Portrait*
1958, oil on canvas, 450 × 370 mm, The Charleston Trust

14

LATE WORKS AND LEGACY

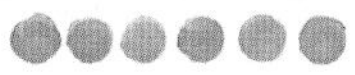

'I have started again on my self portrait which may end up very odd as a likeness of me,' Vanessa wrote to Duncan. 'I see one has no conception of oneself as a whole but bits are very interesting & one works away like a beetle & can't bother much about likeness.'[1] From her first retrospective exhibition in 1964, three years after her death, Vanessa's importance and her creative output were assessed in 'bits' rather than 'as a whole'. The retrospective focused 'wholly on the easel-pictures' because her decorative work had been included in a recent show commemorating the foundation of the Omega Workshops.[2] Vanessa's Bloomsbury family supported the organisation of the retrospective and, conspicuously, they owned many of her finest paintings. Duncan loaned *Iceland Poppies* and *Studland Beach*, and the faceless portraits of Virginia belonged to Leonard. The list of loans shows how Vanessa's experimental paintings were valued by those closest to her during her lifetime.

Vanessa's poignant late *Self-Portrait* was reproduced on the title page to the exhibition catalogue and listed as the last painting in the show (fig. 14.1). Kenneth Clark had bought it soon after her death from a memorial exhibition at the Adams Gallery where Vanessa's friend, André Dunoyer de Segonzac, described it as 'a token of farewell. This masterpiece, steeped in an emotion deep but contained and pervaded by a moving sense of resignation, could be compared with those last portraits that Rembrandt painted of himself – here is the same grandeur, the same beauty.'[3] He cast Vanessa within a European context, comparing the reserve in her paintings with the humility of a Cézanne or a Bonnard. He mentioned her work 'in the minor arts', designing and decorating fabrics, ceramics and book covers and as a muralist. Three years later the retrospective recognised the influence of French Post-Impressionism on Vanessa's work but not her own contribution to modernism beyond 'some of the key pictures' that would 'surely emerge' when English Post-Impressionism was fully assessed. 'There are no great changes of style in the last four decades', the curator wrote.[4] The 1961 exhibition included three self-portraits from the 1950s, asserting Vanessa's continuing vitality as a woman in her seventies. Her last solo exhibition was held in 1956.[5] She painted herself in the attic studio that she had built at Charleston with canvases stacked behind her. She holds a fistful of brushes ready for use and leans forwards in the act of painting. But in the retrospective these provocative self-portraits were passed over in favour of a more retiring reflection of her old age.[6]

The modest retrospective interpreted the facts of Vanessa's achievements to establish a patriarchal narrative that would limit her status within the historiography of modernism. 'Her husband, Clive Bell had met Roger Fry early in 1910 and had helped him to organise the first Post-Impressionist exhibition', according to the catalogue. Clive was a lender to the retrospective. Vanessa had 'helped to found the Friday Club', she had 'visited' Asheham, 'the home of Leonard and Virginia Woolf', she was 'Represented in the first exhibition of the Grafton Group' and Roger Fry had founded the Omega Workshops for which her designs, 'from July 1913 onwards . . . acted as a stimulus' for her own paintings.[7] Her role as a pioneer, initiating or shaping these loci of modernist practice, was overlooked. Perhaps most significantly, her contribution to abstraction was ignored. Although her abstract paintings and collages remained in her estate and were available for exhibition, they were excluded. The catalogue provides invaluable insights into the body of work that was regarded as representative of Vanessa's paintings in 1964 and their provenance. It was dominated by later works: the still lifes and landscapes that were the product of her daily practise and that remained unsold after her numerous group and solo exhibitions. A brief bibliography highlights her marginalisation. It includes monographs on Leslie Stephen, Duncan Grant and Roger Fry, Clive Bell's *Old Friends* and Sir John Rothenstein's *Modern English Painters*. The latter dedicated only 3 of its 33 chapters, each discussing the work of a single artist, to women. Vanessa was not one of them.[8]

The catalogue describes a 'period of retrenchment and readjustment' after the First World War, giving little indication that Vanessa continued to experiment in her painting or that the firm of Grant and Bell expanded the work that she had initiated collaboratively at the Omega Workshops. Through to the 1950s, when she served on the jury for the Prix de Rome awards, Vanessa continued to engage in new initiatives, to represent her own generation and to support the work of younger artists. She was an enthusiastic and capable driver and the *Daily Mail* listed her among the 'brilliant artists' who designed posters for Shell. Vanessa described the process of painting *Alfriston. See Britain First on Shell* 'in size in a pointillist technique with only a few colours' and she was consistently singled out for praise when the posters and original paintings for them were exhibited. 'Mrs Vanessa Bell transports us to Sussex; and gives us a glimpse of Alfriston shimmering in the summer light'.[9] Later in the 1930s she supported an enterprise to make contemporary art more widely accessible through limited-edition prints. 'Duncan and I have spent the last two days at the Baynard Press at Camberwell where we are doing lithographs for Contemporary Lithographs Ltd', she wrote to Clive. The firm had recently been established by John Piper with Robert Wellington, who ran the Zwemmer Gallery. 'They hope to sell to people who can't afford paintings & pay the artist by results.'[10] The prints were issued in large editions and Vanessa's *The Schoolroom* was immediately acquired by the Victoria and Albert Museum's Circulation Department for its touring exhibitions.[11]

Vanessa's involvement with the British Institute of Industrial Art continued through their pioneering *Exhibition of Modern British Embroidery* at the V&A. It was 'a watershed moment' for embroidery as a modern art form.[12] Allan Walton manufactured more of her textile designs, and having supported Duncan's stage designs for many years, she was commissioned to design sets for the ballet *High Yellow*.[13] Duncan was designing for the Camargo Society in 1932. Maynard was the Society's treasurer and Lydia was on the executive committee. Vanessa described the experience as 'rather terrifying, having so little experience of such things' when they commissioned her; by contrast, 'Duncan seems to do his so light-heartedly'. She made a model stage and wrote to Roger that she was spending 'a lot of time carpentering & trying to master wings etc.'. The music was jazz, there were Black dancers and the ballet was set on an island: 'Lydia was convinced I couldn't be hot enough! I doubt if I can be – but it's rather fun doing it', she wrote.[14] She designed a tropical beach with palm trees, boats and a cocktail bar with a striped awning. The challenges, she wrote, were 'really just the same as those in any kind of decoration, only one has to be prepared for everything round the edges being chopped & changed & concealed'. Vanessa quickly 'made great friends with Freddy Ashton, their chief choreographer & Billy Chappell, who does the dresses & dances'.[15] This led to a second commission for sets and costumes for Ashton's *Pomona*, performed the following year at the Sadler's Wells Theatre in London. Virginia described the contrast with *High Yellow*: 'all very pale & bright – I mean Fra Angelico against a background of Cassis'.[16] Virginia relayed an invitation from the composer Ethel Smyth to Vanessa to design sets for her *Fête Galante* and although Virginia and Ethel were friends she described her as 'a plague of locusts . . . fine, vigorous insects, whom I respect and admire, but they leave me bent and broken'.[17] Vanessa wrote to her sister in May 1933: 'I had a visit from Dame Ethel who still goes on about her ballet & made Miss Wendy Toye & her mama also come & visit me.' Wendy Toye was a dancer. 'The dame herself sate with her skirt well above her knees & her legs wide apart & described the mating of her dog with a bitch several sizes too small in great detail. It wasn't really very amusing but Wendy almost became hysterical.'[18]

As successful mainstream artists and designers Vanessa and Duncan were commissioned to design interiors for Cunard's flagship liner, RMS *Queen Mary*, in 1935. Laura Knight and Edward Wadsworth were among the other artists employed. 'I have been given a room to do', Vanessa wrote to Virginia, explaining that it was much smaller, 'of course', than the main lounge that Duncan was to decorate but it included a large panel, decorated doors and all the textiles and carpets.[19] Three weeks later her sketches for the sitting room adjoining the ship's Roman Catholic chapel were approved but within months her contract was cancelled. 'The excuse given in my case is that the Roman Catholics don't approve', she wrote.

> But I think that's only part of the reason. No doubt the committee
> of directors who have now come on the scene are horrified by
> our doings. I suspect they think they can down me entirely and

are trying to put Duncan into a position in which he'll have to throw up the job.[20]

Duncan was required to reduce the size of his panels and of his female figures. Vanessa immediately consulted Maynard, who wrote to Cunard's chairman, explaining the reputational damage that the cancellation of such a prestigious commission would cause. Vanessa was awarded compensation and a new commission for an elite private dining room on the ship. Her panel, representing a view through a window to the Borghese gardens in Rome, is reproduced in a scathing article by Clive on the mismanagement of the interiors. She was disappointed by the scale of the cabin and the absence of carpets and textiles that she and Duncan had designed or selected, but Duncan's decorations were eventually rejected entirely.[21]

Vanessa's *Queen Mary* panel is one of a number of lost or altered paintings, known only from black-and-white illustrations in catalogues and the press, that chart a coherent new direction in her style. Beginning with *The Visit* (exhibited in the *Nameless Exhibition* in 1921), it developed her interest in the domestic lives of women and children. Vanessa assimilated the influence of recent paintings by Matisse such as *Interior at Nice* (which she knew from Paris exhibitions and from Mary's collection), adapting his sun-drenched palette and flattening of forms. In these profoundly still images she often combined an interior scene or still life with a view through an open door or window. They often incorporate extravagant still lifes of flowers or food. Painted curtains frame the images, evoking the impression of a stage set, a dream or a memory. Vanessa's women and children in these paintings are self-absorbed and surreal in their detachment from one another. She was aware of the *International Surrealist Exhibition* in London, writing to Julian that 'one may find oneself one of them before one knows what's happening', but she remained aloof from the movement.[22]

Her *Schoolroom* lithograph and *The Other Room* explore the interior worlds that women inhabit (fig. 14.2). When it was exhibited in a survey exhibition of contemporary British artists *The Other Room* was described as 'the largest picture in the show . . . enormous, not only in area but also in its decorative power. Perhaps it has a faint affinity to Matisse, perhaps a reminiscence of Bonnard, but the relationship is too distant to be of any importance.'[23] In both images, three women occupy a room together without engaging with one another. They are absorbed in reading, writing, playing the piano or they have set aside their books and their faces are averted in thought. In *The Other Room* the interior is abstracted. This is not an actual room in real time and each woman is set within her own environment of space and pattern and colour. Vanessa repeats the compositional device of *Studland Beach* and *Nursery Tea*, creating a vacuum at the centre of the composition around which the viewer's gaze rotates. The foreground figure, reclining on a couch, has an abstract backdrop of intense red. A second figure in the middle ground of the composition faces away from the viewer, sitting forward in a brightly patterned armchair, perhaps reading, with one hand to her face. Her hair and white dress suggest that she is a child or adolescent, while a third figure stands behind the curtain to the semi-glazed door or window, looking out. The palette surrounding her is sombre and she wears a long black dress, but the landscape that she faces is animated by vibrant green and yellow brushstrokes. Like *Studland Beach* the painting alludes to a narrative. There is a vase of bright flowers on a small circular table between the three figures and an incongruous swag of drapery behind it that imply a memento mori or a reflection on the circle of life.

While Vanessa was working on her commission for the *Queen Mary* her eldest son, Julian, now 27, accepted a teaching job at the National University of Wuhan and set sail for China. Her letters to him document their exceptionally close relationship as well as the details of her daily life. He returned in March 1937 but within a few months, determined to fight fascism in the Spanish Civil War, he joined the Spanish Medical Aid as an ambulance driver and was killed. Devastated, Vanessa suffered a complete breakdown. Virginia was constantly at her side in London and then an almost daily visitor to Charleston. 'I cannot ever say how Virginia has helped me', Vanessa wrote to Vita Sackville-West, and Virginia, unable to write about Vanessa in her diary, simply wrote down her sister's own words: 'I shall be cheerful, but I shall never be happy again'.[24]

Gradually, Vanessa began to resume her work. She had written to Julian before his departure for China, when she was grieving Roger's death, that 'in painting one seems to get into another world altogether,

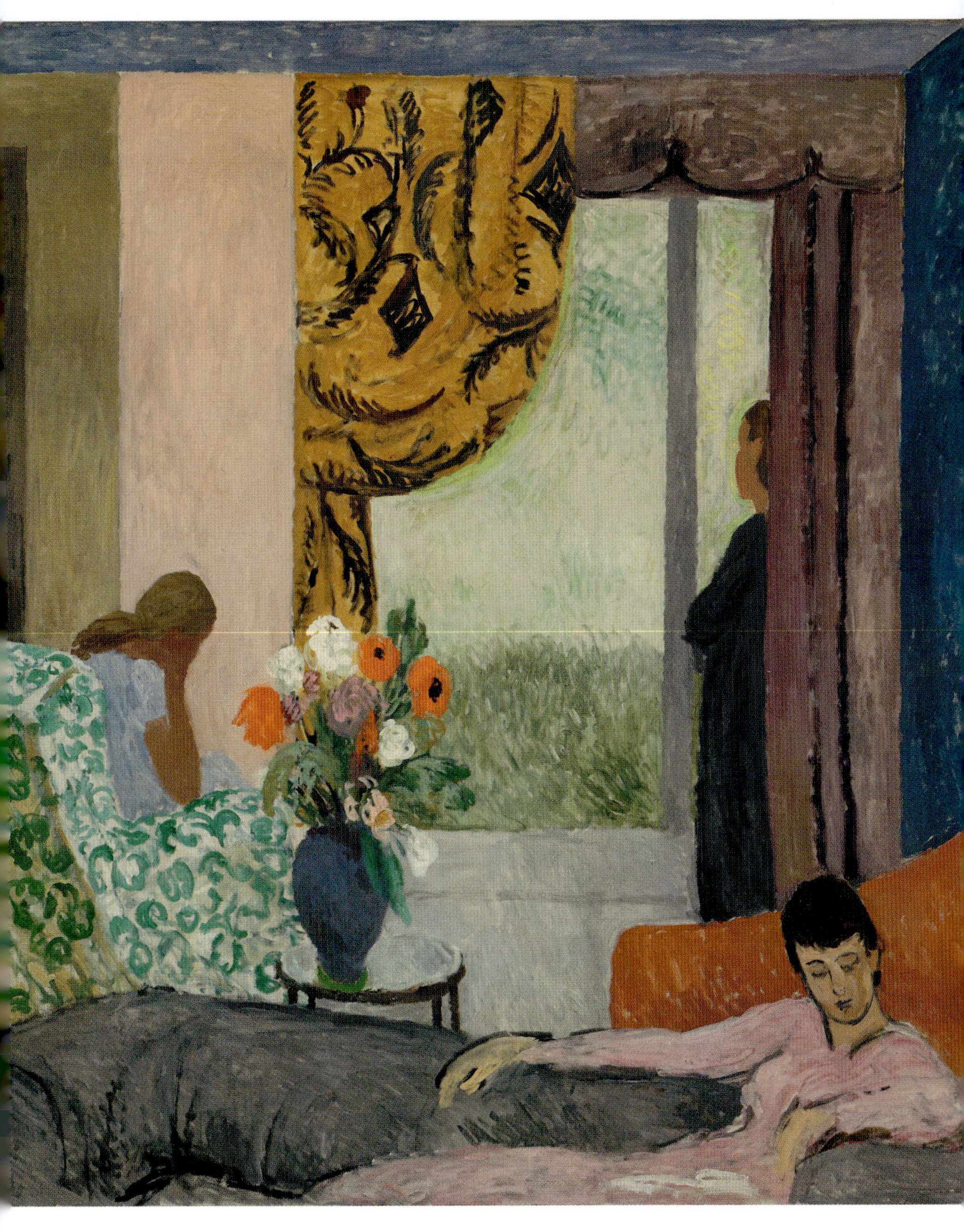

14.2. Vanessa Bell, *The Other Room*

c.1937, oil on canvas, 1610 × 1740 mm, private collection

separate from the ordinary human emotions and ideas . . . It seems such a relief to have this other world to plunge into.'[25] *The Other Room* and *The Schoolroom*, painted before and after Julian's death, may have been manifestations of this escapism. Initially, however, when Virginia offered her a serious commission to paint a portrait of Clive – 'I feel I must get my Bloomsbury gallery started before we're all old and bald and bleareyed' – Vanessa replied that she wasn't ready to paint portraits: 'It needs a special kind of effort which I don't think I'm capable of. Sketching Angelica is different, as she's not sitting specially to me . . . I'm only working at small things which matter to no one but myself.'[26] Many years later, Angelica wrote a penetrating autobiography, *Deceived with Kindness*, describing a second trauma, after her brother's death, when Vanessa chose this time to tell her that her father was Duncan and not Clive.[27] It was one of the factors that made her reject Vanessa and welcome Bunny (David Garnett)'s advances. Vanessa and Duncan were appalled when Angelica became involved with Bunny. It drove a wedge between mother and daughter, but they felt powerless to prevent it: 'the whole thing is rather like what it used to be when one saw a nurse being foolish with one's child & had to wait till it stopped', Vanessa wrote to Duncan, 'he is an upsetting element between her & me. Well, I suppose it won't last.'[28] Ignorant of his former relationship with Duncan, Angelica married Bunny in 1942. Vanessa continued to paint her and, from the 1950s, her four daughters. When Bunny told Vanessa that he planned to publish his memoirs, including a volume on the First World War and life at Charleston, she wrote to Duncan: 'It seemed to me rather alarming – how can he discreetly account for the household here?'[29]

Vanessa encouraged Quentin to become an artist, arranging for him to paint in Paris and Rome, and to have a studio in Fitzroy Street. Her involvement in his early career formed part of a wider engagement with emerging artists. 'Yesterday we spent the afternoon judging the London Group pictures', she wrote to Clive. 'Quentin sent two, one accepted & one rejected. The younger generation are appearing'.[30] She and Duncan went through the show 'looking carefully for the promising young who might be considered for the Artists' Association & marked down several'.[31] Together with Keith Baynes they curated an exhibition for Agnews Gallery in Old Bond Street (which represented them from 1931) surveying modern British painting: 'they have been remarkably broadminded in their selection', Graham Bell (no relation) observed in a review for the *Listener*.[32] William Rothenstein, Augustus John and Walter Sickert were included alongside young realist painters William Coldstream, Victor Pasmore, Claude Rogers and Graham Bell himself. Vanessa helped these young artists, who would become known as the Euston Road School, to initiate a new school of painting and drawing. She lent her reputation to their cause, writing to potential patrons, hosting a fundraising party in her studio and persuading Virginia to be one of the guarantors for their school.[33] Initially it was close to her own studio at Fitzroy Street and she and Duncan, together with Augustus John and John Nash, committed to teaching there informally without pay. When they had models she painted alongside the students.

Vanessa was a member of the Artists' International Association that campaigned against fascism. Two months before Julian's death in 1937 she visited Picasso's studio where he was at work on *Guernica*.[34] She was a founder member of the British Society of Mural Painters in 1939 and her work was again shown within the broader context of contemporary British painting in Tate's exhibition *Mural Painting in Great Britain, 1919–1939* that summer. It recorded the renaissance of this art form in Britain but Vanessa was also aware of a highly charged modern movement in muralism that was political and international in the 1930s.[35] 'I had expected the Tate Gallery to be filled with enormous panels, vast schemes of decoration detached from their surroundings, and brought together like pictures in a gallery', one reviewer wrote.[36] Instead, original sketches were accompanied by photographs of murals in situ by John Banting, Edward Bawden, Eric Ravilious and others. Vanessa and Duncan showed their decorations for Raymond and murals from Penns-in-the-Rocks (fig. 13.6).

Vanessa was 60 when the Second World War began. She had made preparations at Charleston: 'I've had the estimates', she wrote to Clive, for two new studios and a pottery. They enabled Quentin to pursue his career as a ceramicist and painter in the relative safety of Sussex, and gave Vanessa a large new workspace at the top of the house.[37] 'I am sitting here surrounded by great beauty but also by chaos', she wrote: 'Piles of brick and rubble arise and then disappear . . . If one's on the spot at the right moment one can suddenly order a wall to stop building and put in an extra door or window.'[38]

She was ready to fill the house with friends and family: 'you asked me to offer Janice a room in case of war', she wrote to Clive of one of his girlfriends. 'I have also had to arrange to take in Mrs Grant & Aunt Violet . . . Duncan feels responsible for them.'[39] They would be easier, she reasoned, than unknown evacuees. Clive was given a suite of rooms and Vanessa had a new ground-floor bedroom built for herself next to the 1925 studio. Three months later the work was almost complete. 'I may say that you are considered rather cowardly for not having faced the deluge here', she wrote to Duncan, having organised two vanloads of paintings and furniture to be removed from London to Charleston. She had arranged for contractors to distemper the 'outhouse studio' and because it was unfinished she had nowhere to store their paintings: 'However as its fine it doesn't matter leaving paintings outside', she wrote to Duncan. 'The real difficulty is that we very much doubt if there'll be room for more than a fraction of them . . . Anyway we are almost ready for Clive's deluge'.[40]

Vanessa and Duncan sublet their studios in Fitzroy Street to Victor Pasmore and William Coldstream but the latter 'made such a mess of it I had to turn him out and he now lives next door', Vanessa wrote.[41] In September 1940 they were burnt out in a bombing raid. Virginia wrote to Ethel that Vanessa and Duncan had lost around 100 canvases: 'Happily they'd brought most valuables down here. But its odd, being destroyed.'[42] Vanessa wrote that it was 'sad, but doesn't really seem to matter very much'.[43] Many of the paintings that were packed into the outhouse studio at Charleston were also ruined, over the years, by damp and mould. Virginia's letters and diaries vividly describe the community spirit, the anxieties and visceral experiences of wartime Sussex, when bombs shook the windows so violently that the pen jumped out of her hand.[44] Vanessa shut herself up resolutely, she wrote, and painted 'several hours a day' in her attic studio. She and Duncan were commissioned to decorate the neighbouring church of St Michael and All Angels at Berwick. 'What a war time occupation! It needed Hitler to bring such things to pass', she wrote to her friend Jane Bussy in France. The story of the Berwick murals has been told elsewhere.[45] Although the historic interior for which they were designed has recently been ripped out, they remain among the most complete and important ecclesiastical commissions of the twentieth century. Duncan was initially recommended for the scheme but

Bishop Bell of Chichester, who was committed to reviving a tradition of the arts serving the community through the Church, would also have been aware of the Tate exhibition of murals. Vanessa had been raised as an atheist and neither she nor Duncan were churchgoers but they conceived a scheme that located the biblical stories of hope, which every church celebrates at Christmas and Easter, within their own time and place.

Vanessa's *Nativity* revisited a theme that had fascinated her for nearly 30 years. In this instance it was radical in its assertion that birth and motherhood were specific and prosaic as well as being universal symbols of regeneration. Her Virgin and Child, illuminated by a shepherd's lantern, dominate the composition. The local congregation would have recognised the men and schoolboys who modelled

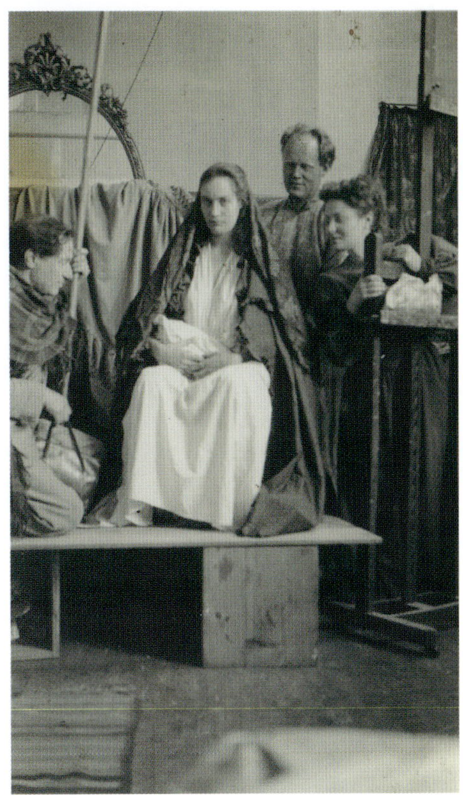

14.3. Vanessa Bell, archive photograph of Duncan Grant, Angelica and Quentin Bell and Chattie Salaman in costume, taken for the Berwick murals, 1941, Tate, London

for shepherds and children in contemporary dress surrounding them. A lamb in the foreground is a local breed, the shepherds hold distinctive Pyecombe hooks crafted in a forge a few miles away and the profile of Mount Caburn in the background locates the scene within the South Downs. Duncan's mural of *Christ in Glory* above the chancel arch carries the analogy further. The risen Christ is flanked by portraits of local servicemen: a sailor, an airman and a soldier all in uniform facing 'defenders of the Faith' Bishop Bell and the Berwick rector. 'Perhaps Duncan gave Vanessa the subjects of *The Annunciation* and *The Nativity* because they were smaller and more manageable', the current guide to the paintings speculates, controversially, 'but it certainly seems fortuitous that she should have painted the scenes relating to motherhood and family life.'[46] Quentin was commissioned to paint

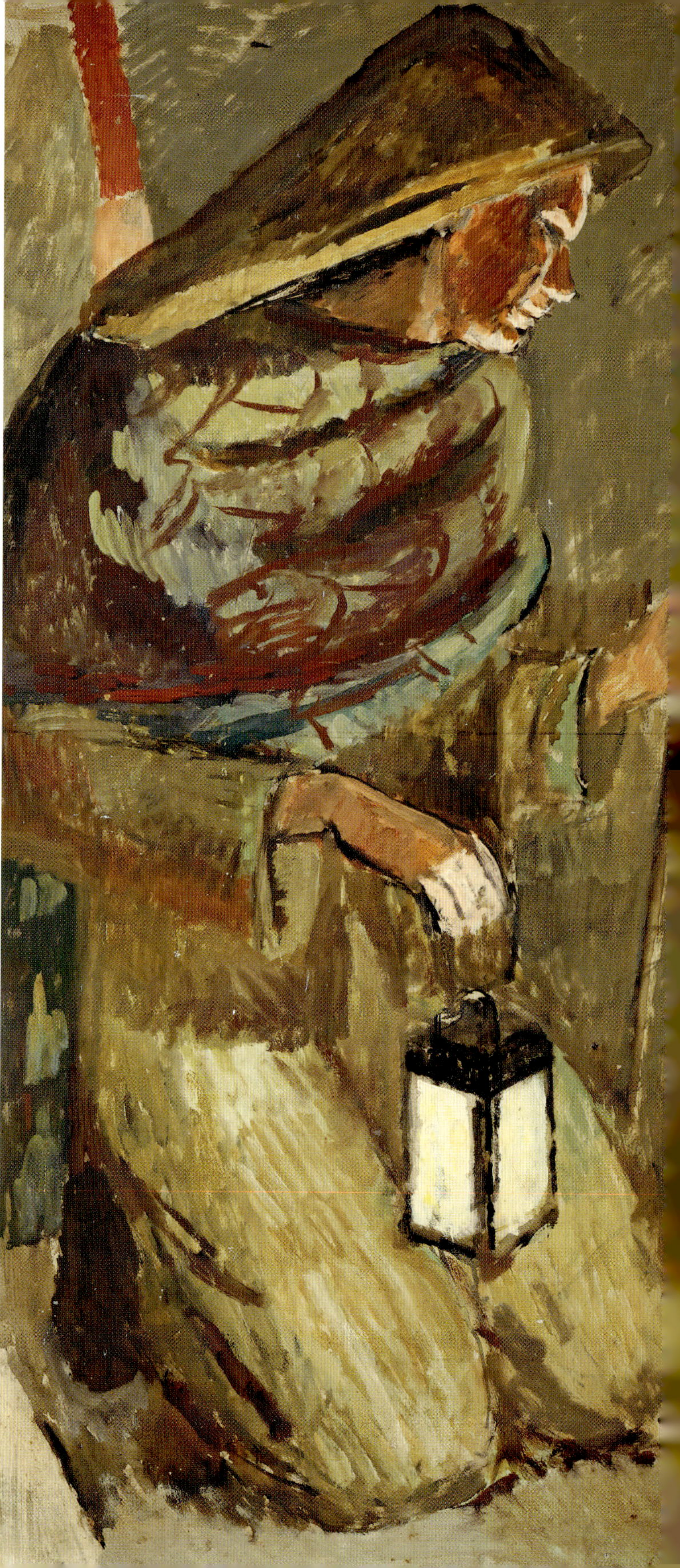

14.4. Vanessa Bell, *Study for Berwick Church: The Shepherd*

1941, oil on wood, 1210 × 590 mm, from the Royal West of England Academy Permanent Collection

The Wise and Foolish Virgins, and on the opposite side of the nave to her *Nativity*, Vanessa painted the *Annunciation*. Photographs and sketches document the collaborative process through which the mural compositions evolved at Charleston (fig. 14.3).[47] Duncan modelled for the kneeling shepherd in the *Nativity* and Angelica for the Virgin in both of Vanessa's murals. Angelica's friend Chattie Salaman, who trained with her to become an actress, modelled for the angel Gabriel and for angels in *Christ in Glory*, and both young women were photographed posing as wise and foolish virgins. Together, the photographs and sketches for the murals provide an insight into Vanessa's creative and alternative household during the war. Her sketch of Duncan kneeling before Angelica with the lamplight illuminating his face is a testament to the personal as political, to Vanessa's achievement in transgressing the heteronormative boundaries of gender and authority in her own family life (fig. 14.4).

Virginia committed suicide in March 1941, soon after work on the murals began. Vanessa had written, urging her to be sensible: 'What shall we do when we're invaded if you are a helpless invalid – what should I have done all these last 3 years if you hadn't been able to keep me alive and cheerful. You don't know how much I depend on you.'[48] 'You can't think how I loved your letter', Virginia replied in her suicide note. 'If I could I would tell you what you and the children have meant to me. I think you know.'[49]

Vanessa's dark group portrait *The Memoir Club* responds, belatedly, to her sister's interest in a 'Bloomsbury gallery'.[50] She includes a back view of herself, seated between Bunny and Duncan, and commemorates the deaths of Virginia, Lytton and Roger by including paintings of them by Duncan and herself on the wall above the assembled company. The Memoir Club was one of the forums through which Bloomsbury defined itself as a group, meeting from 1920 until Clive's death in 1964. Vanessa was diagnosed with breast cancer in 1944. 'Everyone here has come to the rescue', she wrote to Leonard, 'Grace doing all the cooking and others coming in to help, so that I need do nothing but live like a lady if I only knew how. I fear the garden will be weedier than ever.'[51] She hoped that Leonard would lend her books and visit when she had a mastectomy.

Throughout the war, Vanessa remained involved with the mural society. She and Duncan were commissioned to paint murals for the

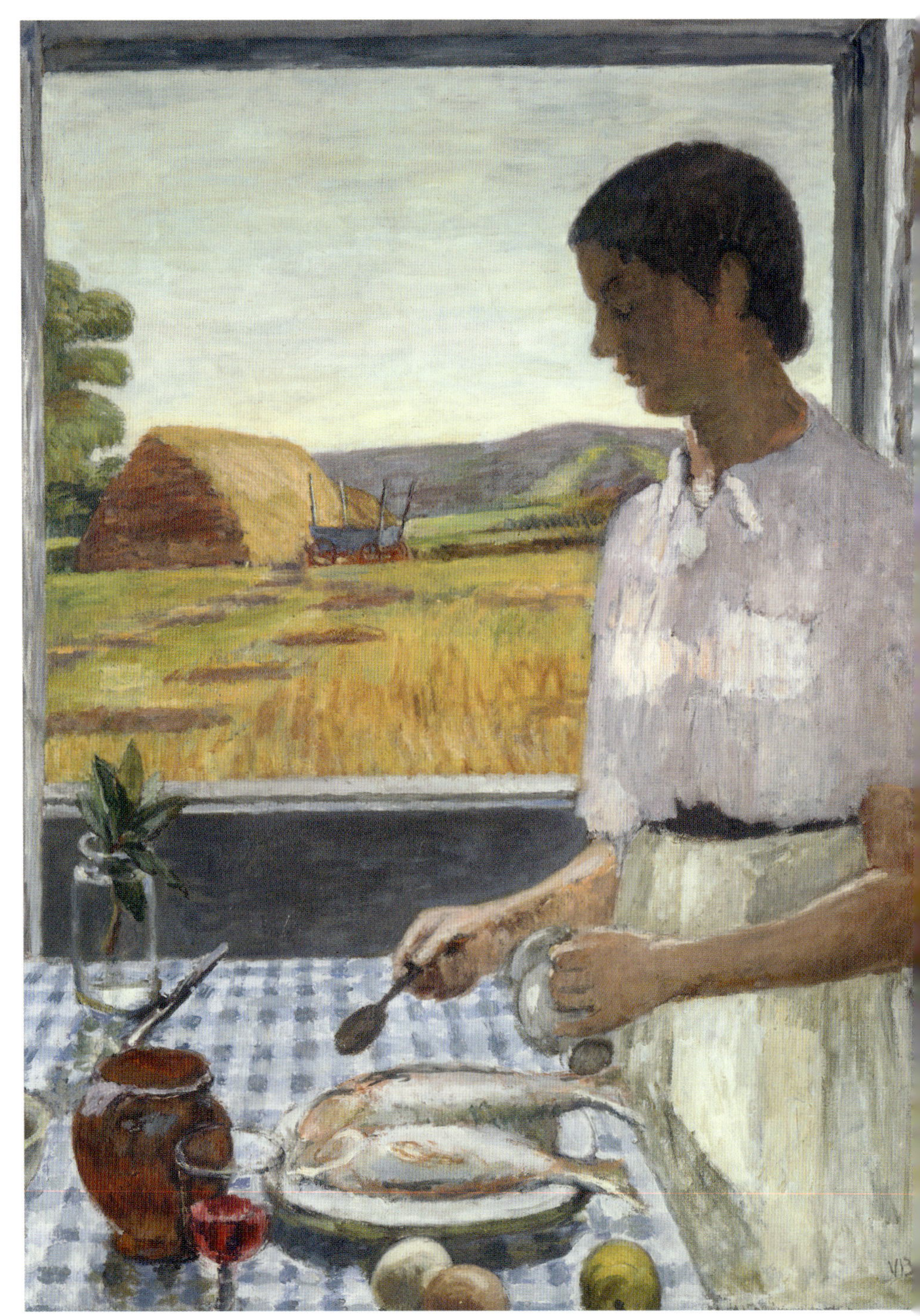

14.5. Vanessa Bell, *The Cook*

1948, oil on canvas, 1003 × 747 mm, Arts Council Collection, London

dining hall of Devonshire Hill School in Tottenham by the Council for the Encouragement of Music and the Arts (a precursor of the Arts Council) and the British Institute of Adult Education.[52] In 1946 they produced murals for the exit to the 'Shopwindow Street' at *Britain Can Make It* and in 1950 they were included in the *Society of Mural Painters First Exhibition*, organised by the Arts Council.[53] They exhibited, too, in an Arts Council exhibition of recent tapestries woven by the Edinburgh Tapestry Company and one of Vanessa's paintings, *The Cook*, was an early acquisition for the Arts Council Collection (fig. 14.5).[54] The painting is not a literal representation of Grace or any of Vanessa's former cooks. Rather, it may combine sketches and memories from different locations. The view through the window, which was not visible from any room at Charleston, appears to represent a Sussex haystack with the downs beyond. But the light airy kitchen and the cook marinating fish with her glass of wine and jar of bay leaves to hand are more likely to be reminiscent of Elise in Cassis.[55] The painting describes another revolution in Vanessa's lifetime, culinary and cultural, away from the dark basement kitchen of her childhood and its hierarchies. By the 1940s Vanessa was cooking dinners at Charleston, adapting the simple meals they enjoyed in France.

Vanessa was one of the artists selected by the Arts Council to represent contemporary painting and sculpture in the Festival of Britain. She showed in their survey exhibition *British Painting 1925–1950* and in *60 Paintings for '51*.[56] This was a limited competition, she wrote to Clive, initially inviting 50 artists 'to paint large pictures, 5 of which they will buy for £500 each, the others to be for sale, and all to be shown at the New Burlington Galleries'. Canvas had been in short supply during the war and the paintings were to measure at least 45 by 60 inches. 'They give one canvases so one will have no expense', Vanessa wrote, 'and I suppose some chance of selling and some egging on to paint large pictures.'[57] She invited Anne Olivier Bell, who was employed by the Arts Council at that time, to model for her at Charleston. Quentin stood outside in the garden, looking in through the open door to model her head in clay, and when he drove her back to Lewes station Olivier kissed him, initiating a relationship that would culminate in a long and happy marriage. Vanessa's painting for *60 Paintings* is characteristic of the elusive images that complicate assessments of her importance. It returns to the theme of women and children in an interior, but Olivier recalled that her figure was later repainted to resemble Angelica and the dynamics of the composition were completely altered as a consequence.[58]

Increasingly through the 1940s and 1950s Vanessa witnessed the writing of Bloomsbury into history. Virginia's biography of Roger was published in 1940: 'you have brought him back to me. Although I cannot help crying, I can't thank you enough', Vanessa wrote to her.[59] The following year Nikolaus Pevsner interviewed Winifred Gill and others about the Omega Workshops. He acknowledged Vanessa's support for an article, 'Ω', in the *Architectural Review*.[60] It excludes her work entirely, mentioning only that Roger 'chose Vanessa Bell and Duncan Grant' as 'nominal co-directors'. When Winifred offered to help with 'an Omega room' for the V&A in 1946 Vanessa was cool in her response, writing to her that it was 'in fact quite a vague idea still'.[61] She was unimpressed by Roy Harrod's biography of Maynard and wrote to Leonard that 'if Bloomsbury is to be written about it must be by its own members (most of whom have done so) . . . I don't mind telling what I can about the past generation, but not about my own – except to my own family and friends.'[62]

Vanessa's regard for Roger's memory, her insistence on the pre-eminence of Duncan's reputation and the predominant culture of patriarchy that determined who qualified for inclusion in the canon and what constituted work restrained her from recounting her role as a modernist woman. She was recorded, however, for a BBC broadcast about Virginia, writing to Clive, 'It was really rather fascinating as after I had done my bit I was allowed to listen to all or nearly all the rest of the programme'.[63] Raymond wrote a short monograph on Duncan for the Penguin Modern Painters series and a chapter was dedicated to him in John Rothenstein's *Modern English Painters*. Rothenstein was director of Tate from 1938 to 1964. He condemned Bloomsbury for the 'venomous attacks' it had launched against his father, William Rothenstein, and other artists, believing they had effectively ruined his father's reputation. Duncan, he wrote, 'has never associated himself with the vendettas and intrigues so ruthlessly pursued by certain of his friends'. He favoured Wyndham Lewis's account of the *Ideal Home Exhibition* row and he may have disliked Vanessa for her influence on Roger and Clive as critics. Even the origin of Bloomsbury, in his text, was located at 'the house of Sir Leslie Stephen'.[64] Clive's *Old Friends*, published in the same year, addressed the inaccuracies in Rothenstein's book but made no attempt to rectify his omission of Vanessa as a significant artist.

The self-effacing nature of Vanessa's work, managing and organising her family's domestic arrangements, went unnoticed – inevitably. Her skilful networking and support for Duncan's as well as her own professional opportunities were also conducted below the radar. She was actively, although perhaps not obviously, involved in selecting works for Duncan's retrospective at Tate in 1959. She described a visit with Alan Clutton-Brock, Duncan and Claude Rogers to Maynard's collection, in Lydia's care since his death, 'to look at paintings by Duncan which might be useful for his Tate show'. She was horrified to find work by Degas, Cézanne and Seurat 'hung almost invisible in high dark corners. And masses of others lying on the floor in passages at the mercy of any strange dog or servant.'[65] Alan's carefully considered catalogue essay and chronology for Duncan's retrospective applied almost equally to Vanessa's work and informed his obituary for her two years later. Her work as an artist, nevertheless, would become almost invisible for the next decade. Her name would be dropped from the lists of male painters with whom she had regularly exhibited and her canvases, rolled and stacked in the damp and inadequate stores at Charleston, would be neglected.

Vanessa died at Charleston after a brief illness with bronchitis on 7 April 1961 at the age of 81. She was buried in the graveyard at Firle without ceremony. Her obituary in the *Daily Telegraph* recorded that she was 'in the forefront of that very select band of outstanding women artists of the 1930s . . . she was acknowledged by the critics as a master of both colour and drawing.'[66] Alan Clutton-Brock located her within the Bloomsbury Group as 'a family of exceptional brilliance . . . There was a family kind of painting as well as of thinking.' He described her work and Duncan's as 'very much alike both in spirit and in style, but it could not be said that either was the imitator of the other; both had devised a way of painting that was an expression of their habit, Bloomsbury's habit, of thought and feeling'. The main distinction between Vanessa and Duncan, he wrote, was that 'she was the less ambitious artist of the two'. He didn't recognise the cultural conditions that resulted in their inequality. But he described her 'fearlessness' and compared her 'sharp and destructive wit' with that of her sister, regarding these qualities as symptoms of the security that she had inherited from 'the great line of Victorian intellectuals to which she belonged'.[67] *The Times* and the *Sunday Telegraph* consigned her firmly to the category of 'women artists': 'She may be considered a typical woman artist in attaching no aggressive importance to theory of any kind', William Gaunt wrote. He imagined her late *Self-Portrait* 'taking its place with dignity and appropriateness, alongside those of Berthe Morisot and Gwen John'.[68]

Vanessa's disruptive, radical practice as a modernist regardless of gender began to emerge in an article by Quentin, written to coincide with an Omega exhibition at the V&A. 'I remember vividly the enthusiastic way in which my mother and Duncan Grant used to paint', he wrote, describing them at Wissett:

> They covered the walls with decoration, quite recklessly . . . There was paint everywhere, and not only paint but dyes – they covered yards of material with brilliant patterns . . . I remember, too, my mother and Duncan throwing paint at a wall and letting it run down, a process which they described, quite inaccurately, as 'marbling'.[69]

In the ensuing years he related these memories only to Duncan's work but he also questioned whether critics of Omega would be equally contemptuous if its abstract rugs had been signed by 'some fashionable American artist'. In 1973 a series of small, beautifully curated exhibitions was initiated by Anthony d'Offay.[70] Tate curator Richard Morphet described Vanessa as 'one of the boldest innovators in British art of this century' in his catalogue essay for *Vanessa Bell: Paintings and Drawings*: 'it is increasingly apparent that her achievement has far greater richness, individuality and historical significance than was generally claimed at the time of her death in 1961'.[71] The exhibition included some of her most important early work, including her *Abstract Painting* which d'Offay subsequently sold to Tate, as well as designs for tiles and the Hogarth Press dust jackets. In 1983 Frances Spalding's encyclopaedic biography of Vanessa was published. Charleston opened as a house museum in 1986, preserving some of her interiors and her potency as a place maker. Her *Selected Letters*, edited by Regina Marler, were published in 1993 and her paintings and decorative arts are now in public collections from London to Adelaide.[72]

In assessing Vanessa's complex contribution to modernism as a whole this book builds on an increasing number of excellent studies and exhibitions exploring her work.[73] It questions what constitutes work in the life of an artist. It surfaces some of the hidden work that distinguished Vanessa's life as a modernist, providing an important role model for her sister and for other women in her circle. Her determination to create and exhibit work on equal terms with men and her life choices were instructive. The leadership with which she founded and co-founded the Friday Club, the Grafton Group, the Omega Workshops and the firm of Grant and Bell, paving the way for Virginia's partnership with Leonard at the Hogarth Press, was masked by discretion and collaboration. Even within the radical Bloomsbury Group there were limits to the authority that a woman could openly exert. Vanessa's self-fashioning as a European distinguished her from most of her British contemporaries. It was crucial to her art as a Post-Impressionist painter and designer, and to her role as a connector, promoting and exploring abstraction. Her disregard for boundaries between progressive painting and decoration compromised her reputation as an abstract painter, and the absence of a supportive environment for this new direction in her painting during and after the war effectively restricted its subsequent expression to her decorative designs. She invented a new style of decorative painting, not only as a colourist, colour-washing walls, but also through her freedom of expression.

Vanessa was an innovator as a place maker and matriarch, as Frances Partridge recalled (see p. 231). She created spaces, in collaboration with Virginia and later with Duncan, which welcomed and enabled alternative ideas and relationships. From Gordon Square to the South of France where, she wrote to Clive, 'one leads a purely sensual & unintellectual existence', she established a distinctive identity for Bloomsbury homes where people were free to be and to express themselves.[74] Vanessa resisted the label of 'a woman painter', understanding its derisory implications.[75] She opened up opportunities for women as a facilitator, providing platforms where they could meet and debate as well as show at the Friday Club, the Grafton Group and the Omega Workshops. As a dress designer she promoted a distinctive brand for feminists and her graphic designs ensured that Virginia's work was seen as well as read. Vanessa's paintings debunked canonical representations of the nude and of women's domestic lives. When Roger selected work for the *Nameless Exhibition* she checked with him – 'Did you let in anything by Carrington or [Dorothy] Brett?' – and she encouraged Carrington to show with the London Group.[76] She was persuaded to exhibit, in 1922, in the *Daily Express Women's Exhibition* at Olympia, where Laura Knight's *Painter and Model* and music hall scenes by Thérèse Lessore attracted particular press attention and her own 'genius for expression in paint' was recognised.[77] Her greatest influence on the lives and work of other modernist women, however, was by example. They saw her prominence in *Twentieth Century Art*, her solo exhibitions and her status within the London Group. *Vogue* opened her work to a wider audience of women and her insistence on embroidery as a modern art form, in books, magazines and exhibitions, was transformative. Vanessa did not retire into obscurity as an older woman. She continued to engage with contemporary creative practice and to encourage and inspire younger generations. As a rule-breaker, subverting patriarchy and reinventing the parameters for art and life, she still inspires.

ACKNOWLEDGEMENTS

●●●●●●

My understanding of Vanessa Bell has been shaped by conversations, texts and events that span several decades. Working at Charleston through all seasons and weathers, caring for its fragile collection, I gained a visceral sense of what her life might have been like there. My office was in her studio at the top of the house. Charleston is beautiful and profoundly affecting but the job was less glamorous than people may suppose. In a letter to Mary Hutchinson, Clive Bell describes Vanessa and Maynard, nightly setting out cubes of bread that she had spread 'with a substance that looks like potted ham' to poison the rats. My role as curator included pest-control and the pungent smell of a mouse or rat decaying beneath floorboards still brings to mind his words, 'the rats are strong in death; but they are passing.'

I was privileged to talk in depth about Vanessa's life and work with her daughter and daughter-in-law, Angelica Garnett and Anne Olivier Bell, as well as her grandchildren. Charleston's trustees included many of the leading Bloomsbury authorities and when visiting scholars, artists, writers and researchers came to Charleston it was my job to show them the house. I am grateful to them for their knowledge and insights, which challenged and enriched my own in so many ways. I thank the staff at Charleston, past and present, for their friendship and expertise. Darren Clarke, Miriam Phelan, Emily Hill, and Nathaniel Hepburn gave me unrestricted access to Charleston's collections and were unfailingly helpful and encouraging as my research progressed.

For several years while I was researching and writing this book, I transcribed three or four of Vanessa's unpublished letters every day so that I always had her voice in my ear. I've quoted from them extensively (and used Virginia's writings, which are very different in tone, sparingly) to infuse the text with her personality and to expand the knowledge base for Bloomsbury studies. I am deeply grateful to Sophie Partridge for her permission to reproduce images and hitherto unpublished quotations by Vanessa. This book would not have been possible without her generous support.

I was immensely fortunate to be awarded a Harry Ransom Center Fellowship. This enabled me to spend a month working with Bloomsbury archives in Austin, Texas and I thank the Center's archivists and staff, in particular Danica Obradovic. Among the other archives I consulted, staff at the Berg Collection, New York Public Library; Tate Archives; Patricia McGuire, Archivist at the Modern Archive Centre, King's College, Cambridge; and Karen Watson and Richard Wragg at the The Keep in East Sussex have been especially helpful. I thank the staff at the University of Sussex Library; the British Library; the National Art Library and the Harvard Theatre Collection, Houghton Library.

I have benefited from the observations and analytical reasoning of numerous curators, conservators, dealers and academics over the years. In particular I thank Richard Morphet, Debo Gage, Frances Spalding, Richard Shone, Simon Watney, Christopher Reed, Maggie Humm, Alexandra Gerstein, Sarah Milroy, Rosalind McKeever, Tony and Frances Bradshaw, Heather Wood and Wilma Day. Cecily Langdale and Caroline Cuthbert generously shared their memories with me of the making of Vanessa's posthumous reputation in Britain and America. I thank the staff at the Museum of Modern Art's Drawings and Prints Study Center in New York and Grey Baker for his close reading of Vanessa's *Abstract Composition*. The people who have given me access to their private collections over the years and who have generously helped me to secure the necessary permissions and images for this book are too numerous to name. I thank them all, and in particular David Herbert, the late Lindy Guinness, Sir Christopher and Valda Ondaatje, Jans Ondaatje Rolls, Will Emmett and Bryan Ferry.

It has been a pleasure to work with the team at Yale University Press. Sophie Neve was responsible for commissioning the book and shaped its progress through to production with tact and determination. I thank Mark Eastment, Daphne Fordham-Smith, Robert

Davies and Alex Billington for their care and professional expertise. I am indebted to my colleagues at the University of Sussex, especially Maurice Howard.

I offer my warmest thanks to the friends and family who encouraged me throughout the writing of this book. Paul Davis, Yoshimi Bucknell, Jane Penny, my sister Sally and my two sons, Matthew and Grey with their partners Thea and Alix, were always ready to listen as I talked through my ideas. I am deeply grateful for their kindness and their love.

NOTES

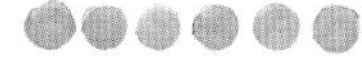

INTRODUCTION

1 Vanessa wrote that Desmond MacCarthy 'seems to be reconciled' to Clive's affair with his wife and that 'He has Mrs R[aven]. H[ill]. & Amber [Blanco-White] going too'. V. Bell to R. Fry, Monday [*c.* October 20, 1913], GB181 SxMs56/1/28, VBRF 108.

2 V. Bell to D. Grant, Jan. 14 [1914], *SLVB*, p. 155. Their plans to travel in January were deferred to March 1914.

3 V. Bell to R. Fry, Wednesday [*c.* January 25, 1914], [mistakenly dated March 25, 1914], *SLVB*, p. 160.

4 Ibid., pp. 160–1.

5 See V. Bell to R. Fry, June 9 [1915], GB181 SxMs56/1/28, VBRF 135.

6 Quoted in John Rothenstein, *Modern English Painters: Sickert to Moore* (London: Eyre & Spottiswoode, 1957), p. 270. For a discussion of women and Vorticism see B. Peppin, 'Women that a Movement Forgot: The Vorticists 1', *Tate Etc.*, 22 (Summer 2011), https://www.tate.org.uk/tate-etc/issue-22-summer-2011/women-movement-forgot (accessed 3 May 2022).

7 V. Woolf, 'Sketch of the Past', in Woolf, *Moments of Being: Autobiographical Writings*, ed. Jeanne Schulkind (1978; repr. London: Pimlico, 2002), p. 106.

8 See Hermione Lee, *Virginia Woolf* (London: Chatto & Windus, 1996), pp. 100–4. See also K. Koutsantoni and M. Oakley, 'Hypothesis of Autism and Psychosis in the Case of Laura Makepeace Stephen', *Disability Studies*, vol. 4, no. 3 (2014), doi:10.2139/ssrn.2418709.

9 V. Bell, 'Notes on Virginia's Childhood', in Bell, *Sketches in Pen and Ink*, ed. Lia Giachero (London: Pimlico, 1997), p. 63.

10 V. Bell, 'Life at Hyde Park Gate after 1897', in Bell, *Sketches in Pen and Ink*, p. 67.

11 See, for example, V. Woolf, Wednesday, November 28 [1928], *TDVW*, vol. 3, p. 208.

12 Woolf, 'Sketch of the Past', p. 117.

13 Bell, 'Life at Hyde Park Gate after 1897', pp. 73–4.

14 Bell, 'Life at Hyde Park Gate after 1897', p. 75.

15 See V. Woolf, 'Reminiscences', written in 1907–8; her Memoir Club papers, '22 Hyde Park Gate' and 'Old Bloomsbury', which she read in 1920 and 1928; and 'Sketch of the Past', written in 1939 and 1940. These are all in Woolf, *Moments of Being*.

16 Woolf, 'Sketch of the Past', pp. 146 and 116.

17 Woolf, '22 Hyde Park Gate', p. 42. The memoir is believed to have been read to the Memoir Club on 17 November 1920, after which she quarrelled with Vanessa and Duncan. See V. Woolf, Tuesday, 23 November and Sunday, 5 December [1920], *TDVW*, vol. 2, pp. 75–7. See also Woolf, 'Sketch of the Past', pp. 82–3. For an objective, evidence-based account of sexual abuse in the Stephen family see Lee, *Virginia Woolf*, pp. 146–59.

18 Frances Spalding, *Vanessa Bell* (London: Weidenfeld & Nicolson, 1983).

19 V. Bell to R. Fry, September 13 [1911], GB181 SxMs56/1/28, VBRF 37.

20 V. Bell to R. Fry, Friday [28 December 1917], GB181 SxMs56/1/28, VBRF 245.

21 V. Bell, 'Notes on Bloomsbury', in Bell, *Sketches in Pen and Ink*, p. 99.

22 See 'At Home' invitation to 'Mr Sydney Turner', 1st March [1906], ink on card, 90 × 112 mm, Charleston Trust Collection.

23 Woolf, 'Sketch of the Past', p. 125; Bell, 'Notes on Bloomsbury', p. 100.

24 Bell, 'Notes on Bloomsbury', p. 101.

25 V. Bell to C. Bell, [September 1905], *SLVB*, p. 36.

26 V. Bell to M. Snowdon, 5 March [1922], GB181 SxMs56/1/31, VBMS 36A.

27 C. Bell to V. Bell, [*c.* May 1919] GB181 SxMs56/1/18, CBVB 75. See also V. Bell to D. Grant, Monday [5 May 1919], TGA 20078/1/44/92.

28 V. Bell to D. Grant, [spring 1919], TGA 20078/1/44/79.

29 See, for example, V. Bell to D. Grant, [June 9, 1919], TGA 20078/1/44/104.

30 V. Bell to D. Grant, Tuesday [27 May 1919], TGA 20078/1/44/93.

31 See R. Fry to V. Bell, May 19 and May 23, 1919, in *Letters of Roger Fry*, vol. 2, ed. Denys Sutton (London: Chatto & Windus, 1972), pp. 451–2.

32 D. Grant to V. Bell, June 7 [1919], TGA 8010/5/1188. The 'tray picture' was V. Bell, *Tea Things*, *c.*1919, oil on panel, 375 × 940 mm, private collection. It remained in Clive's collection until his death.

33 V. Bell to D. Grant, [July 30, 1919], TGA 20078/1/44/98.

34 V. Bell to R. Fry, Monday [October 30, 1913], GB181 SxMs56/1/28, VBRF 108.

35 V. Bell, *Dancing Couple*, 1913, bodycolour and oil on paper, 765 × 480 mm, Victoria and Albert Museum, London, E.734-1955. See V&A catalogue entry, V1747, https://collections.vam.ac.uk/item/O130535/dancing-couple-drawing-bell-vanessa/?carousel-image=2019MA7776 (accessed 14 April 2022).

36 V. Bell to R. Fry, Sep. 18 [1913], *SLVB*, pp. 144–5.

37 *Britain Can Make It*, Victoria and Albert Museum, London, 24 September–31 October 1946.

38 Quentin Bell, *Elders and Betters* (London: John Murray, 1995), p. 53.

39 Angelica Garnett, 'Prologue', in Bell, *Sketches in Pen and Ink*, p. 3.

40 I am indebted to Rosalind McKever for her insights into the curatorial challenges of attributing Vanessa's work in the V&A's collection and to Caroline Cuthbert, formerly of Anthony d'Offay Gallery, who described to me the process of attributing

Vanessa and Duncan's work in the 1970s. Attributions were important, not least, because the beneficiaries of their estates were different. She described a small team comprising Anthony d'Offay, Richard Morphet, Angelica Garnett and herself (in the background), working together on attributions at the d'Offay store at Thames House in *c*.1973 (in conversation with the author, 25 August 2023).
41 V. Bell to C. Bell, June 25 [1910], GB181 SxMs56/1/25, VBCB 7.
42 V. Woolf, 'Foreword', *Recent Paintings by Vanessa Bell with a Foreword by Virginia Woolf*, exh. cat. (London: London Artists' Association, 1930), unpaginated.
43 C. Bell, *Old Friends: Personal Recollections* (London: Chatto & Windus, 1956), p. 85.
44 R. Fry to V. Bell, September 16 [1917], in *Letters of Roger Fry*, vol. 2, pp. 415–16.
45 V. Bell, 'Memories of Roger Fry', in Bell, *Sketches in Pen and Ink*, p. 118.
46 R. Fry to V. Bell, September 16 [1917], in *Letters of Roger Fry*, vol. 2, p. 416. D. Grant to V. Bell, 10 June [1919], TGA 8010/5/1189.

CHAPTER 1: FAMILY AND SOCIAL IDENTITY

1 *Fair Women*, Grafton Galleries, 8 Grafton Street, London, 12 May–December 1894. See Meaghan Clarke, *Fashionability, Exhibition Culture and Gender Politics* (New York: Routledge, 2020). See also Leslie Stephen, *Sir Leslie Stephen's Mausoleum Book*, ed. Alan Bell (Oxford: Clarendon Press, 1977), pp. 31–2.
2 V. Woolf, Tuesday, 16 March 1897, in Woolf, *A Passionate Apprentice: The Early Journals, 1897–1909*, ed. Mitchell A. Leaska (London: Hogarth Press, 1990), p. 55.
3 V. Woolf, Thursday, 11 March 1897, in Woolf, *A Passionate Apprentice*, p. 52.
4 John Singer Sargent, *Ellen Terry as Lady Macbeth*, 1889, oil on canvas, 2210 × 1143 mm, Tate NO2053.
5 V. Woolf and V. Bell with Thoby Stephen, *Hyde Park Gate News: The Stephen Family Newspaper*, ed. Gill Lowe (London: Hesperus Press, 2005), pp. 8 and 11.
6 George Frederic Watts, *Sir Leslie Stephen*, 1878, oil on canvas, 660 × 530 mm, National Portrait Gallery, London, NPG L238. Woolf, 'Sketch of the Past', p. 124.
7 George Frederic Watts, *Julia Duckworth*, *c*. 1870, oil on canvas, 710 × 595 mm, Charleston Trust Collection, CHA/P/342. Its location at Charleston is listed in an inventory of pictures, June 1959, Charleston Trust Archive, uncatalogued, p. 6.
8 Vanessa's interest in this family resemblance is discussed in Wendy Hitchmough, *The Bloomsbury Look* (New Haven and London: Yale University Press, 2020), pp. 23–9.
9 V. Woolf, *Jacob's Room* (1922; repr. Letchworth: Hogarth Press, 1945), p. 141.
10 V. Woolf to E. Smyth, 12 January 1941, *TLVW*, vol. 6, p. 461.
11 See, for example, George Frederic Watts, *The Sisters*, 1856, oil on canvas, 2311 × 1448 mm, Watts Gallery – Art Village, gift from Mrs Michael Chapman (née Lilian Macintosh), 1946, COMWG 137.
12 V. Woolf and R. Fry, *Victorian Photographs of Famous Men and Fair Women by Julia Margaret Cameron* (London: L. and V. Woolf, 1926); V. Woolf, *To the Lighthouse* (London: Hogarth Press, 1927). V. Bell, *The Red Dress*, 1929, oil

on canvas, 733 × 605 mm, Royal Pavilion and Museums, Brighton and Hove, FA000394.

13 Woolf, 'Sketch of the Past', p. 98.

14 G. Burne-Jones, *Memorials of Edward Burne-Jones* (1906; repr. London: Macmillan, 1912), vol. 1, p. 188. Edward Burne-Jones, *The Annunciation*, 1879, oil on canvas, 2500 × 1045 mm, Lady Lever Art Gallery, LL 3634.

15 V. Woolf to M. Vaughan, [early January 1905], *TLVW*, vol. 1, p. 174.

16 Woolf et al., *Hyde Park Gate News*, 14 December 1891, p. 12.

17 Woolf, 'Sketch of the Past', p. 159.

18 British Library, Add. MS 70725–6.

19 Bell, 'Notes on Virginia's Childhood', p. 64.

20 Woolf et al., *Hyde Park Gate News*, 14 December 1891, p. 12.

21 Ibid., 16 May 1892, p. 64.

22 Ibid., 'Cristmas number' [1891], pp. 18–19.

23 Ibid., 30 May and 6 June 1892, pp. 67, 69.

24 Sylvia Milman was born at 22 The Grove, The Boltons, South Kensington on 30 October 1878. Census returns show that she was still living there in 1901. She was admitted to the Royal Academy Schools with Vanessa in July 1901 and both women were recommended by J.W. Nicol, indicating that Sylvia, like Vanessa, had first studied at the Cope and Nicol School of Painting.

25 Woolf et al., *Hyde Park Gate News*, 6 June 1892, p. 69.

26 Bell, 'Notes on Virginia's Childhood', p. 64.

27 Bell, 'Notes on Bloomsbury', p. 97.

28 V. Bell, 'Lecture Given at Leighton Park School', in Bell *Sketches in Pen and Ink*, p. 154.

29 Ibid., pp. 154–5.

30 L. Stephen to J. Duckworth, 19 July 1877, quoted in Noel Annan, *Leslie Stephen, the Godless Victorian* (New York: Random House, 1984), p. 119.

31 Bell, 'Notes on Virginia's Childhood', p. 61.

32 Ibid., p. 60.

33 Bell, 'Life at Hyde Park Gate after 1897', p. 73.

34 Woolf et al., *Hyde Park Gate News*, 6 June 1892, p. 69.

35 Ibid., 25 July 1892, p. 81.

36 Ibid., 26 September 1892, p. 86; Stella Duckworth's diary, October 1893, quoted in Anthony Curtis (ed.), *Before Bloomsbury: The 1900s Diaries of Three Kensington Ladies* (London: Eighteen Nineties Society, 2002), pp. 37–8.

37 The image is in an album of photographs catalogued as by Stella (Duckworth) Hills, Berg, https://digitalcollections.nypl.org/items/35201890-6026-013a-9048-0242ac110002. The album was not compiled by Stella, but rather assembled at a later date.

38 Woolf, 'Sketch of the Past', p. 140.

39 Spalding, *Vanessa Bell*, p. 11.

40 Leslie Stephen, *Sir Leslie Stephen's Mausoleum Book* (Oxford: Clarendon Press, 1977), p. 3.

41 Ibid., p. xiii.

42 See Hitchmough, *The Bloomsbury Look*, pp. 28–43.

43 V. Bell to C. Bell, Dec. 27 [1912], *SLVB*, p. 131.

44 See Lee, *Virginia Woolf*, p. 151.

45 See Woolf, *A Passionate Apprentice*, 2, 12, 13 and 14 February 1897, pp. 28, 34–5. Adrian was given his own Kodak camera as a birthday present from Stella and Jack in 1896. See Stella Duckworth, Tuesday 27 October 1896, Diary, Berg, MSS Woolf, Manuscripts and Typescript relating to Woolf.

46 Bell, 'Life at Hyde Park Gate after 1897', p. 71.

47 Ibid., p. 72.

48 See Lee, *Virginia Woolf*, pp. 146–59.

49 Bell, *Elders and Betters*, p. 46.

50 V. Bell to V. Woolf, Monday [Dec 5, 1904], Berg, Folder 5. See also V. Bell to V. Woolf, Sep. 8, [1904], Berg, Folder 1.

51 F. Shove to V. Bell, 4 December [1918], GB181, SxMs56/1/204, FSVB 11.

52 D. Carrington to L. Strachey, [13 February 1920], in Dora Carrington, *Carrington's Letters*, ed. Anne Chisholm (London: Chatto & Windus, 2017), pp. 143–4.

53 Bell, 'Life at Hyde Park Gate after 1897', p. 67.

54 Ibid., p. 68.

55 See Lee, *Virginia Woolf*, p. 139.

56 Bell, 'Life at Hyde Park Gate after 1897', p. 75.

57 Ibid., p. 77.

58 George Duckworth was unpaid secretary to the social reformer Charles Booth from 1892 to 1902. Gerald founded Gerald Duckworth and Company in 1898.

59 Woolf, 'Sketch of the Past', p. 151.

60 Bell, 'Life at Hyde Park Gate after 1897', p. 81.

61 L. Strachey to L. Woolf, September 10th 1901, in Lytton Strachey, *The Letters of Lytton Strachey*, ed. Paul Levy (London: Penguin, 2006), p. 6.

62 Bell, 'Memories of Roger Fry', p. 118.

63 V. Bell to M. Snowdon, April 18 [1903], GB181 SxMs56/1/31, VBMS 4.

64 Ibid.

65 V. Woolf to V. Dickinson, Monday night [December? 1903], *TLVW*, vol. 1, p. 112.

66 Saturday 1 January, 1898, Woolf, *A Passionate Apprentice*, p. 134.

67 Woolf, 'Reminiscences', p. 25.

CHAPTER 2: TRAINING AND TRAVEL

1 Woolf, 'Reminiscences', p. 2. See V. Bell to V. Woolf, April 20th [1908], *SLVB*, p. 62.

2 See Donata Levi and Paul Tucker, '"J after J. Ruskin": Line in the Art Teaching of John Ruskin and Ebenezer Cooke', *Journal of Art Historiography*, no. 22 (June 2020), pp. 1–16. See also Arthur Ebenezer Cooke, 'Ebenezer Cooke', in Foster Watson (ed.), *The Encyclopedia and Dictionary of Education*, vol. 1 (London: Pitman, 1921), p. 385.

3 Prospectus, Lent Term 1885, 'Grosvenor Select Classes for Ladies', Archive of the Institute for Education, CO/1/11.

4 John Ruskin, *The Elements of Drawing: Three Letters to Beginners* (London: Smith, Elder & Co., 1857).

5 Woolf, 'Reminiscences', p. 4.

6 Ruskin, *The Elements of Drawing*, p. 5.

7 Whitechapel Craft School, Annual Report 1897, quoted at https://fairfaxcholmeley. com/east-end-and-toynbee/the-craft-school-1890-1915/ (accessed 5 September 2022).

8 V. Bell, 'Lecture Given at Leighton Park School', pp. 157–8. See R. Fry to R. Vildrac, April 4, 1917 and R. Fry to M. Fry, May 2, 1917, in *Letters of Roger Fry*, vol. 2, pp. 408–9.

9 Bell, 'Life at Hyde Park Gate after 1897', p. 70.

10 See Royal Academy Schools admissions register, Royal Academy Archives. Margaret Kemplay Snowdon was admitted on 31 July 1900 and continued to study at the Schools until July 1905.

11 Stella Duckworth, Wednesday April 1, 1896, Diary, Berg Coll MSS Woolf, Manuscripts and Typescript relating to Woolf.

12 Woolf, *A Passionate Apprentice*, 3 March 1897, p. 47.

13 V. Bell to J.T. Stephen, Sunday [14 February 1897], GB181 SxMs56/1/32, VBTS 15.

14 See Duckworth, Diary, October 13 and 21, November 18 and 25, and December 4 1896; Woolf, *A Passionate Apprentice*, 29 April 1897, p. 78.

15 V. Bell to M. Snowdon, Monday [May 2, 1904], *SLVB*, p. 16.

16 Spalding, *Vanessa Bell*, p. 19.

17 Woolf, 'Reminiscences', pp. 2–3. V. Bell to J.T. Stephen, [June 1901], GB181 SxMs56/1/32, VBTS 11.

18 V. Bell to J.T. Stephen, [June 1901], GB181 SxMs56/1/32, VBTS 14.

19 V. Bell to J.T. Stephen, July 26 [1901], GB181 SxMs56/1/32, VBTS 19.

20 V. Bell to J.T. Stephen, [June 1901], GB181 SxMs56/1/32, VBTS 14.

21 Sylvia Whitman (née Milman), Catherine Ouless, Daisy Radcliffe Beresford (née Clague), Ethel Everett and Margaret (Margery) Snowdon were among Vanessa's cohort of students who went on to exhibit their work in London and elsewhere.

22 See Stephen, *Mausoleum Book*, p. 18n.

23 See Woolf et al., *Hyde Park Gate News*, pp. 100, 107 and 125. See also Stella Duckworth, Diary, 4 October 1893, quoted in Curtis, *Before Bloomsbury*, p. 38.

24 See Woolf, *A Passionate Apprentice*, 24 January, 19 and 28 February 1897, pp. 20, 39 and 44. Stella took 'Lisa's picture of Nessa' to the New Gallery in April 1896, suggesting that Vanessa sat to Lisa Stillman on previous occasions. Duckworth, Diary, Monday, April 13, 1896.

25 V. Bell to V. Woolf, July 3 [1918], *SLVB*, p. 215.

26 Bell, *Elders and Betters*, p. 48. The 14 January 1894 issue of *Hyde Park Gate News* describes a gift of '5 tickets for Santa Clause at the Lyceum' from Mrs Wickham Flower to Adrian Stephen, denoting a long-standing family connection: Woolf et al., *Hyde Park Gate News*, p. 167. See also Duckworth, Diary, January 10 and 31, February 21 and March 6, 1896.

27 V. Bell to J.T. Stephen, Monday [c.1897], GB181 SxMs56/1/32, VBTS 17.

28 Woolf, *A Passionate Apprentice*, 2 February, 23 February, 2 March, 23 March, 30 March, 11 May, 18 May and 1 June 1897, pp. 27, 41, 46, 58, 62, 84, 87, 94. Anon., 'The National Gallery: Sir Edward Poynter's Report', *Evening Standard*, 6 April 1899, p. 2.

29 James McNeill. Whistler, *Nocturne in Blue and Silver*, 1872–8, oil on canvas, 445 × 610 mm, Yale Centre for British Art, Paul Mellon Fund, B1994.19. The Flowers also owned Whistler's *Note in Blue and Opal – The Sun Cloud*, 1884, oil on wood panel, 124 × 217 mm, Freer Gallery of Art, Washington, DC, and *An Orange Note: Sweet Shop*, 1884, oil on wood panel, 122 × 215 mm, Freer Gallery of Art, Washington, DC.

30 V. Bell to M. Snowdon, [August 13, 1905], *SLVB*, p. 35.

31 James Abbott McNeill Whistler, *Arrangement in Grey and Black, No. 2: Portrait of Thomas Carlyle*, 1872–3, oil on canvas, 1711 × 1435 mm, Kelvingrove Art Gallery and Museum, Glasgow, 671. Although the painting was acquired by the museum in 1891, Vanessa would have seen it exhibited. There is a print of it in the Charleston Collection, CHA/PH/275. See also V. Bell to M. Snowdon, Monday [May 2, 1904], *SLVB*, p. 17.

32 Woolf, *A Passionate Apprentice*, 2 March 1897, p, 46.

33 See V. Woolf to E. Vaughan, October 23rd [1900], *TLVW*, vol. 1, pp. 28–39.

34 See Duckworth, Diary, Sunday, April 12, 1896.

35 See Woolf, *A Passionate Apprentice*, 6 and 7 March 1897, pp. 49–50. By 1897 Watts had a new house and studio, also named 'Little Holland House', in Melbury Road and a country house and studio, 'Limnerslease', in Compton, Surrey.

36 V. Bell to J.T. Stephen, [31 January 1897], GB181 SxMs56/1/32, VBTS 13.

37 Bell, 'Life at Hyde Park Gate after 1897', p. 74.

38 V. Bell to M. Snowdon, Saturday [March 17, 1903], GB181 SxMs56/1/31, VBMS 2 and V. Bell to M. Snowdon, [March 15, 1903], *SLVB*, p. 8.

39 V. Bell to M. Snowdon, [March 15, 1903], *SLVB*, pp. 8–11.

40 V. Bell to M. Snowdon, Saturday [March 17, 1903], GB181 SxMsVBMS56/1/31, VBMS 2.

41 Ibid.

42 Woolf, *A Passionate Apprentice*, 19 January 1997, p. 16.

43 V. Bell to M. Snowdon, Wednesday [April 6, 1904], *SLVB*, p. 12.

44 V. Bell to M. Snowdon, Friday [early April 1904], GB181 SxMs56/1/21, VBMS 6.

45 J.T. Stephen to C. Bell, [early April 1904], GB 181 SxMs56/1/221, JTSCB 15.

46 Ibid.

47 V. Bell to M. Snowdon, [April 6, 1904], *SLVB*, p. 14.

48 J.T. Stephen to C. Bell, [early April 1904], GB 181 SxMs56/1/221, JTSCB 15.

49 J.T. Stephen to C. Bell, [early April 1904], GB 181 SxMs56/1/221, JTSCB 15. V. Bell to M. Snowdon, [April 6, 1904], *SLVB*, pp. 13–14.

50 V. Bell to M. Snowdon, [April 6, 1904], *SLVB*, p. 13.

51 Photographer unknown, Tintoretto, *The Crucifixion*, detail, photograph, 310 × 430 mm, Charleston Trust Collection, CHA/PH/55.

52 V. Bell to M. Snowdon, Tuesday [April 19, 1904], GB181 SxMs56/1/21, VBMS 7.

53 V. Bell to J.T. Stephen, Monday [November 1896], *SLVB*, p. 6.

54 V. Bell to M. Snowdon, Friday [early April 1904], GB181 SxMs56/1/21, VBMS 6.

55 V. Bell to M. Snowdon, Tuesday [April 19, 1904], GB181 SxMs56/1/21, VBMS 7.

56 Ibid.

57 V. Bell to M. Snowdon, [April 25?, 1904], *SLVB*, p. 15.

58 V. Bell to M. Snowdon, Tuesday [April 19, 1904], GB181 SxMs56/1/21, VBMS 7.

59 V. Bell to M. Snowdon, [April 25?, 1904], *SLVB*, p. 15.

60 V. Bell to M. Snowdon, Sept 6th [1906], GB181 SxMs56/1/21, VBMS 16.

61 V. Bell to M. Snowdon, Tuesday [April 19, 1904], GB181 SxMs56/1/21, VBMS 7.

62 V. Bell to M. Snowdon, Sept 6th [1906], GB181 SxMs56/1/21, VBMS 16.

63 V. Bell to M. Snowdon, [May 2, 1904], *SLVB*, p. 16.

64 V. Woolf to V. Dickinson, [May 6?, 1904], *TLVW*, vol. 1, p. 140.

65 Mark Hussey, *Clive Bell and the Making of Modernism* (London: Bloomsbury, 2021), pp. 23–5.

66 V. Bell to M. Snowdon, [May 2, 1904], *SLVB*, p. 16.

67 C. Bell, 'Paris 1904', in Bell, *Old Friends*, pp. 141, 143–4.

68 C. Bell, untitled paper on Paris in 1904, presented to the Memoir Club, n.d., Trinity College, Cambridge, Papers of Clive Bell, BELL/3/8. This passage is not included in the published version of the memoir.

69 Bell, 'Paris 1904', p. 168.

70 See V. Woolf to V. Dickinson, [May 6?, 1904], *TLVW*, vol. 1, p. 140.

71 V. Bell to C. Bell, [May 11, 1904], GB181 SxMs56/1/25, VBCB b. See also V. Woolf to V. Dickinson, [May 6?, 1904], *TLVW*, vol. 1, p. 140.

72 V. Bell to M. Snowdon, [May 2, 1904], *SLVB*, p. 16.

73 Ibid.

74 Bell, 'Memories of Roger Fry', p. 129. Camille Mauclair, *The French Impressionists. 1860–1900*, trans. P.G. Konody (London: Duckworth & Co., 1903), was first published in English in the Popular Library of Art series.

75 V. Bell to M. Snowdon [May 2, 1904], *SLVB*, p. 17.

76 See Deborah Cherry, *Beyond the Frame: Feminism and Visual Culture 1850–1900* (London and New York: Routledge, 2000), pp. 15–20.

77 S.S. Beale, *Recollections of a Spinster Aunt* (London: Heinemann, 1908) pp. 140–1.

78 V. Bell to M. Snowdon, Jan 4th [1902], GB 181 SxMs56/1/21, VBMS 1.

79 V. Bell to M. Snowdon, [October–November 1903], *SLVB*, p. 11.

80 Woolf, 'Old Bloomsbury', pp. 45–6.

81 Bell, 'Notes on Bloomsbury', p. 98.

82 Bell, 'Memories of Roger Fry', p. 118.

83 See V. Bell to V. Woolf, Dec. 7th [1904], *SLVB*, p. 27, and Bell, 'Memories of Roger Fry', p. 118.

84 V. Bell to M. Snowdon, Jan. 11th [1905], *SLVB*, p. 28.

85 Woolf, *A Passionate Apprentice*, Friday 24 March [1905], p. 256.

CHAPTER 3: EARLY WORK, ART CLUBS AND EXHIBITIONS

1 V. Bell to V. Woolf, March 22 [1907], Berg, Folder 8.

2 Snowdon lived at Alexandra House, Bremner Road, Kensington Gore, a hostel built for women students in 1884.

3 Bell, 'Notes on Bloomsbury', pp. 98–9.

4 V. Woolf to V. Dickinson, [February 27, 1910], *TLVW*, vol. 1, p. 422.

5 V. Bell to V. Woolf, [October 1904], Berg, Folder 1.

6 V. Woolf to V. Dickinson, [8 November 1904] and 30 Oct. [1904], *TLVW*, vol. 1, pp. 153 and 147.

7 Bell, 'Notes on Bloomsbury', p. 99.

8 Woolf, 'Old Bloomsbury', p. 46.

9 V. Bell to V. Woolf, [Nov. 5, 1904], Berg, Folder 2.

10 Ibid.

11 V. Bell to V. Woolf, Nov. 1 [1904], Berg, Folder 2.

12 Bell, 'Notes on Bloomsbury', p. 99.

13 Woolf, 'Old Bloomsbury', p. 46.

14 V. Bell to V. Woolf, [Oct. 29, 1904], Berg, Folder 2.

15 V. Bell to V. Woolf, Friday [Nov. 25, 1904], Berg, Folder 4. V. Woolf to M. Vaughan, *TLVW*, vol. 1, p. 161.

16 V. Bell to V. Woolf, Saturday [Oct. 29, 1904], Berg, Folder 2.

17 V. Woolf to V. Dickinson, [January 14, 1905], *TLVW*, vol. 1, p. 175.

18 See L. Strachey to L. Woolf, February 28, 1905, in *The Letters of Lytton Strachey*, p. 54; V. Woolf to E. Vaughan, Feb. 23, [1905] and V. Woolf to V. Dickinson, [February 28, 1905], *TLVW*, vol. 1, pp. 179–81.

19 See for example, V. Bell to J.M. Keynes, Sunday [1907], GB181 SxMs56/1/30, VBMK 1.

20 Bell, 'Notes on Bloomsbury', pp. 99–100.

21 Ibid., p. 101.

22 V. Bell to M. Snowdon, Jan. 11 [1905], *SLVB*, p. 28.

23 'Eleanor Cecil (Lady)', *Mapping Women's Suffrage*, https://map.mappingwomens suffrage.org.uk/items/show/300 (accessed 28 October 2022).

24 V. Bell to V. Woolf, Thursday [December 8?, 1904], Berg, Folder 6.

25 V. Bell to V. Woolf, Saturday [April 14, 1906], Berg, Folder 7.

26 V. Bell to V. Woolf, Sunday [April 15, 1906], *SLVB*, p. 38.

27 V. Bell to V. Woolf, Friday [April 13, 1906], Berg, Folder 7.

28 V. Bell to V. Woolf, Tuesday [April 17, 1906], Berg, Folder 7.

29 V. Bell to V. Woolf, Wednesday [April 18, 1906], Berg, Folder 8.

30 V. Bell to M. Snowdon, Wednesday [August 23, 1906], GB181 SxMs56/1/31, VBMS 15.

31 V. Bell to V. Woolf, Friday [March 1908], Berg, Folder 11.

32 V. Bell to C. Bell, Friday [July 1905], GB181 SxMs56/1/25, VBCB e.

33 V. Bell to M. Snowdon, Mar. 5 [1922], GB181 SxMs56/1/31, VBMS 36A.

34 V. Bell to C. Bell, Friday [July 1905], GB181 SxMs56/1/25, VBCB e.

35 V. Bell to C. Bell, Monday [September (?) 1905], *SLVB*, pp. 36–7. Vanessa was in Cornwall in September, making it more likely that this letter, which lists the rooms that Vanessa had viewed and anticipates a second committee meeting, dates from July 1905.

36 V. Bell to C. Bell, Friday [July 1905], GB181 SxMs56/1/25, VBCB f.

37 V. Bell to L. Woolf, July 20 [*c*.1950], *SLVB*, p. 527.

38 V. Bell to C. Bell, Friday [July 1905], GB181 SxMs56/1/25, VBCB e.

39 C. Bell to L. Strachey, July 20 [1905], quoted in Hussey, *Clive Bell and the Making of Modernism*, p. 35.

40 V. Woolf to V. Dickinson, Aug. 27 [1905], *TLVW*, vol. 1, p. 206.

41 V. Woolf to V. Dickinson, Oct. 1 [1905], *TLVW*, vol. 1, pp. 208–9. Her Cornwall diary is published in Woolf, *A Passionate Apprentice*, pp. 281–99.

42 V. Woolf to V. Dickinson, Nov. 9 [1905], *TLVW*, vol. 1, p. 210.

43 Ibid., and V. Woolf to Lady Robert Cecil, Nov. 10 [1905], *TLVW*, vol. 1, pp. 210–11.

44 V. Woolf, *Night and Day* (1919; repr. Oxford and New York: Oxford University Press, 1999), p. 44.

45 V. Woolf to V. Bell, April 22 [1918], *TLVW*, vol. 2, p. 232.

46 Woolf, *Night and Day*, pp. 48–52.

47 V. Woolf to V. Dickinson, Sunday [December 3, 1905], *TLVW*, vol. 1, p. 213.

48 The support is a French artists' board retailed in Paris. Vanessa used 'prepared canvas board' such as those produced by Winsor & Newton when she needed to work quickly outdoors or for sketch portraits such as, for example, *Julian Bell*, 1908, oil on board, 160 × 215 mm, Charleston Trust Collection CHA/P/68. The subject of *Cornish Cottage* is the seventeenth-century building now known as The Mariners, Church Cove, The Lizard, Penzance. When Vanessa and her siblings were staying at Carbis Bay, Cornwall, in August 1905 Virginia wrote: 'We went for a walk this afternoon which we used to go every Sunday, and saw the Lizard and Michaels Mount.' V. Woolf to V. Dickinson, [August 13?, 1905], *TLVW*, vol. 1, p. 204. This, however, would have been a distant view. The Lizard is 23 miles from Carbis Bay. Vanessa's itinerary on her visit to Cornwall in August/September 1905 is unknown but when she returned to Cornwall in March 1909 and stayed at The Lizard she wrote, 'This house of course is very uncomfortable. I didn't realise it last time.' V. Bell to L. Strachey, [March 8, 1909], *SLVB*, p. 79. On this second visit she wrote that 'A melancholy watercolour of a sunset is my only achievement'. V. Bell to V. Woolf, Friday [March 12, 1909], *SLVB*, p. 81.

49 V. Bell to M. Snowdon, Sunday [August 13, 1905], *SLVB*, p. 35.

50 L. Strachey to L. Woolf, Thursday, December 7, 1905, in *The Letters of Lytton Strachey*, p. 86.

51 Nina Euphemia Forrest was inventive about the details of her romantic and sexual encounters, as were the artists with whom she was involved. See Michael Holroyd, *Augustus John* (London: Chatto & Windus, 1996), pp. 248–51.

52 V. Bell to M. Snowdon, Dec. 21 [1905], GB181 SxMs56/1/31, VBMS 12.

53 Ibid.

54 V. Woolf to V. Dickinson, [January 3?, 1906], *TLVW*, vol. 1, p. 215. V. Bell to M. Snowdon, Friday [April 1907], GB181 SxMs56/1/31, VBMS 20.

55 V. Bell to C. Bell, Monday [n.d.], GB181 SxMs56/1/25, VBCB T.

56 See, for example, V. Bell to V. Woolf, Saturday [April 14, 1906], Berg, Folder 7. Bison was a word she used for Bishop.

57 V. Woolf to M. Vaughan, [April 27, 1906], *TLVW*, vol. 1, p. 224.

58 L. Strachey to L. Woolf, January 26, 1906, in *The Letters of Lytton Strachey*, p. 95.

59 L. Strachey to L. Woolf, February 2, 1906, in *The Letters of Lytton Strachey*, p. 98.

60 L. Strachey to L. Woolf, January 26, 1906, in *The Letters of Lytton Strachey*, p. 95.

61 L. Strachey to L. Woolf, February 2, 1906, in *The Letters of Lytton Strachey*, p. 98.

62 V. Woolf to M. Vaughan, [April 27, 1906]. See also V. Woolf to Lady Robert Cecil, [December 1907], *TLVW*, vol. 1, pp. 224 and 321.

63 V. Bell to J.M. Keynes, Dec. 5 [1907], GB181 SxMs56/1/30, VBMK 2.

64 See V. Woolf to V. Dickinson, Monday [November 14, 1910], and V. Woolf to C. Bell, [January 23, 1911], *TLVW*, vol. 1, pp. 437–8 and 450.

65 R. Fry to V. Bell, Jan. 19, 1910, GB181 SxMs56/1/83, RFVB 1.

66 See R. Shone, 'The Friday Club', *Burlington Magazine*, vol. 117, no. 866 (May 1975), p. 279, n.1.

67 V. Woolf to V. Dickinson, [June 1906], *TLVW*, vol. 1, p. 228.

68 V. Woolf to V. Dickinson, [May 1907], *TLVW*, vol. 1, p. 295.

69 V. Bell to C. Bell, June 22nd [1910], GB181 SxMs56/1/25, VBCB 2. Elmslie is listed as Honorary Secretary in the catalogue to the 1912 Friday Club exhibition.

70 *Catalogue of an Exhibition of Pictures by Members of the Friday Club*, 10–24 February 1912, Alpine Club Galleries, Mill Street, Conduit Street, London. National Art Library, Victoria and Albert Museum, 200.B.168/2.

71 See V. Bell to D. Grant, Feb. 25 [1914], *SLVB*, p. 156. David Bomberg, *Vision of Ezekiel*, 1912, oil on canvas, 2103 × 1435 mm, Tate, T01197.

72 V. Bell to C. Bell, Thursday [June 23, 1910], *SLVB*, p. 92.

73 D. Grant, *Lemon Gatherers*, 1910, oil on board, 5650 × 8130 mm, Tate, N03666.

74 V. Bell to M. Snowdon, Sunday [August 13, 1905], *SLVB*, p. 34.

75 V. Bell to M. Snowdon, Aug. 11 [1906], GB181 SxMs56/1/31, VBMS 14.

76 V. Bell to C. Bell, Monday [July 30, 1906], *SLVB*, p. 41.

77 A. Stephen to C. Bell, Wed. October 24 [1906], GB181 SxMs56/1/215, ASCB 1.

78 V. Bell to M. Snowdon, Thursday [November 1, 1906], *SLVB*, p. 42.

79 V. Bell to C. Bell, Wednesday [November 7, 1906], *SLVB*, pp. 43–4. See also V. Bell to C. Bell, October 24 and November 2, 1906, GB181 SxMs56/1/25, VBCB P and VBCB Q.

80 V. Woolf to V. Dickinson, Friday night [November 16, 1906], *TLVW*, vol. 1, p. 246. L. Strachey to L. Woolf, July 4, 1905, in *The Letters of Lytton Strachey*, p. 73.

81 L. Strachey to L. Woolf, Monday, November 26 1906, Strachey 2006, pp. 213–16.

82 L. Strachey to L. Woolf, Monday, November 26 1906, in *The Letters of Lytton Strachey*, p. 115. They moved to 29 Fitzroy Square in Bloomsbury.

83 V. Bell to V. Woolf, March 22 [1907], Berg, Folder 8.

84 V. Bell to M. Snowdon, Friday [April 1907], GB181 SxMs56/1/31, VBMS 20.

85 See Christopher Reed, *Bloomsbury Rooms* (New Haven and London: Yale University Press, 2004), pp. 29–30; Richard Shone, *The Art of Bloomsbury* (London: Tate Gallery, 1999), p. 61; Christopher Reed, 'Apples: 46 Gordon Square', *Charleston Newsletter*, 23 June 1989, pp. 20–4.

86 V. Bell to M. Snowdon, Oct. 21 [1908], *SLVB*, pp. 75–7.

87 V. Bell, *Sketchbook with Drawings of the Infant Julian Bell,* 1908, pencil on paper, 380 × 245 mm, Charleston Trust Collection, CHA/P/4161.

88 Hussey, *Clive Bell and the Making of Modernism*, pp. 51–80, 103.

89 See C. Bell to V. Woolf, [December 25, 1909], in *Selected Letters of Clive Bell: Art, Love and War in Bloomsbury*, ed. Mark Hussey (Edinburgh: Edinburgh University Press, 2023), p. 45.

90 V. Bell to M. Snowdon, Sep. 26 [1908], GB181 SxMs56/1/31, VBMS 25.

91 V. Bell to M. Snowdon, Oct. 7 [1908], GB181 SxMs56/1/31, VBMS 26.

92 See *The London Salon of the Allied Artists' Association Ltd*, Royal Albert Hall, July 1908, exh. cat. V. Bell is correctly listed in the index but her work, *Portrait*, is listed under the name of Clive Bell, cat. no. 1421, p. 68. https://archive.org/details/AAALondonSalon1908/page/n1/mode/2up (accessed 21 November 2022).

93 V. Bell to M. Snowdon, June [1908], GB181 SxMs56/1/31, VBMS 21.

94 Frank Rutter, 'Foreword', *The London Salon of the Allied Artists' Association*, 1908, p. 5.

95 The New English Art Club showed 95 works by 46 men and 5 women in October 1905. In May 1909 it showed 270 works by 73 men and 35 women.

96 V. Bell, *Iceland Poppies*, 1908–9, oil on canvas, 540 × 450 mm, Charleston Trust Collection, CHA/P/468. V. Bell to M. Snowdon, Oct. 7 [1908], GB181 SxMs56/1/31, VBMS 26.

97 Augustus John, *The Childhood of Pyramus*, c.1908, oil on canvas, 1206 × 1505 mm, Johannesburg Art Gallery.

98 V. Bell to M. Snowdon, Oct. 7 [1908], GB 181 SxMs56/1/31, VBMS 26.

99 V. Bell to M. Snowdon, May 18 [1909], GB 181 SxMs56/1/31, VBMS 30. Henry Lamb exhibited six works in the *Forty-First Exhibition of Modern Pictures. New English Art Club* from 22 May 1909, Sylvia Milman none.

100 Spalding, *Vanessa Bell*, p. 82.

101 See Shone, *The Art of Bloomsbury*, p. 59, although this species of *Papaver nudicaule* was not a source of opium.

102 G. [Duncan Grant], 'The New English Art Club at Suffolk Street', *Spectator*, 19 June 1909, p. 977.

103 W. Sickert to V. Bell, [undated, *c.* May/June 1909], private collection.

CHAPTER 4: PLACE MAKING

1 V. Bell to C. Bell, Sunday [December 1910], GB181 SxMs56/1/25, VBCB 76.

2 The premiere of *Salome*, Op. 54 by Richard Strauss at the Royal Opera House, London, was on 8 December 1910. *Manet and the Post-Impressionists*, Grafton Galleries, 8 Grafton Street, London, 8 November 1910–11 January 1911.

3 See V. Bell to R. Fry, Aug. 9 [1911], GB181 SxMs56/1/28, VBRF 15.

4 Bell, 'Memories of Roger Fry', p. 118.

5 Ibid., pp. 118–19.

6 Fry accepted this role at the Metropolitan Museum in January 1906. The following year his title was changed to that of European advisor to the Department of Paintings.

7 Bell, 'Memories of Roger Fry', p. 121.

8 Ibid., p. 124.

9 See R. Fry to O. Morrell, Sept. 22, 1910, Ottoline Morrell Collection, Harry Ransom Center, Box 7, Folder 7.2. V. Bell to C. Bell, Oct. 9 [1910], *SLVB*, p. 95. See also Anna Greutzner Robins, '"Manet and the Post-Impressionists": A Checklist of Exhibits', *Burlington Magazine*, vol. 152, no. 1293 (December 2010), pp. 782–93. V. Bell to C. Bell, Oct. 11 [1910], GB181 SxMs56/1/25, VBCB 73.

10 V. Woolf, 'Mr Bennett and Mrs Brown' (1924), in her *Collected Essays*, vol. 1 (London: Hogarth Press, 1966), pp. 319–37.

11 Bell, 'Memories of Roger Fry', pp. 129–30.

12 V. Bell to V. Woolf, Friday [August 9, 1907], Berg, Folder 10.

13 V. Bell to C. Bell, Sunday [5 February, 1911], GB181 SxMs56/1/25, VBCB 43.

14 V. Woolf to M. MacCarthy, [April 1911], *TLVW*, vol. 1, p. 456.

15 V. Bell to C. Bell, Sunday [5 February 1911], GB181 SxMs56/1/25, VBCB 43.

16 Bell, 'Memories of Roger Fry', p. 130.

17 V. Bell to R. Fry, Monday [13 November? 1911], GB181 SxMs56/1/28, VBRF 23.

18 V. Bell to V. Woolf, Monday [4 March? 1912], Berg, Folder 34. See Shone, *The Art of Bloomsbury*, pp. 84–5.

19 *Exposition de Quelques Indépendants Anglais*, Galerie Barbazanges, Paris, 1–15 May 1912. Although the only appropriate catalogue entry would be 'La Chaise', cat. no. 4, the catalogue may not include all the exhibits. The painting is inscribed on the back 'Galerie Barbazanges . . . par Vanessa Bell (Mme)'. In addition, it was catalogued in *Vanessa Bell: A Memorial Exhibition of Paintings*, Arts Council, 1964, as 'Exhibited at the Galerie Barbazanges, Paris, July 1912'.

20 Bell, 'Memories of Roger Fry', p. 127.

21 Ibid., pp. 132–3.

22 V. Bell to R. Fry, Sunday [August 27, 1911], GB181 SxMs56/1/28, VBRF 63.

23 V. Bell to R. Fry, Sep. 27 [1911], GB181 SxMs56/1/28, VBRF 43.

24 V. Bell to R. Fry, Aug. 16 [1911], GB181, SxMs56/1/28, VBRF 17.

25 V. Bell to R. Fry, Nov. 15 [1911], GB181, SXMs56/1/28, VBRF 51.

26 V. Bell to C. Bell, Oct. 9 [1911], GB181, SxMs56/1/25, VBCB 17.

27 Pablo Picasso, *Pots et Citron*, 1907, oil on canvas, 550 × 460 mm, Albertina Museum, Vienna, Batliner Collection, GE96DL.

28 V. Bell to R. Fry, Nov. 15 [1911], GB181 SXMs56/1/28, VBRF 51.

29 R. Fry to O. Morrell, Apr. 22, 1911, Ottoline Morrell Collection, Harry Ransom Center, Box 7, Folder 7.2.

30 V. Bell to C. Bell, Tuesday [16 January 1912], GB181 SxMs56/1/25, VBCB 14.

31 V. Bell to V. Woolf, Jan 13 [1912], Berg, Folder 35.

32 D. Grant in conversation with R. Shone, August 1965, quoted in Shone, *The Art of Bloomsbury*, p. 70.

33 V. Bell to M. Snowdon, June 7 [1908], GB181 SxMs56/1/31, VBMS 21.

34 V. Bell to M. Snowdon, Oct. 21 [1908], *SLVB*, p. 77.

35 Virginia Woolf [unsigned], '"The Post-Impressionists" by C. Lewis Hind', *Nation*, 14 October 1911, p. 108. V. Bell to V. Woolf, October 20 [1911] *SLVB*, pp. 110–11.

36 V. Bell to V. Woolf, Sunday [October 22, 1911], Berg, Folder 34.

37 V. Bell, *Virginia Woolf*, *c.* 1911–12, oil on board, 550 × 450 mm, National Trust, Monk's House, 468417. R. Fry, *Virginia Woolf*, *c.* 1911–12, oil on board, 402 × 310 mm, private collection.

38 Paul Cézanne, *Madame Cézanne in a Red Armchair*, *c.*1877, oil on canvas, 724 × 559 mm, Museum of Fine Arts, Boston, bequest of Robert Treat Paine, 2nd, 44.776. See Robins, 'Checklist of Exhibits', p. 785, n. 38.

39 See, for example, Paul Cézanne, *Seated Man*, 1905–6, oil on canvas, 648 × 546 mm, Museo Nacional Thyssen–Bornemisza, Madrid, 488(1976.68).

40 V. Woolf to L. Woolf, Tuesday [March 5, 1912], *TLVW*, vol. 1, p. 491.

41 Frances Spalding, 'Vanessa, Virginia and the Modern Portrait', in Sarah Milroy and Ian A.C. Dejardin (eds), *Vanessa Bell* (London: Philip Wilson, 2017), pp. 65–71.

42 V. Bell to V. Woolf, Tuesday [April 30, 1912; erroneously dated May 17], *SLVB*, p. 115.

43 V. Bell, *Portrait d'un Peintre, Exposition de Quelques Indépendants Anglais*, cat. no. 3 (listed by artist).

44 V. Bell to D. Grant, May 10 [1912], TGA 20078/1/44/8.

45 D. Grant, *The Queen of Sheba*, 1912, oil on board, 1200 × 1200 mm, presented by the Contemporary Art Society, 1917, Tate, N03169.

46 V. Bell to D. Grant, May 15 [1912], TGA 20078/1/44/9.

47 V. Bell to R. Fry, June 6 [1912], *SLVB*, p.120.

48 V. Bell to R. Fry, Sep. 14 [1911], GB181 SXMs56/1/28, VBRF 38.

49 See Vanessa's comments on Frederick and Duncan's mural at 38 Brunswick Square, V. Bell to R. Fry, June 6 [1912], *SLVB*, p. 119.

50 Leonard Woolf, *Beginning Again: An Autobiography of the Years 1911 to 1918* (London: Hogarth Press, 1972), pp. 56–61. His account of finding the house while walking from Little Talland House with Virginia omits Vanessa's essential role, combining her income and organisational skills with those of her sister to negotiate and manage the lease. Leonard and Virginia were not even engaged to be married when these negotiations began. Although Virginia and Leonard used Asheham extensively in 1913 due to Virginia's illness, a letter from Vanessa clarifies their arrangement: 'I suppose that as things are I have a half share in the letting, but if you want to we could probably come to some arrangement about my taking it. In any case, if you don't want to be there I should like to have it for such weekends as are due to me. You see except for 6 weeks in the winter we have had no good at all out of it this year, but as you have wanted it for special reasons all this time of course there is every reason why you should have had it.' V. Bell to V. Woolf, July 3 [1913], Berg, Folder 40. See also V. Bell to V. Woolf, Sep. 2 [1912], Berg, Folder 38.

51 V. Bell to C. Bell, Aug. 17 [1912], GB181 SxMs56/1/25, VBCB 27.

52 Frederick and Jessie Etchells stayed at Asheham from 28 August to 4 September 1912.

53 V. Bell to C. Bell, Aug. 20 [1912], GB181 SxMs56/1/25, VBCB 34.

54 V. Bell to V. Woolf, Aug. 19 [1912], *SLVB*, p. 124. V. Bell to R. Fry, Aug. 19 [1912], GB181 SxMs56/1/28, VBRF 71.

55 V. Bell, *The Studio: Duncan Grant and Henri Doucet Painting at Asheham*, 1912, oil on board, 572 × 445 mm, private collection, reproduced in Reed, *Bloomsbury Rooms*, fig. 51.

56 V. Bell to C. Bell, Saturday [August 24, 1912], GB181 SxMs56/1/25, VBCB 30. V. Bell to D. Grant, Sep. 1 [1912], TGA 20078/1/44/11; V. Bell to R. Fry, Sep. 4 [1912], GB181 SxMs56/1/28, VBRF 73. V. Bell to R. Fry, Sep. 4 [1912], GB181 SxMs56/1/28, VBRF 73.

57 D. Grant, *Second Post-Impressionist Exhibition*, 1912, line block print poster, 856 × 576 mm, Victoria and Albert Museum, Given by Miss Margery Fry, JP, E.737-1955.

58 Reed, *Bloomsbury Rooms*, p. 89.

59 V. Bell to M. Snowdon, Sep. 18 [1912], GB181 SxMs56/1/31, VBMS 33.

60 V. Bell to V. Woolf, Sep. 2 [1912], Berg, Folder 38.

61 V. Bell to V. Woolf, Sep. 14 [1912], Berg, Folder 38.

CHAPTER 5: WOMEN AND CHILDREN

1 Walter Richard Sickert, 'The naked and the Nude', *The New Age*, 21 July 1910, pp. 276–7. Critics were outraged by Sickert's two *Camden Town Murder* paintings exhibited in *The First Exhibition of the Camden Town Group*, June 1911, Carfax Gallery, London, cat. nos 10 and 12. Vanessa described a meeting with him soon after the exhibition in which she 'had a long and intimate and interesting conversation with him . . . we talked of painting'. V. Bell to R. Fry, Sunday [July 2, 1911], *SLVB*, p. 102.

2 R. Fry, 'The French Group', *The Second Post-Impressionist Exhibition*, exh. cat. (London: Grafton Galleries, 1912), p. 27.

3 Maurice Denis and R. Fry, 'Cézanne – I', *Burlington Magazine*, vol. 16, no. 82 (January 1910), pp. 207–19, and Maurice Denis, 'Cézanne –II', *Burlington Magazine*, vol.16, no. 83 (February 1910), pp. 275–80. As Frances Spalding has noted, Roger also praised recent work by Denis exhibited in Paris in June 1911: R. Fry, 'The Salons and Van Dougen [sic]', *Nation*, 24 June 1911, pp. 463–4.

4 D. Grant, *Bathing*, 1911, oil on canvas, 2286 × 3061 mm, Tate, N04567. Bell, 'Memories of Roger Fry', pp. 145–6.

5 Vanessa stayed at Harbour View, Studland, managed by the Gibbons family, from 16 September to 7 October 1909, from *c*.25 March to 15 April 1910, from 13 September to 13 October 1910, and from 1 to 29 September 1911. V. Bell to V. Woolf, [Aug. 8] and [Aug. 17, 1909], Berg, Folders 21 and 22. Quentin Bell recalled a fifth visit after April 1912: see V. Bell to R. Fry, Feb. 7 [1912 or 1913], GB181, SxMs56/1/28, VBRF 2. There is further evidence that the children and their nurses were at Studland in May 1912: V. Bell to V. Woolf, [May 1912] and May 10 [1912], Berg, Folder 36. See also V. Bell to V. Woolf, Sunday [January 26, 1913], Berg, Folder 39. See also the online catalogue entry for *Studland Beach*, https://www.tate.org.uk/art/artworks/bell-studland-beach-verso-group-of-male-nudes-by-duncan-grant-t02080 (accessed 12 January 2022). Harbour View has subsequently been renamed 'Seacombe'.

6 V. Bell to V. Woolf, Oct. 3 [1910], Berg, Folder 31.

7 V. Bell, *Figure on the Beach, Studland Bay*, *c*.1910, oil on board, 350 × 255 mm, private collection; V. Bell, *The Beach, Studland*, *c*.1912 (fig. 5.2).

8 V. Bell, *Bathers*, 1911 (fig. 5.3); V. Bell, *Studland Beach*, *c*.1912 (fig. 5.1).

9 V. Bell to R. Fry, Sep. 7 [1911], GB181 SxMs56/1/28, VBRF 34.

10 Lisa Tickner, 'Vanessa Bell: Studland Beach, Domesticity, and "Significant Form"', *Representations*, 65 (Winter 1999), p. 68.

11 Minutes for Studland Parish Council meeting, 15 April 1907, *Studland Parish Council Minute Book, 1894–1927*, Dorset History Centre, Dorchester, PC/STD/1/1/1, quoted in Martin Ferguson Smith, 'A Complete Strip-Off: A Bloomsbury Threesome in the Nude at Studland', *British Art Journal*, vol. 20 (2019), no. 2, p. 75.

12 See, for example, Paul Cézanne, *Three Bathers*, oil on canvas, 550 × 520 mm, Musée de la Ville de Paris, Petit Palais, Paris, PPP2099. The painting was acquired by Matisse from Ambroise Vollard in 1899.

13 Tickner, 'Vanessa Bell: Studland Beach', pp. 63–92.

14 Piero della Francesa, *Madonna del Parto*, *c*.1455, detached fresco, 2600 × 2030 mm, Musei Civici Madonna del Parto, Monterchi. See Sarah Milroy, 'Some Rough Eloquence', in Milroy and Dejardin, *Vanessa Bell*, p. 32. Piero della Francesca, *Madonna della Misericordia*, 1460–2, tempera and oil on panel, 2730 × 3300 mm, Museo Civico di Sansepolcro. Spalding, *Vanessa Bell*, p. 124.

15 V. Bell to R. Fry, Nov. 2 [1912], GB181 SxMs56/1/28, VBRF 81.

16 V. Bell to V. Woolf, July 29 [1910], Berg, Folder 30.

17 See V. Bell to V. Woolf, Aug. 6 [1910], Berg, Folder 31.

18 V. Bell to C. Bell, Sep. 7 [1910], GB181 SxMs56/1/25, VBCB 64.

19 V. Bell to C. Bell, Sunday [August 28, 1910], GB181 SxMs56/1/25, VBCB 60.

20 V. Bell to V. Woolf, Sunday [July 1910], Berg, Folder 30. See also V. Bell to V. Woolf, Dec. 31 [1926], Berg, Folder 61.

21 V. Bell to V. Woolf, Sunday [July 1910], Berg, Folder 30.

22 Vanessa Bell's photograph album CH 1 (TGA 9020/1). For an analysis of this album see Hitchmough, *The Bloomsbury Look*, pp. 41–50. I was unaware of Vanessa's letter to Virginia establishing the date of this album until I visited the Berg Collection in September 2022. There is an 'H.J. Ryman, stationer' sticker inside the album's cover that correlates with Vanessa's letter to Virginia: 'I have spent

most of my time arranging my family album. I bought one from your stationer.'
V. Bell to V. Woolf, Sunday [July 1910], Berg, Folder 30. See also Maggie Humm,
Snapshots of Bloomsbury: The Private Lives of Virginia Woolf and Vanessa Bell
(London: Tate, 2006).

23 V. Bell, photograph album CH 1 (TGA 9020/1), p. 39.

24 V. Bell to V. Woolf, July 27 [1910], Berg, Folder 30.

25 V. Bell to V. Woolf, Tuesday [August 30, 1910], Berg, Folder 31.

26 V. Bell to V. Woolf, July 27 [1910], Berg, Folder 31.

27 V. Bell to C. Bell, Sep. 6 [1910], GB181 SxMs56/1/25, VBCB 63.

28 V. Bell, photograph album CH 1 (TGA 9020/1), p. 35.

29 This theme was developed in the London Borough Polytechnic murals. For
an analysis of the beach as a gendered modern subject see Tickner, 'Vanessa Bell:
Studland Beach', pp. 72–4.

30 V. Bell to C. Bell, Sunday [October 9, 1910], GB181 SxMs56/1/25, VBCB 68.

31 V. Bell to C. Bell, Oct. 9 [1910] *SLVB*, p. 95.

32 V. Bell to C. Bell, Oct. 7 [1910], GB181 SxMs56/1/25, VBCB 8.

33 V. Bell to C. Bell, Thursday [June 23, 1910], *SLVB*, p. 93. V. Bell to V. Woolf,
Oct. 3 [1910], Berg, Folder 31.

34 V. Bell to R. Fry, Aug. 31 [1911], GB181 SxMs56/1/28, VBRF 33. V. Bell to
R. Fry, Aug. 25 [1911], GB181 SxMs56/1/28, VBRF 30.

35 An archive of Bloomsbury photographs and negatives, 1908–1965 (1910–1913),
Berg Coll+ Bloomsbury ZP8 A73 1908. See Ferguson Smith, 'A Complete Strip-
Off', pp. 72–7.

36 See Jane Garrity, 'Nude Bloomsberries', in Derek Ryan (ed.), *A History of
the Bloomsbury Group* (Cambridge: Cambridge University Press, forthcoming).

37 V. Bell to R. Fry, Sep. 5 [1911], GB181 SxMs56/1/28, VBRF 35.

38 V. Bell to R. Fry, Sep. 7 [1911], GB181 SxMs56/1/28, VBRF 34.

39 V. Bell to D. Grant, Sep. 7 [1911], TGA 20078/1/44/4.

40 V. Bell to R. Fry, Sep. 7 [1911], GB181 SxMs56/1/28, VBRF 34.

41 V. Bell to D. Grant, Sep. 7 [1911], TGA 20078/1/44/4.

42 V. Bell to D. Grant, Sep. 27 [1911], TGA 20078/1/44/5. L. Strachey to J.
Strachey, Sep. 24 [1911], in *Letters of Lytton Strachey*, p. 203.

43 V. Bell to R. Fry, Sep. 27 [1911], GB181 SxMs56/1/28, VBRF 43.

44 V. Bell to D. Grant, Sep. 27 [1911], TGA 20078/1/44/5.

45 See V. Bell to R. Fry, Oct. 10 [1911], GB181 SxMs56/1/28, VBRF 45; V. Bell
to R. Fry, Sunday [20 August 1911] and Aug. 25 [1911], GB181 SxMs56/1/28,
VBRF 64 and VBRF 30. V. Bell to R. Fry, Sep. 26 [1911], GB181 SxMs56/1/28,
VBRF 42.

46 V. Bell to V. Woolf, Oct. 19 [1911], *SLVB*, p. 109.

47 V. Bell to V. Woolf, Oct. 20 [1911], *SLVB*, p. 110.

48 Bell, 'Memories of Roger Fry', p. 126.

49 Fry, 'The Salons and Van Dougen [sic]', pp. 463–4.

50 Maurice Denis, *Décor*, 1891, present whereabouts and details unknown. See
Allison Morehead, 'Defending Deformation: Maurice Denis's Positivist Modernism',
Art History, 38 (November 2015), pp. 890–915.

51 Maurice Denis, *Ulysses and Calypso*, 1905, oil on canvas, 820 × 1170 mm, Ateneum Art Museum, Helsinki. Maurice Denis, *Orpheus and Eurydice*, 1910, oil on canvas, 1149 × 1651 mm, Minneapolis Institute of Art, The Putnam Dana McMillan Fund, 68.1.

52 Emile Bernard, *Baigneuses à la vache rouge*, 1887, oil on canvas, 920 × 730 mm, Musée d'Orsay, Paris, RF 1984 21. This was part of a frieze of three paintings in Bernard's studio in Asnières. Denis saw it there in 1891.

53 V. Bell to R. Fry, Nov. 5 [1911], GB181 SxMs56/1/28, VBRF 47.

54 *Exposition de Quelques Indépendants Anglais*, Galerie Barbazanges, Paris, 1–15 May 1912, exh. cat. V. Bell, *Au Bord de la Mer* was cat. no. 1 (listed by artist).

55 V. Bell to R. Fry, Oct. 10 [1911], GB181 SxMs56/1/28, VBRF 45.

56 V. Bell to R. Fry, Sunday [20 October 1912], GB181 SxMs56/1/28, VBRF 132.

57 *Twentieth Century Art: A Review of Modern Movements*, Whitechapel Art Gallery, London, 8 May–20 June 1914, cat. no. 12.

58 See V. Bell to V. Woolf, Sep. 26 [1912], Berg, Folder 39.

59 Paul Gauguin, *The Spirit of the Dead Watching*, 1892, oil on jute mounted on canvas, 724 × 924 mm, Albright Knox Art Gallery Art Museum, Buffalo, NY, A. Conger Goodyear Collection, 1965, 1965:1, exhibited in *Manet and the Post-Impressionists* as *L'Esprit veille*, cat. no. 42. Paul Gauguin, *Tahitian Women Bathing*, 1892, oil on paper laid down on canvas, 1110 × 895 mm, Metropolitan Museum of Art, New York, Robert Lehman Collection, 1975, Accession No. 1975.1.179, exhibited in *Manet and the Post-Impressionists* as *Grandes baigneuses*, cat. no. 86. Paul Gauguin, *Maternité II*, 1899, oil on burlap, 947 × 610 mm, private collection, exhibited in *Manet and the Post-Impressionists* as *Négresses*, cat. no. 41. See Reed, *Bloomsbury Rooms*, pp. 31–4 for a comparison between Gauguin's paintings and *Women and Baby*.

60 V. Bell to R. Fry, Nov. 6 [1911], GB181 SxMs56/1/28, VBRF 48.

61 Henri Matisse, *The Red Studio*, 1911, oil on canvas, 1810 × 2191 mm, Museum of Modern Art, New York, Mrs Simon Guggenheim Fund, 8.1949, exhibited in the *Second Post-Impressionist Exhibition* as *Le panneau rouge*, cat. no. 35. Henri Matisse, *Dance (1)*, 1909, oil on canvas, 2597 × 3901 mm, Museum of Modern Art, New York, Gift of Nelson A. Rockefeller in honour of Alfred H. Barr, Jr, 201.1963, exhibited in the *Second Post-Impressionist Exhibition* as *Les Danseuses. Design for a decoration in Prince Tschoukine's Palace at Moscow*, cat. no. 185. Vanessa's painting includes *The Red Studio* and *Nu au bord de la mer* by Matisse: V. Bell, *A Room at the Second Post-Impressionist Exhibition*, 1912, oil on board, 505 × 605 mm, Musée d'Orsay, Paris, AM3677. See also V. Bell to R. Fry, Nov. 17 [1912], GB181 SxMs56/1/28, VBRF 82.

62 V. Bell to R. Fry, Oct. 17 [1912] and Sunday [October 20, 1912], GB181 SxMs56/1/28, VBRF 78 and VBRF 132.

63 V. Bell to R. Fry, Oct. 17 [1912], GB181 SxMs56/1/28, VBRF 78.

64 V. Bell to R. Fry, Sunday [October 20, 1912], GB181 SxMs56/1/28, VBRF 132.

65 V. Bell to R. Fry, Oct. 22 [1912], GB181 SxMs56/1/28, VBRF 79.

66 V. Bell to R. Fry, Oct. 24 [1913], GB181 SxMs56/1/28, VBRF 111.

67 R. Fry, 'The Work of a Woman Painter: Vanessa Bell', *Vogue* [London], early February 1926, pp. 33–5, 78.

68 *Twentieth Century Art*, exh. cat., p. 26. V. Bell, *Women and Baby* (lender Roger Fry, Esq.) is cat. no. 12. R. Fry, 'A Possible Domestic Architecture', *Vogue* [London], late March 1918, p. 40. See Hitchmough, *The Bloomsbury Look*, p. 139.

69 V. Bell to D. Grant, Thursday [31 December? 1914], TGA 20078/1/44/27. V. Bell to R. Fry, Christmas Day [1914], GB181 SxMs56/1/28, VBRF 151.

70 V. Bell to D. Grant, May 10 [1912], TGA 20078/1/44/8.

71 V. Bell to R. Fry, June 5 [1912], *SLVB*, p. 119.

72 Ibid.

73 Mabel was one of seven sisters, Elsie, Ada, Beatrice, Mabel, Marion, Florence and Daisy. For a summary of their work as servants for members of the Bloomsbury Group see Alison Light, *Mrs Woolf and the Servants* (London: Penguin, 2007), pp. 124–5. Virginia's servant, Mabel Haskins, should not be confused for Mabel Selwood.

74 V. Bell to V. Woolf, Friday [June 2, 1911], Berg, Folder 26.

75 Vanessa established with Clive that he might on occasion sleep in the day nursery at Studland: V. Bell to C. Bell, Sunday [September 11, 1910], GB181 SxMs56/1/25, VBCB 67.

76 V. Bell to R. Fry, Aug. 19 [1912], GB181 SxMs56/1/28, VBRF 71. See also V. Bell to C. Bell, Aug. 17 [1912], GB181 SxMs56/1/25, VBCB 27.

77 V. Bell to C. Bell, Sunday [October 9, 1910], GB181 SxMs56/1/25, VBCB 68.

CHAPTER 6: OMEGA DESIGNS

1 V. Bell to R. Fry, Aug 16 [1911], GB181 SxMs56/1/28, VBRF 17. See also R. Fry to W. Lewis, February 21 [1912], in *Letters of Roger Fry*, p. 355.

2 V. Bell to R. Fry, Jan. 7 [1912], GB181 SxMs56/1/28, VBRF 66.

3 V. Bell to R. Fry, Sunday [June 2, 1912], GB181 SxMs56/1/28, VBRF 5.

4 V. Bell to R. Fry, Monday [June 3, 1912], GB181 SxMs56/1/28, VBRF 6.

5 Walter Richard Sickert, *Jacques-Emile Blanche*, c.1910, oil on canvas, 601 × 508 mm, Tate, NO4912, exhibited as *Portrait of Mr Jacques Blanche* in the *Forty-Seventh Exhibition of Modern Pictures. New English Art Club*, Galleries of the Royal Society of British Arts, London, May–June 1912, cat. no. 163, https://exhibitions.univie.ac.at/exhibition/468 (accessed 3 February 2022).

6 V. Bell to R. Fry, Monday [June 3, 1912], GB181 SxMs56/1/28, VBRF 6.

7 V. Bell to C. Bell, Aug. 15 [1912], *SLVB*, p. 122.

8 Vanessa and Clive had acquired Augustus John's *Childhood of Pyramus* for 100 guineas. See V. Bell to C. Bell, Aug. 15 [1912], *SLVB*, pp. 122–3; V. Bell to C. Bell, Aug. 20 [1912], GB181 SxMs56/1/25, VBCB 35; V. Bell to R. Fry, Oct. 23 [1912], GB181 SxMs56/1/28, VBRF 80.

9 V. Bell to R. Fry, Jan. 6 [1912], GB181 SxMs56/1/28, VBRF 65.

10 V. Bell to V. Woolf, Sep. 18 [1912], Berg, Folder 39. See also A. John to C. Bell [undated, 1912], GB181 SxMs56/1/117, AJCB 1.

11 Fry, 'The French Group', pp. 25–9.

12 V. Bell to M. Snowdon, Aug. 20 [1912], GB181 SxMs56/1/34, VBMS 32.

13 Vanessa's exhibits in the *Second Post-Impressionist Exhibition* were *Asheham*, cat. no. 77; *Nosegay*, cat. no. 109; *The Spanish Model*, cat. no. 119; and *The Mantelpiece*, cat. no. 155.

14 V. Bell to M. Snowdon, Oct. 15 [1912], GB181 SxMs56/1/31, VBMS 34.

15 V. Woolf to L. Strachey, Boxing Day [1912], and V. Woolf to V. Dickinson, 24 Dec. [1912], *TLVW*, vol. 2, pp. 16 and 14. See also Bell, 'Memories of Roger Fry', p. 144.

16 See V. Bell to V. Woolf, Dec. 23 [1912], Berg, Folder 39.

17 V. Bell to C. Bell, Sunday [December 22, 1912], GB181 SxMs56/1/25, VBCB 41.

18 V. Bell to R. Fry, Nov. 23 [1911], *SLVB*, p. 112.

19 V. Bell to R. Fry, Nov. 2 [1912], GB181 SxMs56/1/28, VBRF 81.

20 V. Bell to C. Bell, Dec 24 [1912], GB181 SxMs56/1/25, VBCB 45.

21 V. Bell to C. Bell, Dec. 25 [1912], GB181 SxMs56/1/25, VBCB 46.

22 R. Fry, 'Omega Workshops Fundraising Letter', Dec. 11, 1912, in *A Roger Fry Reader*, ed. Christopher Reed (London and Chicago: University of Chicago Press, 1996), pp. 196–7.

23 V. Bell to C. Bell, Dec. 26 [1912], GB181 SxMs56/1/25, VBCB 47.

24 R. Fry, 'Art and Socialism', in his *Vision and Design* (London: Chatto & Windus, 1920), pp. 41 and 43. First published in H.G. Wells (ed.), *The Great State: Essays in Construction* (London: Harper & Brothers, 1912).

25 Fry, 'Omega Workshops Fundraising Letter' and 'Prospectus for the Omega Workshops', in *A Roger Fry Reader*, pp. 196–200.

26 For an analysis of the relationship between Paul Poiret's Ecole Martine, his showroom the Maison Martin and the Omega Workshops see Reed, *Bloomsbury Rooms*, pp. 122–5.

27 Fry, 'Omega Workshops Fundraising Letter', p. 196.

28 V. Woolf to L. Strachey, Boxing Day [1912], and V. Woolf to V. Dickinson, 24 Dec. [1912], *TLVW*, vol. 2, pp. 16 and 14.

29 V. Bell to C. Bell, Dec. 27 [1912], *SLVB*, p. 131.

30 D. Grant, *Cat on a Cabbage*, *c.* 1913, gouache on paper, design for cross-stitch chair seat, 480 × 610 mm, Charleston Trust Collection, CHA/P/101. See also D. Grant, *Design for Embroidered Chair Seat*, 1913, gouache and pencil on paper, 723 × 624 mm, Courtauld Gallery Collection, D.1958.PD.97. V. Bell to R. Fry, Jan. 10 [1913] GB181 SxMs56/1/28, VBRF 86. See also V. Bell to D. Grant, Jan. 14 [1913], TGA 20078/1/44/14.

31 V. Bell to V. Woolf, Sunday [January 26, 1913], Berg, Folder 39.

32 Ibid.

33 V. Bell to R. Fry, Feb. 6 [1913], *SLVB*, p. 135.

34 V. Bell to R. Fry, Feb. 17 [1913], GB181 SxMs56/1/28, VBRF 94.

35 V. Bell to R. Fry, Jan. 21 [1913], GB181 SxMs56/1/28, VBRF 91.

36 V. Bell to C. Bell, Aug. 21 [1913], GB181 SxMs56/1/28, VBCB 101. For details of the original shareholders see J. Collins, *The Omega Workshops* (London and Chicago: University of Chicago Press, 1984), p. 50.

37 D. Grant, Diary, 8 January 1912, quoted in Collins, *The Omega Workshops*, p. 34.

38 V. Bell to R. Fry, Jan. 10 [1913], GB181 SxMs56/1/28, VBRF 86. See also V. Bell to M. Snowdon, Sep. 18 [1912], GB181 SxMs56/1/31, VBMS 33, and V. Bell to C. Bell, Ap. 6 [1912], GB181 SxMs56/1/25, VBCB 28.

39 See V. Bell to R. Fry, Nov. 5 [1911], GB181 SxMs56/1/28, VBRF 47. *An Exhibition of Pictures by Members of the Friday Club*, exh. cat. (Alpine Club Gallery, London, February 1912), National Art Library, Victoria and Albert Museum, 200 Box 168.

40 V. Bell to R. Fry, March 6 [1912], GB181 SxMs56/1/28, VBRF 25.

41 Anon., 'Our London Letter: The Grafton Group', *Manchester Courier*, 21 March 1913, p. 6. See also Claude Phillips, 'The Grafton Group', *Daily Telegraph*, 22 March 1913, p. 6.

42 *The Grafton Group. Vanessa Bell. Roger Fry. Duncan Grant. Second Exhibition*, exh. cat. (Alpine Club Gallery, London, January 1914), National Art Library, Victoria and Albert Museum, 200.B.5.15.

43 *Women and Baby* was not for sale. Unlike Picasso's *Tête d'homme* and André Derain's *Sous Bois*, it was not yet identified as 'Lent by Roger Fry'. *Grafton Group Second Exhibition*, exh. cat. *Women and Baby* was cat. no. 34.

44 W. Gill to D. Grant, Letter II, June 1966, Tate Archive, TAM 24M, p. 2.

45 See R. Fry to Lady Fry, July 9, 1913, in *Letters of Roger Fry*, p. 371.

46 Winifred Gill and Pamela Diamand, interview with Stephen Chaplin, n.d. [1958–9]. Transcripts of the interview with manuscript additions by Pamela Diamand are in the Courtauld Gallery Archives and in the Quentin Bell Papers GB181 SxMs74/1/76. The Workshops also sold needlepoint and batik hand-dyed cushion covers.

47 Vanessa would have seen Kandinsky's work at Allied Artists' Association exhibitions and two of his abstract 'Compositions' were loaned by Michael Sadler to the first Grafton Group exhibition. She may also have seen *Exhibition of works by the Italian Futurist Painters*, Sackville Gallery, London, March 1912. See Barbara Pezzini, 'The 1912 Futurist Exhibition at the Sackville Gallery, London: An Avant-Garde Show within the Old-Master Trade', *Burlington Magazine*, vol. 155, no. 1324 (July 1913), pp. 471–9.

48 V. Bell to R. Fry, Sunday [July 21? 1912], *SLVB*, p. 121.

49 V. Bell to C. Bell, Monday [March 31, 1913], GB181 SxMs56/1/25, VBCB 98.

50 V. Bell to C. Bell, Ap. 2nd [1913], GB181 SxMs56/1/25, VBCB 95.

51 Anon., 'Art Notes', *Illustrated London News*, 13 September 1913, p. 408.

52 See Mary Schoeser, 'Omega Textiles: A Sea-Change into Something Strange', in Alexandra Gerstein (ed.), *Beyond Bloomsbury: Designs of the Omega Workshops 1913–19* (London: Fontanka, 2009), pp. 17–25.

53 Gill and Diamand, transcript, [1958–9]. W. Gill to Q. Bell, May 6, 1967, Quentin Bell Papers, GB181 SxMs74/1/7/6.

54 W. Gill to N. Pevsner, March 3, 1941, TGA 8022.8.

55 See W. Gill to D. Grant, Letter II, June 1966, Tate Archive, TAM 24M, pp. 2–3.

56 See W. Gill to N. Pevsner, March 3, 1941, TGA 8022.8; W. Gill to Alan Bowness, February 4, 1959, TGA 8022.6; correspondence between W. Gill and

Q. Bell, 1967–9, GB181 SxMs74/1/7/6; and her extensive correspondence with D. Grant, 1966–7, Tate Archive, TAM 24M.

57 W. Gill to Q. Bell, April 15, 1967, Quentin Bell Papers, GB181 SxMs74/1/7/6.

58 W. Gill to Q. Bell, May 6, 1967, Quentin Bell Papers, GB181 SxMs74/1/7/6.

59 V. Bell to D. Grant, [November 30, 1913], TGA 20078/1/44/16.

60 W. Gill to D. Grant, Letter III, July 4, 1966, Tate Archive, TAM 24M, p. 4.

61 V. Bell, designer, John Joseph Kalleborn, maker, *Omega Workshops Tray with Abstract Design*, 1913, mahogany carcase, with marquetry of oak, walnut and ebony, 63 × 725 × 680 mm, National Trust Collection, NT1274867. See https://www.nationaltrustcollections.org.uk/object/1274867 (accessed 14 February 2022). Richard Shone reiterates the Shaw quote in relation to Duncan's elephant tray: Shone, *The Art of Bloomsbury*, p. 176.

62 V. Bell to R. Fry, Saturday [26 July 1913], GB181 SxMs56/1/28, VBRF 131.

63 See Hitchmough, *The Bloomsbury Look*, pp. 84–8.

64 V. Bell to V. Woolf, Sunday [August 17, 1913], Berg, Folder 41; V. Bell to C. Bell, [August 14?, 1913] and Aug. 20 [1913], GB181 SxMs56/1/25, VBCB 89 and VBCB 100.

65 V. Bell to C. Bell, Aug. 18 [1913], GB181 SxMs56/1/25, VBCB 99. V. Bell to C. Bell, [August 19?, 1913], GB181 SxMs56/1/25, VBCB 93.

66 George Bernard Shaw quoted in Frances Spalding, *Roger Fry: Art and Life* (London: Granada, 1980), p. 177.

67 V. Bell to R. Fry, Sep. 17 [1913], GB181 SxMs56/1/28, VBRF 147.

68 V. Bell to R. Fry, Sep. 23 [1913], GB181 SxMs56/1/28, VBRF 101.

69 V. Bell to R. Fry, Sep. 18 [1913], *SLVB*, p. 144.

70 V. Bell to D. Grant, Monday [September 29, 1913], TGA 20078/1/44/15.

71 Gill and Diamand, transcript, [1958–9].

72 See Quentin Bell and Stephen Chaplin, 'The Ideal Home Rumpus', *Apollo*, vol. 80, no. 32 (October 1964), pp. 284–91.

73 V. Bell to R. Fry, Sunday [October 12, 1913], *SLVB*, pp. 146–7.

74 F.G. Bussy to V. Bell, Oct. 22nd, 1913, published in Bell and Chaplin, 'The Ideal Home Rumpus', p. 290.

75 V. Bell to R. Fry, Oct. 13 [1913], *SLVB*, p. 148.

76 See Rothenstein, *Sickert to Moore*, pp. 256–7, 268–70. Vanessa defended Jessie Etchells when the Workshops manager wanted to 'discharge' her on the grounds of disloyalty. She wrote that Jessie was 'too valuable as an artist not to keep her': V. Bell to R. Fry, Tuesday [October 14, 1913], *SLVB*, p. 149.

77 V. Bell to R. Fry, Sunday [October/November 1913], GB181 SxMs56/1/28, VBRF 121. Duncan was one of the 32 founder members in October 1913, of whom only six were women. Roger and Nina Hamnett were admitted in 1917.

78 See W. Gill to N. Pevsner, March 3, 1941, Tate Archive, TGA 8022.8.

79 W. Gill to D. Grant, Letter II, June 1966, Tate Archive, TAM 24M, p. 3.

80 Anon., 'Beethoven's "Moonlight Sonata": A Watteau Picture and Post-Impressionism as Inspiration for Schemes of Decoration', *Illustrated London News*, 25 October 1913, pp. iv–v.

CHAPTER 7: MODERN FIGURE STUDIES

1 V. Bell to D. Grant, Dec. 5 [1913], TGA 20078/1/44/17.

2 V. Bell to D. Grant, Sunday [November 30, 1913], TGA 20078/1/44/16.

3 P.G. Konody, 'Post-Impressionism in the Home', *Observer*, 14 December 1913, p. 8.

4 See W. Gill to D. Grant, Letter VII, October 10, 1966, Tate Archive, TAM 24M, pp. 1–2.

5 V. Bell to V. Woolf, Sunday [August 17, 1913], Berg, Folder 41.

6 V. Bell to R. Fry, Saturday [July 26, 1913], GB181 SxMs56/1/28, VBRF 131.

7 V. Bell to D. Grant, Sunday [November 30, 1913], TGA 20078/1/44/16. R. Fry, *Dolls' House*, 1913, wood and plywood, painted; glass, 658 × 962 × 300 mm. Victoria and Albert Museum, London, MISC.2:10-1934.

8 Konody, 'Post-Impressionism in the Home', p. 8. See also Anon., 'The Omega Workshops: Decorative Form and Colour', *The Times*, 10 December 1913, p. 13.

9 V. Bell, *Madonna and Child*, *c.*1915 [I propose 1913], glazed ceramic, Omega Workshops, 225 × 190 × 115 mm, Charleston Trust Collection, CHA/C/142.

10 V. Bell to R. Fry, Sunday [late October 1913], *SLVB*, pp. 150–1.

11 See Judith Collins, *The Omega Workshops* (London and Chicago: University of Chicago Press, 1984), pp. 70–5.

12 V. Bell, *Painted Tray*, oil on wood, 460 mm diameter, private collection.

13 See V. Bell to D. Grant, [September 29, 1913], TGA 20078/1/44/15. V. Bell to R. Fry, Sunday [late October 1913], *SLVB*, pp. 150–1.

14 V. Bell to D. Grant, Feb. 25 [1914], *SLVB*, p. 156.

15 V. Bell to D. Grant, Wednesday [March 25, 1914], *SLVB*, p. 162.

16 V. Bell to R. Fry, Ap. 8 [1914], GB181 SxMs56/1/28, VBRF 97.

17 See V. Woolf to V. Bell, Friday [July 21, 1911], *SLVW*, vol. 1, pp. 469–71 for an account of Walter Lamb's relationship with Virginia. This may have been one of the letters shown to Leonard.

18 V. Bell to D. Grant, Jan. 14 [1913], TGA 20078/1/44/13.

19 V. Bell to V. Woolf, Jan. 22 [1913] and Sunday [January 26, 1913], Berg, Folder 39.

20 V. Bell to R. Fry, Saturday [July 26, 1913], GB181 SxMs56/1/28, VBRF 131.

21 V. Bell to L. Woolf, Thursday [September 11, 1913], *SLVB*, p. 143.

22 See V. Bell to C. Bell, Aug. 18 [1913], GB181 SxMs56/1/25, VBCB 99; V. Bell to R. Fry, Friday [September 19. 1913], GB181 SxMs56/1/28, VBRF 102.

23 See V. Bell to R. Fry, Oct 22 and Sunday [November 1913], GB181 SxMs56/1/28, VBRF 109 and VBRF 121.

24 Leonard Woolf, *The Wise Virgins* (1914; repr. London: Persephone Books, 2013), pp. 98–9.

25 V. Bell to R. Fry, Christmas Day [1913], GB181 SxMs56/1/28, VBRF 112.

26 Lyndall Gordon, 'Preface', in Woolf, *The Wise Virgins*, p. xvi.

27 V. Bell to R. Fry, Apr. 7 [1914], GB181 SxMs56/1/28, VBRF 96.

28 Ibid.

29 C. Bell, *Art* (London: Chatto & Windus, 1914), p. 8.

30 Quentin Bell, interview with D. Grant, 1969, GB181 SxUOS1/2/3/1/10, University of Sussex Collection, University of Sussex Special Collections at The Keep.

31 David Garnett, *The Flowers of the Forest* (London: Chatto & Windus, 1955), p. 26.

32 C. Bell, *Art*, pp. i, viii and xi.

33 V. Bell to R. Fry, Dec. 28 [1913], GB181SxMs56/1/28, VBRF 115.

34 V. Bell to R. Fry, Dec. 27 [1913], GB181SxMs56/1/28, VBRF 114.

35 V. Bell to R. Fry, Dec. 28 [1913], GB181 SxMs56/1/28, VBRF 115; R. Fry to C. Vildrac, January 1, 1914, in *Letters of Roger Fry*, pp. 376–7.

36 Anon., 'The Grafton Group', *The Times*, Saturday 3 January 1914, p. 11.

37 Claude Phillips, 'More Post-Impressionism', *Daily Telegraph*, 5 January 1914, p. 8.

38 V. Bell to C. Bell, Aug. 21 [1913], GB181 SxMs56/1/25, VBCB 101.

39 V. Bell, photograph album CH2, TGA 9020/3, pp. 29–33.

40 See Hitchmough, *The Bloomsbury Look*, pp. 84–8.

41 V. Bell to R. Fry, Monday [October 20? 1913], GB181 SxMs56/1/28, VBRF 108.

42 V. Bell to V. Woolf, Sunday [August 17, 1913?], Berg, Folder 41.

43 See also V. Bell, *Preliminary Design for Lady Hamilton Rug*, 1914, gouache on squared paper, 419 × 803 mm, Samuel Courtauld Trust, Courtauld Gallery, D.1958.PD.88, and V. Bell, *Preliminary Design for Lady Hamilton Rug*, 1914, gouache and pencil on squared paper, 627 × 402 mm, Samuel Courtauld Trust, Courtauld Gallery, D.1958.PD.89.

44 See V. Bell to D. Grant, Sunday [November 30, 1913], TGA 20078/1/44/16.

45 V. Woolf to V. Dickinson, [11? February 1914], *TLVW*, vol. 2, p. 39.

46 See V. Bell to R. Fry, Apr. 7 [1914], GB181 SxMs56/1/28, VBRF 96; V. Bell to D. Grant, Thursday [March 5, 1914], *SLVB*, p. 157.

47 See catalogue entry for D. Grant, *Head of Eve*, 1913, oil on board, 756 × 635 mm, Tate, T03847, https://www.tate.org.uk/art/artworks/grant-head-of-eve-t03847 (accessed 28 March 2023).

48 See Collins, *The Omega Workshops*, pp. 86–90.

49 See Hitchmough, *The Bloomsbury Look*, pp. 70–4.

50 V. Bell, *The Tub*, 1917–18, oil and gouache on canvas, 1803 × 1664 mm, Tate T02010.

51 See, for example, the standing figure apparently based on that of Molly MacCarthy in R. Fry, *Female Nudes in a Landscape* (verso), 1915, oil on cardboard, 458 × 558 mm, Samuel Courtauld Trust, Courtauld Gallery, P.1958.PD.144. See also V. Bell to C. Bell, Sunday [October 9, 1910], GB181 SxMs56/1/25, VBCB 68.

52 See Hitchmough, *The Bloomsbury Look*, p. 73. See also V. Bell, photograph of *Naked Female Standing in Studio*, c.1914 (TGA VB/AD30); D. Grant, *Nude with a Flute*, 1914, oil on panel, 612 × 1800 mm, private collection and D. Grant, *Standing Nude with Bird*, 1914, oil on panel, 1830 × 625 mm, private collection, both reproduced in Shone, *The Art of Bloomsbury*, p. 157.

53 D. Carrington to M. Gertler, 27 November 1917, Dora Carrington Collection, Harry Ransom Center, Box 1, Folder 1.6. She may have been referring to *A Conversation* which Vanessa had recently sold to Roger.

54 V. Bell to D. Grant, July 23 [1939], TGA 20078/1/44/210.

55 D. Grant, *Reclining Nude (Vanessa Bell)*, *c*.1919, oil on canvas, 616 × 819 mm, whereabouts unknown, reproduced in Shone, *The Art of Bloomsbury*, p. 17, fig. 9. D. Grant, *Vanessa Bell*, 1917, oil on canvas, 1270 × 1664 mm, National Portrait Gallery, London, NPG 5541.

56 R. Fry to V. Bell [October 9, 1911?], GB181 SxMs56/1/83, RFVB 5. R. Fry to V. Bell, Oct. 12, 1911, GB181 SxMs56/1/83, RFVB 11.

57 V. Bell to R. Fry, Nov. 6 [1911] and Mar. 12 [1912?], GB 181 SxMs56/1/28, VBRF 48 and 26.

58 Fry, 'Prospectus for the Omega Workshops', p.199.

59 See V. Bell to D. Grant, Thursday [March 5, 1914], *SLVB*, p. 157; Collins, *The Omega Workshops*, pp. 86–90; Anon., 'More Peaceful than the Dardanelles: The London Home of General Sir Ian and Lady Hamilton', *Sketch*, 23 June 1915, pp. 240–1.

60 C. Bell, *Art*, p. 130.

61 V. Bell to C. Bell, Wednesday [April 22, 1914], GB181 SxMs56/1/25, VBCB 108.

62 Fry, 'A Possible Domestic Architecture', pp. 40–1, 66, 68. See also Reed, *Bloomsbury Rooms*, pp. 46–9.

63 *Twentieth Century Art*, cat. nos 49–64.

64 *Twentieth Century Art*, cat. no. 110. The catalogue includes three Omega Workshops screens and three rugs in the Lower Gallery.

65 Claude Phillips, 'Art in Whitechapel. Twentieth Century Exhibition', *Daily Telegraph*, 12 May 1914, p. 14.

66 Vanessa exhibited: *Women and Baby*, cat. no. 12; *Landscape and Figures*, cat. no. 304; *Design for a Screen*, cat. no. 305; *The Girlhood of Thisbe*, cat. no. 313; *Still Life*, cat. no. 317. *The Girlhood of Thisbe* was credited as belonging to the Contemporary Art Society. See *Twentieth Century Art*, exh. cat.

67 V. Bell to V. Woolf, July 3 [1918], *SLVB*, p. 214.

68 Spencer Gore, *The Balcony at the Alhambra*, 1911–12, oil on canvas, 480 × 350 mm, York Art Gallery, YORAG: 1384.

69 See Wendy Baron, *Sickert. Paintings and Drawings* (New Haven and London: Yale University Press, 2006), pp. 328–43. Jessie Etchells, *The Opera Box*, *c*.1912, oil on board, 330 × 277 mm, Charleston Trust Collection, CHA/P/82. *Twentieth Century Art*, the painting was exhibited as *The Theatre Box*, cat. no. 158.

70 See, for example, F. Matania, 'The Wagner Cycles at Covent Garden: Specially Illustrated for "The Sphere"', *The Sphere*, 31 May 1913, pp. 240–1.

71 M. Hutchinson to V. Bell, Au. 17 [1916], GB 181 SxMs56/1/112, MHVB 3.

72 The painting was finished by October 1917, when Vanessa wrote that Monty Shearman wanted to buy it: 'I'm telling him it's sold to you.' V. Bell to R. Fry, [May or June 1916] and V. Bell to R. Fry, Oct. 4 [1917], GB181 SxMs56/1/28, VBRF 215 and VBRF 240.

73 M. Hutchinson to V. Bell, Au. 17 [1916], GB 181 SxMs56/1/112, MHVB 3.

74 *The London Group Retrospective Exhibition*, New Burlington Galleries, London, April–May 1928. Vanessa exhibited three paintings: *Three Women*, 1913,

cat. no. 19; *Portrait of Mrs St John Hutchinson*, 1915, cat. no. 20; and *Arum & Iris*, 1925, cat. no. 21. All three were 'Lent by Roger Fry, Esq.'.
75 V. Woolf to V. Bell, Saturday May 12th [1928], *TLVW*, vol. 3, p. 498.

CHAPTER 8: ABSTRACT COMPOSITIONS AND MODERN PORTRAITS

1 W. Gill to D. Grant, Letter V, August 29, 1966, Tate Archive, TAM 24M, pp. 1–2. 'The Show' was the *Sixth London Salon of the Allied Artists' Association*, Royal Albert Hall, London, 5–30 July 1913. Reviewing the exhibition, Roger wrote that Brancusi's sculptures 'have not, I think, been seen before in England'. R. Fry, 'The Allied Artists', *Nation*, 2 August 1913, pp. 676–7.
2 V. Bell to R. Fry, October 22 [1913], GB181 SxMs56/1/28, VBRF 109. Wyndham Lewis, *Kermesse* was exhibited in *Post-Impressionist and Futurist Exhibition*, Doré Gallery, London, 12 October 1913–16 January 1914, cat. no. 84.
3 V. Bell to D. Grant, Feb. 25 [1914], *SLVB*, p. 156. David Bomberg, *Vision of Ezekiel*, 1912, oil on canvas, 1140 × 1370 mm, Tate, T01197 was exhibited at *Friday Club*, Alpine Club Gallery, London, February–March 1914, cat. no. 19.
4 V. Bell to R. Fry, Apr. 7 [1914], GB181 SxMs56/1/28, VBRF 96.
5 Grace Brockington, 'Bell in Europe', *Research in Focus: Abstract Painting, c.1914 by Vanessa Bell*, https://www.tate.org.uk/research/in-focus/abstract-painting-vanessa-bell/relationships (accessed 13 April 2023).
6 *Exhibition of Works by the Italian Futurist Painters*, Sackville Gallery, London, March 1912.
7 Wassily Kandinsky, *Improvisation 21a*, 1911, oil on canvas, 960 × 1050 mm, Lenbachhaus, Munich, GMS 82 was exhibited in *Internationale Kunstausstellung des Sonderbundes Westdeutscher Kunstfreunde und Künstler zu Cöln*, Städtische Ausstellungshalle am Aachener Tor, Cologne, 25 May–30 September 1912, cat. no. 425. Vanessa would have seen Kandinsky's purely abstract work, too, the following year at the Allied Artists' Exhibition.
8 V. Bell to V. Woolf, Aug. 14 [1912], Berg, Folder 38.
9 František Kupka, *Amphora: Fugue in Two Colours*, 1912, gouache and ink on paper, 216 × 225 mm, Gift of Mr and Mrs František Kupka, Museum of Modern Art, New York, 569.1956.18. Roger saw Vanessa soon after his return from Paris, where he would have visited the Salon d'Automne. See V. Bell to R. Fry, Oct. 22 [1912], GB181 SxMs56/1/28, VBRF 79. I have found no evidence that Vanessa visited the exhibition.
10 R. Fry, 'Preface', *Second Post-Impressionist Exhibition Catalogue*, 1912, reprinted in Fry, *Vision and Design*, pp. 156–7.
11 W. Kandinsky to F. Marc, October 2, 1911, quoted in Leah Dickerman, 'Inventing Abstraction', in Leah Dickerman (ed.,), *Inventing Abstraction 1910–1925: How a Radical Idea Changed Modern Art*, exh. cat. (London and New York: Thames & Hudson/Museum of Modern Art, 2012), p. 15.
12 Anon., catalogue entry, D. Grant, *Interior at Gordon Square*, c.1915, oil on

wood, 400 × 321 mm, Tate, T01143, https://www.tate.org.uk/art/artworks/grant-interior-at-gordon-square-t01143 (accessed 17 April 2023).

13 *The London Salon of the Allied Artists Association*, Holland Park Hall, London, 12 June–2 July 1914.

14 Fry, *Vision and Design*, p. 156.

15 David Blayney Brown, catalogue entry, V. Bell, *Abstract Painting*, https://www.tate.org.uk/art/artworks/bell-abstract-painting-t01935 (accessed 14 April 2023). The entry draws on a transcript of a conversation between Tate curator David Blayney Brown and D. Grant, 28 May 1976, Tate Artist Catalogue File, Vanessa Bell, A22109, item 6.

16 V. Bell to R. Fry, Monday [August 24, 1914], *SLVB*, pp. 169–70. See also V. Bell to R. Fry, Monday [September 1, 1914], GB181 SxMs56/1/28, VBRF 140. The work described is D. Grant, *Abstract Kinetic Collage Painting with Sound*, 1914, paper on canvas, 279 × 4502 mm, Tate, T01744.

17 These are: *Composition*, *c*.1914, gouache, watercolour and coloured paper on cut-and-pasted paper, 551 × 437 mm, Joan and Lester Avnet Collection, Museum of Modern Art, New York, 9.1978; *Abstract Painting*, *c*.1914, oil on canvas, 441 × 381 mm, Tate, T01935; *Abstract Composition*, 1914, oil on canvas, 925 × 620 mm, Collection of Ivor Braka, reproduced in Milroy and Dejardin, *Vanessa Bell*, p. 91; *Abstract Composition*, *c*.1913–14, oil, gouache and collage on paper, 19¼ × 24 ⅛ in., exhibited in *Vanessa Bell 1879–1961: A Retrospective Exhibition*, 18 April–24 May 1980, Davis & Long Company in association with Anthony d'Offay Ltd, New York, cat. no. 22. In addition, untraced large abstracts by Vanessa are referenced in R. Fry to V. Bell, Apr. 6. 1919, in *Letters of Roger Fry*, p. 449, and D. Grant to V. Bell, Friday [June 2, 1916], TGA 8010/5/1127. Tate notes that 'an unfinished work on the back of a portrait also by Bell, was seen by a member of the Tate Gallery staff on 30 September 1969', in the online catalogue entry to T01935.

18 V. Bell to D. Grant, May 10 [1912], TGA 20078/1/44/8.

19 V. Bell to D. Grant, [March 25, 1914], *SLVB*, p. 160.

20 Claudia Tobin, 'Decoration, Abstraction and the Influence of Middle Eastern Textiles', *Research in Focus: Abstract Painting, c.1914 by Vanessa Bell*, https://www.tate.org.uk/research/in-focus/abstract-painting-vanessa-bell/decoration-abstraction (accessed 13 April 2023).

21 D. Grant, *Interior at Gordon Square*, *c*.1914–15, collage of papier collé on board, 600 × 720 mm, private collection. Reproduced in Shone, *The Art of Bloomsbury*, pp. 137, 152.

22 Anon., catalogue entry, D. Grant, *Interior at Gordon Square*, *c*.1915, oil on wood, 400 × 321 mm, Tate, T01143, https://www.tate.org.uk/art/artworks/grant-interior-at-gordon-square-t01143 (accessed 19 April 2023). The entry draws on a transcript of a conversation between the compiler and D. Grant, 30 September 1969, and was subsequently approved by the artist.

23 V. Bell to V. Woolf, Tuesday [March 24, 1914], Berg, Folder 41.

24 R. Fry, 'The Artist as Decorator', reprinted from *Colour*, April 1917, in Fry 1996, p. 209. See Nina Hamnett, *Omega Interior, Illustration to Fry's 'The Artist* *as Decorator', Colour, April 1917,* 1917, oil and pencil on cardboard, 469 × 307 mm, Samuel Courtauld Trust, Courtauld Gallery, D.1958.PD.81. See also Reed, *Bloomsbury Rooms*, pp. 152–63.

25 Caroline Cuthbert, who knew Duncan through her work at the Anthony d'Offay Gallery from 1973, in conversation with the author, 25 August 2023.

26 D. Grant, *Design for a Fire Screen Panel*, c.1916, mixed media and gouache on board, 740 × 620 mm, Charleston Trust Collection, CHA/P/233.

27 See Anon., catalogue entry, D. Grant, *Abstract Kinetic Collage Painting with Sound*, https://www.tate.org.uk/art/artworks/grant-abstract-kinetic-collage-painting-with-sound-t01744 (accessed 19 April 2023).

28 Text including part of a date is visible through brown paint on one strip showing the top of the newspaper page: 'H 10. 1914.', suggesting that the newspaper was dated 10 March 1914. This newspaper pre-dates Vanessa's visit to Picasso's studio. Duncan may have used an old newspaper for his collage or he may have been exploring collage before Vanessa wrote to him from Paris.

29 V. Bell to V. Woolf, May 3 [1913], *SLVB*, p. 139.

30 V. Bell to R. Fry, Thursday [1914], GB181 SxMs56/1/28, VBRF 157.

31 V. Bell to R. Fry, July 2 [1915], GB181 SxMs56/1/28, VBRF 181. See also Frances Spalding, *Duncan Grant* (London: Chatto & Windus, 1997), pp. 163–6.

32 V. Bell to R. Fry, July 2 [1915], GB181 SxMs56/1/28, VBRF 181.

33 V. Bell to R. Fry, Tuesday [August 1915?], GB181 SxMs56/1/28, VBRF 177.

34 V. Bell to R. Fry, Aug. 6 [1915], GB181 SxMs56/1/28, VBRF 182.

35 See, for example, V. Bell to V. Woolf, Sunday [January 26, 1913], Berg, Folder 39.

36 V. Bell to R. Fry, Tuesday [February 9, 1915], GB181 SxMs56/1/28, VBRF 119.

37 See D. Grant to M. Hutchinson, [11 July 1914], Mary Hutchinson Papers, Harry Ransom Center, Box 14, Folder 14.3.

38 V. Bell, *Lytton Strachey*, 1913, oil on board, 915 × 610 mm, Ivor Braka Collection, reproduced in Hitchmough, *The Bloomsbury Look*, p. 77. V. Bell, *David Garnett*, 1915, oil and gouache on cardboard, 764 × 526 mm, National Portrait Gallery, London, NPG 6046.

39 The painting was first exhibited in *Vanessa Bell: Drawings and Designs*, Folio Fine Art Ltd, London, 10–24 November 1967, cat. no. 36. A catalogue note states: 'All the items come from the artist's studio.' The painting may have been made in 1920, however. It is similar to Georges Rouault, *Profile*, reproduced in Fry, *Vision and Design*, Plate XIX and captioned as 'Author's Collection'. Roger described Rouault in December 1919 as 'a young artist hitherto almost unknown to me . . . surely one of the great geniuses of all times'. The following year he described an interview with Rouault: 'He seems very grateful for all the good things I've said about him and very pleased that I have such good works of his.' R. Fry to M. Mauron, [December 31, 1919] and R. Fry to P. Fry, Saturday [October 1920], in *Letters of Roger Fry*, pp. 476 and 492.

40 Anon., 'A Harmony of the Furnishing of Two Centuries at River, House, Upper Mall', *Vogue* [London], early February 1919, pp. 40–1.

41 D. Grant, *David Garnett in Profile*, 1915, oil on canvas, 670 × 388 mm, private collection, reproduced in Shone, *The Art of Bloomsbury*, p. 109.

42 V. Bell to D. Grant, Dec. 31 [1927], TGA 20078/1/44/151. In addition to the Rollins Museum work shown here as fig. 8.3 there are two oil portraits by Duncan, taken from a vantage point slightly to the right of Vanessa's: D. Grant, *Portrait of Mary Hutchinson*, 1915, oil on board, 614 × 448 mm, Piano Nobile – this painting was inscribed at a later date, 'Grant/17'; D. Grant, *Portrait of Mary Hutchinson*, 1915, oil on board, 762 × 635 mm, private collection, is a less finished version of this portrait. The Rollins Museum portrait was formerly in Roger's collection and is likely to be the version exhibited as 'Portrait, M.H.', which he loaned to *The New Movement in Art*, Mansard Gallery, Heal and Son, London, October 1917, cat. no. 5, and to *The London Group Retrospective Exhibition*, New Burlington Galleries, London, April–May 1928, cat. no. 20. A very similar version by V. Bell, retained in her own collection, is *Mrs St John Hutchinson*, 1915, oil on board, 737 × 578 mm, Tate, T01768. This is likely to be the painting that Vanessa exhibited in *Eleventh Exhibition of the London Group*, Mansard Gallery, Heal and Son, London, 1–29 November 1919, listed as *Portrait*, cat. no. 10.

43 C. Bell to M. Hutchinson, October 3. 1915, Mary Hutchinson Papers, Harry Ransom Center, Box 3, Folder 3.4.

44 C. Bell to M. Hutchinson, Jan. 31, 1916, Mary Hutchinson Papers, Harry Ransom Center, Box 3, Folder 3.5.

45 V. Bell to R. Fry, Oct. 29 [1919], GB 181 SxMs56/1/29, VBRF 296. Vanessa had first exhibited with the London Group in April 1919.

46 Quoted in Shone, *The Art of Bloomsbury*, p. 160. There are two abstracts by Vanessa in this inventory and seven abstracts by Duncan. 'Abstract test for chrome yellow' is listed as an unstretched oil. The second abstract is simply listed as 'Abstract', either a stretched canvas or a work on board measuring 36 × 24½ in., matching the dimensions of the work now in Ivor Braka's collection. I am indebted to Richard Shone for providing this information.

47 C. Bell, *Art*, p. 28.

48 V. Bell to D. Grant, May 11 [1954], TGA 20078/1/44/227.

49 V. Bell to R. Fry, Sep. 19 [1923], *SLVB*, p. 272.

50 V. Bell to R. Fry, June 9 [1915], GB181 SxMs56/1/28, VBRF 135.

51 V. Bell to R. Fry, Wednesday [April 21, 1915?], GB181 SxMs56/1/28, VBRF 167.

52 D. Grant, *In Memoriam: Rupert Brooke*, 1915, oil and collage on panel, 548 × 298 mm, Yale Center for British Art, Paul Mellon Fund, B1985.3.3.

53 D. Grant to V. Bell, Friday [June 2, 1916], TGA 8010/5/1127.

54 V. Bell to R. Fry, Sep. 7 [1924], *SLVB*, p. 280.

55 V. Bell to R. Fry, Sep. 19 [1923], *SLVB*, p. 272.

56 V. Bell to V. Woolf, Tuesday [August 31, 1915], *SLVB*, p. 189.

57 R. Fry to V. Bell, Apr. 6. 1919, in *Letters of Roger Fry*, p. 449.

58 Matthew Affron, 'Decoration and Abstraction in Bloomsbury', in Dickerman, *Inventing Abstraction*, p. 184.

59 V. Bell, *Omega Paper Flowers in a Bottle*, *c*.1915, oil on canvas, 305 × 330 mm, private collection, reproduced in Hitchmough, *The Bloomsbury Look*, p. 140.

60 D.H. Lawrence to O. Morrell, January 27 [1915], *The Letters of D.H. Lawrence*, vol. 2, ed. George J. Zytaruk and James T. Boulton (Cambridge: Cambridge University Press, 1981), p. 263. For an account of this visit see also David Garnett, *The Flowers of the Forest* (London: Chatto & Windus, 1955), pp. 34–7.

61 See Shone, *The Art of Bloomsbury*, p. 155.

62 V. Bell to R. Fry, Sep. 25 [1925], GB181 SxMs56/1/29, VBRF 363.

63 D. Grant, *The White Jug*, 1914–18, oil on panel, 1067 × 445 mm, Southampton City Art Gallery, 36/2002; see catalogue entry, Tate T01143.

64 Blayney Brown, catalogue entry, Tate T01935. The painting with the additional circle is illustrated in *Vanessa Bell: Paintings and Drawings*, exh. cat., Anthony d'Offay Gallery, London, 20 November–12 December 1973, p. 31.

CHAPTER 9: VANESSA BELL – DUNCAN GRANT

1 V. Bell to R. Fry, Saturday [March 27, 1915], GB181 SxMs56/1/28, VBRF 133.

2 See V. Bell to R. Fry Tuesday [February 9, 1915], GB181 SxMs56/1/28, VBRF 119.

3 V. Bell to R. Fry, Saturday [March 27, 1915], GB181 SxMs56/1/28, VBRF 133.

4 V. Bell to V. Woolf, Saturday [April 1915], Berg, Folder 42.

5 See V. Bell to C. Bell, Thursday [March 25, 1915?], GB 181 SxMs56/1/25, VBCB 52; V. Bell to R. Fry, Friday [April 9, 1915?], *SLVB*, p. 174.

6 V. Bell to R. Fry, Monday [January 1914], GB181 SxMs56/1/28, VBRF 122.

7 D. Grant, *Vanessa Bell*, 1942, 1016 × 610 mm, Tate, N05405.

8 D. Grant, *Lytton Strachey in the Garden at Asheham*, 1913, oil on plywood, 910 × 590 mm, Charleston Trust, CHA/P/2; and V. Bell, *Lytton Strachey*, 1913, oil on board, 915 × 610 mm, Ivor Braka Collection. The paintings are reproduced together in Hitchmough, *The Bloomsbury Look*, p. 77.

9 C. Bell, 'Duncan Grant', *Athenaeum*, 6 February 1920, p. 182.

10 V. Bell, *Still Life (Triple Alliance)*, 1914, collage, newsprint, oil and pastel on canvas, 819 × 603 mm; D. Grant, *Still Life, Asheham House*, 1914, oil and collage on board, 790 × 615 mm, both in the University of Leeds Art Collection, LEEUA 1923.001 and LEEUA 2011.001.

11 V. Bell to R. Fry, [August 1912?], GB181 SxMs56/1/28, VBRF 128.

12 V. Bell to R. Fry, Sep. 11 [1912], GB 181SxMs56/1/28, VBRF 74.

13 V. Bell to R. Fry, Thursday [September 25, 1913], GB181 SxMs56/1/28, VBRF 125.

14 R. Fry to V. Bell, May 12, 1921, Fry 1972, p. 507. *Nameless Exhibition of Modern British Painting*, Grosvenor Gallery, London, 20 May–2 July 1921. See also R. Fry to V. Bell, May 18–20, 1921, in *Letters of Roger Fry*, p. 510. For a discussion of the exhibition see Samuel Elmer, 'The "Nameless Exhibition", London, 1921', *Burlington Magazine*, vol. 153, no. 1302 (September 2011), pp. 583–90.

Denys Sutton, in *Letters of Roger Fry*, p. 507, suggests that *The Visit* may have been *A Conversation*. He was mistaken, as Elmer notes: *The Visit* is illustrated in Anon., '"The Nameless Exhibition": Representative British Art Subjected to the Test of Anonymity', *Illustrated London News*, 21 May 1921, pp. 684–5. Its current whereabouts are unknown.

15 V. Bell to R. Fry, Monday [May 1921], GB181 SxMs56/1/29, VBRF 304.

16 Rupert Brooke, 'The Post-Impressionists – II', *Cambridge Magazine*, 30 November 1912.

17 Frank Rutter, *Since I Was Twenty-Five* (London: Constable, 1927), p. 146.

18 R. Fry to V. Bell, April 6, 1919; R. Fry to V. Bell, December 26, 1918, in *Letters of Roger Fry*, pp. 449 and 441.

19 Leonard Woolf, transcript of interview by Quentin Bell, 5 April 1967, GB181 SxMs-18/4/23/1, R.3/2.

20 V. Bell to C. Bell, Sunday [December 1910], GB181 SxMs56/1/25, VBCB 76. See Chapter 4.

21 Duncan's self-portrait from this sitting is in a private collection.

22 The painting can be dated with accuracy to 1915 by the setting and Vanessa's red dress, matching the one in Duncan's portrait, *At Eleanor: Vanessa Bell*.

23 V. Bell to C. Bell, Thursday [March 25, 1915?], GB181 SxMs56/1/25, VBCB 52.

24 V. Bell to R. Fry, Friday [April 9, 1915?], *SLVB*, p. 174.

25 Gill and Diamand, transcript, [1958–9].

26 V. Bell to R. Fry, Monday [May 10, 1915?], GB181 SxMs56/1/28, VBRF 173.

27 See R. Fry to V. Bell, Apr. 11. [19]15, GB181 SxMs56/1/83, RFVB 27.

28 V. Bell to R. Fry, Monday [May 10, 1915?], GB181 SxMs56/1/28, VBRF 173.

29 V. Bell to R. Fry, June 12 [1915], GB181 SxMs56/1/28, VBRF 171. For an analysis of Omega dress design see Hitchmough, *The Bloomsbury Look*, pp. 91–128.

30 V. Bell to C. Bell, Monday [March 29, 1915], GB181 SxMs56/1/25, VBCB 118.

31 V. Bell to C. Bell, Wednesday [April 28, 1915], GB181 SxMs56/1/25, VBCB 86.

32 V. Bell to R. Fry, May 2 [1915], *SLVB*, p. 177.

33 See V. Bell to R. Fry, May 21 [1915], GB181 SxMs56/1/28, VBRF 166. V. Bell to C. Bell, [23 May 1915], GB181 SxMs56/1/25, VBCB 128.

34 V. Bell to R. Fry, Monday [June 7, 1915?], GB181 SxMs56/1/28, VBRF 154.

35 V. Bell to C. Bell, Wednesday [June 16, 1915], GB181 SxMs56/1/25, VBCB 88.

36 V. Woolf to V. Bell, August 16 [1916], *TLVW*, vol. 2, p. 111. See also V. Bell to R. Fry, Monday [June 14, 1915], GB181 SxMs56/1/28, VBRF 170.

37 V. Bell to R. Fry, June 9 [1915], GB181 SxMs56/1/28, VBRF 135.

38 For an analysis of Omega flowers see Wendy Hitchmough, 'Omega Flowers', *Charleston Press*, 3 (2019), pp. 72–9.

39 R. Fry to V. Bell, Jan. 20. [19]19, GB 181 SxMs56/1/83, RFVB 164. The artificial flowers were for an 'East African play'.

40 Described by her son, Jeremy Hutchinson, born 28 March 1915, interview by the author, 19 May 2009, Charleston Trust Collection, Sound Archive.

41 See Anon., 'Unity in Diversity: The House of Mr Osbert and Mr. Sacheverell Sitwell', *Vogue* [London], late October 1924, p. 54. The Sitwell interiors are discussed in Lawrence Mynott, 'Unity in Diversity: Edith, Osbert & Sacheverell Sitwell, Interior Innovators', *Journal of the Decorative Arts Society 1890–1940*, 8 (1984), pp. 29–39, although the relevant photograph is not reproduced. This is the only photograph of Omega flowers that I have found.

42 V. Bell, *Iris Tree*, 1915, oil on canvas, 1220 × 915 mm, private collection; V. Bell, *Helen Dudley*, c.1915, oil on canvas, 724 × 610 mm, presented by the Trustees of the Chantrey Bequest 1969, Tate, T01123.

43 V. Bell to R. Fry, Jan 4 [1916], GB181 SxMs56/1/28, VBRF 189.

44 See Collins, *The Omega Workshops*, p. 126. V. Bell, *Still Life on Corner of a Mantelpiece*, c.1914, oil on canvas, 559 × 457 mm, Tate, T01133; D. Grant, *The Mantelpiece*, 1914, oil and paper on board, 457 × 394 mm, Tate, T01328.

45 See C. Bell to M. Hutchinson, Jan. 31, 1916, Mary Hutchinson Papers, Harry Ransom Center, Box 22, Folder 22.8; W. Sickert, 'A Monthly Chronicle: O Matre Pulchrâ', *Burlington Magazine*, vol. 29, no. 157 (April 1916), p. 35.

46 Anon., 'Modern Art: Post-Impressionism of Mr S.F. Gore' and 'The Omega Workshops', *The Times*, 11 February 1916, p. 9.

47 V. Woolf to Katherine Cox, Feb. 12 [1916], *TLVW*, vol. 2, p. 78. V. Bell to V. Woolf, Monday [February 1916?], Berg, Folder 42.

48 Ibid.

49 V. Bell to R. Fry, Sep. 19 [1923], *SLVB*, p. 272.

50 D. Grant, *Vanessa Bell*, 1917, oil on canvas, 1270 × 1016 mm, National Portrait Gallery, London, NPG 5541. For evidence of the 1917 pregnancy and its influence on Vanessa's work as a dress designer see Hitchmough, *The Bloomsbury Look*, pp. 118–20.

51 D. Grant, *Vanessa Bell*, c.1918, oil on canvas, 940 × 606 mm, National Portrait Gallery, London, NPG 4331.

52 D. Grant, *The Room with a View*, 1919, oil on canvas, 760 × 570 mm, private collection; D. Grant, *Venus and Adonis*, 1919, oil on canvas, 635 × 940 mm, Tate, T01514.

53 Anon., 'Lyrics and Jingles in Paint: An Artist's Two Phases', *The Times*, 10 February 1920, p. 10.

54 C. Bell, 'Duncan Grant', *Athenaeum*, 6 February 1920, p. 182.

55 R. Fry, 'Mr Duncan Grant's Pictures at Patterson's Gallery', *New Statesman*, 21 February 1920, p. 586.

56 See D. Grant to compiler of Tate catalogue, 22 March 1972, quoted in Anon., catalogue entry, D. Grant, *Venus and Adonis*, https://www.tate.org.uk/art/artworks/grant-venus-and-adonis-t01514 (accessed 10 May 2023).

CHAPTER 10: CHARLESTON

1 V. Bell to D. Grant, Aug. 3 [1921], *SLVB*, p. 253.

2 V. Woolf, Tuesday 2 September [1930], *TDVW*, vol. 3, p. 316.

3 V. Bell to R. Fry, May 27 [1915], GB181 SxMs56/1/28, VBRF 169.

4 V. Bell to R. Fry, Sunday [May 9? 1915], *SLVB*, pp. 178–9. See also V. Bell to R. Fry, June 25 [1915], GB181 SxMs56/1/28, VBRF 175.

5 V. Bell to R. Fry, Thursday [1915], GB181 SxMs56/1/26, VBRF 190.

6 V. Bell to D. Grant, Monday [March 14, 1916], TGA 20078/1/44/47.

7 See V. Bell to D. Grant, Monday [March 14, 1916], TGA 20078/1/44/47. Garnett erroneously recollects that Duncan rented Wissett, in *The Flowers of the Forest*, p. 111.

8 V. Bell to O. Morrell, Friday [March 17, 1916], *SLVB*, p. 192.

9 Clive's exemption on medical grounds is questionable. See C. Bell to V. Bell, Monday [June 24, 1918?], in *Selected Letters of Clive Bell*, pp. 207–8.

10 V. Woolf to V. Bell, May 14 [1916], *TLVW*, vol. 2, p. 95.

11 V. Bell to V. Woolf, Sep. 14 [1916], Berg, Folder 43.

12 V. Bell to V. Woolf, [September 1916], Berg, Folder 43.

13 Ibid.

14 V. Bell to D. Grant, Sunday [September or October 1916], TGA 20078/1/44/42.

15 V. Bell to D. Grant, Wednesday [September or October 1916], TGA 20078/1/44/53.

16 Quentin Bell, interview with D. Grant, 1969, GB181 SxUOS1/2/3/1/10, University of Sussex Special Collections at The Keep.

17 V. Bell to R. Fry, May 10 [1916], GB181 SxMs56/1/28, VBRF 196.

18 Fra Angelico, *Visitation*, 1433–4, tempera on panel, 230 × 1830 mm, Museo Diocesano del Capitolo, Cortona.

19 V. Bell to R. Fry, May 10 [1916], GB181 SxMs56/1/28, VBRF 196.

20 *Exhibition of Copies & Translations*, Omega Workshops, London, May 1917.

21 V. Bell to R. Fry, Thursday [1916], GB181 SxMs56/1/28, VBRF 194.

22 V. Bell to R. Fry, June 22 [1916], GB181 SxMs56/1/28 VBRF 200.

23 V. Bell to R. Fry, Monday [April 1924], GB181 SxMs56/1/29, VBRF 346.

24 D. Garnett to L. Strachey, [September 1916], quoted in Spalding, *Vanessa Bell*, p. 155.

25 V. Bell to R. Fry, Feb 22 [1918], GB181 SxMs56/1/28, VBRF 259. The letter is incorrectly dated 1917 and reproduced in Quentin Bell and Virginia Nicholson, *Charleston: A Bloomsbury House and Garden* (London: Frances Lincoln, 1997), p. 112.

26 D. Grant, *Still Life*, private collection.

27 Garnett, *The Flowers of the Forest*, pp. 128, 151, 175–6.

28 Garnett wrote 'for the first year, we worked the same hours': Garnett, *The Flowers of the Forest*, p. 132. However, Vanessa's letters demonstrate that Duncan worked 'half time' from February 1917. V. Bell to R. Fry, Saturday [February 1917], GB181 SxMs56/1/28, VBRF 247, and V. Bell to V. Woolf, June 5 [1917], Berg, Folder 45.

29 V. Bell to R. Fry, Tuesday [7 November 1916?], GB181 SxMs56/1/28, VBRF 210.

30 V. Bell to D. Grant, Wednesday [September or October 1916], TGA 20078/1/44/53. See also V. Bell to D. Grant, Thursday [19 October 1916?] and Oct. 20 [1916], TGA 20078/1/44/52 and 20078/1/44/48.

31 See Garnett, *The Flowers of the Forest*, p. 46.

32 V. Bell to R. Fry, Tuesday [30 January 1917], GB181 SxMs56/1/28, VBRF 246.

33 V. Bell to D. Grant, Tuesday [February 29, 1916], TGA 20078/1/44/44.

34 See R. Fry to V. Bell, March 11, 1919, in *Letters of Roger Fry*, p. 448.

35 Angelica Garnett, interviewed by Wendy Hitchmough, 28 April 2003, British Library National Life Story Collection: Artists' Lives, C466/167, Tape 1 Side B.

36 D. Grant, *Lemon Gatherers*, 1910, oil on board, 565 × 813 mm, Tate, N03666.

37 V. Bell to R. Fry, Aug. 15 [1921], GB181 SxMs56/1/29, VBRF 315.

38 See V. Bell to D. Grant, Aug, 3 [1921], *SLVB*, p. 252.

39 V. Bell to R. Fry, Sep. 21 [1924], GB181 SxMs56/1/29, VBRF 355.

40 V. Bell to R. Fry, Aug. 11 [1925], GB181 SxMs56/1/29, VBRF 362.

41 Ibid.

42 V. Bell to D. Grant, Thursday [August 1926], TGA 20078/1/44/139.

43 When the original fireplace decorations, painted onto plaster, were spoiled by smoke from the stove Duncan painted a second version onto panels but the artists preserved the original. It remains in situ underneath.

44 When bookshelves were removed from the chimney wall during conservation work in 2005 the wall behind them was found to be unpainted. There is also a rectangle above the bookshelves showing only the base coat of brown distemper.

45 The brown and grey painted walls to the right of the chimneybreast, when facing the fireplace, and the exterior wall with the door into the Folly Garden were replastered and painted by conservators in the 1980s, as was the wall beneath the large window. The chimney wall and the adjoining wall between the studio and the main body of the house are substantially original.

46 I am indebted to Heather Wood and Wilma Day for sharing their knowledge of Charleston's wallpapers and painted walls as well as the restoration of the house with me.

47 V. Bell to D. Grant, Oct. 20 [1916], TGA 20078/1/44/48.

48 Burnt orange and green paint from an early scheme are evident in the above-ground archaeology.

49 V. Bell to D. Grant, Tue. Oct 11 [1927], TGA 20078/1/44/149.

50 See Barbara Bagenal, photograph of the studio at Charleston, *c*.1934, Charleston Trust Archive. D. Grant, *Cover for an Armchair*, 1932, printed linen, 740 × 840 × 550 mm, Charleston Trust Collection, CHA/T/247.

51 D. Grant, *Little Urn*, 1932, block-printed cotton and rayon curtains, 1860 × 1450 mm, Charleston Trust Collection, CHA/T/70a and b; V. Bell, *Pelmet*, *c*.1932, cotton with woollen rope swag, 180 × 3030 mm, Charleston Trust Collection, CHA/T/70c.

52 V. Bell to R. Fry, Monday [October 16, 1916], *SLVB*, p. 200.

53 V. Woolf, Friday November 2 [1917], *TDVW*, vol. 2, p. 69.

54 Garnett, *The Flowers of the Forest*, p. 144.

55 V. Bell to D. Grant, Tuesday [October 30, 1916?], TGA 20078/1/44/49.

56 V. Bell to R. Fry, Saturday [February 1917?], GB181 SxMs56/1/28, VBRF 247.

57 V. Bell to D. Grant, March 31 [1942], TGA 20078/1/44/219.

58 Vanessa calculated the costs of running Charleston to be around £235 a year in 1921. This included 'household books' for two months of £120; rent of £65 a year; repairs and garden costs of £37; £7 for coal; and £6 for caretaking. She

deducted £32 for the children's keep and Angelica's nurse, which she and Clive had already agreed to divide. Maynard contributed £60 towards the costs, Clive paid £30, Vanessa £70 and Duncan paid £42.10.0 'for rent & keep this year'. V. Bell to C. Bell, Nov. 21 [1921], GB181 SxMs56/1/25, VBCB 133. See also V. Bell to J.M. Keynes, November 26 [1921], GB181 SxMs56/1/30, VBMK 61.

59 V. Bell to V. Woolf, Feb 1 [1917], Berg, Folder 44.

60 See V. Bell to R. Fry, Mar. 5 and Monday [March 1918], GB181 SxMs56/1/28, VBRF 280 and 281.

61 Vanessa's plan to manage a small school at Charleston lasted only a term. V. Bell to R. Fry, Saturday [February 1917?], GB181 SxMs56/1/28, VBRF 247.

62 V. Bell to D. Grant, July 25 [1928], TGA 20078/1/44/154.

63 V. Bell to R. Fry, Oct. 10 [1925], GB181 SxMs56/1/29, VBRF 364.

CHAPTER 11: STILL LIFE

1 V. Bell to M. Snowdon, Mar. 5 [1922], GB181 SxMs56/1/31, VBMS 36A.

2 V. Bell to V. Woolf, Thursday [summer 1921], Berg, Folder 56.

3 V. Bell to M. Snowdon, Dec. 4 [1921], GB181 SxMs56/1/31, VBMS 41.

4 R. Fry to V. Woolf, October 24, 1921, in *Letters of Roger Fry*, p. 515.

5 Ibid.

6 V. Bell to M. Snowdon, Dec. 4 [1921], GB181 SxMs56/1/31, VBMS 41.

7 Ibid. V. Bell, *Vineyard in Winter* was cat. no. 3, *Catalogue of Paintings and Drawings by Vanessa Bell*, Independent Gallery, 7a Grafton Street, May–June 1922. V. Bell to M. Keynes, Nov. 1 [1921], GB181 SxMs56/1/30, VBMK 59.

8 V. Bell to M. Keynes, Nov. 1 and Nov. 11 [1921], GB181 SxMs56/1/30, VBMK 59 and VBMK 60.

9 V. Bell, *The Pond at Charleston*, c.1916, oil on canvas, 295 × 348 mm, Charleston Trust Collection, CHA/P/78.

10 V. Bell to M. Snowdon, Sept. 6 [1906], GB181, SxMs56/1/31, VBMS 16.

11 V. Bell to R. Fry, Monday [May 1921], GB181 SxMs56/1/29, VBRF 304. Johannes Vermeer, *Girl with a Pearl Earring*, c.1665–7, oil on canvas, 465 × 400 mm, and *View of Delft*, c.1660–3, oil on canvas, 985 × 1175 mm, Koninklijk Kabinet van Schilderijen, Mauritshuis, The Hague.

12 V. Bell to M. Keynes, October 23 [1921], GB181, SxMs56/1/30, VBMK 58.

13 V. Bell to M. Keynes, Nov. 26 [1921], GB181 SxMs56/1/30, VBMK 61.

14 V. Bell to C. Bell, Nov. 21 [1921], *SLVB*, p. 260.

15 R. Fry to J. Marchand, December 19, 1921, in *Letters of Roger Fry*, pp. 519–20.

16 V. Bell to R. Fry, Monday [May 16, 1921], *SLVB*, p. 247.

17 See Hitchmough, *The Bloomsbury Look*, pp. 91–128.

18 V. Bell to D. Grant, Wednesday [September 1917], TGA 20078/1/44/66. The paintings exhibited in *The New Movement in Art*, Mansard Gallery, Heal & Son, London, October 8–26, 1917 are listed in *Letters of Roger Fry*, pp. 413–14. See also Peter Risdon, 'Still-Life (Triple Alliance) by Vanessa Bell (1879–1961)', *British Art Journal*, vol. 19, no. 3 (2018/19), pp. 114–16. R. Fry to V. Bell, Aug. 20 and Sept. 20, 1917, GB181 SxMs56/1/83, RFVB 104 and RFVB 106.

19 Anon., 'Exhibition of Modern Paintings and Drawings at the Omega Workshops', *Burlington Magazine*, vol. 33, no. 189 (December 1918), p. 233.

20 V. Bell to R. Fry, Feb. 18 [1919], GB181 SxMs56/1/29, VBRF 287.

21 C. Bell to V. Bell, November 20, 1919, in *Selected Letters of Clive Bell*, pp. 139–40. The London premiere of *Parade* with scenery, front cloth and costumes by Picasso, music by Erik Satie and choreography by Léonide Massine was at the Empire Theatre on 14 November 1919. Vanessa's letter to Clive appears to be lost but she also described her impressions in V. Bell to R. Fry, Nov. 15 [1919], GB181 SxMs56/1/29, VBRF 297.

22 V. Bell to R. Fry, Dec. 17 [1919], GB181 SxMs 56/1/29, VBRF 299.

23 V. Bell to R. Fry, Oct. 29 [1919], GB181 SxMs56/1/29, VBRF 296.

24 V. Bell to R. Fry, Nov. 15 [1919], GB181 SxMs56/1/29, VBRF 297.

25 V. Bell to R. Fry, Nov. 30 [1919], GB181 SxMs56/1/29, VBRF 298.

26 V. Bell to R. Fry, Ap. 11 [1920], GB181 SxMs56/1/29, VBRF 301, and V. Bell to R. Fry, March 24 [1920], *SLVB*, p. 238.

27 V. Bell to R. Fry, Ap. 11 [1920], GB181 SxMs56/1/29, VBRF 301.

28 V. Bell to R. Fry, Sunday Ap. 18 [1920], GB181 SxMs56/1/29, VBRF 302.

29 V. Bell to R. Fry, May 17 [1920], *SLVB*, p. 244.

30 M. Vaughan to V. Bell, Mond. March 7 [1920], GB181 SxMs56/1/33, MVVB 18.

31 V. Bell to M. Vaughan, Mar. 10 [1920], *SLVB*, p. 235.

32 M.V. to M. Vaughan, March 21 [1920], GB181 SxMs56/1/33, MVVB 22.

33 V. Bell to R. Fry, Sunday [undated], GB181 SxMs56/1/29, VBRF 310. V. Bell, *Clive Bell and Family*, 1924, oil on canvas, 1270 × 1015 mm, Leicester Museum & Art Gallery, L.F23.1927.0.0.

34 V. Bell to R. Fry, Wednesday [May 25, 1921], *SLVB*, pp. 250–51.

35 See V. Bell to R. Fry, Sep. 9 [1921], GB181 SxMs56/1/29, VBRF 319 and V. Bell to C. Bell, Dec. 22 [1921], GB181 SxMs56/1/25, VBCB 135.

36 V. Bell to R. Fry, Jan. 6 [1922], GB181 SxMs56/1/29, VBRF 324.

37 V. Bell to M. Snowdon, Mar 5 [1922], GB 181 SxMs56/1/31, VBMS 36A.

38 V. Bell to R. Fry, Feb. 4 [1922], GB181 SxMs56/1/29, VBRF 325.

39 *Catalogue of Paintings and Drawings by Vanessa Bell*, 1922, cat. nos. 26, 4, 24 and 23. Of these, two are now in public collections: V. Bell, *On the Seine*, 1921, oil on canvas, 270 × 460 mm, Fitzwilliam Museum, Cambridge, 2375, and V. Bell, *Le Pont Neuf, Paris*, 1921, oil on canvas, 380 × 550 mm, Ashmolean Museum, Oxford, WA1940.1.26, both bequeathed by Frank Hindley Smith. The composition of *Le Pont Neuf, Paris* suggests a direct inspiration from Vermeer's *View of Delft*.

40 V. Bell to R. Fry, Aug. 16 [1921], GB181 SxMs56/1/29, VBRF 316.

41 V. Bell to R. Fry, Sunday [*c.* February 1923], GB181 SxMs56/1/29, VBRF 312.

42 V. Bell to R. Fry, Dec. 14 [1921] and Feb. 24 [1922], GB181 SxMs56/1/29, VBRF 322 and VBRF 327.

43 V. Bell, *Still Life at a Window*, 1922, oil on canvas, 598 × 357 mm, Courtauld Gallery, London (Samuel Courtauld Trust), gift of Samuel Courtauld, P.1932. SC.26. *Catalogue of Paintings and Drawings by Vanessa Bell*, 1922, cat. no. 11. The same white urn is painted in a very different composition in D. Grant, *Still Life*, 1922, oil on canvas, 533 × 660 mm, Southampton City Art Gallery, 2/1972.

44 V. Bell to R. Fry, Nov. 30 [1919], GB181 SxMs56/1/29, VBRF 298.

45 V. Bell to R. Fry, Monday [February 1922] and Feb. 24 [1922], GB181 SxMs56/1/29, VBRF 326 and VBRF 327.

46 See V. Bell to R. Fry, Feb. 24 and March 2 [1922], GB181 SxMs56/1/29, VBRF 327 and VBRF 328.

47 V. Bell to R. Fry, Feb. 24 [1922], GB181 SxMs56/1/29, VBRF 327.

48 V. Bell to R. Fry, March 2 [1922], GB181 SxMs56/1/29, VBRF 328.

49 V. Bell to R. Fry, March 2 [1922], GB181 SxMs56/1/29, VBRF 328.

50 V. Bell to R. Fry, Ap. 5 [1922], GB181 SxMs56/1/29, VBRF 329.

51 *Catalogue of Paintings and Drawings by Vanessa Bell*, 1922, cat. nos 1, 19 and 27.

52 V. Bell to C. Bell, Friday [May 19, 1922], GB181 SxMs56/1/25, VBCB 137. V. Bell to R. Fry, Ap. 5 [1922], GB181 SxMs56/1/29, VBRF 329.

53 V. Bell to C. Bell, Thursday [May 25, 1922], GB181 SxMs56/1/25, VBCB 137.

54 Walter Sickert, 'Vanessa Bell', *Burlington Magazine*, vol. 41, no. 232 (July 1922), pp. 32–5.

55 V. Bell to R. Fry, Feb. 6 [1919], *SLVB*, p. 230.

56 V. Bell to R. Fry, Wednesday [May 1919], GB181 SxMs56/1/29, VBRF 290.

57 V. Bell to R. Fry, Dec. 17 [1919], GB181 SxMs56/1/29, VBRF 299.

58 See D. Grant, *Dr Marie Moralt*, 1919, oil on canvas, 455 × 405 mm, private collection, reproduced in Shone, *The Art of Bloomsbury*, p. 188.

59 R. Fry, 'Independent Gallery. Vanessa Bell and Othon Friesz', *New Statesman*, vol. 19, no. 477 (3 June 1922), pp. 237–8. The remaining quotations in this chapter are all from the same review.

60 *Interior with a Table* may also have been exhibited as *Interior* with the London Group in April – May 1923, cat. no. 68, and acquired by Hindley Smith from that exhibition.

CHAPTER 12: DECORATIVE DESIGNS

1 For Bell and Grant's interior designs see Reed, *Bloomsbury Rooms*, and Darren Clarke, 'The Politics of Partnership: Vanessa Bell and Duncan Grant, 1912–1961', doctoral thesis, University of Sussex, 2012.

2 See, for example, V. Woolf to V. Bell, Saturday May 18, 1929, *TLVW*, vol. 4, p. 60.

3 V. Bell to R. Fry, May 10 [1928], GB181 SxMs56/1/29, VBRF 386.

4 V. Bell to V. Woolf, Thursday [April 26, 1924], Berg, Folder 58.

5 *Embroideries from New Designs by Vanessa Bell, Roger Fry, Duncan Grant & Wyndham Tyron*, Independent Gallery, London, 6–26 October 1925. The catalogue is in the National Art Library, 607.AZ.0054. Robert R. Tatlock, 'Modern Designs in Needlework', *Burlington Magazine*, vol. 47, no. 271 (October 1925), pp. 208–10.

6 Anon., 'The London Group', *Burlington Magazine*, vol. 37, no. 212 (November 1920), p. 260.

7 R.R. Tatlock, 'The London Group', *Burlington Magazine*, vol. 43, no. 248 (November 1923), p. 250.

8 R.R. Tatlock, 'The London Group. Passing of Abstract Art', *Daily Telegraph*, 21 October 1924, p. 13.

9 'Modern Designs in Needlework', 1925.

10 Anon., 'Modern Embroidery', *Daily Telegraph*, 5 December 1925, p. 15. The display at the Victoria and Albert Museum continued until 12 January 1926.

11 V. Bell to R. Fry, Monday [February 1922], GB181 SxMs56/1/29, VBRF 326.

12 V. Bell to R. Fry, Thursday [1925], GB181 SxMs56/1/29, VBRF 372.

13 Anon., 'Art Exhibitions. A Survey of the Past Fortnight', *The Times*, 19 May 1926, p. 14.

14 V. Bell to R. Fry, Sep. 8 [1926], GB181 SxMs56/1/29, VBRF 367.

15 V. Bell to D. Grant, Wednesday [August 17, 1925], TGA 20078/1/44/128.

16 Anon., 'Art Exhibitions. Miss Vanessa Bell', *The Times*, 22 February 1927, p. 12.

17 V. Bell to V. Woolf, March 2 and March 17 [1927], Berg, Folder 62.

18 V. Woolf to V. Bell, March 5, 1927, *TLVW*, vol. 3, pp. 340–1.

19 V. Bell to D. Grant, Dec. 22 [1925], 20078/1/44/131.

20 V. Bell to D. Grant, Dec. 27 [1925], *SLVB*, p. 288.

21 V. Bell to D. Grant, Dec. 29 [1925], 20078/1/44/126.

22 V. Bell to D. Grant, Monday [December 28, 1925] and Dec. 29 [1925], TGA 20078/1/44/125 and 20078/1/44/126.

23 C. Bell, 'The London Group and Sargent', *Vogue* [London], late February 1926, pp. 54–5, 80. *The London Group, 23rd Exhibition*, exh. cat., R.W.S. Gallery, London, 9–30 January 1926, cat. nos 107a and 107b.

24 Fry, 'The Work of a Woman Painter', pp. 33–5 and 78.

25 Anon., 'Modern English Decoration,' *Vogue* [London], early November 1924, pp. 43–5, 106.

26 V. Bell to V. Woolf, Tuesday [April 1917], Berg, Folder 45.

27 V. Bell to V. Woolf, Dec. 6 [1918], Berg, Folder 53.

28 V. Woolf, *Kew Gardens* (London: Hogarth Press, 1919).

29 V. Bell to W. Woolf, Thursday [October 24, 1918], Berg, Folder 52.

30 V. Woolf, *Monday or Tuesday* (London: Hogarth Press, 1921).

31 V. Woolf to V. Bell, Thursday [September 3, 1925], *TLVW*, vol. 3, p. 202.

32 V. Woolf to V. Bell [March? 1929], *TLVW*, vol. 4, p. 33.

33 V. Bell to V. Woolf, Wednesday [April 17, 1929], Berg, Folder 67.

34 V. Woolf to V. Bell, April 24, 1929, *TLVW*, vol. 4, p. 41.

35 See Raymond Mortimer, 'Electric', *Architectural Review*, vol. 67, no. 402 (May 1930), p. 295.

36 V. Bell, circular painted table, *c.*1933, painted wood, 705 × 1990 mm diameter, Charleston Trust Collection, CHA/F/8. See also V. Bell, *Design for Dining Room Table, Charleston*, *c.*1952, pencil and gouache, 438 × 438 mm, private collection.

37 V. Bell to R. Fry, Aug. 17 [1933], GB181 SxMs56/1/29, VBRF 423.

38 Marianne Mayfayre, 'Curtain Goes Up on New Spring Fashions', *Daily Telegraph*, 27 January 1931, p. 7.

39 V. Bell and D. Grant to M. Hutchinson, February 4, 1926. Harry Ransom Center, Mary Hutchinson Papers, Box 14, Folder 14.5.

40 The tiles were illustrated and described as part of a 'collection of modern British Pottery' exhibited at the V&A in *Studio*, vol. 95, no. 418 (January 1928), pp. 45, 47.

41 A.D., 'Decorative Work. Stage and Other Designs', *Daily Telegraph*, 11 January 1930, p. 17.

42 Paul Nash, 'Modern English Textiles – I', *Listener*, vol. 7, no. 172 (27 April 1932), p. 607.

43 1957 advertisement, reproduced in Anon., 'John Walton of Glossop, Charlestown and Longdendale Works', *Glossop Heritage*, 21 August 2020, https://glossopheritage.co.uk/ghtarchive/jwalton/ (accessed 1 July 2023).

44 Cyril Connolly, 'Genuine Arts & Crafts', *Architectural Review*, vol. 71, no. 422 (1 January 1932), p. 23.

45 Ibid.

46 Anon., 'The London Artists' Association', *The Times*, 8 December 1931, p. 12.

47 Connolly, 'Genuine Arts & Crafts', p. 23.

48 *Room and Book*, Zwemmer Gallery, London, 2–25 April 1932.

49 Nash, 'Modern English Textiles – I', p. 607.

50 Allan Walton, 'Furnishing Textiles', *Journal of the Royal Society of Arts*, vol. 83, no. 4285 (4 January 1935), p. 173.

51 Cyril Connolly, 'Orpheus in Bloomsbury: A Music Room Decorated, Furnished and Painted by Vanessa Bell and Duncan Grant', *Architectural Review*, vol. 73, no. 435 (1 February 1933), p. 74. See also Reed, *Bloomsbury Rooms*, pp. 267–72.

52 T.L.H., 'Modern Design for China and Earthenware', *Apollo*, vol. 20, no. 119 (1 November 1934), p. 283.

53 Clarice Cliff, 'Design Quiz No. 2', *Pottery Gazette and Glass Trade Review*, April 1951, pp. 572–3. Nikolaus Pevsner, *An Enquiry into Industrial Art in England* (Cambridge: Cambridge University Press), 1937, p. 77.

54 V. Bell to D. Grant, July 29 [1930], TGA 20078/1/44/168. For an illustration of Vanessa's glassware manufactured by Stuart & Sons of Stourbridge for the exhibition see W.W. Winkworth, 'China with Consideration', *Listener*, vol. 12, no. 303 (31 October 1934), p. 733.

55 *Exhibition of British Art in Industry*, Royal Academy, London, 5 January–9 March 1935. The ceramics display is illustrated in Christopher Hussey, 'The Art in Industry Exhibition', *Country Life*, 19 January 1935, p. 77.

56 See Hana Leaper, 'Talk of the Table: Vanessa Bell and Duncan Grant's Famous Dinner Service', in S. Ketteringham and M. Travers (eds), *From Omega to Charleston: The Art of Vanessa Bell and Duncan Grant, 1910–34* (London: Piano Nobile); Reed, *Bloomsbury Rooms*, pp. 265–6.

57 V. Bell to R. Fry, Oct. 2 [1932], GB181 SxMs56/1/29, VBRF 421.

58 V. Bell to R. Fry, June 19 [1933], GB181 SxMs56/1/29, VBRF 419.

59 V. Bell to C. Bell, Jan. 31 [1930], GB181 SxMs56/1/25, VBCB 211. V. Bell to D. Grant, Saturday [January or early February 1930], TGA 20078/1/44/167.

60 V. Woolf, 'Foreword', *Recent Paintings by Vanessa Bell with a Foreword by Virginia Woolf* (London: London Artists' Association, 1930), unpaginated.

61 V. Bell to C. Bell, Jan. 31 [1930], GB181 SxMs56/1/25, VBCB 211.

62 Anon. [Charles Marriott], 'Mrs Vanessa Bell', *The Times*, 7 February 1930, p. 12.
63 V. Bell to D. Grant, Feb. 7 [1930], *SLVB*, p. 351.

CHAPTER 13: INTERIOR WORLDS

1 Frances Partridge, 'From a Paper Given at a Charleston Open Day at the Victoria and Albert Museum, London, 1985', reprinted in Quentin Bell, Angelica Garnett, Henrietta Garnett and Richard Shone, *Charleston Past and Present* (London: Hogarth Press, 1987), p. 143.

2 Henrietta Garnett, 'Visits to Charleston: Vanessa', in Quentin Bell et al., *Charleston Past and Present*, pp. 153–4.

3 Reed, *Bloomsbury Rooms*.

4 V. Bell to V. Woolf, June 5 [1917], Berg, Folder 45.

5 V. Bell to D. Grant, Monday [18 June, 1917], [erroneously dated *c*.1916], TGA 20078/1/44/43.

6 Anon., 'A Harmony of the Furnishing of Two Centuries', *Vogue* [London], early February 1919, pp. 40–1. See also Reed, *Bloomsbury Rooms*, pp. 201, 203.

7 See V. Bell, *Nude with Poppies*, 1916, oil on canvas, 234 × 424 mm, Swindon Museum and Art Gallery, AG1973/294.

8 V. Bell to V. Woolf, July 4 [1917], Berg, Folder 45.

9 V. Bell to D. Grant, Friday [*c*. September 1917], TGA 20078/1/44/70.

10 Anon., 'Modern English Decoration', pp. 45, 106.

11 V. Bell to R. Fry, Saturday [June 2, 1917], GB181 SxMs56/1/28, VBRF 226. See also R. Fry to V. Bell, June 1 [1917], GB181 SxMs56/1/83, RFVB 91.

12 R. Fry to V. Bell, June 11 1917, in *Letters of Roger Fry*, pp. 411–12.

13 V. Bell to D. Grant, Tuesday [*c*. late 1917], TGA 20078/1/44/77.

14 R.F. Harrod, *The Life of John Maynard Keynes* (London: Macmillan, 1951), pp. 317–18.

15 V. Bell to R. Fry, Aug. 20 [1918], GB181 SxMs56/1/28, VBRF 265. J.M. Keynes to F.A. Keynes, September 21, 1918, quoted in Harrod, *Life*, p. 227.

16 V. Bell to R. Fry, Aug. 20 [1918], GB181 SxMs56/1/28, VBRF 265.

17 V. Bell to D. Grant, Sunday [September 22, 1918], TGA 20078/1/44/75.

18 V. Bell to D. Grant, Saturday [September 28, 1918], TGA 20078/1/44/83.

19 V. Bell to D. Grant, Saturday and Sunday [28 and 22 September 1918], TGA 20078/1/44/83 and 20078/1/44/88. See also V. Bell to V. Woolf, [October 4, 1918], Berg, Folder 52.

20 See D. Grant to D. Garnett, letters postmarked 6, 9 and 10 October 1918, quoted in Garnett, *The Flowers of the Forest*, pp. 187–8. See also Harrod, *Life*, p. 228.

21 For a detailed analysis of this scheme see Reed, *Bloomsbury Rooms*, pp. 205–11.

22 See V. Bell to D. Grant, Thursday [*c*. June 15, 1923], TGA 20078/1/44/124.

23 See Reed, *Bloomsbury Rooms*, pp. 208–9.

24 V. Bell to R. Fry, Aug. 26 [1920], GB181 SxMs56/1/29, VBRF 317.

25 See Richard Shone, essay on 'Duncan Grant and Vanessa Bell, *Eight Studies for Murals at John Maynard Keynes' rooms, Webb Court, King's College, Cambridge; The Muses of Arts and Sciences*', 1920, oil on canvas, each 838 × 355 mm, Modern

British Art Evening Sale, Christie's, 12 December 2012, lot 60: https://www.christies.com/en/lot/lot-5640049 (accessed 16 July 2023). Shone erroneously speculates that the eight figures were divided by gender: 'the males by Grant, the females by Bell'. See also Trancred Borenius, 'Bono da Ferrara', *Burlington Magazine*, vol. 35, no. 200 (November 1919), pp. 178–9.

26 Anon., 'An Economist and Modern Art. The Cambridge Rooms of Mr Keynes', *Vogue* [London], early March 1925, pp. 46–7.

27 See sketches in V. Bell to R. Fry, Aug. 26 [1920], GB181 SxMs56/1/29, VBRF 317, and D. Grant, sketchbook, 1920, Charleston Trust Collection, CHA/P/2620/2, CHA/P/2620/19 and CHA/P/2620/20 in support of these attributions.

28 V. Bell to R. Fry, Aug. 26 [1920], GB181 SxMs56/1/29, VBRF 317.

29 See V. Bell to R. Fry, Aug. 15 [1920], GB181 SxMs56/1/29, VBRF 315.

30 V. Bell to R. Fry, Aug. 16 [1921], GB181 SxMs56/1/29, VBRF 316.

31 V. Bell to D. Grant, Thursday [August 4, 1921], TGA 20078/1/44/108.

32 V. Bell to R. Fry, Aug. 26 [1920], GB181 SxMs56/1/29, VBRF 317.

33 Q. Bell, *Elders and Betters*, p. 55. V. Bell to D. Grant, Thursday [August 4, 1921], TGA 20078/1/44/108.

34 See Reed, *Bloomsbury Rooms*, pp. 220–2.

35 Anon., 'An Economist and Modern Art', p. 47.

36 V. Bell to V. Woolf, Ap. 16 [1927], Berg, Folder 62.

37 V. Bell to D. Grant, July 27 [1928], TGA 20078/1/44/155. This must have been an advance copy of D. Todd, 'Mural Decoration To-Day', *Studio*, vol. 96, no. 425 (August 1928), pp. 108–16.

38 Dorothy Todd and Raymond Mortimer, *The New Interior Decoration* (London: Batsford, 1929). V. Bell to V. Woolf, [*c.* April 26, 1928], Berg, Folder 66.

39 'Preface' [dated April 1929], in Todd and Mortimer, *The New Interior Decoration*, p. v.

40 V. Bell to V. Woolf, [*c.* April 26, 1928], Berg, Folder 66.

41 See Todd and Mortimer, *The New Interior Decoration*, Plate 74.

42 For a summary of this issue see Anon., 'Interior Decoration: The Work of Modern English Artists', *Architects' Journal*, vol. 71, no. 401 (30 April 1930), pp. 690–1. See also Reed, *Bloomsbury Rooms*, pp. 261–4.

43 V. Bell to D. Grant, Saturday [February 15, 1930], TGA 20078/1/44/167.

44 John Betjeman, '1830–1930 Still Going Strong: A Guide to the Recent History of Interior Decoration', *Architectural Review*, vol. 67, no. 402 (1 May 1930), pp. 240–72. Mortimer, 'Electric', pp. 282–300.

45 For details of this scheme, attributed exclusively to Vanessa, see Anon., 'Lord Benbow's Apartments: The Architectural Review Competition', *Architectural Review*, vol. 68, no. 409 (1 December 1930), pp. 242–42a.

46 V. Bell to V. Woolf, March 17 [1927], Berg, Folder 62.

47 V. Bell, *A Garden Scene*, fig. 13.5; V. Bell, *Mural Painting, Decorative Border with Red Curtain*, 1925, oil on panel, 2515 × 580 mm; V. Bell, *Mural Painting, Decorative Border with Red Curtain*, 1925, oil on panel, 2518 × 380 mm; three of five panels given by Raymond Mortimer when he moved house in 1953, Victoria and Albert Museum, London, P.2-1953; P.4-1953 (set); P.4-1953.

48 V. Bell to V. Woolf, Feb. 2 [1928], Berg, Folder 65.

49 V. Bell to V. Woolf, March 9 [1928], Berg, Folder 65.

50 V. Bell to V. Woolf, Feb. 24 [1928], Berg, Folder 65.

51 See V. Bell to C. Bell, May 31 and July 1 [1929], GB181 SxMs56/1/25, VBCB 171 and 242.

52 See V. Bell to C. Bell, Feb. 19 [1930], GB181 SxMs56/1/25, VBCB 227.

53 Robert Medley, *Drawn from the Life: A Memoir* (London: Faber & Faber, 1983), p. 105.

54 V. Bell to V. Woolf, [*c.* May 1928], Berg, Folder 66.

55 V. Bell to D. Grant, February 5 [1930], TGA 20078/1/44/162.

56 V. Bell to D. Grant, July 29 [1930], TGA 20078/1/44/168.

57 V. Bell to D. Grant, Feb. 13 [1930], TGA 20078/1/44/166.

58 V. Bell to D. Grant, February 5 [1930], TGA 20078/1/44/162.

59 V. Bell to D. Grant, Feb. 6 [1930], TGA 20078/1/44/163.

60 See V. Bell to C. Bell, Jan. 28 [1930], GB181 SxMs56/1/25, VBCB 209; V. Bell to D. Grant July 29 and July 30 [1930] TGA 20078/1/44/169 and 20078/1/44/170 and Medley, *Drawn from Life*, p. 119 for references to 'the room'. See also V. Bell to D. Grant, Feb. 10 [1930], TGA 20078/1/44/165.

61 V. Bell to C. Bell, Aug. 3 [1929], GB181 SxMs56/1/25, VBCB 245. See also Reed, *Bloomsbury Rooms*, pp. 256–8.

62 V. Bell to Q. Bell, Nov. 27 [1929], *SLVB*, pp. 345–6. See also Victor Rienaecker, 'An Interesting Experiment', *Apollo*, vol. 43, no. 252 (1 February 1946), pp. 34, 35, 38.

63 Madge Garland, 'A Room Decorated by Duncan Grant and Vanessa Bell', *Studio*, vol. 100, no. 449 (August 1930), pp. 142–3.

64 V. Bell, *Interior with Duncan Grant*, 1934, oil on canvas, 1122 × 973 mm, Williamson Art Gallery & Museum, Birkenhead, BIKGM:2332. V. Bell, *Interior Scene with Clive Bell and Duncan Grant Drinking Wine*, n.d., oil on canvas, 1220 × 1520 mm, private collection on loan to Birkbeck, University of London, 26.

CHAPTER 14: LATE WORKS AND LEGACY

1 V. Bell to D. Grant, Thursday [September 20, 1928], TGA 20078/1/44/156.

2 'G.W.', 'Foreword', *Vanessa Bell: A Memorial Exhibition of Paintings*, exh. cat. (London: Arts Council, 1964), p. 3. The exhibition was held at the Arts Council Gallery, London (29 February–28 March); City Art Gallery, Plymouth (11 April–2 May); Museum and Art Gallery, Bolton (9–30 May); City Art Gallery, Leeds (6–27 June); Castle Museum, Norwich (4–25 July); Art Gallery, Brighton (1–22 August) 1964. Cat. nos 3, 4, 5, 6, 18, 119, 22, 30, 31, 41, 46 and 47 were owned by Duncan. Leonard owned cat. nos 8, 10, 13, 49, 61 and 63.

3 André Dunoyer de Segonzac, 'Foreword', *Exhibition of Paintings by Vanessa Bell (1880–1961)*, exh. cat., Adams Gallery, London, 6–27 October 1961. Bell, *Self Portrait*, 1958 was cat. no. 61.

4 Ronald Pickvance, 'Introduction' and 'Chronology', *Vanessa Bell: A Memorial Exhibition* 1964, p. 7.

5 *Paintings by Vanessa Bell*, Adams Gallery, London, 2–25 February 1956.

6 See Vanessa V. Bell, *The Artist in Her Studio*, 1952, oil on canvas, 610 × 508 mm, Yale Center for British Art, Louise Wheatley Collection, Gift of Alison, Kit, and Christopher Wheatley, B2017.12, and V. Bell, *Self-Portrait*, *c*.1952, oil on canvas, 422 × 310 mm, private collection, reproduced in Milroy and Dejardin, *Vanessa Bell*, p. 178. These were included in *Exhibition of Paintings by Vanessa Bell (1880–1961)*, cat. nos 46 and 39, in addition to V. Bell, *Self-Portrait*, 1958, cat. no. 61.

7 Pickvance, 'Introduction' and 'Chronology', pp. 5–10. Some of the dates given in the catalogue are inaccurate.

8 Ethel Walker, Frances Hodgkins and Gwen John were the three women given their own chapters in Rothenstein, *Modern English Painters: Sickert to Moore*.

9 Anon., 'Art in Advertising', *Daily Mail*, 16 June 1931, p. 13. V. Bell, *Alfriston. See Britain First on Shell*, 1931 (issued), colour lithograph poster issued by Shell-Mex and BP Ltd, 757 × 1117 mm, Victoria and Albert Museum, London, E.1491-1931. V. Bell to R. Fry, Sep. 29 [1930], GB181 SxMs56/1/129, VBRF 413. *An Exhibition of Modern Pictorial Advertising by Shell*, exh. cat., New Burlington Galleries, London, June 1931, cat. no. 21. Malcolm C. Salaman, 'The Spirit of "Shell" in Posters', *Apollo*, vol. 14, no. 79 (1 July 1931), pp. 38–9. See also R.R. Tatlock, 'Art and Advertising', *Daily Telegraph*, 17 June 1931, p. 10, and Anon., 'Shell Advertising', *The Times*, 16 June 1931, p. 12.

10 V. Bell to C. Bell, March 9 [1938], GB181 SxMs56/1/25, VBCB 177.

11 V. Bell, *The Schoolroom*, 1938, colour lithograph, 508 × 660 mm, Victoria and Albert Museum, London, CIRC.209-1938.

12 *Exhibition of Modern British Embroidery*, Victoria and Albert Museum, London, 1–30 July 1932. See Joseph McBrinn, 'Queer Hobbies: Ernest Thesiger and Interwar Embroidery', *Textile: Cloth and Culture*, vol. 15, no. 3 (2017), pp. 292–323. See also Mary Hogarth, *Modern Embroidery* (London: The Studio, 1933).

13 For stage designs see V. Bell to R. Fry, Wednesday [May 1917], GB181 SxMs56/1/28, VBRF 221; V. Bell to R. Fry, Aug 22 [1917], GB181 SxMs/56/1/28, VBRF 232; V. Bell to V. Woolf, Wednesday [September 19, 1917], Berg, Folder 46; V. Bell to V. Woolf, Monday [September 24, 1917], Berg, Folder 47; V. Bell to D. Grant, Sunday [September 22, 1918], TGA 20078/1/44/75.

14 V. Bell to R. Fry, May 13 and May 31 [1932], GB181 SxMs56/1/29, VBRF 416 and VBRF 417.

15 V. Bell to R. Fry, June 12 [1932], GB181 SxMs56/1/29, VBRF 418.

16 V. Woolf, Thursday January 19 [1933], *TDVW*, vol. 4, p. 144.

17 V. Woolf to V. Bell, Monday, May 2 [1932], *TLVW*, vol. 5, p. 58. V. Woolf to O. Morrell, [early January 1933], *TLVW*, vol. 5, p. 146.

18 V. Bell to V. Woolf, May 14 [1933], Berg, Folder 70.

19 V. Bell to V. Woolf, June 14 [1935], Berg, Folder 70.

20 V. Bell to J. Bell, Sep. 24 [1935], *SLVB*, p. 397.

21 C. Bell, 'Inside the "Queen Mary", a Business Man's Dream', *Listener*, vol. 15, no. 378 (8 April 1936), p. 659. V. Bell to J. Bell, Nov. 1 [1935], *SLVB*, p. 402.

22 V. Bell to J. Bell, Saturday, June 13 [1936], *SLVB*, p. 414.

23 Graham Bell, 'Contemporary British Art at Its Best', *Listener*, vol. 18, no. 444 (14 July 1937), p. 74.

24 V. Bell to V. Sackville-West, Aug. 16 [1937], *SLVB*, p. 439. V. Woolf, Friday 6 August [1937], *TDVW*, vol. 5, p.106.

25 V. Bell to J. Bell, June 9 [1935], *SLVB*, p. 392.

26 V. Woolf to V. Bell, Wednesday [September 8, 1937], *TLVW*, vol. 6, p. 168. V. Bell to V. Woolf, Sep. 9 [1938], *SLVB*, p. 441.

27 Angelica Garnett, *Deceived with Kindness: A Bloomsbury Childhood* (London: Chatto & Windus, 1984).

28 V. Bell to D. Grant, [July 28, 1939], TGA 20078/1/44/211. See also Spalding, *Vanessa Bell*, pp. 304–11.

29 V. Bell to D. Grant, June 24 [1953], TGA 20078/1/44/234.

30 V. Bell to C. Bell, Oct. 8 [1929], GB181 SxMs56/1/25, VBCB 215. *The London Group Twenty-Seventh Exhibition*, New Burlington Galleries, London, 14 October–1 November 1929.

31 V. Bell to Q. Bell, Oct. 30 [1929], GB181 SxMs56/1/25, VBCB 217 (erroneously filed with letters to Clive).

32 G. Bell, 'Contemporary British Art at Its Best', p. 74.

33 Virginia committed to guarantee £50 a year for two years. See V. Bell to V. Woolf, Nov. 6 [1938], Berg, Folder 74.

34 Pablo Picasso, *Guernica*, 1937, oil on canvas, 3493 × 7766 mm, Museo Nacional Centro de Arte Reina Sofia, Madrid.

35 *Mural Painting in Great Britain, 1919–1939: An Exhibition of Photographs*, Tate Gallery, London, 25 May–30 June 1939.

36 W.W. Winkworth, 'Decorating the Wall', *Listener*, vol. 21, no. 543 (8 June 1939), pp. 1224–5.

37 V. Bell to C. Bell, Ap. 11 [1939], GB181 SxMs56/1/25, VBCB 302.

38 V. Bell to V. Woolf, June 9 [1939], *SLVB*, pp. 454–5.

39 V. Bell to C. Bell, Ap. 11 [1939], GB181 SxMs56/1/25, VBCB 302.

40 V. Bell to D. Grant, July 23 and [July 28, 1939], TGA 20078/44/1/210 and 20078/1/44/211. Virginia noted 'Duncan's 480 canvases': V. Woolf, Sunday 31 July, *TDVW*, vol. 5, p. 228.

41 V. Bell to J. Bussy, June 6 [1940], *SLVB*, p. 470.

42 V. Woolf to E. Smyth, Sat. Oct. 12 [1940], *TLVW*, vol. 6, p. 439.

43 V. Bell to J. Bussy, Jan. 13 [1941], *SLVB*, p. 473.

44 See, for example, V. Woolf, Sunday, 15 September–Wednesday, 2 October [1940], *TDVW*, vol. 5, pp. 321–7, and V. Woolf to H. Walpole, 29 Sept 40, *TLVW*, vol. 6, p. 435.

45 See Richard Shone, *The Berwick Church Paintings* (Eastbourne: Towner Art Gallery, 1986); Anon., 'Berwick Church Murals – Preliminary Sketches by Duncan Grant', *Charleston Attic*, https://thecharlestonattic.wordpress.com/category/berwick-murals/berwick-church-murals/ (accessed 10 August 2023), and Peter Blee, *The Bloomsbury Group in Berwick Church: A Decorative Scheme by Duncan Grant, Vanessa Bell & Quentin Bell* (Berwick: St Michael & All Angels, 2016).

46 Reverend Peter Blee, 'Christ in Glory by Duncan Grant', Berwick Church, https://www.berwickchurch.org.uk/page/christ-in-glory-by-duncan-grant (accessed 10 August 2023).

47 V. Bell, archive photograph of D. Grant, Angelica and Quentin Bell, and Chattie Salaman in costume, taken for the Berwick murals, 1941 (TGA VB/R39), included in Vanessa Bell, photograph album CH9 (TGA 9020/10).

48 V. Bell to V. Woolf, March 20 [1941], *SLVB*, p. 474.

49 V. Woolf to V. Bell, Sunday [23? March 1941], *TLVW*, vol. 6, p. 485.

50 V. Bell, *The Memoir Club*, *c*.1943, oil on canvas, 608 × 816 mm, National Portrait Gallery, London, purchased with help from the Dame Helen Gardner Bequest, 2005, NPG 6718.

51 V. Bell to L. Woolf, Friday Aug. 5 [error for Aug. 4, 1944], *SLVB*, pp. 482–3.

52 See Anon., 'The Bell of the Ball', *Charleston Attic*, https://thecharlestonattic. wordpress.com/2015/04/30/the-bell-of-the-ball/ (accessed 13 August 2023).

53 *Society of Mural Painters: First Exhibition 1950*, New Burlington Galleries, Arts Council of Great Britain, London, 18 April–10 May; Brighton Art Gallery, 27 May–11 June; Wednesbury Museum and Art Gallery, 24 June–5 July; Lincoln, 12 July–12 August; Plymouth Art Gallery, 19 August–9 September; Ferens Art Gallery, Hull, 16 September–7 October; Graves Art Gallery, Sheffield, 14 October–4 November; Laing Art Gallery, Newcastle, 9–30 December 1950). Vanessa exhibited four studies in oil for *Marriage at Canaa (Design for a Church)*, cat. nos 10–13, pl. V.

54 *Recent Tapestries Woven by the Edinburgh Tapestry Company,* (dates and venues not given in the catalogue), The Arts Council, 1950. Bell, *The Cook,* 1948, oil on canvas, 1003 × 747 mm, Arts Council Collection, Accession No. 138.

55 See, for example, V. Bell, photograph of Elise Anghilante, 'The Cook with Dog', 1928 (TGA VB/P28).

56 *British Painting 1925–1950: Second Anthology*, New Burlington Galleries, London, 20 June–28 July 1951, and Manchester City Art Gallery, 4 August–16 September 1951. See Philip James, foreword, *60 Paintings for '51: The Arts Council – Festival of Britain*, exh. cat. (London: Arts Council of Great Britain, 1951), unpaginated. The exhibition opened in London before touring to regional galleries, 1 January–1 December 1951.

57 V. Bell to C. Bell, Jan. 14 [1950], GB 181 SxMs56/1/25, VBCB 263.

58 See V. Bell, *The Garden Room*, *c*.1951, oil on canvas, 2032 × 1676 mm, *60 paintings for '51:* exh. cat, cat. no. 6, fig. 11. This painting is also reproduced in Alan Clutton-Brock, 'Vanessa Bell and Her Circle', *Listener,* vol. 65, no. 1675 (4 May 1961), p. 790. V. Bell, *Figure Group with the Artist, Another Woman and Two Children by French Windows,* c.1951, oil on canvas, 2010 × 1650 mm., on loan from the artist's estate to Birkbeck, University of London. Accession No. 24 is the repainted version in which pentimenti show the original composition.

59 V. Bell to V. Woolf, Wednesday – midnight [March 13, 1940], *SLVB*, p. 461.

60 Nikolaus Pevsner, 'Ω', *Architectural Review*, vol. 90, no. 536 (1 August 1941), pp. 45–8. The interview with Winifred took the form of an exchange of letters. See W. Gill to N. Pevsner, March 3, 1941, TGA 8022.8.

61 V. Bell to W. Gill, July 7, 1946, National Art Library, OCLC 1008543539.

62 V. Bell to L. Woolf, July 20 [c.1950], *SLVB*, p. 527. See also V. Bell to A. Garnett, May 4 [1950], *SLVB*, p. 527.

63 V. Bell to C. Bell, March 25 [1950], GB181 SxMs56/1/25, VBCB 280.

64 Rothenstein, *Modern English Painters: Sickert to Moore*, pp. xi, 287, 290. A more vitriolic attack was published in the second volume of the first edition of John Rothenstein, *Modern English Painters: Lewis to Moore* (London: Eyre & Spottiswoode, 1956), pp. 14–15.

65 V. Bell to J. Bussy, Dec. 29 [1958], *SLVB*, p. 546.

66 Anon., 'Vanessa Bell, Bloomsbury Group Artist of 1930s', *Daily Telegraph*, 10 April 1961, p. 14.

67 Clutton-Brock, 'Vanessa and Her Circle', p. 790.

68 William Gaunt, 'The Bloomsbury Painter', *Sunday Telegraph*, 8 October 1961, p. 11.

69 Quentin Bell, 'The Omega Revisited', *Listener*, vol. 71, no. 1818 (30 January 1964), pp. 200–1.

70 See, for example, *Vanessa Bell: Paintings and Drawings*, Anthony d'Offay, London, 20 November–12 December 1973; *Vanessa Bell, Paintings from Charleston*, Dering Street, 26 July–25 August 1979; *Vanessa Bell 1879–1961: A Retrospective Exhibition, 1879–1961*, Davis and Long, New York, 18 April–24 May 1980.

71 Richard Morphet, 'The Art of Vanessa Bell', in *Vanessa Bell: Paintings and Drawings*, exh. cat., p. 5.

72 Spalding, *Vanessa Bell*; *SLVB*.

73 See Grace Brockington, 'A "Lavender Talent" or "The Most Important Woman Painter in Europe"? Reassessing Vanessa Bell', *Art History*, vol. 36, no. 1 (2013), pp. 128–53.

74 V. Bell to C. Bell, Aug. 3 [1929], GB181 SxMs56/1/25, VBCB 245.

75 See, for example, V. Bell to D. Grant, Friday [c. May 1940], TGA 20078/1/44/217.

76 V. Bell to R. Fry, May 16 [1921], *SLVB*, p. 249. D. Carrington to L. Strachey, 12 October 1920, *Carrington's Letters*, p. 155.

77 *Daily Express Women's Exhibition*, Olympia, London, 12–29 July 1922. See P.G. Konody, 'The Women's Academy at Olympia', *Observer*, 16 July 1922, p. 8.

BIBLIOGRAPHY

ABBREVIATIONS AND UNPUBLISHED SOURCES

SLVB   *Selected Letters of Vanessa Bell*, ed. Regina Marler (New York: Pantheon, 1993)

TDVW   *The Diary of Virginia Woolf*, ed. Anne Olivier Bell and Andrew McNeillie (Harmondsworth: Penguin Books, 1977–84), 5 vols

TLVW   *The Letters of Virginia Woolf*, ed. Nigel Nicolson and Joanne Trautmann (London: Hogarth Press, 1975–80), 6 vols

Public collections of letters and manuscripts are cited in the notes with the following abbreviations:

Berg   New York Public Library, Berg Collection, MSS Woolf, Manuscript box (Woolf). In: Bell, Vanessa

British Library   Department of Manuscripts, British Library, London

Charleston Trust Archive   Uncatalogued collection of photographs and ephemera, formerly in the collection of Quentin and Anne Olivier Bell and of Angelica Garnett

GB181 SxMs   University of Sussex Special Collections at The Keep, Brighton

TGA   Vanessa Bell's photograph albums and letters are catalogued and in the Hyman Kreitman Research Centre, Archive and Special Collections, Tate.

A.D., 1930, 'Decorative Work. Stage and Other Designs', *Daily Telegraph*, 11 January, p. 17

Adams Gallery, 1961, *Exhibition of Paintings by Vanessa Bell (1880–1961)*, exh. cat., Adams Gallery, London

Affron, Matthew, 2012, 'Decoration and Abstraction in Bloomsbury', in Leah Dickerman (ed.), *Inventing Abstraction 1910–1925: How a Radical Idea Changed Modern Art*, exh. cat. (London and New York: Thames & Hudson/ Museum of Modern Art), pp. 182–7

Alpine Club Gallery, 1913, *The Grafton Group*, exh. cat., Alpine Club Gallery, London

———, 1914, *The Grafton Group: Vanessa Bell. Roger Fry. Duncan Grant. Second Exhibition*, exh. cat., Alpine Club Gallery, London

Annan, Noel, 1984, *Leslie Stephen, the Godless Victorian* (New York: Random House)

Anon., 1899, 'The National Gallery: Sir Edward Poynter's Report', *Evening Standard*, 6 April, p. 2

———, 1906, *Exhibition of Pictures & Sketches by Charles Wellington Furse, ARA*, exh. cat., Burlington Fine Arts Club, London

———, 1910, 'Manet and the Post-Impressionists', *Athenaeum*, 12 November, pp. 598–9

———, 1912, *An Exhibition of Pictures by Members of the Friday Club*, exh. cat., Alpine Club Gallery, London

———, 1913, 'The Grafton Group', *The Times*, 20 March, p. 4

———, 1913, 'Our London Letter: The Grafton Group', *Manchester Courier*, 21 March, p. 6

———, 1913, 'The Grafton Group', *Pall Mall Gazette*, 27 March, p. 4

———, 1913, 'A New Venture in Art: Exhibition at the Omega Workshops', *The Times*, 9 July, p. 4

———, 1913, 'Post-Impressionist Furniture', *Daily News and Leader*, 7 August, p. 10

———, 1913, 'Art Notes', *Illustrated London News*, 13 September, p. 408

———, 1913, 'Beethoven's "Moonlight Sonata": A Watteau Picture and Post-Impressionism as Inspiration for Schemes of Decoration', *Illustrated London News*, 25 October, pp. iv–v

———, 1913, 'The Omega Workshops: Decorative Form and Colour', *The Times*, 10 December, p. 13

———, 1914, 'The Grafton Group', *The Times*, 3 January, p. 11

———, 1914, 'The Grafton Group at the Alpine Club Gallery', *Athenaeum*, 10 January, p. 70

———, 1915, 'In the Great World: Lady Hamilton', *Sketch*, 21 April, p. 52

———, 1915, 'More Peaceful than the Dardanelles: The London Home of General Sir Ian and Lady Hamilton', *Sketch*, 23 June, pp. 240–1

———, 1916, 'Modern Art: Post-Impressionism of Mr S.F. Gore', *The Times*, 11 February, p. 9

———, 1916, 'The Omega Workshops', *The Times*, 11 February, p. 9

———, 1918, 'Exhibition of Modern Paintings and Drawings at the Omega Workshops', *Burlington Magazine*, vol. 33, no. 189, p. 233

———, 1919, 'A Harmony of the Furnishing of Two Centuries at River House', *Vogue* [London], early February, pp. 40–1

———, 1920, 'Lyrics and Jingles in Paint: An Artist's Two Phases', *The Times*, 10 February, p. 10

———, 1920, 'The London Group', *Burlington Magazine*, vol. 37, no. 212, p. 260

———, 1921, '"The Nameless Exhibition": Representative British Art Subjected to the Test of Anonymity', *Illustrated London News*, 21 May, pp. 684–5

———, 1923, 'The Art of Duncan Grant', *Vogue* [London], late February, pp. 50–1, 70

———, 1923, 'Modern Embroidery', *Vogue* [London], late October, pp. 66–7, 78

———, 1924, 'The Contemporary Style of Decoration', *Vogue* [London], early January, pp. 50–1, 74

———, 1924, 'Unity in Diversity: The House of Mr Osbert and Mr Sacheverell Sitwell', *Vogue* [London], late October, pp. 53–5, 92

———, 1924, 'Modern English Decoration', *Vogue* [London], early November, pp. 43–5, 106

———, 1925, 'An Economist and Modern Art', *Vogue* [London], early March, pp. 46–7

———, 1925, 'A Bachelor Flat in Bloomsbury', *Vogue* [London], late April, pp. 44–5

———, 1925, 'Modern Embroidery', *Daily Telegraph*, 5 December, p. 15

———, 1926, 'Art Exhibitions: A Survey of the Past Fortnight', *The Times*, 19 May, p. 14

———, 1927, 'Art Exhibitions: Miss Vanessa Bell', *The Times*, 22 February, p. 12

——— [Charles Marriott], 1930, 'Mrs Vanessa Bell', *The Times*, 7 February, p. 12

———, 1930, 'Interior Decoration: The Work of Modern English Artists', *Architects' Journal*, vol. 71, 30 April, pp. 690–1

———, 1930, 'Lord Benbow's Apartments: The Architectural Review Competition', *Architectural Review*, vol. 68, 1 December, pp. 242–242a

———, 1931, 'Art in Advertising', *Daily Mail*, 16 June, p. 13

———, 1931, 'Shell Advertising', *The Times*, 16 June, p. 12

———, 1931, 'The London Artists' Association', *The Times*, 8 December, p. 12

———, 1940, 'Sir A.S. Cope, RA: A Successful Portrait Painter', *The Times*, 6 July, p. 7

———, 1940, 'Sir Arthur Cope, RA', *Daily Telegraph*, 6 July, p. 6

———, 1961, 'Vanessa Bell, Bloomsbury Group Artist of 1930s', *Daily Telegraph*, 10 April, p. 14

Anthony d'Offay Gallery, 1973, *Vanessa Bell: Paintings and Drawings*, exh. cat., Anthony d'Offay Gallery, London

———, 1979, *Vanessa Bell: Paintings from Charleston*, exh. cat., Anthony d'Offay Gallery, London

———, 1984, *The Omega Workshops: Alliance and Enmity in English Art*, exh. cat., Anthony d'Offay Gallery, London

Arts Council, 1964, *Vanessa Bell, 1879–1961: A Memorial Exhibition of Paintings*, exh. cat., Arts Council Gallery, London

Baron, Wendy, 2006, *Sickert. Paintings and Drawings* (New Haven, CT, and London: Yale University Press)

Beale, S.S., 1908, *Recollections of a Spinster Aunt* (London: Heinemann)

Beechey, James, and Chris Stephens, 2012, *Picasso and Modern British Art* (London: Tate)

Bell, Clive, 1912, 'The English Group', in *Second Post-Impressionist Exhibition*, exh. cat., Grafton Galleries, London

———, 1914, *Art* (London: Chatto & Windus)

———, 1915, *Peace at Once* (London: National Labour Press)

———, 1920, 'Duncan Grant', *Athenaeum*, 6 February, p. 182

———, 1926, 'The London Group and Sargent', *Vogue* [London], late February, pp. 54–5, 80

———, 1934, 'Duncan Grant', *New Statesman and Athenaeum*, 19 May, pp. 763–4

———, 1936, 'Inside the "Queen Mary"', *Listener*, 8 April, pp. 658–60

———, 1956, *Old Friends: Personal Recollections* (London: Chatto & Windus)

———, 2023, *Selected Letters of Clive Bell: Art, Love & War in Bloomsbury*, ed. Mark Hussey (Edinburgh: Edinburgh University Press)

Bell, Graham, 1937, 'Contemporary British Art at Its Best', *Listener*, 14 July, p. 74

Bell, Quentin, 1964, 'The Omega Revisited', *Listener*, 30 January, pp. 200–1

———, 1968, *Bloomsbury* (London: Weidenfeld & Nicolson)

———, 1972, *Virginia Woolf: A Biography*, vol. 1: *Virginia Stephen, 1882–1912* (London: Hogarth Press)

———, 1973, *Virginia Woolf: A Biography*, vol. 2: *Mrs Woolf, 1912–41* (London: Hogarth Press)

———, 1995, *Elders and Betters* (London: John Murray)

Bell, Quentin, and Stephen Chaplin, 1964, 'The Ideal Home Rumpus', *Apollo*, October, pp. 284–91

Bell, Quentin, and Angelica Garnett, 1981, *Vanessa Bell's Family Album* (London: Jill Norman & Hobhouse)

Bell, Quentin, and Virginia Nicholson, 1997, *Charleston: A Bloomsbury House and Garden* (London: Frances Lincoln)

Bell, Vanessa, 1974, 'Notes on Bloomsbury' [1951], in S.P. Rosenbaum (ed.), *The Bloomsbury Group: A Collection of Memoirs, Commentary and Criticism* (London: Croom Helm), pp. 74–84

———, 1993, *Selected Letters of Vanessa Bell*, ed. Regina Marler (New York: Pantheon)

———, 1997, *Sketches in Pen and Ink*, ed. Lia Giachero (London: Hogarth Press)

Betjeman, John, 1930, '1830–1930 Still Going Strong: A Guide to the Recent History of Interior Decoration', *Architectural Review*, vol. 67, 1 May, pp. 240–72

Birrell, Rebecca, 2021, *This Dark Country: Women Artists, Still Life and Intimacy in the Early Twentieth Century* (London: Bloomsbury)

Blee, Peter, 2016, *The Bloomsbury Group in Berwick Church: A Decorative Scheme by Duncan Grant, Vanessa Bell & Quentin Bell* (Berwick: St Michael & All Angels)

Bonett, Helena, Ysanne Holt and Jennifer Mundy (eds), 2012, *The Camden Town Group in Context*, Tate Research Publications, https://www.tate.org.uk/art/research-publications/camden-town-group (accessed 18 January 2023)

Borenius, Trancred, 1919, 'Bono da Ferrara', *Burlington Magazine*, vol. 35, no. 200, pp. 178–9

Boyd Haycock, David, 2009, *A Crisis of Brilliance* (London: Old Street)

Brockington, Grace, 2010, *Above the Battlefield: Modernism and the Peace Movement in Britain, 1900–1918* (New Haven, CT, and London: Yale University Press)

———, 2013, '"A Lavender Talent" or "The Most Important Woman Painter in Europe"? Reassessing Vanessa Bell', *Art History*, vol. 36, no. 1, pp. 128–53

———, 2017, 'Relationships: Formal, Creative and Political', in her *In Focus: 'Abstract Painting' c.1914 by Vanessa Bell*, Tate Research Publications, www. tate.org.uk/research/publications/in-focus/abstract-painting-vanessa-bell/ relationships (accessed 18 January 2019)

Brooke, Rupert, 1912, 'The Post-Impressionists – II', *Cambridge Magazine*, 30 November

Bullen, J.B. (ed.), 1988, *Post-Impressionists in England: The Critical Reception* (London: Routledge)

Burlington Galleries, 1931, *An Exhibition of Modern Pictorial Advertising by Shell*, exh. cat., Burlington Galleries, London

Burne-Jones, Georgiana, 1906, *Memorials of Edward Burne-Jones* (London: Macmillan)

Carrington, Dora, 2017, *Carrington's Letters*, ed. Anne Chisholm (London: Chatto & Windus)

Caws, Mary Ann, 1990, *Women of Bloomsbury: Virginia, Vanessa, and Carrington* (New York: Routledge)

Caws, Mary Ann, and Sarah Bird Wright, 2000, *Bloomsbury and France: Art and Friends* (Oxford: Oxford University Press)

Cherry, Deborah, 2000, *Beyond the Frame: Feminism and Visual Culture 1850– 1900* (London and New York: Routledge)

Clarke, Darren, 2012, 'The Politics of Partnership: Vanessa Bell and Duncan Grant, 1912–1961', doctoral thesis, University of Sussex

Clarke, Meaghan, 2020, *Fashionability, Exhibition Culture and Gender Politics* (New York: Routledge)

Clarke, Meaghan, and Francesco Ventrella, 2017, 'Women's Expertise and the Culture of Connoisseurship', *Visual Resources*, vol. 33, no. 1, pp. 1–10

Cliff, Clarice, 1951, 'Design Quiz No. 2', *Pottery Gazette and Glass Trade Review*, April, pp. 572–3

Clutton-Brock, Alan, 1961, 'Vanessa Bell and Her Circle', *Listener*, 4 May, p. 790

Collins, Judith, 1984, *The Omega Workshops* (London and Chicago: University of Chicago Press)

Collins, Judith, and Fiona MacCarthy, 1984, *The Omega Workshops, 1913–19*, exh. cat., Crafts Council, London

Connolly, Cyril, 1932, 'Genuine Arts & Crafts', *Architectural Review*, vol. 71, 1 January, p. 23

———, 1933, 'Orpheus in Bloomsbury: A Music Room Decorated, Furnished and Painted by Vanessa Bell and Duncan Grant', *Architectural Review*, vol. 73, February, pp. 74–5

Constable, W.G., 1920, 'Lotiron, Duncan Grant and Vanessa Bell', *Burlington Magazine*, vol. 37, no. 213, p. 326

Cooke, Arthur Ebenezer, 1921, 'Ebenezer Cooke', in Foster Watson (ed.), *The Encyclopedia and Dictionary of Education*, vol. 1 (London: Pitman), p. 385

Cox, Julian, and Colin Ford, 2003, *Julia Margaret Cameron: The Complete Photographs* (Los Angeles: Getty)

Curtis, Anthony (ed.), 2002, *Before Bloomsbury: The 1900s Diaries of Three Kensington Ladies* (London: Eighteen Nineties Society)

Davies, Randall, 1914, 'The Grafton Group', *New Statesman*, 10 January, pp. 436–7

Davis & Long Company, 1980, *Vanessa Bell 1879–1961: A Retrospective Exhibition*, exh. cat., Davis & Long Company in association with Anthony d'Offay Ltd, New York

Denis, Maurice, and Roger Fry, 1910, 'Cézanne – I', *Burlington Magazine*, vol. 16, no. 82, pp. 207–19

———, 1910, 'Cézanne – II', *Burlington Magazine*, vol.16, no. 83, pp. 275–80

Dickerman, Leah (ed.), 2012, *Inventing Abstraction 1910–1925: How a Radical Idea Changed Modern Art*, exh. cat., (London and New York: Thames & Hudson/Museum of Modern Art)

Dunn, Jane, 1990, *A Very Close Conspiracy: Vanessa Bell and Virginia Woolf* (London: Jonathan Cape)

Dunoyer de Segonzac, André, 1961, 'Foreword', in *Exhibition of Paintings by Vanessa Bell (1880–1961)*, exh. cat., Adams Gallery, London

Elkin, Lauren, 2018, 'Bloomsbury and Feminism', in Derek Ryan and Stephen Ross (eds), *The Handbook to the Bloomsbury Group* (London: Bloomsbury Academic), pp. 109–20

Elmer, Samuel, 2011, 'The "Nameless Exhibition", London, 1921', *Burlington Magazine*, vol. 153, no. 1302, pp. 583–90

Ferguson Smith, Martin, 2019, 'A Complete Strip-Off: A Bloomsbury Threesome in the Nude at Studland', *British Art Journal*, vol. 20, no. 2, pp. 72–7

Forster, E.M., 1942, *Virginia Woolf* (Cambridge: Cambridge University Press)

Frost, Abigail, 1984, 'Omega Anonymous', *Crafts*, vol. 66, pp. 40–4

Fry, Roger, 1911, 'The Salons and Van Dougen [sic]', *Nation*, 24 June, pp. 463–4

———, 1912, 'The French Group', in *The Second Post-Impressionist Exhibition*, exh. cat., Grafton Galleries, London, pp. 25–9

———, 1913, 'The Allied Artists', *Nation*, 2 August, pp. 676–7

———, [1917], *Catalogue of an Exhibition of Works Representative of the New Movement in Art, Selected and Arranged by Mr Roger Fry*, exh. cat., Mansard Galleries, London

———, 1917, *Exhibition of Omega Copies and Translations* (London: Omega Workshops)

———, 1918, 'A Possible Domestic Architecture', *Vogue* [London], late March, p. 40

———, 1920, 'Mr Duncan Grant's Pictures at Patterson's Gallery', *New Statesman*, 21 February, pp. 586–7

———, 1920, *Vision and Design* (London: Chatto & Windus)

———, 1922, 'Independent Gallery: Vanessa Bell and Othon Friesz', *New Statesman*, 3 June, pp. 237–8

———, 1923, *Duncan Grant* (London: Hogarth Press)

———, 1926, *Transformations: Critical and Speculative Essays on Art* (London: Chatto & Windus)

———, 1926, 'The Work of a Woman Painter: Vanessa Bell', *Vogue* [London], early February, pp. 33–5, 78

———, 1932, *Characteristics of French Art* (London: Chatto & Windus)

———, 1939, *Last Lectures* (Cambridge: Cambridge University Press)

———, 1969, *Reflections on British Painting* [1934] (Freeport, NY: Books for Libraries Press)

———, 1972, *Letters of Roger Fry*, ed. Denys Sutton (London: Chatto & Windus), 2 vols

———, 1989, *Cézanne* [1927] (Chicago: University of Chicago Press)

G. [Duncan Grant], 1909, 'The New English Art Club at Suffolk Street', *Spectator*, 19 June, p. 977

G.R.H., 1914, 'The Grafton Group at the Alpine Gallery', *Pall Mall Gazette*, 8 January, p. 5

G.W., 1964, 'Foreword', in *Vanessa Bell, 1879–1961: A Memorial Exhibition of Paintings*, exh. cat., Arts Council Gallery, London

Garland, Madge, 1930, 'A Room Decorated by Duncan Grant and Vanessa Bell', *Studio*, vol. 100, no. 449, pp. 142–3

———, 1972, 'Recollections of Virginia Woolf', in Joan Russell Noble (ed.), *Recollections of Virginia Woolf* (London: Peter Owen), pp. 171–4

Garnett, Angelica, 1984, *Deceived with Kindness: A Bloomsbury Childhood* (London: Chatto & Windus/Hogarth Press)

Garnett, David, 1953, *The Golden Echo* (London: Chatto & Windus)

———, 1955, *The Flowers of the Forest* (London: Chatto & Windus)

———, 1962, *The Familiar Faces* (London: Chatto & Windus)

Garnett, Henrietta, 1987, 'Visits to Charleston: Vanessa', in Quentin Bell, Angelica Garnett, Henrietta Garnett and Richard Shone, *Charleston Past and Present* (London: Hogarth Press), pp. 153–60

Garrity, Jane, 1999, 'Selling Culture to the "Civilized": Bloomsbury, British *Vogue*, and the Marketing of National Identity', *Modernism/Modernity*, vol. 6, no. 2, pp. 29–58

———, 2000, 'Virginia Woolf, Intellectual Harlotry, and 1920s British *Vogue*', in P. Caughie (ed.), *Virginia Woolf in the Age of Mechanical Reproduction* (New York: Garland), pp. 185–218

———, 2010, 'Virginia Woolf and Fashion', in Maggie Humm (ed.), *The Edinburgh Companion to Virginia Woolf and the Arts* (Edinburgh: Edinburgh University Press), pp. 195–211

———, forthcoming, 'Nude Bloomsburies', in Derek Ryan (ed.), *A History of the Bloomsbury Group* (Cambridge: Cambridge University Press, forthcoming)

Gaunt, William, 1961, 'The Bloomsbury Painter', *Sunday Telegraph*, 8 October, p.11

Gerstein, Alexandra, 2009, *Beyond Bloomsbury: Designs of the Omega Workshops, 1913–19*, exh. cat., Courtauld Gallery, London

Gerzina, Gretchen Holbrook, 1989, *Carrington: A Life* (New York: W.W. Norton)

Gillespie, Diane, 1991, *The Sisters' Arts: The Writing and Painting of Virginia Woolf and Vanessa Bell* (Syracuse, NY: Syracuse University Press)

Glendinning, Victoria, 2006, *Leonard Woolf: A Biography* (New York: Free Press)

Grafton Galleries, 1910, *Manet and the Post-Impressionists*, exh. cat., Grafton Galleries, London

———, 1912, *Second Post-Impressionist Exhibition*, exh. cat., Grafton Galleries, London

Grant, Duncan, 1941, 'Virginia Woolf', *Horizon*, vol. 2, no. 18, pp. 403–4

Green-Lewis, Jennifer, 2017, *Victorian Photography, Literature, and the Invention of Modern Memory: Already the Past* (London: Bloomsbury Academic)

Hamnett, Nina, 1932, *Laughing Torso* (New York: Ray Long & Richard R. Smith)

Harrison, Charles, 1981, *English Art and Modernism, 1900–1939* (London: Allen Lane)

Harrod, R.F., 1951, *The Life of John Maynard Keynes* (London: Macmillan)

Haule, James (ed.), 2014, *The Bloomsbury Group Memoir Club* (Basingstoke: Palgrave Macmillan)

Helt, Brenda, and Madelyn Detloff (eds), 2016, *Queer Bloomsbury* (Edinburgh: Edinburgh University Press)

Hitchmough, Wendy, 2019, 'Omega Flowers', *Charleston Press*, no. 3, pp. 72–9

———, 2020, *The Bloomsbury Look* (New Haven, CT, and London: Yale University Press)

Hogarth, Mary, 1933, *Modern Embroidery* (London: The Studio)

Holroyd, Michael, 1976, *Augustus John: A Biography* (Harmondsworth: Penguin)

———, 1980, *Lytton Strachey: A Biography* [1967] (Harmondsworth: Penguin)

Howells, Richard, 2015, 'Copies and Translations: Roger Fry, Old Masters and the Omega Workshops', *British Art Journal*, vol. 16, no. 1, pp. 47–57

Hulme, T.E., 1914, 'Modern Art – I: The Grafton Group', *The New Age*, 15 January, pp. 341–2

Humm, Maggie, 2002, *Modernist Women and Visual Cultures: Virginia Woolf, Vanessa Bell, Photography and Cinema* (Edinburgh: Edinburgh University Press)

———, 2006, *Snapshots of Bloomsbury: The Private Lives of Virginia Woolf and Vanessa Bell* (London: Tate)

——— (ed.), 2010, *The Edinburgh Companion to Virginia Woolf and the Arts* (Edinburgh: Edinburgh University Press)

Hussey, Christopher, 1935, 'The Art in Industry Exhibition', *Country Life*, 19 January, p. 77

Hussey, Mark, 2021, *Clive Bell and the Making of Modernism* (London: Bloomsbury)

James, Philip, 1951, 'Foreword', in *60 Paintings for '51: The Arts Council – Festival of Britain*, exh. cat., Arts Council, London

Keynes, John Maynard, 1971, *The Collected Writings of John Maynard Keynes* (London: Macmillan)

———, 1974, 'My Early Beliefs' [1949], in S.P. Rosenbaum (ed.), *The Bloomsbury Group: A Collection of Memoirs, Commentary and Criticism* (London: Croom Helm), pp. 48–64

Knights, Sara, 2015, *Bloomsbury's Outsider: A Life of David Garnett* (London: Bloomsbury)

Konody, P.G., 1910, 'Post-Impressionists at the Grafton Galleries', *Observer*, 13 November, p. 9

———, 1913, 'Post-Impressionism in the Home', *Observer*, 14 December, p. 8

———, 1922, 'The Women's Academy at Olympia', *Observer*, 16 July, p. 8

Koutsantoni, K., and M. Oakley, 2014, 'Hypothesis of Autism and Psychosis in the Case of Laura Makepeace Stephen', *Disability Studies*, vol. 4, no. 3, doi:10.2139/ssrn.2418709

Laing, Donald, 1979, *Roger Fry: An Annotated Bibliography of the Published Writings* (New York: Garland)

Lawrence, D.H., 1981, *The Letters of D.H. Lawrence*, ed. George J. Zytaruk and James T. Boulton (Cambridge: Cambridge University Press), 2 vols

Leaper, Hana, 2017, 'Between London and Paris', in S. Milroy and I.A.C. Dejardin (eds), *Vanessa Bell* (London: Philip Wilson), pp. 41–53

——— (ed.), 2017, *The Famous Women Dinner Service: A Critical Catalogue* (London: Paul Mellon Centre), https://universalviewer.io/uv.html?manifest=https:// raw.githubusercontent.com/paulmelloncentre/manifest/master/bas/famous_ women#?c=0&m=0&s=0&cv=0&xywh=-1023%2C236%2C4231%2C2233 (accessed 3 August 2023)

———, 2018, 'Talk of the Table: Vanessa Bell and Duncan Grant's Famous Dinner Service', in S. Ketteringham and M. Travers (eds), *From Omega to Charleston: The Art of Vanessa Bell and Duncan Grant, 1910–34* (London: Piano Nobile)

Lee, Hermione, 1996, *Virginia Woolf* (London: Chatto & Windus)

Levi, Donata, and Paul Tucker, 2020, '"J after J. Ruskin": Line in the Art Teaching of John Ruskin and Ebenezer Cooke', *Journal of Art Historiography*, no. 22, pp. 1–16

Lewis, Wyndham, 1930, *Apes of God* (London: Arthur Press)

———, 1969, *Wyndham Lewis on Art: Collected Writings, 1913–1956*, ed. Walter Michel and C.J. Fox (New York: Funk and Wagnalls)

Light, Alison, 2007, *Mrs Woolf and the Servants* (London: Penguin)

M.M.B., 1913, 'Post-Impressionist Furniture', *Daily News and Leader*, 7 August, p. 10

[MacCarthy, Desmond], 1910, 'The Post-Impressionists', introduction to *Manet and the Post-Impressionists*, exh. cat., Grafton Galleries, London

MacCarthy, Desmond, 1949, *Portraits* (London: MacGibbon and Kee)

———, 1974, 'The Post-Impressionist Exhibition of 1910' [1953], in S.P. Rosenbaum (ed.), *The Bloomsbury Group: A Collection of Memoirs, Commentary and Criticism* (London: Croom Helm), pp. 68–73

MacGibbon, Jean, 1997, *There's the Lighthouse: A Biography of Adrian Stephen* (London: James and James)

Maitland, Frederic William, 1906, *The Life and Letters of Leslie Stephen* (London: Duckworth)

Matania, F., 1913, 'The Wagner Cycles at Covent Garden: Specially Illustrated for "The Sphere"', *The Sphere*, 31 May, pp. 240–1

Mauclair, Camille, 1903, *The French Impressionists. 1860–1900*, translated by P.G. Konody (London: Duckworth & Co.)

Mayfayre, Marianne, 1931, 'Curtain Goes Up on New Spring Fashions', *Daily Telegraph*, 27 January, p. 7

McBrinn, Joseph, 2017, 'Queer Hobbies: Ernest Thesiger and Interwar Embroidery', *Textile: Cloth and Culture*, vol. 15, no. 3, pp. 292–323

Medley, Robert, 1983, *Drawn from the Life: A Memoir* (London: Faber & Faber)

Milroy, Sarah, and Ian A.C. Dejardin (eds), 2017, *Vanessa Bell* (London: Philip Wilson)

Morehead, Allison, 2015, 'Defending Deformation: Maurice Denis's Positivist Modernism', *Art History*, vol. 38, no. 5, pp. 890–915

Morphet, Richard, 1973, 'The Art of Vanessa Bell', in *Vanessa Bell: Paintings and Drawings*, exh. cat., Anthony d'Offay Gallery, London, pp. 5–13

Morrell, Ottoline, 1963, *Ottoline: The Early Memoirs of Lady Ottoline Morrell*, ed. Robert Gathorne-Hardy (London: Faber & Faber)

———, 1974, *Ottoline at Garsington: Memoirs of Lady Ottoline Morrell, 1915–1918*, ed. Roger Gathorne-Hardy (London: Faber & Faber)

Mortimer, Raymond, 1923, 'Duncan Grant at the Independent Gallery', *Vogue* [London], late June, pp. 56–7

———, 1930, 'Electric', *Architectural Review*, vol. 67, 1 May, pp. 282a, 283–6, 286a, 287–92, 292a, 293–300

———, 1930, 'Modern Furniture and Decoration', *Architectural Review*, vol. 68, 1 December, pp. 252–3

———, 1944, *Duncan Grant* (Harmondsworth: Penguin)

———, 1956, 'Lively Portraits: The Bloomsbury Set from the Inside', *Sunday Times*, 11 November, p. 4

Mynott, Lawrence, 1984, 'Unity in Diversity: Edith, Osbert & Sacheverell Sitwell, Interior Innovators', *Journal of the Decorative Arts Society 1890–1940*, no. 8, pp. 29–39

Nash, Paul, 1932, 'Modern English Textiles – I', *Listener*, 27 April, p. 607

Naylor, Gillian, 1990, *Bloomsbury: The Artists, Authors and Designers by Themselves* (London: Pyramid)

Nead, Lynda, 1992, *The Female Nude: Art, Obscenity and Sexuality* (London and New York: Routledge)

Nicholson, Virginia, 2003, *Among the Bohemians: Experiments in Living, 1900–1939* (London: Penguin)

Ondaatje Rolls, Jans, 2014, *The Bloomsbury Cookbook: Recipes for Life, Love and Art* (New York: Thames & Hudson)

Partridge, Frances, 1987, 'From a Paper Given at a Charleston Open Day at the Victoria and Albert Museum, London, 1985', reprinted in Quentin Bell, Angelica Garnett, Henrietta Garnett and Richard Shone, *Charleston Past and Present* (London: Hogarth Press), pp. 142–4

Patmore, Derek, 1933, *Colour Schemes for the Modern Home* (London: The Studio)

Pepler, H.D.C., 1950, 'Hampshire House Workshops', *Blackfriars*, vol. 31, no. 359, pp. 70–4

Peppin, B., 2011, 'Women That a Movement Forgot: The Vorticists 1', *Tate Etc.*, no. 22, https://www.tate.org.uk/tate-etc/issue-22-summer-2011/women-movement-forgot (accessed 3 May 2022)

Pevsner, Nikolaus, 1936, *Pioneers of the Modern Movement* (London: Faber & Faber)

——, 1937, *An Enquiry into Industrial Art in England* (Cambridge: Cambridge University Press)

——, 1941, 'Omega', *Architectural Review*, vol. 90, August, pp. 45–8

Pezzini, Barbara, 1913, 'The 1912 Futurist Exhibition at the Sackville Gallery, London: An Avant-Garde Show within the Old-Master Trade', *Burlington Magazine*, vol. 155, no. 1324, pp. 471–9

Phillips, Claude, 1913, 'The Grafton Group', *Daily Telegraph*, 22 March, p. 6

——, 1914, 'More Post-Impressionism', *Daily Telegraph*, 5 January, p. 8

——, 1914, 'Art in Whitechapel. Twentieth Century Exhibition', *Daily Telegraph*, 12 May, p. 14

Pickvance, Ronald, 1964, 'Introduction' and 'Chronology', in *Vanessa Bell, 1879–1961: A Memorial Exhibition of Paintings*, exh. cat., Arts Council Gallery, London

Poiret, Paul, 1930, *En habillant l'époque* (Paris: Bernard Grasset)

Pollock, Griselda, 1988, *Vision and Difference: Femininity, Feminism, and the Histories of Art* (London: Routledge)

——, 1999, *Differencing the Canon: Feminist Desire and the Writing of Art's Histories* (London: Routledge)

Porter, Charlie, 2023, *Bring No Clothes: Bloomsbury and the Philosophy of Fashion* (London: Penguin)

Porter, David H., 2008, *The Omega Workshops and the Hogarth Press: An Artful Fugue* (London: Cecil Woolf)

Reed, Christopher, 1990, 'The Fry Collection at the Courtauld Institute Galleries', *Burlington Magazine*, vol. 132, no. 1052, pp. 766–72

——, 1999, *Roger Fry's Durbins: A House and Its Meanings* (London: Cecil Woolf)

——, 2004, *Bloomsbury Rooms: Modernism, Subculture, and Domesticity* (New Haven, CT, and London: Yale University Press)

——, 2006, 'A *Vogue* That Dare Not Speak Its Name: Sexual Subculture during the Editorship of Dorothy Todd, 1922–26', *Fashion Theory*, vol. 10, nos 1–2, pp. 39–72

——, 2016, 'Bloomsbury Bashing: Homophobia and the Politics of Criticism in the Eighties', in Brenda Helt and Madelyn Detloff (eds), *Queer Bloomsbury* (Edinburgh: Edinburgh University Press), pp. 36–63

—— (ed.), 1996, *A Roger Fry Reader* (Chicago: Chicago University Press)

Reinaecker, Victor, 1946, 'An Interesting Experiment', *Apollo*, 1 February, pp. 34–5, 38

Risdon, Peter, 2018/19, 'Still-Life (Triple Alliance) by Vanessa Bell (1879–1961)', *British Art Journal*, vol. 19, no. 3, pp. 114–16

Robins, Anna Gruetzner, 1997, *Modern Art in Britain, 1910–1914*, exh. cat., Barbican Art Gallery, London

———, 2010, '"Manet and the Post-Impressionists": A Checklist of Exhibits', *Burlington Magazine*, vol. 152, no. 1293, pp. 782–93

Rodker, John, 1914, 'The New Movement in Art', *Dial Monthly*, May, pp. 184–8

Rosenbaum, S.P., 2014, 'Old Bloomsbury', in J.M. Haule (ed.), *The Bloomsbury Group Memoir Club* (London: Palgrave Macmillan), pp. 151–3

——— (ed.), 1974, *The Bloomsbury Group: A Collection of Memoirs, Commentary and Criticism* (London: Croom Helm)

Rosner, Victoria (ed.), 2014, *The Cambridge Companion to the Bloomsbury Group* (Cambridge: Cambridge University Press)

Rothenstein, John, 1956, *Modern English Painters: Lewis to Moore* (London: Eyre & Spottiswoode)

———, 1957, *Modern English Painters: Sickert to Moore* (London: Eyre & Spottiswoode)

Ruskin, John, 1857, *The Elements of Drawing: Three Letters to Beginners* (London: Smith, Elder & Co.)

Rutter, Frank, 1908, 'Foreword', *The London Salon of the Allied Artists Association, Ltd*, exh. cat., Royal Albert Hall, London, p. 5

———, 1910, *Revolution in Art: An Introduction to the Study of Cézanne, Gauguin, Van Gogh, and Other Modern Painters* (London: Art News Press)

———, 1927, *Since I Was Twenty-Five* (London: Constable)

Ryan, Derek, and Stephen Ross (eds), 2018, *The Handbook to the Bloomsbury Group* (London: Bloomsbury Academic)

Salaman, Malcolm, C., 1931, 'The Spirit of "Shell" in Posters', *Apollo*, 1 July, pp. 38–9

Schoeser, Mary, 2009, 'Omega Textiles: A Sea-Change into Something Strange', in Alexandra Gerstein (ed.), *Beyond Bloomsbury: Designs of the Omega Workshops 1913–19* (London: Fontanka), pp. 17–25

Schwabe, Randolph, 1943, 'Reminiscences of Fellow Students', *Burlington Magazine*, vol. 82, no. 478, pp. 6–9

Scrase, David, and Peter Croft, 1983, *Maynard Keynes: Collector of Pictures, Books and Manuscripts* (Cambridge: Fitzwilliam Museum)

Shone, Richard, 1975, 'The Friday Club', *Burlington Magazine*, vol. 117, no. 866, pp. 278–84

———, 1976, *Bloomsbury Portraits: Vanessa Bell, Duncan Grant and Their Circle* (Oxford: Phaidon)

———, 1986, *The Berwick Church Paintings* (Eastbourne: Towner Art Gallery)

———, 1999, *The Art of Bloomsbury: Roger Fry, Vanessa Bell and Duncan Grant*, exh. cat., Tate Gallery, London

———, 2017, 'Vanessa Bell's Late Self-Portraits', in S. Milroy and I. Dejardin (eds), *Vanessa Bell* (London: Philip Wilson)

Sickert, Walter, 1910, 'The naked and the Nude', *The New Age*, 21 July, pp. 276–7

[Sickert, Walter], 1915, 'A Monthly Chronicle: Roger Fry', *Burlington Magazine*, vol. 28, no. 153, p. 117

———, 1916, 'A Monthly Chronicle: O Matre Pulchrâ', *Burlington Magazine*, vol. 29, no. 157, p. 35

———, 1922, 'Vanessa Bell', *Burlington Magazine*, vol. 41, no. 232, pp. 32–5

Skidelsky, Robert (ed.), 2015, *The Essential Keynes* (London: Penguin)

Southworth, Helen (ed.), 2010, *Leonard and Virginia Woolf, the Hogarth Press and the Networks of Modernism* (Edinburgh: Edinburgh University Press)

Spalding, Frances, 1980, *Roger Fry: Art and Life* (London: Granada)

———, 1983, *Vanessa Bell* (London: Weidenfeld & Nicolson)

———, 1997, *Duncan Grant* (London: Chatto & Windus)

———, 2013, *The Bloomsbury Group* (London: National Portrait Gallery)

———, 2022, *The Real and the Romantic: English Art Between the Two World Wars* (London: Thames & Hudson)

Spink, 1991, *Duncan Grant and Vanessa Bell: Design and Decoration, 1910–1960*, exh. cat., Spink Gallery, London

Stansky, Peter, 1996, *On or About 1910: Early Bloomsbury and its Intimate World* (London and Cambridge, MA: Harvard University Press)

———, 2008, *Bloomsbury as Publisher: Virginia and Leonard Woolf and the Hogarth Press* (San Francisco: Arion Press)

Stephen, Leslie, 1977, *Sir Leslie Stephen's Mausoleum Book* (Oxford: Clarendon Press)

———, 1996, *Selected Letters of Leslie Stephen*, ed. J.W. Bicknell, 2 vols (Basingstoke & London: Macmillan Press)

Strachey, Lytton, 2006, *The Letters of Lytton Strachey*, ed. Paul Levy (London: Penguin)

Strachey, Nino, 2018, *Rooms of Their Own* (London: Pitkin)

T.L.H., 1934, 'Modern Design for China and Earthenware', *Apollo*, 1 November, p. 283

Tate Gallery, 1959, *Duncan Grant*, exh. cat., Tate Gallery, London

———, 1975, *Duncan Grant: A Display to Celebrate His 90th Birthday*, exh. cat., Tate Gallery, London

Tatlock, R.R., 1923, 'The London Group', *Burlington Magazine*, vol. 43, no. 248, pp. 250, 253

———, 1924, 'The London Group: Passing of Abstract Art', *Daily Telegraph*, 21 October, p. 13

———, 1925, 'Modern Designs in Needlework', *Burlington Magazine*, vol. 47, no. 271, pp. 208–10

———, 1931, 'Art and Advertising', *Daily Telegraph*, 17 June, p. 10

Tickner, Lisa, 1999, 'Vanessa Bell: Studland Beach, Domesticity, and "Significant Form"', *Representations*, no. 65, pp. 63–92

———, 2000, *Modern Life and Modern Subjects: British Art in the Early Twentieth Century* (New Haven, CT, and London: Yale University Press)

———, 2002, 'Mediating Generation: The Mother–Daughter Plot', *Art History*, vol. 25, no. 1, pp. 23–46

Tobin, Claudia, 2017, 'Decoration, Abstraction and the Influence of Middle Eastern Textiles', in Grace Brockington (ed.), *In Focus: 'Abstract Painting' c.1914 by Vanessa Bell*, Tate Research Publications, https://www.tate.org.uk/research/in-focus/abstract-painting-vanessa-bell/decoration-abstraction (accessed 13 April 2023)

Todd, Avery, 2015, *Saxon Sydney-Turner: The Ghost of Bloomsbury* (London: Cecil Woolf)

Todd, Dorothy, 'Mural Decoration To-Day', *Studio*, vol. 96, no. 425, pp. 108–16

Todd, Dorothy, and Raymond Mortimer, 1929, *The New Interior Decoration: An Introduction to Its Principles, and International Survey of Its Methods* (London: B.T. Batsford)

Walton, Allan, 1935, 'Furnishing Textiles', *Journal of the Royal Society of Arts*, vol. 83, no. 4285, p. 173

Watney, Simon, 1980, *English Post-Impressionism* (London: Studio Vista)

Weld-Blundell, C.J., 1910, 'Manet and the Post-Impressionists', *The Times*, 7 November, pp. 11–12

Whitechapel Art Gallery, 1914, *Twentieth Century Art: A Review of Modern Movements, Summer Exhibition*, exh. cat., Whitechapel Art Gallery, London

Wilcox, Denys J., 1995, *The London Group, 1913–39: The Artists and Their Works* (Aldershot: Scolar Press)

Williams, Raymond, 1980, 'The Significance of "Bloomsbury" as a Social and Cultural Group', in Derek Crabtree and A.P. Thirlwall (eds), *Keynes and the Bloomsbury Group: The Fourth Keynes Seminar Held at the University of Kent at Canterbury, 1978* (London: Macmillan), pp. 40–57

Williams, Val, 1991, 'Carefully Creating an Idyll: Vanessa Bell and Snapshot Photography, 1907–46', in Jo Spence and Patricia Holland (eds), *Family Snaps: The Meanings of Domestic Photography* (London: Virago), pp. 186–98

Winkworth, W.W., 1934, 'China with Consideration', *Listener*, 31 October, p. 733

———, 1939, 'Decorating the Wall', *Listener*, 8 June, pp. 1224–5

Wolfe, Jesse, 2011, *Bloomsbury, Modernism and the Reinvention of Intimacy* (Cambridge: Cambridge University Press)

Woolf, Leonard, 1914, *The Wise Virgins* (London: Edward Arnold)

———, 1961, *Growing: An Autobiography of the Years 1904 to 1911* (London: Hogarth Press)

———, 1964, *Beginning Again: An Autobiography of the Years 1911 to 1918* (London: Hogarth Press)

———, 1967, *Downhill All the Way: An Autobiography of the Years 1919 to 1939* (London: Hogarth Press)

———, 1969, *The Journey not the Arrival Matters* (London: Hogarth Press)

———, 1989, *The Letters of Leonard Woolf*, ed. Frederick Spotts (San Diego, CA: Harcourt Brace Jovanovich)

[Woolf, Virginia], 1911, '"The Post-Impressionists" by C. Lewis Hind', *Nation*, 14 October, p. 108

Woolf, Virginia, 1915, *The Voyage Out* (London: Duckworth)

———, 1919, *Kew Gardens* (Richmond: Hogarth Press)

———, 1919, *Night and Day* (London: Duckworth)

———, 1921, *Monday or Tuesday* (London: Hogarth Press)

———, 1922, *Jacob's Room* (Richmond: Hogarth Press)

———, 1925, *Mrs Dalloway* (London: Hogarth Press)

———, 1927, *To the Lighthouse* (London: Hogarth Press)

———, 1928, *Orlando* (London: Hogarth Press)

———, 1930, 'Foreword', *Recent Paintings by Vanessa Bell with a Foreword by Virginia Woolf*, exh. cat., London Artists' Association, London

———, 1931, *The Waves* (London: Hogarth Press)

———, 1934, *Walter Sickert: A Conversation* (London: Hogarth Press)

———, 1934, 'Foreword', *Catalogue of Recent Paintings by Vanessa Bell with a foreword by Virginia Woolf*, exh. cat., Alex, Reid and Lefevre, London

———, 1937, *The Years* (London: Hogarth Press)

———, 1938, *Three Guineas* (London: Hogarth Press)

———, 1940, *Roger Fry: A Biography* (London: Hogarth Press)

———, 1966–7, *Collected Essays* (London: Hogarth Press), 4 vols

———, 1973, *A Room of One's Own* [1929] (Harmondsworth: Penguin)

———, 1975–80, *The Letters of Virginia Woolf*, ed. Nigel Nicolson and Joanne Trautmann (London: Hogarth Press), 6 vols

———, 1976, *Freshwater: A Comedy*, ed. Lucio P. Ruotolo (London: Hogarth Press)

———, 1977–84, *The Diary of Virginia Woolf*, ed. Anne Olivier Bell and Andrew McNeillie (Harmondsworth: Penguin), 5 vols

———, 1985, *The Complete Shorter Fiction*, ed. Susan Dick (London: Triad Grafton Books)

———, 1987, *Essays 2, 1912–1918*, ed. Andrew McNeillie (London: Hogarth Press)

———, 1990, *A Passionate Apprentice: The Early Journals, 1897–1909*, ed. Mitchell Leaska (London: Hogarth Press)

———, 1995, *Killing the Angel in the House* (Harmondsworth: Penguin)

———, 2002, *Moments of Being: Autobiographical Writings* [1978], ed. Jeanne Schulkind (London: Pimlico)

———, 2008, *The Platform of Time: Memoirs of Family and Friends*, ed. S.P. Rosenbaum (London: Hesperus Press)

Woolf, Virginia, and Vanessa Bell, with Thoby Stephen, 2005, *Hyde Park Gate News: The Stephen Family Newspaper*, ed. Gill Lowe (London: Hesperus Press)

Woolf, Virginia, and Roger Fry, 1973, *Victorian Photographs of Famous Men and Fair Women by Julia Margaret Cameron* [1926] (Boston: David R. Gordine)

Woolf, Virginia, and Leonard Woolf, 1917, *Two Stories* (Richmond: Hogarth Press)

PICTURE CREDITS

Vanessa Bell artwork images © Estate of Vanessa Bell. All rights reserved, DACS 2024. Duncan Grant artwork images © Estate of Duncan Grant. All rights reserved, DACS 2024.

Published in Architectural Review, 1 May 1930 246

Arts Council Collection, Southbank Centre, London, UK© Arts Council Collection/©Estate of Vanessa Bell. All rights reserved, DACS 2024/Bridgeman Images 264

Courtesy of Bonhams 135

Brighton & Hove Museums 19

The Charleston Trust 14, 17, 42, 47, 53, 60, 66, 68, 71, 84, 102, 114, 124, 125, 134, 157, 185, 186, 187, 191, 193, 220, 222, 225, 250

The Charleston Trust, purchased with assistance from the Arts Council England/V&A Purchase Grant Fund, the Art Fund and supporters of The Charleston Trust in memory of Lord Jeremy Hutchinson QC 159

Private Collection. Photo © Christie's Images Limited 102

The Courtauld, London (Samuel Courtauld Trust).

Photo © Estate of Vanessa Bell. All rights reserved, DACS 2024/Bridgeman Images 134, 142

The Courtauld, London (Samuel Courtauld Trust). Gift of Samuel Courtauld. Photo © Estate of Vanessa Bell. All rights reserved, DACS 2024/Bridgeman Images 207

© Fitzwilliam Museum, Cambridge 206, 209

David Herbert Collection 229

Henry W. and Albert A. Berg Collection of English and American Literature, The New York Public Library 24

Leicester Museum & Art Gallery, Leicestershire, UK© Leicester Museum & Art Galleries. Photo © Estate of Vanessa Bell. All rights reserved, DACS 2024/Bridgeman Images 107

© Mary Evans Picture Library 121

The Metropolitan Museum of Art, New York. Bequest of William S. Lieberman, 2005. Image © The Metropolitan Museum of Art/ Art Resource/Scala, Florence 170

The Museum of Modern Art, New York. Joan and Lester Avnet Collection. Digital image, The Museum of Modern Art, New York/Scala, Florence 150

National Galleries of Scotland. Purchased 1965 172

© National Portrait Gallery, London 79, 179

© National Portrait Gallery, London, purchased with help from the Art Fund 82

Courtesy of Piano Nobile, London vi, 33

Private Collection 97, 132, 235, 257

Private Collection. Photo © Estate of Vanessa Bell. All rights reserved, DACS 2024/Bridgeman Images 132

With the permission of the Provost and Scholars of King's College, Cambridge 238

Collection of Rollins Museum of Art, Orlando, Florida. Gift of Kenneth Curry, Ph.D. '32 156

From the RWA Permanent Collection 262

© Sheffield Museums Trust 200

Smith College Museum of Art, Northampton, MA 81

Photo © Sotheby's 2024 54, 91

PICTURE CREDITS

INDEX